All rights reserved. No part of this publication may be reproduced or transmitted in any form or by any means, electronic or mechanical, including photocopy, recording, or any information storage and retrieval system, without permission in writing from Todd Kachinski Kottmeier.

ISBN-13:
978-1724593474

ISBN-10:
1724593471
Copyright © 2014 and 2018 Todd Kachinski

DRAG411's Ten Black Books

Book 1:	DRAG411's "DRAG Bully, A Survivor's Guide"
	Copyright © 2015 and 2018
Book 2:	DRAG411's "Original DRAG Handbook"
	Copyright © 2010, 2011, 2012, 2014, and 2018
Book 3:	DRAG411's "Crown Me! Winning Pageants"
	Copyright © 2013, 2014, and 2018
Book 4:	DRAG411's "DRAG King Guide"
	Copyright © 2014 and 2018
Book 5:	DRAG411's "DRAG Stories"
	Copyright © 2011, 2014, and 2018
Book 6:	DRAG411's "DRAG Mother, DRAG Father"
	Copyright © 2012, 2014, and 2018
Book 7:	DRAG411's "SPOTLIGHT TODAY"
	Copyright © 2012 and 2018
Book 8:	DRAG411's "DRAG Queen Guide"
	Copyright © 2014 and 2018
Book 9:	Two Comedy Scripts:
	DRAG411's "Best Said Dead"
	Copyright © 2011, 2014, and 2018
	"Following Wynter"
	Copyright © 2012, 2014, and 2018
Book 10:	DRAG411's "DRAG World"
	Copyright © 2012 and 2018

From the best-selling author of "CommUnity of Transition,"
"Two Days Past Dead," The Novel and the sequel,
"Turn Around Bright Eyes, The DRAG Queen Killer,"
and "Joey Brooks, The Show Must Go On."

DRAG411's

DRAG
King Guide

Another Book By InfamousTodd.com

2nd Edition

I am not a fan of the term "drag" as applied across this entire art form, but until they find a single word "more accepting," I will have to use it. The drag community has helped me earn twenty LGBT world records. I created DRAG411 to document this form of entertainment. We are the world's largest organization for male, female, and androgynous impersonators with over 7,000 current or former impersonators in 32 countries. The Todd Kachinski Kottmeier

(sic)

Latin adverb: thus"; in full: sic erat scriptum, thus was it written indicates DRAG411 transcribed the comments into this book exactly as found in the original source, complete with any erroneous or archaic spelling or other nonstandard presentation. We try to print the responses using the same words sent to us, ensuring the reader DRAG411 did not change the tone, reflection, or character of each response.

> We print verbatim, without editing
>
> ver·ba·tim   vərˈbātəm/
> adverb: verbatim; adjective
> in exactly the same words as used originally.

Go to our website at Drag411.com to locate any name listed in any of the books in our Ten Black Book series and the details of each book, entertainer, and chapter.

Dedication

To Vinnie Marconi, for teaching me the positive traits of this craft and inspiring this Guide dedicated to male impersonators. Also to "My Michael," for giving me love, unconditional love, and time to complete this journey with DRAG411.

Todd Kachinski Kottmeier
Founder of DRAG411

From the Impersonators, in their own writing

CHAPTERS
❀❀❀

Chapter One
Your first paydays.

Chapter Two
"Where was your first gig?

Chapter Three
"Name the best show bars in your town? What were the best show bars in your life?"

Chapter Four
"When did you know you had the confidence and talent to perform in front of an audience?"

Chapter Five
"How should a newbie get on stage the first few years,
until they have enough experience to have venues contacting them?"

Chapter Six
"What stage names did you have since the beginning?
How did you get them? Why did you change it?"

Chapter Seven
"How do you get a venue to appreciate you enough as an entertainer to actually book you?
How do you catch their attention? What tricks will help someone find bookings into venues?"

Chapter Eight
"When did you become interested in dressing in the opposite sex?
Explain the details including the reaction of your family and friends?
When was the first time you took it to the next level as a performer?"

Chapter Nine
"Define your relationship with dating or live in partners in regards performing."

Chapter Ten
"What has a spouse/partner done for your craft? How did you handle the negative?"

Chapter Eleven
"How did you handle negative people in the beginning? How did they affect you?
Looking back through today's eyes, how would have you handled it differently?"

Chapter Twelve
"How do you handle anger in the dressing room?
Explain what you determine as the biggest problem with bitter words exchanged amongst entertainers? What advice do you share to those dishing out the hurtful words and to those performers struggling to survive the bullying?"

Chapter Thirteen
"Do you currently have a DRAG parent or mentor?
Who are they? Why are they your mentor? What do they do for you?"

Chapter Fourteen
"Who did you look up to as you began your first number on stage?"

Chapter Fifteen
"How do you handle your anger with a venue no longer interested in you?"

Chapter Sixteen
"Which key people in your life are oblivious to the fact, that you perform as an impersonator? Why?"

Chapter Seventeen
"How did your family handle you performing by cross dressing in the beginning of your craft? How do they handle it now? Are you the only impersonator in your family?"

Chapter Eighteen
"Explain your inner circle"

Chapter Nineteen
"Who was your support group in the beginning for you as an entertainer? What did they offer?"

Chapter Twenty
"What tricks with tape should every performer learn before heading on stage? What are the biggest mistakes with binding? Any experiences you wish to share?"

Chapter Twenty-One
"DRAG Boxes become DRAG Rooms, which eventually take over your home. How much space does your craft consume in your home, car, and venue? How much is it worth? Where do you go to retire it?"

Chapter Twenty-Two
"Where do you purchase wigs? How do you clean them? How are they stored? What do you do when you retire them from your DRAG room?"

Chapter Twenty-Three
"What rules apply for padding and binding?"

Chapter Twenty-Four
"What is the best procedure for applying makeup to include performers with acne?"

Chapter Twenty-Five
"What is the most effective way to remove makeup?"

Chapter Twenty-Six
"Where is the best place to find clever outfits for a production?"

Chapter Twenty-Seven
"Where are the best places to find perfect shoes? What are the biggest mistakes in purchasing foot wear as an impersonator? Any experiences you wish to share?"

Chapter Twenty-Eight
"What do you say about shaving?"

Chapter Twenty-Nine
"Make-up!"

Chapter Thirty
"What procedures do you have in place to ensure your belonging
are safe and secure in the dressing room? "

Chapter Thirty-One
"What are the top three things a performer can do to impress an audience? Why are they
important enough to be the top three on your list?"

Chapter Thirty-Two
"How do you handle an aggressively affectionate or groping patron?"

Chapter Thirty-Three
Music makes you dance!

Chapter Thirty-Four
"What is the most embarrassing mistake done on stage?
What advice do you give the entertainers believing mistakes are career killers?"

Chapter Thirty-Five
"Many performers ignore the patron tipping them. Other entertainers acknowledge the dollar
with intimate gratitude; in the middle, are the rest of the impersonators. Where do place?"

Chapter Thirty-Six
"How do you like to be introduced to the stage?"

Chapter Thirty-Seven
"How do you handle a heckler in the crowd, sidetracking your performance?"

Chapter Thirty-Eight
"When everything is said and done, and you leave the stage for the very last time in life…
what do you hope your audience will say about you?"

Chapter Thirty-Nine
"If you were to sit down with a new performer, one on one,
to say an important message about the craft… what would you say?"

Chapter Forty
"The Pageantry system has adjusted many times since its inception. Explain your belief of
where it is now and what it needs to accomplish in the future."

Chapter Forty-One
"Where do you see this craft in ten years? What do impersonators need to do, to enable it to
positively move in the right direction?"

Contributing Impersonator adding their
Wisdom in this Handbook include...

❦❦❦

Male Impersonators

Aaron Phoenix
Abs Hart
Adam All
Adam DoEve
AJ Menendez
Alec Allnight
Alexander Cameron
Alik Muf
Andrew Citino
Anjie Swidergal
Anson Reign
Ashton The Adorable Lover
Atown
Ayden Layne
B J Armani
B J Bottoms
Bailey Saint James
Ben Doverr
Ben Eaten
Bootzy Edwards Collynz
Brandon KC Young-Taylor
Bruno Diaz
Cage Masters
Campbell Reid Andrews
Chance Wise
Chandler J Hart
Chasin Love
Cherry Tyler Manhattan
Chris Mandingo
Clark Kunt
Clint Torres
Cody Wellch Klondyke
Colin Grey
Corey James Caster
Coti Blayne
Crash Bandikok
Dakota Rain
Dante Diamond
Davion Summers
DeVery Bess
Devin G. Dame
Devon Ayers
Dionysus W Khaos
Diseal Tanks Roberts
D-Luv Saviyon
Dominic Demornay
Dominic Von Strap
D-Rex
Dylan Kane

E. M. Shaun
Eddie C. Broadway
Emilio
Erick LaRue
Flex Jonez
Freddy Prinze Charming
Gabe King
Gage Gatlyn
George De Micheal
Greyson Bolt
Gunner Gatlyn
Gus Magendor
Hawk Stuart
Harry Pi
Holden Michael
Howie Feltersnatch
Hurricane Savage
J Breezy St James
Jack E. Dickinson
Jack King
Jake Van Camp
Jamel Knight
Jenson C. Dean
Johnnie Blackheart
Jonah Godfather of DRAG
Jordan Allen
Jordan Reighn
Joshua K. Mann
Joshua Micheals
Juan Kerr
Julius M. SeizeHer
Jude Lawless
Justin Cider
Justin Luvan
Justin Sider
K'ne Cole
Kameo Dupree
Kenneth J. Squires
King Dante
King Ramsey
Jack Inman
Kody Sky
Koomah
Kristian Kyler
Kruz Mhee
Linda Hermann-Chasin
Luke Ateraz
Lyle Love-It
Macximus
Marcus Mayhem
Marty Brown
Master Cameron Eric Leon
Max Hardswell
MaXx Decco
Michael Christian

Mike Oxready
Miles Long
Mr-Charlie Smith
Nanette D'angelo Sylvan
Nolan Neptune
Orion Blaze Browne
Owlejandro Monroe
Papa Cherry
Papi Chulo
Papi Chulo Doll
Persian Prince
Phantom
Pierce Gabriel
Prince Steele Silk
Rasta Boi Punany
Rico M Taylor
Rock McGroyn
Rocky Valentino
Rogue DRAG King
Romeo Sanchez
Rychard "Alpha" Le'Sabre
Ryder Knightly
Ryder Long
Sam Masterson
Sammy Silver
Santana Romero
Scorpio
Shane Rebel Caine
Shook ByNature
SirMandingo Thatis
Smitty O'Toole
Soco Dupree
Spacee Kadett
Starr Masters
Stefan LeDude
Stefon Royce Iman
Stefon SanDiego
Stormm
Teddy Michael
Thug Passion
Travis Luvermore
Travis Hard
Trey C. Michaels
Trigger Montgomery
Tyler Manhattan
Viciouse Slick
Vinnie Marconi
Welland Dowd
William Vanity Matrix
Wulf Von Monroe
Xander Havoc
Xavier Bottoms

❦❦

Chapter One
"How much money should a new performer expect to earn from the venue the first 3 years?"

❦❦❦

This book is produced with limited editing to allow the reader to understand the entertainer through their words and not our interpretation.

❦**Dakota Rain:** Depends on the venue and person. Sometimes I will work only for tips. I do this because I enjoy it. I love making people smile.

❦**Travis Hard:** This all depends on the quality of their performance. I do not believe you should expect anything besides making a name for yourself... You need to earn a level a respect first

❦**Koomah:** Factors include like the performer, type of performance, venues, budgets, locations, etc. Some people make money within the first 3 years, some breakeven; some lose money but gain experience.

❦**Dominic:** Some venues make you win a few talent nights before being able to grasp a spotlight! It's usually $25 plus tips, not worth it really!

❦**D-Luv Saviyon:** It depends on their work, reputation (booking ability), and titles can help, but usually only National titles (and contracted current reigning) are guaranteed a paid booking. Your ability to make money depends on you and how hard you work/build yourself (you are a brand within yourself if you choose to be).

❦**Orion Blaze Browne:** Never expect money. What you earn when you start is usually tips and maybe a small booking fee. When establish yourself you will make a name and reputation than your pay depends on an agreed amount. Different venues have different budgets. Bar also pay differently in different areas. Best advice, get your name out there, and work hard. Once you prove yourself, accept no less than your Queen counter parts. If you entertain at the same caliber, you deserve the same pay.

❦**Kenneth J. Squires:** I think it would depend on the entertainer, and how well they entertain. The first thing to think about would be yourself, and how to make your performance better.

❦**Coti Blayne:** Depends on the venue. Depends on the night. I do not do this for money though so I do not really sweat things like pay. If I get enough to cover my gas is all I really care about. However, if you are at an open night do not expect too much if anything. Just be reasonable.

❦**Stormm:** To be paid depends on the places you perform. I think it is up to the person, if you are good and people like you u get the tips.

❦**Travis Luvermore:** I started with tips until I got a one night for $25 a show.

🎭**Joshua Micheals:** Expect to do many talent nights and other pro bono work. You have to show that deserve to be before you should worry about money if you are doing for money it is the reason anyway do for love off the art

🎭**Clint Torres:** As new performers I have never made more than 25 plus tips from a venue and I personally feel that that is fair. We are new and upcoming whereas the others are older, have put in more time, and should be paid more

🎭**Shook ByNature:** I generally accepted what was offered. Show up and focus on earning tips; since you work for a few years you can base what you will accept based on knowing a venue and what the owners can afford.

🎭**Campbell Reid Andrews:** What is money? I did not really start being paid until 2012. I started in '05. I would be surprised if a bar or club offers a new king compensation but hey if they do take it. Titles help because it is contracted you make x amount per booking. If you are not offered, do not ask because your new just be happy with your tips put on an outstanding show and I guarantee you the audience will make the venue pay you next time. They would not be able to say no when you are bringing in the crowd.

🎭**Ben Eaten:** None. This is not a hobby for the sake of making money. Yes, there are people who get to make money doing what they love, but they did not get there overnight. I would say expect many tip only spots and many non-paying shows.

🎭**Adam All:** We do not get tips in the United Kingdom; we tend to get free drinks or nothing at all. It depends on what you offer the venue and how established you can make yourself look. I was charging and I got some gigs but only locally and now, I do more free gigs to promote my work. A general UK price for a half hour or 45 minute set would be in the region of £150 but expect less to begin with and expect people to be surprised you charge. DRAG Queens in the UK get a hell of a lot more and have far more opportunities. The more Kings like those and myself that have pushed their way into the cabaret scene fight for equal pay and respect the better it will be for Kings across the UK. My work as a king a king is considered a hobby, as I have to work a day job to pay my bills. It is a second income

🎭**AJ Menendez:** How often they perform, how consistent they are. Do not quit their day job and just do DRAG. It is a very long process.

🎭**Chance Wise:** I have always work, and probably will always have to have a job to perform. It would be nice to live off DRAG, but I still have my job.

🎭**Justin Cider:** Little to none. We do not do it for the money. If you are in it for that, you will probably be disappointed. I spend much more on my outfits then I get back. Mot saying there is not money Being a DRAG king is more of my expensive hobby.

🎭**Hurricane Savage:** Nothing! Do it because you love it not for the money!

🎭**Jonah Godfather of DRAG**: A new king works for tips only. Tips only spots may graduate to paid spots but that depends on the quality of the king and the show budget. The quality of the king is a major factor. The director is looking for male illusion, lip-syncing, costuming, audience appeal and interaction, etc. Whatever money comes from tips and pay should be reinvested in the next performance.

🎭**Marcus Mayhem:** Here for fun and the money is a bonus, if not just your gas money.

🎭**Rychard "Alpha" Le'Sabre:** Never expect to earn anything more than the TIPS you work your ass off to earn. I was making $10 a night. After three years, I made almost $100 a night. Seven years later I have three shows I do regularly and make on Average $10 at one, $40 at another, and $100-$150 at the main venue. When I travel things I get expenses paid, food covered, drinks covered, really just depends on the Venue.

🎭**Dixon Heat: I** have no idea. I have never been paid.

🎭**Shane Rebel Caine:** First few years expect tips only. You will be lucky to make $10. You have to prove yourself to make the big bucks.

Place Faces Without Peeking At The Answer Key In Book Two

Name the performers without checking on DRAG411.com

🎭**Atown:** Are you are in a group or crew? If the crew is booked, you would divide cover at the door, or the manager or promoter pays a flat rate.

🎭**Freddy Prinze Charming:** Never "expect" to make anything. If you get tips, great! Be appreciative. If you are lucky enough to get show pay, even better... be even more appreciative.

🎭**Rasta Boi Punany:** I never expect to earn anything from a venue. I have considered my place of enjoyment as my bread and butter. I negotiate my booking fee according to the venue and what they have to offer.

❀Ashton The Adorable Lover: Depends on venue. If it is a show th
If invited tips and small pay. If you are a cast member, equal pay.
expect anything. Tips vary. I do this craft for the enjoyment not pay although it can get expensive

❀Spacee Kadett: DRAG will almost *never* equate to "making money." Be humble. Be hardworking. Be willing to do many shows FREE. Then again, outside of "zero," all numbers are arbitrary in our business, from booking fees to time onstage. It is not the years you put into your DRAG, but the DRAG you put into your years. I earned a major national title when I was two years into DRAG, and signed a contract promising a strong booking fee for all related events. During my year of reign, this proved to be a lie, and I compromised myself to promote my name and title. I drove dozens of hours to NUMEROUS events and even prelims at a personal cost. Days after national crowning, one of my home bars offered me a booking for $30, half of what it offered to even an amateur Queen. When I tried to bargain up, I was informed that "no king will ever be worth that" and all of my bookings were cut. I was so scared; I undersold myself for a good two years after. There is a fine line between fair and cocky, reasonable and unreasonable. Benefit shows are also always important, but they fall into a different category. Most local booking fees are $20 to $50. Deliver a good product. Make yourself worth every penny, and do not undersell yourself. Venues will be happy to pay you what you are worth, if they can. The venue that denied me three years ago now pays me what they said I would never be worth.

❀Pierce Gabriel: Depends on venue. Some shows I have been given $20 per show plus tips, but most of the time I have performed for tips only. Just like everywhere, the tipping is highly unpredictable. In any case, do not expect to actually make a profit. You are lucky if your tips pay for gas and new outfits.

❀Vinnie Marconi: I am into this almost three years now and have put a LOT more IN than I have made. I have never had a booking for under $50 plus tips. Those actual bookings are FAR less than the benefits. I do not promote myself or ask for bookings. I 'might' get more if I tried harder, but the benefits keep me busy and is my heart.

❀Kruz Mhee: Depends on the state; in Alabama you should not expect much. There are those that have been able to make a living but mostly those have been DRAG Queens. What I have seen at least in Alabama, if your pay covers your costuming and makeup and a bar tab you are doing really well! For me the craft is a creative outlet but unfortunately not a paycheck.

❀Alec Allnight: Many different factors. A performer's commitment being the greatest one. Please do not expect huge tips and payday if you cannot put in the time to prepare and perfect your performance. As you gain experience and a following, everything else will follow. Be patient!

Remember: awesome costumes and props do not need to cost a lot if you get creative enough.

🎭**B J Bottoms:** If you are doing DRAG just for the money it is time for a new outlet. You are going to put more money into it if you are truly passionate about your craft. Never expect to be worth a fixed dollar amount know in your heart that no matter how much money you do or do not make it is not a reflection on you or your art. Be happy with every tip and thankful for every paycheck because being an MI is hard and even someone giving you dollar shows that they appreciate you and your art.

🎭**Silk Steele Prince:** Do not expect to make money. Do benefit or charity shows to get recognition and experience. You may make $10 in tips. As you grow, the money grow.

🎭**SirMandingo Thatis:** I perform at so many venues I am never booked at only one and I only leave with what I make in tips. I have only had two bar titles in the short amount of time I have been doing DRAG but when I earn my national title. I will definitely have a booking fee. Anyway, the most I have left a bar with was $338 in tips

🎭**Flex Jonez:** Expect nothing but tips. In bars, expect no more than $50. As you mature at best with the craft you can then hold booking contracts and more and then once the following of fans begins the booking fees becomes no issue.

🎭**Cody Wellch Klondyke:** At first was doing spotlight for only tips. After a year, I started being paid booking which started at $50.00 plus tips.

🎭**Viciouse Slick:** It varies because each show will have different amount of people show up. A popular show may pay you more than a show with a fickle attendance. My biggest pay was $50, the rest as mostly tips.

🎭**George De Micheal:** About £40 to £60 pounds in the United Kingdom depending upon travel and how many numbers you are performing.

🎭**DeVery Bess:** Nothing, lots, and lots of charity work.

🎭**Thug Passion:** You will spend your first six months to a year earning your audience and fellow entertainers respect. They want to know the type of person you are on and off the stage. You should not expect money from the owner of the venue, but depending on the venue, the type of music, whether or not the audience has some type of attraction to you, yes I said it attraction to the entertainer whether it be the clothes, the hair, the way you smell, your smile, shoes, your facial hair or even if you go without facial hair does the baby face really give the illusion of a male, would depend on how much money a new king could make. I did not have trouble when I started out as a king, I think you could make anywhere from $10- $50 within your first year. Do not forget to be helpful back stage because this is a brotherhood. There is competition but its friendly competition. We want to up lift and have each other's backs. Besides that entertain because you love it, to make someone's day, or just even get some emotions off your chest. Not for the money.

🎭**Bootzy Edwards Collynz**: Do not expect to earn much. This is the time toyou're your wardrobe together. It takes a bit to get a base for costumes. I have done shows that range from $35-$100. It all depends on the venue, their budget, and how good of a performer you work to become. Overall, you should be doing DRAG for the joy of it. The money should be the added bonus. This does not pay much at the start. The more you work you craft, the better it can get. For making it full time, congratulations and keep pushing. Some cannot, but this is all a hustle. The harder you work, the better.

🎭**Colin Grey:** If you are doing it for the money, you are doing it for the wrong reasons. Do not get me wrong, I love a good haul on a show night and it is even better having paid bookings but money is not why I am in it.

🎭**Eddie C. Broadway:** A new performer should not expect any amount. However, if they are networking, getting out there, and doing things well, then they can expect show pay $25-$100. Probably more on the $30-$60 range.

🎭**Sam Masterson:** Depends on your shows; if good you will receive more

🎭**Kameo Dupree:** Do DRAG because you enjoy it not for any financial expectations. I have titles and still perform in venues as "Tips Only." I honestly believe some of the best performers or performances come from tip only performers. They give 100% every show than those that know they have a pay no matter what they do.

🎭**Xavier Bottoms:** Most of the kids now do not get a booking but they make solely tips. If they are doing DRAG for money, they are in it for all the wrong reasons. For my first two years, I put all my tips in a jar for a charity known as Grandma's house.

🎭**Stefan LeDude:** This is not something you get into for money. In addition, you especially should not expect much the first few years.

🎭**Jamel Knight:** Do not expect to be paid much than exposure. How much depends on the standard booking fees in your area. Nevertheless, you should never expect to be paid as much as other more established and seasoned entertainers.

🎭**Bruno Diaz:** This is fun for me; I do not expect to get money when I try to expose Bruno, networking, and to connect with venues. I performed without expectation of pay, which is a bonus. If people think this is lucrative, they are wrong. I have spent more money on my wardrobe than I earned, but this is the love for the Art. Some places pay depending of titles. Some have a show budget. Friday/Saturday in my home bar, with tips is $150 to $180 which is not bad for two hours of fun

🎭**Howie Feltersnatch:** The troupe I perform with is strictly volunteer. All the money the show makes goes a safe place for youth to hang out once a week. After performing with the troupe for a year, you have a chance to travel with the troupe.

❀Master Cameron Eric Leon: I am happy to pay for my materials. The more I make, the more elaborate my costumes. It will be a while before I break even.

❀Welland Dowd: Definitely not about money. It depends on the gig and venue. I am happy to get a token of appreciation, cover a few drinks or my props/costume, I am happy. If we are doing a bigger stage with a large audience, it is nice to be valued higher. I definitely think venues should not assume Kings will perform for free!

❀Julius M. SeizeHer: This is just a fun thing. As a performer with a little over a year under the belt. A few bucks here and there, but not a whole lot.

❀Adam DoEve: I did not even know that people were paid to do it. I thought that we only got tips and that was your pay. I have come to learn diff, but I still do not really care about the money. I like what I do and have fun with it.

❀Jack E. Dickinson: Depends on venue and context. Many shows are fundraising initiatives so, in those cases, no payment at all, except maybe cab fare and drink tickets. If people put on a show themselves and it is not a fundraiser, then it is up to them how much goes to cover troupe expenses and how much goes to individual performers. With our troupe, over the years, we developed formula to determine these kinds of things. An individual's pay was determined by the number of acts, the size of their roles, the organizational responsibilities they accomplished, and so forth.

❀Travis Hard: Unless you hold a title or are well known, do not expect anything. Even tips. Money is not why I do DRAG. It should not be your reason. You should expect to make are friends and contacts!

❀Clark Kunt: I started in talent competitions where you only were paid if you won - in that context do not expect to make money. With a group or troupe, where you can organize your own shows and are paid to do that, you might get a small take home. Iif you do DRAG for the money, good luck!

❀Emilio: I did not make much. It was fair, since I was learning the craft. I make my wifeager/manager negotiate my payment.

❀Juan Kerr: I do not tend to be paid. I receive some expenses. The scene's just not that big in the United Kingdom. I am sure if I looked I could get some paid gigs somewhere. I am not sure what the going rate is though.

❀Trey C. Michaels: I never expect anything. If I make five dollars, I am grateful. I perform because I love it not to just get paid. Over time, you can expect the tips to become more and hopefully show pay someday.

❀Bailey Saint James: I believe that you should perform for the love of it and the awareness it brings to the human misconception that gender is binary. However, after a while, if you are spending more on costuming and travel than your tips and wages...you may wish to consider a career/hobby change.

❀Aaron Phoenix: An entertainer should expect to do free guest/"hot spots", benefits, and talent contests to build their name before expecting any kind of booking fee. Once established as an entertainer proving their talent, then the approaching venues will decide what they are willing to pay to book them. It really depends on experience and what you bring to the stage. If the audience likes it and the venue likes it and it makes them money/brings people in the door, they are going to pay more.

❀Soco Dupree: Not about earning money, but making a name for yourself. Booking fee is based on yourself value as an entertainer. Stay humble.

❀E. M. Shaun: I never did this for money. It started as a hobby and then became a part of my lifestyle. I realized I was a entertainer, so I would advise a new performer not to be discourage if they do not make a large amount of money at first. It takes time to build a name for yourself. We do it because we love the fans, along with the attention and excitement we bring when we are on stage. Money has never been my focus with DRAG. I have always wanted to do my best, have fun, and just enjoy the ride.

❀Stefon Royce Iman: I started out doing DRAG contests, community events, and benefits and tipping out. I got booked in my first gig for fifty dollars. Than as the years went by I got booked on gigs for 100-200. You need to be established. Always reinvent yourself and the pay will come as long as you are professional.

❀Santana Romero: Never expect much money. Hot spots should be your best friend and you should not expect more than 15-20 dollars in tips. When you gain some experience, notoriety and a decent fan base, bookings come into play. The money grows as you do, so stay humble and appreciative of what you receive.

❀B J Armani: I do not make money at DRAG. Most people do not. If you are going into this craft as a job or moneymaker, find another route. If you have a state or national title, you could ask for more but depends on the region. Never set yourself up for failure by asking for lots of money. If you really are good, tips will come.

❀Smitty O'Toole: New performers should expect to only earn tips. They should expect unpaid cameos to get their name out. I was lucky and landed a weekly gig my first month, then a year into it won a DRAG race where I co-hosted a weekly show, so I have gotten paid quite a bit more than most people in their first year or so.

❀Dionysus W Khaos: I do not except anything. Tips are great; rare show pays are awesome. I do this for the love of the art. I never break even. If you have expectations especially at the beginning you will come out disappointed

❧**Jensen C. Dean:** Many factors are at play. It is better to look at the knowledge gained in the first few years and the experiences as the things you earn, and any cash you pick up along the way is bonus. Performance is an art and it should be about the expression and experiences not the paycheck.

❧**LoUis CYfer:** Perform because you love it not because u was not to be paid. Never ever put a pound sign above your head!

❧**Luke Ateraz:** Wait, you mean there is money in DRAG? If you are in this for the money, GOOD LUCK! Do not quit your day or night job, or any job for that matter. Expect nothing except tips. Benefit events expect nothing.

❧**William Vanity Matrix:** Making money in DRAG where I live is impossible- because by the time you spend money in supplies, the money you make back in tips and such may only cover enough for you to break even.

❧**Devin G. Dame:** Starting performer need to pay dues with free shows and hot spots. As the performer grows and has more costumes and makeup there than a fee is paid for their time. I was making about $75/show within my first three years of performing.

Chapter Two
"Where was your first gig? How did it come about and what were the results?"

❀❀❀

❀**B J Armani:** Trish our MC at our show was leaving. I had been tossing around the idea to perform since I had been going to the shows. I listened to song after song until I came upon UB40 "Cannot help falling in love with you" a remake of the Elvis song. I did that song complete with four other DRAG Kings with trumpets that I had rented (the music store is used to me now). B J Armani performed for the first and what I thought was last time. However, I was bit by the stage bug. I set out to be as good as I saw around me only a bit different. You could call me the hybrid or as some Queens say the Prius of the DRAG World. Out of my love for Queens came the Elton costumes and out of my love for comedy came the pie plate belt buckle complete with spinner. The result was a backlash from some performers (some still do not get me but they are used to me by now) and an audience that is a bit forgiving at times but mostly loving and, of course, now they expect the unexpected.

❀**Shook ByNature!:** My first Gig as was an amateur show in San Diego. I performed "Cyclone" by Baby Bash and my DRAG Mother was not happy. She wanted me to be more R&B classic. My first Gig as Shook ByNature was due to Tara Nicole Brooks giving me a one number cameo at Ibiza. I performed "Infidelity" by Trey Songz. ❀**Koomah:** My first gig was at Club 20/20 in Houston for a top surgery fundraiser in 2008. I had never done gender performance onstage before and made something up the night before. It was a DRAG-ish gender performance where I transformed from a woman to a man onstage. I was invited by a DRAG troupe that was there to perform it again at a different event the next weekend at a lesbian bar called Chances and have not stopped since. I was immediately sucked into gender performance and DRAG.

❀**Brandon KC Young-Taylor:** Rumors in Springfield, Missouri, USA. It was a Tuesday night talent show. I signed up two weeks before. After the show, another king that asked me if I would be interested in joining a king group and invited me to come to practice that weekend approached me. History was written from there!

❀**D-Luv Saviyon:** A duo gig at a club called Amnesia in Nashville owned by DJ Lil Junior or Junior as everyone knew him...my first backup dancer performance was backup to making good love by Avant. The backup dancing gig came about because I had been doing choreography and teaching anonymous men routines (male impersonator group). My first duo was a result of encouragement from dancing...we did a mix of Playboy like me by Playa into So Anxious by Ginuwine. The duo was called The Original Playbois. The reception was amazing and so it began...

❧**Sammy Silver:** As an activist performance night, there was a feminist cabaret. I performed a slot. at Burdell's Yard in Bath, United Kingdom.

❧**Clint Torres:** My first gig was given to me but my bro Justin Cider to perform at Aldo's Night Club on gay night. I was one of three performers and the only king. I remember that the host and I had to educate the audience on just what a DRAG king was. There were a lot of women in the audience so with me doing "Take You Down" by Chris Brown and adding some floor work, my response was nothing but positive.

❧**Vinnie Marconi:** A charity benefit for the USO in New Port Richey, Florida USA. I was asked to do it because I was just in a Butch Fashion Show for charity and wore my sailor uniform. I had an INTENSE week with Dr. J and then hit the stage. VINNIE MARCONI came to life with the audience response and it made me hungry for more!

❧**Orion Blaze Browne:** A bar in Binghamton, New York, USA. I could not find any local kings in Pittsburgh at the time so through the internet I met two kings who were willing to teach me how to bind, pack, and put on face. I remember practicing my number for hours a day. When I got to New York, USA, I was not even there for 15 minutes and it was "oh by the way you are performing tonight for the open stage." I remember the bar was packed, the stage was their dance floor equipped with stripper pole and two walls of mirrors. I went through my number without interacting with the crowd at all. However, when I was finished the applause was incredible.

❧**Freddy Prinze Charming:** A fundraiser in Tucson for a small, independent art gallery/teaching studio perhaps called Arthouse. I performed with DRAGstar Cabaret, and did Fall Out Boy's 'Dance Dance' with great feedback. I performed with DRAGstar for about the next year before moving to Phoenix.

❧**E. M. Shaun:** Legends in Raleigh, North Carolina, USA. A few months prior, I saw my first DRAG king show during pride weekend. I looked at my best friend. We both were thought I could do that and it seemed like it would be so fun too. Therefore, a month later I step on stage as E. M. Shaun and performed Neyo's "Closer" and M.I.M.S "This is why I am Hot." I had a blast and now seven years later here I am.

❧**Kristian Kyler:** MISS KITTYS in Little Rock, Arkansas, USA. It was talent night I was so nerves but I ended up winning that night! What a rush I had when I came off that stage I will never forget that moment!

❧**Chance Wise:** A benefit show for a Queen to do a national pageant. I was the only king among fifteen Queens. I was nervous. I had to push myself from behind the curtain. I remember it being pitch black and the spotlight hitting me in the face. There may have been a deer in the headlights look for a second...but I stayed out there and did my song. I am sure I at least tried to lip sync but I am not entirely sure. One of the Queens asked me how it was and I was like, 'I do not know' which she responded, 'Welcome to DRAG baby!'

❦Joshua Micheals: Rainbow Room in Detroit, Michigan, USA. It was the Wednesday talent night after Thanksgiving out was on a dare/bet I won the talent night contest

❦Gus Magendor: My first gig was at OYP in Tulsa, Oklahoma, USA. It came about because I came to all the shows every weekend dressed in DRAG and they asked if I wanted to perform some time. It went better than I thought. I got many compliments and made more money than the regulars that night

❦Jonah Godfather of DRAG: My first show was an amateur show at Blake's in St Louis, Missouri, USA. Candy Barr was the show director. I had wanted to perform for quite a few years before I actually did. I finally got up enough courage and signed up. After my first song, Candy called me back to the dressing rooms and booked me with the Saturday night show cast, Jennifer James, Candy James, Tiffany Scott, and Miss Tracy. This was a dream come true, to perform with the people that I admired so much.

❦D-Rex: 20 years ago. San Antonio, Texas, USA, on a dare. I am still hooked.

❦Kameo Dupree: A pageant; Metro East Pride Pageant. It was new, exciting, and even though I did not win (First Alternate.) Such an amazing experience confirmed "Male Illusion" was something I really wanted to continue.

❦Emilio: The Egyptian Room in Portland, Oregon, USA. The DRAG troop had a show.

❦Travis Hard: My first performance was with the Miltown Kings in 2006 or 2007, time flies so I cannot accurately recall. Back then, my name was Gregory Swallows and I had a horrible herniated disc, but I powered through.

❦Dakota Rain: Rainbow Inn in Lake Wylie South Carolina, USA. Country Casniova asked me to do a show. I was nervous as crap but I did it and thrived to better myself. I had Tammy Black and Yvonne Crowder to cheer me on.

❦K'ne Cole: Waterside Landing in New Port Richey, Florida. I was asked to join TNT boi's and performed Paralyzer by Finger Eleven. I was hooked.

❦Rasta Boi Punany: William Way Center in the Mr. Philadelphia DRAG King/Mr. Philadelphia Gay Pride 2011 competition. My wife entered me, gave me my name, outfits we picked out together, theme, music. I won.

❦Jack King: My first appearance was on the Copenhagen town square, with 15,000 people who watched the show. It was AWESOME.

❦Adam All: The London Hotel, Southampton, United Kingdom a haunt for many famous London DRAG Queens, making it the most prominent place to begin. Shat myself as I came from the red curtain and promptly went into autopilot. "Footloose"

✹Davion Summers: Talent night at The Cabaret in Cincinnati, Ohio, USA. I did Suit and Tie by Justin Timberlake and I won rising star. I did it as a joke but I fell in love with DRAG that night and could not stop doing it.

✹Trey C. Michaels: First show was Tuesday, October 25, 2011 at BS West in Scottsdale, Arizona, for the Stars of Tomorrow show. I did "Sexy back" by Justin Timberlake. I did well for a first timer but I knew I had a lot to learn and I think I made like a dollar or two that night.

✹Campbell Reid Andrews: Kourtney Devereaux Rodriguez was the first person to help me get my first gig at the Old Saint. It was a new armature show and she was so sweet. Gave me my first break on a Tuesday stage. I was probably horrible Lmao but I had so much fun danced my little ass off.

✹Coti Blayne: Amateur night at the Wreckroom. "I came to play" because I came to play and because I loved the band. I did a remix of "more" by usher. I practiced a whole ton and the night of I was like a deer in the headlights and tripped on stage. It was wretched. Nevertheless, I had a blast.

✹Lyle: Love-It: Queen invited me after a Halloween costume, I had done

✹Spacee Kadett: I was a student performer at my university's DRAG show in 2007. My intent was to be fabulous and immediately discovered by the professionals at the show, who would whisk me away to their magical world and my career as a famous entertainer would be launched. I learned that my vision of discovery was dead wrong. One show does not a performer make. We DRAGs have busy lives outside the magical world of cross-dressing. There is little money in the craft. For most of us, it is pure passion. Two years later, I started doing open mics, benefit shows, contests (which I never won) and eventually pageants. It was only through my own hard work and persistence that I was able to build a name and open more opportunities for myself.

✹Eddie C. Broadway: My first REAL show was for my pops' birthday.

✹Stormm: Wausau, Wisconsin, USA at Mad Hatter, now Oz. It was a Christmas show.

✹Travis Luvermore: Night Owls in Gastonia North Carolina, USA. A couple DRAG brothers encouraged me to do the weekly amateur night to perfect the art and to gain a fan base. I selected "how do you like me now" by Toby Keith. I was nervous as hell as soon as the crowd started getting into it there was no going back.

✹Marty Brown: Treetops Cabaret now known as Club Cabaret.

✹Dominic Von Strap: Peepshow. My friend Angie Vandine (skate name "Lil Bo Peepshow") was PST in DRAG raisers and put on a show to raise money for the Phoenix pride scholarship fund. She had dinner people that had to back out and my mentor Eddie asked me to fill in. It was not the best, but for my very first time ever performing as Dominic, I think I did damn well.

❁Bens Eaten: My University's amateur DRAG show. I was hesitant, but knew Queens in the area would help. They helped me get taped and painted then gave me pointers. I ended up gaining the confidence I needed to keep on doing it. I got another show about 2 months later at Attitudes Nightclub and that jump-started my career.

❁AJ Menendez: The Norm in Jacksonville, Florida USA, with 100 Degrees Celsius.

❁Atown: Opening for lesbian comedian Sandra Valls, at the North Tower Circle in Fresno, California USA. It went well; Sandra and the crowd enjoyed it. Someone recommended me to a venue in Clovis, California. We were the first gay DRAG group to the area. It was a huge turnout and we did not have any problems with discrimination.

❁Justin Cider: North Tower Circle; it is the only place in town that regularly allows DRAG Kings to perform. Saw photos of Kings the group, "Femznstudz." I thought I could do that. I decided to put my money where my mouth was and reached out to them to perform at their next show.

❁Atown: Lemoore and my first actual "gig" was the Sandra Valls show.

❁Hurricane Savage: Club Majestic Tulsa, Oklahoma, USA. I thought it went great. **❁Marcus Mayhem:** TNT in Tulsa, Oklahoma, USA. The show manager is a friend of mine (Shannon) and I never seen a DRAG show before. She talked me into going and after a month of watching I tried it out and fell in love with the art. First songs were wicked game by him and kiss me deadly by reel big fish.

❁Rychard "Alpha" Le'Sabre: First place in face was in Tacoma, Washington, USA at On The Rocks, but first stage was a college show at TCC. It went well, and I was invited to come back, and made some amazing friends

❁Corey James Caster: My first gig was at Chill Chamber I performed "Friends in Low Places." It was on a talent night and I won.

❁Shane Rebel Caine: My first gig was at the Carousel II for talent night, as was my first paid booking because I would won their talent night. It went decent considering I would only been performing for a little over a month.

❁B J Bottoms: I went to see the show and afterwards spoke with the show director, told her I was interested in performing. She booked me for a show a few weeks later.

❁Stefon SanDiego: My first gig was at Seekers Show Bar in Port Huron, Michigan, USA. It came about during the holidays and Kings were mild and few. Children and families in struggle benefited from food, toys, and clothes for their families. Last year we raised $12,000 in proceeds and indeed the children if St. Clair County flourished!

❊**Pierce Gabriel:** JR's Place in Olathe, Kansas, USA. I had been attending Buttwiser's Bash shows every week. I was surprised and excited when the emcee, Butt Wiser offered a spot the following week. I have been a proud Bashian ever since.

❊**Alec Allnight:** A pride fundraiser at The North Tower Circle in Fresno, California, USA. Many never done DRAG. My roommate, Shannon Price and my outfielder on my softball team, Leilani Price, both performed, so I had many pictures on my Facebook with many of the local Queens. My girlfriend started Ladies' Niight called SheBar with DRAG kings performing once a month. That is why I was asked if I was interested. I had two months to prepare and there was a lot of trial and error! I wanted to do Moves Like Jagger. Nevertheless, it had to be epic. I went all out and duct taped my tits in my armpits, drew on my abs and Adam Levine tats, and went for it! It was awesome! I do not remember a lot of it, but I was slapped in the face with some money so that was good be great it was a fundraiser and all! I have been performing at least once a month at SheBar ever since. In addition, anywhere else I have been invited.

❊**Ryder Knightly:** L4 lounge in Charlotte, North Carolina USA. They were holding their first DRAG king talent show, and needed help. I completely loss, but made two of my closes friend Jamel Knight, and Macximus. Jamel definitely kicked our asses.

❊**Kruz Mhee:** Quest in Birmingham, Alabama, USA. I helped put together a show where entertainers performed opposite their norm. It was called "Alter Ego." Kruz performed "Wake up call" and now refuses to go back to being Paula on stage.

❊**Hawk Stuart:** My first one was a bar in California, USA, but my first one in Florida, USA, was a bar called Georgie's.

❊**Silk Steele Prince:** Club Escape in Chicago, Illinois, USA; a gender blender routine. I came out as Sisco of the R&B group Dru Hill. By the second half of my song, the mustache was in my pocket and my clothes came off. I was in full stripper ware. It was awesome. The crowd was wild, shocked, or confused. By the end of the night, people were congratulating my performance. I knew this is what I wanted to do.

❊**Flex Jonez:** Charle's West New Jersey, USA, with Ms. Jackson. Very positive and was booked for following gigs after as the bar's only King.

❊**SirMandingo Thatis:** First time was at a bar called DC's. It was a disaster. I fell on the slick stage, my dress shoes were new, and I could not see because of the spotlight. Fourteen years ago, I saw a local bar (The Q) in Lincoln, Nebraska, USA (now called Karma). They were having their annual Mr. Q Pageant so I said to myself I can do this and I put in a app paid my entry fee and the rest is history In thirteen months I have been Mr. Q and also Mr. Max Mi.

❦Kenneth J. Squires: My first real gig was at The Bar in Lexington, Kentucky. I was performing for a fundraiser called, DRAGgin for Jesus. It was fun and many people were nice to me. I got a lot of feedback and took it all in.

❦Harry Pi: Open Stage at Masque Nightclub, Ohio USA. I had a blast.

❦Mike Oxready: My first was a show called DRAGnomenon, a contest and a benefit for a couple of youth organizations in town. There was a tryout, I was put on the lineup, and performed with my partner at the time. First place!

❦J Breezy St James: My first time performing was at Panic Bar in Lincoln, Nebraska for their beauty and beast pageant for kings and Queens that had never performed before and to this day, I consider it my home bar.

❦Abs Hart: Boom in Oklahoma City, March 2010. My younger brother was a female illusionist, and recently moved to California, so I thought someone in the family needed to carry on. I signed up for the "talent night" called "trashy Thursdays." The first song I ever performed was Adam Lambert's "For Your Entertainment." I drew facial hair on with brown markers, and a friend of mine helped wrap my chest with three ace bandages. Every Queen in the dressing room hit on me. I looked ridiculous, looking back. I had a blast, and I have been hooked ever since. Adam Lambert actually came up to that bar one night, the night before his concert, and I walked up, introduced myself, and told him the first song I ever did DRAG to was his song.

❦Cody Wellch Klondyke: My very First Gig was In Monroe, Louisiana, USA. In Club Pink we had, the DRAG King Group Boyzz II Men the bar was full of people. It was something new to the Club. .

❦George De Micheal: As part of the DRAG kings of Manchester, England, United Kingdom. I had my first performance at the birdcage nightclub. My first paid gig in London, England, United Kingdom at a place called the Royal Vauxhall Tavern. RVT.

❦Thug Passion: Our Fantasy Complex in Wichita, Kansas, USA. It was on the Brown Sugar Show on a Thursday night. This show is a talent showcase show. It was a competition between eight to twelve people. The talent could be anything live singing, dancing, plays a instrument, or male or female illusion. You could win $25, a chance to perform on a Sunday with the Fantasy Follies. I performed my first song with a good friend of mine. The outcome that night was I won the competition.

❦Colin Grey: Roz Ryan show on a Friday night at Weatherbee's in Kansas City, Missouri, USA. Thankful for Queens like Roz Ryan, Sunny Delight, Gina Blake, and Marvin Nathan. I am even more thankful to Buttwiser for giving me a solid place to hone my craft as a king and entertainer through the years.

❀**Stefan LeDude:** It was at a bar called "Le Drugstore" in Montreal, Canada.

❀**Xavier Bottoms:** I was asked to do a duet with Ophelia Bottoms. It was a benefit show. I had a mullet, rat-tail, and glasses. It went over very well. I was asked to perform at that bar for the regular show the following month.

❀**Jamel Knight:** In 2004. A friend, Monica Simpson started "Jump off Thursdays" at a place we called The Barn, to come out and perform, begged me repeatedly. She loved the way I would just dance in the club and thought I would be a good performer. After about 4 months of her begging, I finally gave in and agreed to perform in their Christmas Eve show. That show was crazy. It was packed and standing room only. Nervous does not describe what I felt that night. I have been on stage before quite a few times since the age of 3 but this was the first time I had ever performed in an LGBT establishment as a DRAG king and I really had no idea what I was doing. But, the funny thing is backstage I was officially introduced to my now girlfriend of 10 years and that kind of helped with the nervousness because at that point it was all about impressing her and I almost forgot about all the people out there. That was actually a great night and I had a ball performing and evidently did not do too bad.

❀**Master Cameron Eric Leon:** A little dive bar here in Ottawa, Canada. I was a regular there for years, and a friend with the house Queen. I dressed up as Gregory House, M.D. for Halloween and popped in to say hi. Alyna did not recognize me and was shocked at how good I was. She told me I had to do a show, to which of course I agreed. I ended up doing DRAG for my birthday a month and a half later.

❀**Welland Dowd:** McGill University Bi-Annual Amateur DRAG and Burlesque night. I ended up being the finale number and even though I was nervous as fuck, people literally jumped out of their seats at the end to give me a huge round of applause. It was incredible. I realized DRAG was something I definitely needed in my life.

❀**DeVery Bess:** Faggity Ass Friday's was the first appearance of DeVery! I performed alongside Ian Po Kerr and Nat King Pole who was singing live, hilarious great night never would forget that night ever! I was in a troop that did a yearly show, and the show hadn't passed yet, but Nat King Pole was asked to do a number at faggity and asked who would like to help him out and I wanted to so that is how that happened.

❀**Michael Christian:** Open mic talent contest at the Rainbow Room in Detroit, Michigan, USA. Hosted by Trixxie Deluxxe. A wonderful outlet to be free to myself.

❀**Julius M. SeizeHer:** OneNTen Phoenix, Arizona, USA. My big gig was Pride 2013. I made $2 on the community stage (not bad for a first timer, in my eyes) and Jensen C. Dean was impressed. Me, a first timer!

❀**Howie Feltersnatch:** An amateur competition three years ago with fake Mustache. I got third place. I came back every show with a new number and willingness to learn.

❀**Jack E. Dickinson:** My first gig was a DRAG king competition, Meow Mix show, a cabaret for bent girls and their buddies in Montreal, Canada. It no longer exists but ran for over 10 years. I won which amazed and thrilled me, though I am not the competitive type. I met some fantastic performers. I made connections and we started to perform together. Eventually led to the creation of a troupe called The Dukes of DRAG, which lasted seven years. We performed in Montreal, Canada at various gigs, put on our own annual show every year and even traveled to perform in Toronto, Quebec City, Ottawa, Canada and some other towns.

❀**Travis Hard:** With the Miltown Kings in Milwaukee, Wisconsin, USA at the Miramar Theatre. These guys are amazing and gave me the chance to get out there. Anytime during the season, give them a look and check them out

❀**Clark Kunt:** Five minutes of Fame at Reflections Cabaret in Halifax, Nova Scotia. I almost threw up on stage and had a panic attack, but the judges gave me great constructive criticism. I did not make it into the second round.

❀**Juan Kerr:** I ran a burlesque night in my hometown called 'Cherry on Top'. My friends and I organized a gay venue, called 'The Hangout' to host it. The first was a charity event. The second one ran better than the first one but the first one was packed out and we raised £400 for the charity so it was a good night.

❀**Trey C. Michaels:** A pageant that I bombed but first non-pageant performance was at BS West in Scottsdale for the stars of tomorrow show.

❀**Bailey Saint James:** Chicago, Illinois, USA, with the former Chicago Boi Toiz, led by Gia and Sebastion Cock Las Vegas, Nevada, USA. I asked to join and was given the opportunity to be involved in a group number.

❀**Aaron Phoenix:** An all-king show at a club called RandD in St. Petersburg, Florida USA. A friend put it together, said I had a great look for DRAG, and convinced me to give it a shot. It was fun putting together, got some great feedback from the audience and other performers, and was hooked.

❀**Soco Dupree:** Play Dance Bar in Nashville, Tennessee, USA.

❀**LoUis CYfer:** At the Admiral Duncan in Soho!

❀**Stefon Royce Iman:** Escuelita in New York City, USA. I did a sexy number and made the men go wild. They were waiting for me to come out the dressing room. I always did well on the gay boys market. They support DRAG.

❀**Santana Romero** A local lesbian bar named Outskirts. The owner, Lexi Staples, asked me to do my first solo number as member of the troupe, Bois W/ Outskirts. I could not have been more pumped. From this came my very first home bar where I met some of the most amazing people on the planet, had opportunities to perform for my community, and really come into myself as an entertainer. Unfortunately, Outskirts is now closed but the experiences (good and bad alike) will always follow me for as long as I am doing DRAG.

❀Jensen C. Dean: A pageant. I competed for the title of Mister Rainbow Cactus (a prelim to the Mister Phoenix Gay Pride pageant). I was so nervous, I was bound for the first time by Freddy Prinze Charming about 30 minutes before the pageant started, and I did not know how to really move in duct tape. In the end it went well I was crowned Mister Rainbow Cactus 2013

❀Smitty O'Toole: EJ's Bar in Houston, Texas, USA. I became a part of the Houston Gendermyn and my first performance was a strip tease to Sexy Back. The bar was packed and it was a Benefit show for a friend who had health issues. It went well and led to a weekly gig there from that week on.

❀William Vanity Matrix: The Bang, Bang Queer Punk Variety Show at the Hidden Castle in Norman, Oklahoma, USA. There are no more DRAG shows there. I miss it dearly. It had a great set up and I wish it were still around

❀MaXx Decco: Open stage The GYPSY in Las Vegas, Nevada, USA.

❀LoUis CYfer: At the Admiral Duncan in Soho. I dressed as a vicar. People thought I was a camp boy, up for a singsong dressed alike the vicar of dibly.

❀Bootzy Edwards Collynz: My first gig was for my friends Matt, Doc, And Starr. I was one of the Hip Hop DJs at this club named 60 South in Denver; Colorado (was on South Broadway). Matt, Doc, and Starr some of were the original founding Kings of the "South Town Kingz" and "The Zu Kingz" here in Denver. They decided to do a monthly show and were producing the whole thing themselves. They had a great cast of DRAG Kings and Queen, even a few variety acts. At that time, I worked with my dance troupe, "RoyalRush" (a dance/Janet Jackson Tribute troupe) at that time. We used the basement for rehearsals at the club, and were there on the weekends. I was not really into DRAG at the time, because of working with my troupe and our schedule was pretty busy. But I would be there for support and cocktails after my dance rehearsal. After all those were my boys and I was excited to see their first show. They named the show "MDS" got flyers and passed them out. Their opening night they had a "no call/no show," and asked if I would do 2 songs to help fill. Starr helped me bind for the first time ever, which looked a little lopsided. I did "Humpin Around" by Bobby Brown and "Do I Do" by Stevie Wonder. It still took a few months before I really started performing more regularly.

❀Devin G. Dame: I lost a bet and performed the first time in a tuxedo at Destiny's in Tacoma, Washington, USA. I loved it and was hooked.

❀Dionysus W Khaos: It was a benefit for CARE in Tucson Arizona, USA, I knew after that moment I never wanted to leave the stage.

Chapter Three
"Name the best show bars in your town? What were the best show bars in your life?"
❀❀❀

❀**D-Luv Saviyon:** Currently the Playbois and Divas of Play Dance Bar's Ladies Night in Nashville, TN. Of my life, The Connection, Club Amnesia*, and The Shute* of all of Nashville, TN (*now closed), Angles in OKC, Hamburger Mary's in Long Beach, CA, Club Masque in Dayton, OH, Club 708 in Atlanta, GA, and The Parliament House in Orlando, Fl. Except Amnesia, I have seen AMAZING entertainers perform in all these venues. Many of these venues are also, where major pageants have been held. It was a huge and humbling honor to be able to perform or be a cast member on these stages.

❀**Clint Torres:** North Tower Circle is my favorite. There is Club Legends, The Red Lantern, The Phoenix, and Club Aldo's. I have performed at NTC, Red, and Aldos but always feel at home with the Fresno Fresbians at NTC

❀**Shook ByNature:** Ibiza in Wilmington, North Carolina, USA is my home bar. Club Generations. Club Cabaret Hickory is my second home. Connections in Charleston, North Carolina, is my third home. DejaVu II, QLounge Greensboro, North Carolina. Chemistry Club Greensboro, North Carolina. Pulse in Myrtle Beach, Virginia, USA. Hershee Bar Ambush in VA. Legends in Raleigh! Club Snap ClubHide Away, Pure in Myrtle Beach, Virginia (all USA).

❀**Gus Magendor:** OpenArms Youth Project, The WreckRoom and Club metro Jacksonville, Florida, USA; these are the only clubs I have been to.

❀**Joshua Micheals:** Sadly, both my home bar in Michigan USA, The Rainbow Room and my home bar in Arkansas, USA have closed. The corner bar in Monroe, Louisiana, USA treats their kings amazingly.

❀**Ben Eaten:** My favorite bar to perform at is SoCo Club in Columbia Missouri, USA. Their show director is professional and treats everyone with respect. The best in my hometown is Attitudes Nightclub in St. Louis Missouri. Their show director, Rydyr Reeves does many shows where people can get a start in this craft. He always has a great show and a variety of talent.

❀**Freddy Prinze Charming:** BS West is a great bar for performers. Zoan, the home of my Spotlight show, is a good venue too.

❀**Coti Blayne:** The Wreckroom is my home bar so I will always be partial to it. I also like the Copa - great hosts and great bartenders. Those are my favorite two right now but we have a ton of great places to perform.

❀**Adam Allok:** The Black Cap in Camden, Massachusetts, USA. Madam JoJo's in Soho, and the Royal Vauxhall Tavern in Vauxhall (All in London). These bars I feel I get the best stage, sound, and audience. There I feel respected as an act and confident to perform. Great legendary venues and it is an honor to perform at any one of them any day of the week. I have played others that are brilliant too but these are my top three.

Spacee Kadett: Club Rainbow Room Detroit, Michigan, USA, formerly the Railroad Crossing and later the Birdcage: When it closed its doors last November, my community and I grieved. We wept as if a family member had died because in essence, she had. Gigi's Cabaret, Menjo's, legendary in Detroit. Menjo's was Madonna's hangout in the '70s. I regret to report that Gigi's never has and never will have kings on Fridays or Saturdays. Stilettos, Inkster Michigan, USA - Detroit is lesbian bar and king showcase: The Malebox (Detroit), Innuendo (Detroit), Seekers Showbar (Port Huron, MI), Club Triangle (Flint, MI), The Mixx (Saginaw, MI), Spiral Dance Bar (Lansing, MI), Rumors Nightclub (Grand Rapids, MI), Outskirts (Lesbian bar, Toledo, Ohio, USA- Closed), and Blush (Toledo, OH). Today I work as a full-time cast member of the gorgeous and glossy Play Dance Bar in Louisville. I also owe credit to the amazing Connection Nightclub, Louisville, KY for my start as a National Entertainer, and Purrswaytions Nightclub.

AJ Menendez: Jacksonville, Florida, Untied States is the town that DRAG goes to die, especially for us boiz. I perform mainly out of town or state.

Adam DoEve: There is nothing very close for me in Volant. I have to drive 40 minutes to Butler at M and J Lounge. This my home bar and is the only gay friendly one there. I was the only king up until a few months ago. The other place is an hour away in Pittsburgh at Cattivo. I would like to go to a few other places in Pittsburgh but it is so far away.

Kenneth J. Squires: Here in Lexington Kentucky, USA there is The Bar Complex, Pulse Nightlife, Crossings, The Sound Bar. There also is in Louisville, Kentucky, USA a few bar's, such as Connections and Purrswations. I am sure there are a few others that I have not listed in Louisville. I have not been there in a while.

Chance Wise: There is a special place in my heart for The Norm in Jacksonville, Florida USA, mostly sentimental since this where I started performing. Most of the best clubs in Florida have closed. I did have a blast at Bill's in Ft Lauderdale, Florida, USA...and would go back in a second.

Orion Blaze Browne: Around Pittsburgh, Pennsylvania, USA you have There Ultra Lounge, Cruze, PTown, The Link, and Cattivo if you want to catch a show. Cattivo is really the only place to finds kings except for a few of us the Queens will let in their shows at the other bars. I have performed at all of them. Cattivo will always be home to me. Other bars I like to perform at are Wild Coyote in Follansbee, West Virginia, USA, Vice Versa in Morgantown WV, and Stallions in Harrisburg Pennsylvania, USA.

Stormm: In Wausau, Wisconsin, USA we only have one bar, OZ … It is always a great time… I really liked performing at Napoleas Lounge in Green Bay, Wisconsin, USA. They made you feel like family.

❀**Cody Wellch Klondyke:** Five Nightclub in Madison, Wisconsin, USA

❀**Marty Brown: I** have always been faithful to Club Cabaret in Hickory

❀**Hurricane Savage:** Tulsa, Oklahoma, USA. New Age Renegades for their stage. The Bamboo Lounge for their crowd and Club Majestic for size of crowd/stage and tips.

❀**Marcus Mayhem:** I hope to walk the stage in Amarillo at Club 212. Beautiful stage and I hope my family who lives there will be able to see me.

❀**Jack King:** Cosy bar.

❀**Travis Hard:** We lost two bars in my Rockford. We have The Mix for Tydetanium and the host is Dymond Ty. My next favorite is in Seattle, Washington, USA at Neighbors Nightclub. They have shows all the time.

❀**Shane Rebel Caine:** The best show bar in Knoxville, Tennessee, USA especially for kings, is Kristopher's. It is mostly a lesbian bar and the ladies go crazy! Carousel II was the best but unfortunately, their legacy ended this past December, was the best bar period around here.

❀**Sam Masterson:** The Garden.

❀**Alexander Cameron:** There are not a ton of show bars in my city but I would say the best is The Cabaret. I have also performed at Masque in Dayton, Ohio, USA and Wall Street in Columbus, Ohio. Both venues are incredible and have a strong fan base as far away as Michigan (USA).

❀**Campbell Reid Andrews:** There are not many show bars here but my order would be The Pegasus (Big stage, great management, newbie friendly), The Heat (Has a nice remodeled stage great crowd), and Saint Show Bar (Big stage, busy most show nights).

❀**Rasta Boi Punany:** Beagle Tavern and Bob and Barbaras. These two bars have given me a chance and continue to support me.

❀**Dakota Rain:** Rainbow IN (now closed) and Club hideaway.

❀**Ashton The Adorable Lover:** In Minnesota's twin cities The Gay 90's, The Brass Rail and The Townhouse. My starting venue The Park Nightclub in Roanoke, Virginia, USA. I would love to travel more.

❀**Vinnie Marconi:** Too many clubs to list in the Tampa Bay region, Florida, USA, however, it would read more like the gay yellow pages!

❀**Kruz Mhee:**In Birmingham the top show clubs are The Quest and Al's. One new club on the rise is Our Place. I started performing in a hole in the wall called Bills. There have been many thru the years but that one holds a special place in my heart. Kruz Mhee was born and started at the Quest.

❀**Hawk Stuart:** Too many to name. However, I will say that at each one I went to I did meet my family each at a different place.

❀**Alec Allnight:** My home is The North Tower Circle with The Fresno Fresbians with SheBar. The Phoenix and The Red Lantern are smaller venues. Shout out to Fresno Pride who provided an air-conditioned trailer to get ready in this year!

🌸**Silk Steele Prince:** The Taste in Chicago, Illinois, USA promoted by KatrinaTruLuv a stud performer of KC Productions. They welcome newcomers with open arms. The crowd is mixed with a variety entertainment needs. The kings are greatly appreciated.

🌸**SirMandingo Thatis:** I do believe that The Max Omaha is the best show bar in town. It is ranked among the top three show bars in the USA.

🌸**Flex Jonez:** NC BAR: W29 and CO2 (Both closed), Scorpios, Club Chemistry, and a new one Club Snap. In my life Charlie's West (Closed) They, all have fabulous dressing room space and dance floors are large

🌸**Atown:** Home bar is North Tower Circle in Fresno, California. Hamburger Mary's Long Beach and Play Dance Bar in Nashville, Tennessee USA.

🌸**Cody Wellch Klondyke:** There is a lot here in Houston, Texas, USA, Meator and Tc's Premier show bar, Fbar, and Neon Boots.

🌸**J Breezy St James:** Karma Night Club and cabaret is the best in Lincoln. But the best I have been to is Missy B's in Kansas City, Missouri, USA.

🌸**George De Micheal:** Too many in the Manchester Village to mention.

🌸**Chasin Love:** Spiral in Lansing, Michigan, USA. The paradise cabaret lounge in Angola Indiana, USA, and Partners bar in Battle Creek, Michigan.

🌸**DeVery Bess:** Montreal, Canada venue: cafe Cleopatra, great stage, back stage, and the staff are awesome. Calgary, Canada Dickens pub, great stage, and staff are awesome! But the best of all time was Montreal's Mado`s.

🌸**Colin Grey:** Best show bar was Tootsie's. It closed a few years back after an owner remodeled. I miss this bar. Sidekick's Saloon is a good close second with a great staff.

🌸**Eddie C. Broadway:** Phoenix, Arizona USA. I love performing at Zoan, BS West and The Rock. The Rock is my favorite because of the atmosphere. They have a room set up for shows only. It is small, but fun.

🌸**Stefan LeDude:** Montreal, Canada it was Cafe Cleopatra and the Sala Rossa. In Halifax, Nova Scotia, I have only performed at Menz. Company House does shows.

🌸**Clark Kunt:** Menz and Mollyz in Halifax (Canada). I love the crowds. I have had the honor of performing at Wetspot - the big outdoor stage party during Halifax Pride, as well as at World Pride 2014 in Toronto. While those were incredible experiences that will always be top on my list, I love the intimacy of Menz and the ability to perform to people. We also have performed at Reflections, Company House, at Universities and other spaces in the city.

🌸**Jamel Knight:** Best show bars in Charlotte, North Carolina, USA, are Scorpio's and Cathode Azure. They have some amazing entertainers that are regularly booked and they book big named performers from other areas.

❀**Jamel Knight:** The up and coming L4 Lounge. They are building their shows around diversity and really have a love for DRAG kings.

❀**Howie Feltersnatch:** Calgary, Canada, we have dickens pub, our stage is big and is able to fit all our group numbers. The servers are amazing. When we started performing there, they only had one server.

❀**Welland Dowd:** In Montréal, Canada most king shows happen at the Café Cleopatra. I have also performed at the Sala Rosa, the Royal Phoenix, and big stages as part of the Just For Laughs festival.

❀**Michael Christian:** Rumors Nightclub, Grand Rapids Michigan, USA. The Mixx, Saginaw Michigan. The Partners Bar Battle Creek Michigan, Stilettos Inkster Michigan, Spiral Lansing Michigan, Gigi's Detroit (though the only time you'll find kings is an off night show. The Saturday Night show in the cabaret is for the Queens currently).

❀**Julius M. SeizeHer:** Charlie's, The Rock, ICE Pics... (Phoenix, AZ USA)

❀**Lyle Love-It:** FIVE In Madison Wisconsin, USA. (Great stage, shows well-promoted, friendly staff and venue owner is very supportive) and The Flame in Superior Wisconsin, USA, great atmosphere and beautiful town.

❀**Jonah Godfather of DRAG:** Rehab in St Louis (Missouri, USA) is the home of the FRatPack where a diverse group of kings that entertain.. We also bring in a Lady of the Evening because everyone loves a queen. Hummel's in St Louis is the actual bar I started performing at. It has went through a few name changes and owners in the 14 years since I started, but it is still the same crowd and entertainers. It is a laid back, older, country crowd. I would like to mention Attitudes and Honey. I do not normally perform there but I have had the chance on a few occasions. I do want to recommend them also because they are so welcoming to kings.

❀**Dante Diamond:** Sue Ellen's in Dallas, Texas, USA is home to the bi-monthly Mustache Envy show, and the weekly Tuesday Tease show; the Rose Room at Station 4 sometimes has kings in the Thursday night "Rising Star" talent night, but the entire cast has been supportive of kings.

❀**Jack E. Dickinson:** The Dukes of DRAG performed most often at Sala Rossa in Montreal, Canada, which hosted the now defunct Meow Mix cabaret evenings. It was an awesome place to perform as it had an actual stage with curtains! Café Cleopatra is also worthy of mention. They have been supporting community groups, amateur performers, and alternative performers of all types for a long time! In addition, with their stage, you are really close to the crowd, which has its own charm.

❀**Xavier Bottoms:** Freddie's Beach Bar and Grill in Crystal City, Virginia, USA for best show with all types of performers. PW's in Laurel, Maryland, USA is the best for the R&B crowd. Cobalt in Washington, District of Columbia, USA also has all types of performers (parking is a pain). Ziegfeld's in Washington, D.C. has the best all DRAG Queen show.

❀**Emilio:** Performing all over the Pacific Northwest for Inferno/Hot Flash Dances. My favorites: Crystal Ballroom in Portland, OR in front of over 3,000 women at Portland Pride, and at Neighbours Nightclub in Seattle, Washington, USA for Seattle Pride.

❀**Juan Kerr:** BOI BOX @ She bar in London. There are other nights in London that I have yet to go to. I quite like another called Bar Wotever in Vauxhall, London, England. They do loads of cool nights.

❀**Brandon KC Young-Taylor:** I travel the USA. My most memorable: Martha's Vineyard, Springfield, Missouri, USA, Spectrum, Memphis, Tennessee, USA, Honey Pot, Ybor City, Florida, USA, Brickhouse, Evansville, Indiana, USA, Play Dance Bar, both Nashville, Tennessee, USA. and Louisville, Kentucky, USA.

❀**Trey C. Michaels:** For Albuquerque, New Mexico, USA there is the Social club (members only) and Sidewinders. They have shows every weekend that are guaranteed to be amazing.

❀**Bailey Saint James:** La Cage, Milwaukee, Wisconsin, USA.

❀**Stefon Royce Iman:** Suite Lounge, Escuelita, El Morocco all in New York City, New York, USA, Liquid 891 in Harrisburg Pennsylvania, USA, Bob and Barbara in Philadelphia, USA, Lana Lounge in Hoboken New Jersey, Omega in Washington DC, USA to name a few. I been all over the USA performing.

❀**E. M. Shaun:** Legends in Raleigh, North Carolina, USA , Time Out in Greensboro, North Carolina, USA, The Q Lounge in Greensboro, North Carolina, USA, Club Cabaret in Hickory, North Carolina, USA

❀**Santana Romero:** Bret'z, Rhouse, Legends, Mojo's and Outskirts are the best only LGBT show/dance bars in Toledo, Ohio USA. I am pretty close with the show directors at most of them and the patrons are awesome. Other venues I haveperformed that are fantastic and have treated me well include Wall Street and Axis in Columbus, OH, Crew Bomb in Canton, OH, Rumors in Grand Rapids, MI, and last but not least Stilettos in Inkster, MI.

❀**Soco Dupree:** All the Nashville, Tennessee, USA bars are fantastic. From Play to Traxx to Chameleons Lounge. All have amazing talent.

❀**B J Armani:** We do not have gay bars in North Dakota (USA) but you can convince any venue to have a show as long as you bring entertainment and fans. Shout to Level 10 in Grand Forks for giving my show it is first home and the American Legion in East Grand Forks for giving us a home when Level 10 got too small.

❀**Luke Ateraz:** Phoenix, Arizona, USA, the best show bars are BS West, Zoan, The Rock, and Rainbow Cactus. Riverside California, USA, the best is VIP Nightclub.

❀**Smitty O'Toole:** Houston, Texas, USA. Love performing at FBar. My home bar was EJ's but it recently closed. I also like the shows at Meteor and TC's.

❀**LoUis CYfer:** Admiral Duncan Soho, Black cap London, England, and Ruby at Vauxhall London, England.

🌸**Jensen C. Dean:** Phoenix, Arizona (USA), I would have to say some of the best bars are Rainbow Cactus, Zoan, Crusin' 7th, The Rock, and BS West

🌸**Kameo Dupree:** Currently the best show bars in town would be Rehab and The Honey Hole. Both are located in the Grove! Best I ever performed in would be Spectrum and they are located in Memphis, Tennessee (USA).

🌸**Mike Oxready:** In Vermont, USA we have Higher Ground, Monkey House, and ArtsRiot as the primary venues for performances.

🌸**William Vanity Matrix:** Oklahoma, USA we have Club Majestics, Renegades, The Pheonix Rising, Angles, and my DRAG 'home' the Wreckroom; a DRAG boot camp.

🌸**Lyle Love-it:** FIVE in Madison, Wisconsin, USA.

🌸**Devin G. Dame:** The Masque Nightclub - Dayton, OH. Stiletto's - Inkster, MI. Angle's - OKC, OK. Touche - Springfield, Missouri, USA (formally The Edge). Rumors - Springfield, MO. and Destiny's - Tacoma, Washington.

🌸**Bailey Saint James:** Scandals in Springfield, Illinois, USA treats kings very well! Circuit of Chicago Illinois and Ricky's in the High Desert of California, USA. Also former clubs Triangle and Monas of Milwaukee, Wisconsin, USA.

🌸**Dionysus W Khaos:** In Tucson, Arizona, USA there are only three bars with shows and one is now a straight bar. Sagebrush, IBTs and Brodie's. My favorite bar I have performed at is Masque in Dayton, Ohio, USA.

This book became a reality for Kings, once Vinnie Marconi convinced me "Kings were ready to take the lead." Boy, was he right!

Chapter Four
"When did you know you had the confidence and talent to perform in front of an audience?"

❀❀❀

❀**Shook ByNature:** I knew I had the confidence to be a stud stripper so DRAG was just an evolution. I had to be more creative and meld the styles... and at the time Kings around me were not doing that... in my first performances I focused too much on playing to the ladies and getting tips... I had to learn how to connect with the crowd in more than just a sexual way... I have fun and make sure that I am able to remain respectful to myself, my girlfriend and my audience.. and I keep it positive!

❀**Freddy Prinze Charming:** I would been performing on stage since I was a toddler. Church plays, school plays, band, choir, musicals, community theatre. The performing was not an issue. I knew I had a certain amount of stage presence and acting skill, both of which are handy to have if you are going to perform in any capacity. What was tricky for me was figuring out how to make myself look like a man. My very first public performance as Freddy was a mess, but not as messy as some. I did use real facial hair, though my skill with the spirit gum was lacking. I bound, badly, with duct tape, but my breasts were hidden. I knew my words and my choreography. By the time I had my second performance, my facial hair was much better, I had purchased a binder. With each performance, I knew I had to research, to learn, to grow. I was not satisfied with my package, and knew it was up to me to make it better.

❀**B J Armani:** I would been in theatre/band/choir all throughout my school years so that in itself prepared me for the stage. What I was NOT prepared for was the fact that you are always changing and having to come up with a new idea or gimmick to "grab" your audience. Many DRAG shows are performed in bar settings and people tend to have short attention spans. SO sequins were utilized and bigger and crazier costumes were created. Now this was after some time that the fedora and sequins became my trademark. I remember first performing "Welcome to the Jungle" in mom jeans, I had shredded. I since learned to ONLY buy men's clothing and make sure the "uniboob" does not happen. (White t-shirts are the DEVIL sometimes with that.) Costumes and the look aside I always tell new performers to pick songs that are TOP 40 of ANY decade. If you perform a song that is obscure than you become the dreaded "smoke/bathroom" break. As far as being "ready" you perform I have always said that if you aren't nervous before EVERY show get your butt off that stage cause being comfortable is one thing but complacency is a killer. Too many performers rest on their laurels. ALWAYS remember that being nervous is a good thing. I am not always sure I am ready, but the costume is usually pretty awesome, it is how I stack the deck.

❦**Orion Blaze Browne:** I was not ready confidence wise for my first performance. I think I took a total of $3 in tip, which came from my friends. The rest of the audience was blank face. After my first performance, I got a rush and wanted to do it again. It took me 2-3 months to be confident enough to actually interact with the crowd and not just grab n run when collecting tips. With more experience, I grew to the performer I am today. I can honestly say I still get butterflies before every number but as soon as the music hits my adrenaline goes and I dance my heart out. Looking back at old videos and pictures, I cannot help but wonder, "What was I thinking?" "It is also because I am my own worst critique. You need to allow yourself to grow and learn from every experience both on and off stage. It does get easier but it never stops being work. I wish I could have started DRAG years ago as the performer I am and with what I know now but each successful and not so successful performance has made me the king I am and I continue to learn and grow more every time.

❦**Dominic:** Jill Horstmann and Amanda Wilkin did not give me much choice. I was terrified but once we finished the show with a few drinks, it was the best feeling in the world and an adrenaline rush! I grew from learning and watching other performers.

❦**D-Luv Saviyon :** First started as a backup dancer and choreographer for an all stud group called Anonymous Men, so I was able to get my nerves under control about being on stage. Although I tried not to, I often stood out in performances and encouraged by the promoter who gave me my first shot about performing. The next step was a duo; I knew I was ready when my performance partner and I had made the perfect mix, followed by weeks of practice of choreography and learning words. I was EXTREMELY blessed to have some of Nashville's best male impersonators at that time to mentor and guide me in the beginning. In hindsight, I would have used real facial hair from the beginning, had better fitting clothes, and more eye contact/crowd interaction. As far as what I brought to the stage in confidence and dance, I would not change a thing because I have always left my heart on the stage.

❦**Clint Torres:** I had done drama all throughout Jr High and High School so I knew at a young age that I was comfortable on stage. It was not until I got the lead role in a local play called "A Kinky Night In Paris" that I really got the confidence to keep going to keep performing. My DRAG dad always overlooked all my performances before I took stage and he critiqued me so that I knew what to do and what not to do. Now I can pretty much tell for myself what is going to work. The audience only responds to confidence in the performers so if you do not have it there be able to tell.

❦**Koomah:** I have always enjoyed entertaining folks, volunteering, and fundraising. First gig was fundraiser and since they were short on performers, I agreed to perform the night before and I made something up. I never considered confidence when I agreed to get onstage, I did not think about talent (I hope I am at least entertaining!), I just thought about helping out. I still get anxious before performances but not nervous. It is good; it is adrenaline and it means I will bring it onstage. I have found that if I ever do not feel anxious excitement before I go onstage it is probably time to put that number on break because I put it on autopilot onstage and just kind of go through the motions without performing it at my best. Now all I do is art and performance - this is my job.

Vinnie Marconi: AFTER my first performance. I try hard not to do something I am not prepared for. I had my real friends at that show, the kind that shoots from the hip, good, bad, or indifferent! They laughed and clapped, they gave me suggestions and encouragement, THEY liked it, (and they are a tough crowd!). I have been a sponge since and sought the best around to learn how to improve… I LISTEN!

Gus Magendor: I had confidence in performing because I had always loved to dance because it was a passion. Everyone I had ever danced in front of told me I should go into dance as a career. The only mistakes I had made in past performances what not having the proper supplies like binding and proper facial hair.

Chance Wise: I have always been a performer. I spent my life on stage in choirs, choruses, and garage bands, and DRAG seemed like the natural progression for me. It is a lot different from having a band or group of singers up there with you, but it was somewhat nice being the only one out there doing me. I had to learn very quickly to be humble and take criticism, cos I was not as good starting out as I thought I was. The more I listened the more I learned and took that to the stage and the better response I got. I still have a lot to learn after 7 years.

Travis Hard: I really never knew, I just kept going out and doing it. I gained confidence over the years. While it did get to my head, I find my confidence has outgrown my ego and just seems to grow humbly as I age.

Rasta Boi Punany: My first time on stage was as a Punk Rocker singing the rap section of Blondie's' Rapture'. I threw up afterwards. My first time on stage as a DRAG King, I became the character. I won the competition and my first title. I realized Rochelle has stage fright, Rasta does not. There lies my confidence.

Jack King: I have stage fright, but when there were no kings here, so I took the plunge and still struggle. I want to go out with and I wanted to show that there were kings and give the Pride something else to look at

Adam All: Never. Never will. I perform because I am always searching for the perfect show and always critiquing myself. Confidence is irrelevant when it is a part of you that MUST be. Every show is magnificently terrifying and fulfills my inner 'Adam' whilst pushing my own creativity.

Atown: I am 100% confident I know my performance front to back, side to side and every single word and motion. When I am feeling the song and

I can put myself in the place (mentally) of the actual performer of the song. The energy of the crowd gets me amped up, and my energy reels them into me. My tips for errors or the viewer's critiques, are know your stage, lighting areas, eye contact, and dramatize your lip sync and movements. Facial expressions are good as well as body language.

❀**Viciouse Slick:** I had performed in theater, speech, and debate for three years in high school so I always had a skill for performing and I would sing to songs. So I was confident in that and even though I knew nothing of how to be a king, I knew if I were confident in my performing, those errors would go away. Before your first show make sure you know what thins to do like binding, makeup and lip-syncing and of course always have fun on stage this makes watching you perform fun

❀**Lyle Love-it: L**ots of practice at home, and support of partner and friends

❀**Joshua Micheals:** I had been doing theatre my whole life and got the jitters out of performing as a male in high school when I performed as Horatio in Hamlet in my small town backwoods city and was given nothing but positive feedback (I was lucky) so a bar fined with friends seemed like nothing.

❀**Eddie C. Broadway:** I knew I had the confidence to perform when I was no longer worried about what other people thought of me. I just acted like me and went for it, without worry about judgment. Looking back, I wish I had been more daring and more courageous. However, I grew very quickly and began to look more confident, feel more confident, and be more confident.

❀**Stormm:** A lot of practice... performing live can be hard... missing words music malfunction... just go out there and have a good time.

❀**Dominic Von Strap:** I did not. I never would have the courage to do it. My mentor had faith and encouraged me to get on that stage at a charity show. He convinced me to go for my first title, which I would not have had the nerve to go alone. I did not think I would win. I did not think I was talented enough, but Eddie had faith in me.

❀**Travis Luvermore:** Friend pressured me to give it a try. I found the right country song, how do you like me now. I was a nervous wreck until the crowd got into it. I learned that knowing your words and making eye contact with the audience, your performing clothes are very important, as your song choice.

❀**Persian Prince:** Mine was more a challenge. People said I was too femme to do it, so I had to prove them wrong. I ended up enjoying the first couple of times. I learned do not put your belt over your binder if you are going to dance.

❀**Kody Sky:** I did not know. It was not planned to become a male impersonator. People seeing me perform, praised and encouraged me to come back. When I first started, I did a lot more dancing than audience interaction; I had to learn that over time. Thinking of then and now, one of the most important things to remember is that you need to PERFORM the song and grab the hearts of the audience, do not just stand there or run around in circles, (as I have seen in some new performers).

❀**AJ Menendez:** I started performing as a Diva. Performing on stage was never a real problem for me but it was not until I performed as a king for the first time that I found my nitch. Even after all these years, I still get nervous before I go on stage for my first number. Do not know why, I just do.

❀**Romeo Sanchez:** I grew up in theatre and dance. I was not confident enough to get on stage in the beginning, but the more I performed, the more confident I became.

❀**King Dante:** I have been gay my whole life it came naturally.

❀**Hurricane Savage:** Really, I JUST WENT FOR IT! I was not sure if I would do well at it or not but I wanted to try it so bad!

❀**Marcus Mayhem:** I tried it to see if I could.

❀**Rychard "Alpha" Le'Sabrel:** I have been a performer since the 1st grade. I did Choir but I had stage fright so solos were always an issue, and I took Salsa and swing dance lessons in my teen years. It is always just been in my blood to perform, but with "DRAG" you can be someone completely different. The stage fright completely vanished; create who you always wished you could be, and "Just Do It."

❀**Corey James Caster:** I was always a performer.

❀**Scorpio:** I started performing at a young age from chorus to color guard/winter guard. Competing nationally as an independent winter guard taught me to convey emotion and to set the "mood" for songs to audiences.

❀**Shane Rebel Caine:** I got my confidence when a Queen who I look up to encouraged me to do it. I spent two months trying to learn what I could to be ready for my first show, I used Halloween makeup to make my beard, and although it was not too bad, looking it was shiny in the stage lights and more smeared looking than hairy. I used ace bandages to bind and struggled with them always rolling up or down on me. There was rarely much of a crowd for the talent nights and instead of putting on my own energetic performance, I tried too hard to perform to the crowd and with a lack of people that proved difficult. No matter how small or how big a crowd is, nor how big or how small the stage is, always give it you are all and act like you are putting on your own concert or making a music video, venues will be more impressed if you can still have stage presence with very little crowd and a huge stage.

❀**B J Bottoms:** I honestly had no idea if I had the confidence or the talent to perform. I just took the risk and let whatever was going to happen, happen. Looking back on my first show to where I am now I would not change a thing. As the years have gone on I evolved as an entertainer the way I am supposed to. With a lot of help from my family I am able to be the entertainer I am today. We all start somewhere I do not feel like I can say I made errors the first few times because if it weren't for first few shows and just getting out there I wouldn't have the career that I do now. It is all about trust yourself and finding mentors who will help you grow. Never be afraid to seek the help and advice from those who have come before you. Do not ever settle for anything less than your best and always look for new ways not only to make your performance better but make yourself as an entertainer better.

Dakota Rain: I am very shy but being on stage changes me. I had no clue I could do it until I stepped on stage. I have learned so much the past five years

Stefon SanDiego: Growing up with my father having a band most my childhood, I became his biggest fan. Music seemed to bring me alive in such a serious sense of expression. My confidence came from the many Queens back 20 years ago who believed my ambition was enough. Therefore, with the support of the Queens back then, while "Kings" were still out the spotlight per say when it came to that stage, I ventured into the world of ace bandages, clear plastic wrap, eyeliners, brown eye shadows and found a passion upon that stage through a great cause raising Toys for Kids. Looking back in those days, I recommend a focal point when performing. Often as entertainers, we find ourselves nervous during the performance, but to have that one focal point finds you back in the realms of your crowd. Quite often entertainers forget their words to their numbers and in doing so can fluke the whole performance. With any great entertainer, he/she picks up that mistake in an instance without being noticed (for the most part). Being a part of the crowd in which one is entertaining is a main attribute to a great show!

Ben Eaten: I have always been able to perform in front of people because of prior things. The talent portion I just went up there and tried it, I asked for a lot of advice and I learn more things with every show. My obvious errors were not know how to move on stage and not to look like a girl on stage. I had to watch myself in a mirror and videos to help correct it.

Spacee Kadett: I have always been a ham. The trick was being a BOY ham. Now that was something I did not want to do. Then I recognized the theatricality in DRAG -- which the art was about portraying any character, so long as it was male, and I found my comfort zone. That is what I recommend to any new entertainer. Find a happy medium between what you like, and what your audience will like. Perform your favorite Top 40 songs from any decade. Be a character that is YOU first, and then branch out. I still struggle with "sexy," but I am learning. My character wears bowties and pants higher than his belly button! It is a big leap for me! However, it goes to show that even seasoned performers have to step outside their comfort zone. You are not alone just because you are a newbie.

❊Pierce Gabriel: Since I would been on stage countless times before, I jumped at the chance to try it in DRAG. I shudder when I remember the first several performances though, and refuse to watch those early videos. After getting plenty of pointers from my DRAG brothers and sisters, I started watching music videos to learn the differences between how males and females move - posture, expressions, every detail. People do not realize that the illusion is more than just clothes, binding and facial hair. A lot of work has to go into the body language as well.

❊Brandon KC Young-Taylor: When I took the stage for the first time I had never been on stage solo. I was part of the band in school, did drama and the praise team at church but nothing solo. I was nervous but something about being on stage as a boy gave me the confidence. Looking back I know I made every mistake every new king makes. My facial hair was not great, I used no makeup and did not have one costume.

❊Alec Allnight: I did not know until the music started. I was asked to perform for a pride fundraiser. All the performers had never done DRAG before. I did "Moves Like Jagger," so I asked my roommate to be my Christina. He has done DRAG for years, so that made me feel a little more confident. I was so nervous I do not remember much. Good thing I got it on video! I have definitely gotten better and more comfortable. My makeup, facial hair, and duct tape skills are way better and always improving.

❊Ryder Knightly: I have always been considered the "entertainer' I say the perks of having ADHD. My friends are the owner of this great Lesbian bar, and they needed more kings for their talent show, and asked if I could do it. I knew they needed help, and it did not sound so bad. Little did I know how big the turnout was going to be I might have re thought it ha-ha. We all have to start somewhere, and mine was with binding showing and not in a good way, with just eye shadow beard, and long hair clearly trying to be hidden under this horrible hat. I would not have changed a single thing, because without that I would not have had a base to learn new things.

❊Kruz Mhee: I have had the confidence since I was a kid. It is not to say that I think I'm all that, but I have always enjoyed the crowd response to whatever I'm doing. I played music, I was on stage and in drama in high school, and I have always enjoyed playing to a crowd. I was nervous the first time I stepped on stage as Kruz. I was not happy with the facial hair, the way my hair came out, or the fact that I had never seen a King perform. There was no one local or even close by that I knew I could ask for help. I did have a couple of friends in local theater that helped with the stage makeup/facial hair. Still, I did not like the fake facial hair on me. It looked extremely fake. My partner suggested I use all make up. After the first year, I started doing a pretty good job of making it look like I grew my own beard. I will admit it is still a learning process and I hope that never changes. Meeting and learning from other male impersonators or DRAG kings just makes me better.

❀Hawk Stuart: First time I took stage, but I still get stage fright every time.

❀Silk Steele Prince: I knew I had confidence and talent to perform in front of an audience the moment I took the stage and the crowd was yelling my name and clapping for me. I knew I was ready to hit the stage after I had practiced repeatedly in front of the mirror and everything felt perfect. Looking back at my first few shows through today's eyes, I should have had a DRAG mother or father to guide me. I would have did more research on other performers performances. I would have ask more questions. I would have learned to sew or be more creative with my wardrobe. I would have learned more about mixing song tracks and took some drama classes.

❀Flex Jonez: Having been taught the skill of stage presence was my secret to being able to perform in any venue. In my youth I had taken plenty of professional acting, dancing classes. With much practice, listening, learning and watching other performers helps. I knew I was ready when I found a signature step and style.

❀SirMandingo Thatis: Even as a child I knew I wanted to be an actress. Originally, I wanted to be an actress on The Young And The Restless. As we can see, that did not happen and so with my love for music and my dancing skills I took to the stage of being a male entertainer. I was always told I look like my dad so I used that to my advantage and I molded my facial hair and clothing style to look like him then I moved on to gather my own style and I have been doing well ever since.

❀Kenneth J. Squires: The first time I stepped out on stage was the beginning of it all. I thought that no one would like me, or what I was doing. I got a few tips and I felt better about my being a DRAG King/MI. My facial hair was not great, and I cannot dance worth anything, so I began practicing makeup on my face and facial hair. Through the years. I have tried many different things, and now, I have it down pat. Practice is the key to it all.

❀Cody Wellch Klondyke: The first time I stepped out on stage I was nervous has heck. I was shaking in my boots. I have learned many different things from my Brothers. My facial hair is a lot easier to put. I have entered many MI Pageants and bar pageants and I learn from the feedback that is given to me.

❀George De Micheal: I was nervous the first time, I still get nervous but I like challenges and with having that drive empowers me to get up and entertain.

❀Colin Grey: I do not think I was ever confident at first. I had an idea and got out there. It was great having friends supporting me. Hardest part of being a king in an all Queen show is not having someone to help seal the deal on the illusion. I spent many of my first performances onstage with no face on what so ever. I let the Queens build me up about how studly I was and got a huge head. I was fortunate enough to have a king group in the city come through and see me perform so I was able to eventually start working with them and work on my image and go through the process of being humbled. I still get nerves to this day as they announce me to the stage.

❀**Sam Masterson:** I have a lot of confidence so I just jumped right in.

❀**DeVery Bess:** I always was good in front of an audience. I have been more shy in smaller group. Very shy and awkward,. but since I was little I loved performing, public speaking, dancing, making a fool of myself.

❀**Jack King:** I always knew.

❀**Xavier Bottoms:** One year at summer camp at age twelve. I was asked to help put on a skit. It was a comedy number. I knew then that making people laugh was my niche. I was not really ever interested on performing on stage but on a softball field or a basketball court. My first performance as Xavier was for a charity event. I have never done DRAG for money, only for the entertainment value. To me, entertaining you is important. I do not want your dollar, but I do want to make you smile. I believe this is missing in today's DRAG. The biggest things I learned, is "know the words to your songs."

❀**Stefan LeDude:** I knew someone who was trying out to perform as a DRAG King in a regular DRAG Queen show they had in a local gay bar. I thought it might be fun to try, though I was not sure I had the guts. Nevertheless, a friend of mine encouraged me, so I decided to give it a shot.

❀**Jamel Knight:** I have always had the confidence to get on stage. It is second nature to me. Nevertheless, I really started believing in myself as a DRAG kings when I was able to fool people I had known for a while. These people would be brutally honest and give critiques for days. So, when they were actually encouraging me to keep going because they saw my potential that is when I knew that I was good at male illusion and could really go far with it.

❀**Welland Dowd:** My first number was in a University amateur DRAG and burlesque show. I brought down the house. I needed this in my life

❀**Kameo Dupree:** Confidence was never the issue with me. It was more of a procrastination within myself. I work out the look, had the clothes, but could not find the motivation to see it through. When I finally hit the stage, almost 4 months had passed. It was the best experience and very grateful for it.

❀**Julius M. SeizeHer:** I have been stage child since I can remember, so confidence was never an issue. When 1n10 Phoenix had their competition to decide performers for Pride 2013, I knew Julius was ready. I took what I had, presented it, and made it. One big error I made, I tend to be stubborn and do not take advice. My advice? Take what is said in all respect. Listen to your DRAG family! It might get you somewhere.

❀Jonah Godfather of DRAG: When I first hit the stage, my performance was years in the making. I had dreamt and visualized about being on stage repeatedly. I had the confidence mentally but I had to get over my hang-up about my body image. I was overweight and I had a problem with my body looking more female than it is now. I learned how to bind and became more accepting of my weight. All my friends were supportive and my first performance went great as they said it would. If I had not had problem with my body image, I would have started performing years earlier. So my advice to any up and coming kings is do not let a little weight keep you from doing what you really want to do.

❀Howie Feltersnatch: Move past your boundaries to gain more confidence and that can be something to live by. When I started I was in a very dark place, and all I wanted was to accept myself. Performing was my first step. Off stage, I was not confident, but on stage, I was able to escape. I was able to show off a side of me that had the confidence to do things I could not do before. You see I am a bigger person. My weight has always played with my image issues. I fell while performing a year ago, and it opened my eyes. It made me realize something needs to change because my weight is affecting the healing of my knee, so I started on a journey. It is been a year since I started this journey, I am 66 pounds lighter, 100% more confident in my own skin and am as happy as I ever been. I feel like I take chances that I never would have taken before. My confidence is no longer just on stage, but every day off stage. Love yourself full heartily and the universe will help you as well. If you feel like you are ready or are just intrigued by performing, I suggest you do it. Watch YouTube to see how other kings do it, and just do it. The confidence may come in time, but you should never put yourself down for not being "as good" as the others that have been performing longer.

❀Jack E. Dickinson: I never really knew for sure if I was ready, I had a strong desire and went with it. A friend convinced me that the crowd where I had my first chance to perform (a local DRAG king competition) would be very receptive and supportive, and that it was not about being a "professional" performer. I had the confidence in my act though because I knew I had the passion for music, knew the lyrics by heart since I had been listening to Iron Maiden's Number of the Beast since I was 14 (I was 33 at the time). I also wanted to bring long hair to the local DRAG King scene. I think I have improved as a performer since those early days, I do not see what I did as "errors." It was all simply part of the path. I think that many DRAG kings start by imitating, to a certain extent, what many DRAG Queens do, which is look convincing and lip-sync. That is fine, but there is so much else we can do, so over the years, along with my troupe, we expanded our horizons to include more dance, theatrics, etc. In addition, like many beginning DRAG kings, I had a bit of a narrow view of masculinity. Over the years, again along with my fellow troupe members, we really opened up to various kinds of masculinity and, ultimately, genderblending. Therefore, I have actually come to a point where I am more of a "DRAG jack" than strictly a DRAG king. I either tend to blend to switch genders on stage, or am sometimes neutral. Nevertheless, I have no regrets about my beginning steps. They were part of the process. Well, maybe one small regret is that sometimes I verged into a slightly macho version of masculinity, which leaves a bad taste in my mouth now.

Clark Kunt: I wanted to perform for years before I actually found the nerve. The day I knew, I was ready, I was at a thrift shop and found an incredible waiter jacket that I just needed for DRAG. That was it. I did not think I was ready even while driving to the venue the first time! I knew myself; I am the type of person that can plan forever without taking action, so I took the plunge during Pride since it was the easiest time for new performers to find a show. The first few performances I was all over the place, number did not organize my costumes, and my make-up was everywhere. When I found my routine that is when things settled. I listen only to my DRAG songs days before a show, packing each costume in a different plastic bag inside my suitcase, make-up used to do my basic face/body on one side, and extra accents on the other.

Lyle Love-it: It is in my blood…it is a rush.

Emilio: I become more confident with every performance. The more comfortable I get on stage, the less I rehearsed prior to shows. I want to explode on the stage when I get up there! I still get nervous, but the nerves are gone once I hit the stage.

Juan Kerr: I have been performing since forever anyway as myself so this was just an extension of that. It is a weird one. The more I stay away from the stage the more nervous I become when I do eventually get back up there. Once I have done a couple of shows in succession I feel better and start enjoying it more, I look way more relaxed in pictures where I have done a few shows than in say my first show back after a month or two.

Bailey Saint James: when I was five years old, I was the lead in a play for the PTA, then again when I was 11. People always told me I dance like a choreographer. I have loved the crowds from birth.

Aaron Phoenix: I have been performing in various forms my whole life, so it was just another art form for me.

Mike Oxready: I did not necessarily think I would be good on stage, but my excitement and passion were enough for me to try. After that, my girlfriend at the time and I decided to form a troupe and perform at the biggest DRAG show of the year. We rehearsed A LOT! Great feedback and positive responses kept us going.

❀**Soco Dupree:** Started DRAG as a way to impress a girl I had been crushing on since high school. After the first night, I knew the stage is where I needed and wanted to be.

❀**Santana Romero** I knew had a burning passion to entertain before I even hit the stage; I just needed to find the right outlet. I knew I was ready as soon as I was allowed my first opportunity to perform and with hardly, any preparation I went for it with all I had. That initial rush of that experience is what pushes me to continue to do what I do. Looking back, I would have definitely made sure my overall appearance was a lot cleaner and that I slowed down a bit more to play with the crowd. I also had a horrible habit of snatching tips, which could have me made me off a little rude to patrons so I quickly changed this when it was brought to my attention.

❀**Stefon Royce Iman:** I said lets go and I was ready I think dancing as an exotic female dancer only made it easy for me to do a show DRAG show. Only thing I can say is I did need help with my face I used to do it wrong and when I taped I thought I would pass out. Now I have learned so much along the way so I am okay.

❀**E. M. Shaun:** I love dancing and always had a secret desire to perform. I used to love working behind the scenes in stage productions but wanted to act. I was scared of doing a Broadway play in school so doing production I felt I gave my contribution. After watching my first DRAG show, I said I could do that. I thought I would have stage fright but instead it felt natural. I said I wanted to have fun and that is what I did.

❀**Smitty O'Toole:** I have been performing since I was in elementary. I started in theater, which transitioned to singing karaoke for years. I wanted to combine the two, and have always been interested in DRAG, so I became involved in it. I had no problem pushing through stage fright, but in the beginning my performances were stiff and I still had feminine movements integrated in my performance, I recorded my shows since the beginning and watch them like game tapes to improve my stage presence.

❀**Papi Chulo Doll:** Been dancing since grade school. I danced for my parents, and family members. So that gave me my confidence.

❀**Jensen C. Dean:** I never had a moment where I knew for sure I could so this I somewhat just jumped in and hoped for the best. Everything came to me in time.

❀**Boi Wonder:** I am very shy. With the help of friends I got on stage. I would not perform alone and certainly not sing. I may consider doing group drama in the near future to build confidence, think slapstick style.

❀**Devin G. Dame:** The first time I was in stage I knew I was born to be on stage. I loved every minute of it and craved it when I was not on it. You do not have success without mistakes and growing from them.

❀**Dionysus W Khaos:** I bet from a friend got me on stage. For me it was a healing process coming out of an abusive relationship.

Chapter Five
"How should a newbie get on stage the first few years, until they have enough experience to have venues contacting them?"
❀❀❀

❀**Koomah:** In my area, there are several fundraiser shows every weekend. They are almost always open to all performers and since they are held at different venues it is a great way to try out acts on different stages, learn different audiences, get to know different club owners and managers. A great way to network for a good cause.

❀**D-Luv Saviyon :** A newbie should be HUNGRY. Get on every stage you can and take in as much information as possible from any and every one you feel has knowledge to help you grow. If possible try to perform in different types of Venus and not just local main clubs, private events, open stage, hole in the wall. The more exposure, the better. If you want to get into pageants, start learning all you can about pageantry, systems, currents, formers. Network. Attend as many pageants as possible.

❀**Orion Blaze Browne:** Fundraisers and benefits are good way to get on stage. Also enter talent nights or open stage nights. Remember to have your performance videotaped by a friend. A promo video is a good way to get booked out of your area. It is easy to send a video to show directors to show them what you can bring to the stage. Your career is like a business. It is all about promoting yourself and networking.

❀**Coti Blayne:** Amateur nights and open talent nights are great. In addition, if you do pageants it is a great way to be recognized and get bookings. I have gotten a ton from that alone. Really, any opportunity is a good one. Have a few spare numbers ready and watch the local clubs and hosts. If they ask for a last minute performer because someone dropped - message them immediately and do a good job. Be consistent too. Do not bail out of performances - flaky performers do not get far

❀**Travis Luvermore:** Where I started, we had one night a week for newcomers to take the stage.in addition enter contest.

❀**Clint Torres:** I was fortunate to have my DRAG father and some of the more seasoned kings in town hook me up with some performances here and there

❀**Shook ByNature:** I did amateur shows and talent nights at clubs outside my city. If I traveled with other entertainers I brought a number just in case...

❀**Alexander Cameron:** Go to open stage venues. Go back so show directors, entertainers, and patrons recognize you. Do charity shows whenever possible and always be prepared to do a show at a moment's notice.

❀**Campbell Reid Andrews:** Be prepared before you get on stage! By doing the necessary research so when you do get the opportunity you would not have to wait years to be on a main stage. Do not be greedy coming onto the scene remember you are just starting out. Networking is your friend it will help you get on any stage you want. Pageantry helps. Titles are sought after for some clubs and bar entertainment. Go win some titles. It might help make you more reputable.

❀**Gus Magendor:** This should be handled as though you are going in for an interview, it is. DRAG is a business and a profession.

❀**Joshua Micheals:** Talent night's charities, spotlight numbers, and any chance to learn and grow is great

❀**Freddy Prinze Charming:** Looking for amateur competitions. Newbies can get great feedback at things like that. Look for talent nights, newbie shows, etc. You need to show the vets, the show directors that you are willing to put the effort in, willing to learn and willing to grow. You are not "entitled" to a booking, so do not act like just because you performed once that everyone owes you a spot in their show.

❀**Adam All:** You can only ask. Get decent photos taken to create a 'press pack' explaining your character and your show. Try to get on stage at showcase nights and seek venues looking for new talent. In London, England, I run a night dedicated to putting new kings on the stage, called BOi BOX. We have open mic so new kings can take part. I started this night because it is hard to get into the scene. Another way is to befriend a DRAG Queen. Cannot help to have someone in your corner.

❀**Romeo Sanchez:** Open stage night is always the best way to get your name out there. Do not get discouraged and give up. It is always to your advantage to have a costume or two in tow; you never know when a venue may ask you to perform.

❀**Hurricane Savage:** I am a Newbie. I am still working it out.

❀**Marcus Mayhem:** Open mic at every place to get your name out there. Cannot stay at one place and hope to make it big overnight. It takes time and when you go be nice to those around you and people will remember that so you will be ask to book.

❀**Travis Hard:** If you want to get on stage have the drive to ask around. Find anywhere you can go and perform. Talent nights, open mic nights, etc...

❀**Rychard "Alpha" Le'Sabre:** Find a DRAG stage. Go and watch for a while, make a relationship with some of the cast. Ask questions, express interest, and it does not hurt to ask the host if they have room for a newbie. In Seattle, Washington, USA there is a show every Tuesday night that is perfect for newbies. Get on stage, a panel of judges gives you advice and critiques, and you can learn and grow from there.

❀**Sam Masterson:** In this town, it is who you know

❀**Shane Rebel Caine:** Perform in as many talent night/open mics at as many clubs as you can. Talk to people and make as many friends at the clubs as you can. The more "fan base" you can get the more likely you are to get a booking.

❀**Atown:** I also encourage newbies to be confident on stage because it shows. Always be professional and have fun at the same time.

❀**Rasta Boi Punany:** I, as a newbie, performed with a troupe so I could get the exposure. To get people to know you, I suggest places in the area of your hometown to ask others to get you on board to hopefully take off from there.

❀**Ashton The Adorable Lover:** I would say talent shows, as many as you can, and battles if they have them and you like them, you never know whose watching. Get out and get your face known. Hard work and perseverance.

❀**Dakota Rain:** I think this depends on the person, some are ready to hit the stage and run others take a little while, so I would say you know how you feel so take your time and do what's right for you.

❀**Adam DoEve:** I started with open stage night and then moved on to performing with a group as a guest. The open stage really helped because the crowds were small and most of the others there were people that were trying something new also so there was no one judging you.

❀**Stormm:** Ask someone performing for contacts. Maybe you can do a duet. Have fun.

❀**Kameo Dupree:** Amateur nights, work on a package to compete in a bar competition, pageant, and benefit shows!

❀**Kenneth J. Squires:** Amateur nights work really well, and will get a performer ready for the stage and give them an idea what to expect.

❀**Pierce Gabriel:** Go to the different DRAG shows in your area, talks to the emcees. Everyone appreciates a little bit of initiative.

❀**Vinnie Marconi:** Benefits and talent nights! I have only done two talent shows before my first crown and not another one since, but BENEFITS are a completely different ball-game! When they can rely on you for a benefit, they will call you to fill in and then you start to get bookings.

❀**Brandon KC Young-Taylor:** Each king's journey is different. Talent nights are usually where everyone starts. Some kings need more practice than others and must continue talent nights until they are able to secure a spot on a show cast or win a title that gives you something to stand behind your name. There are also times when a king steps on stage and shows so much talent that they are immediately brought back for paid shows, etc. Each person has to determine what amount of effort they are going to put into their DRAG career. Side note.. I havealso notice that it is different in every area of the USA that I havetravel to. Some areas are very big on benefits where as others are big on entertainers coming out to support the regular show cast!

✤Anjie Swidergal: It might take some research to find them in your area, but bars all over have open stage/open talent nights monthly or even weekly. You can develop a following, try out new stuff, or simply network with other performers!

✤Kruz Mhee: Always open talent nights. If you know, entertainers then ask about performing a duet with them. When I ran my own performance group the only way in was the talent competition we ran once a month.

✤B J Bottoms: Amateur nights are a great opportunity. Many places hold amateur contests to get a foot in the door. Do benefits often to give yourself as much time on stage as possible. Do not turn down any chance to perform. The more you get your face out there the higher the chance a venue will ask you to perform. Seek help from your mentor. They started somewhere once.

✤Silk Steele Prince: A newbie should get on the stage during benefit shows, amateur nights and talent contest the first few years until they are a well know face or name before having venues contact them.

✤SirMandingo Thatis: Make friends and they will help you. It is not what I know or how I do it but WHO YOU KNOW. Stay connected.

✤Flex Jonez: Talent nights are the best. You can be seen and once acknowledged by a venue scout then you are on your way. Give it time and perfect your craft during time.

✤Cody Wellch Klondyke: Talent Nights and Spot Lights. Are the best

✤Viciouse Slick: Anything that is open for people so if it is a contestant or an open stage for anyone. This is a great way to get on stage and get feedback on what you are doing. In addition, do fundraisers, if someone needs help getting to national or raising money for a charity, ask him or her if you can be in it. My first year as a king I was in a lot of fundraiser to help raise money for the Phoenix Scholarship Program.

✤George De Micheal: Practice on karaoke first or go to DRAG venues. Go to DRAG nights to get familiar with seeing other DRAG performers.

✤DeVery Bess: Make friend with kings, see king shows, join a troupe, do not turn down gigs, exposure!

✤Colin Grey: Go see shows. Create a Facebook account just for your DRAG persona. Befriend many kings. The opportunities will be there.

✤Eddie C. Broadway: Attend shows in face. Meet veteran kings. Participate in amateur competitions or shows. Say yes to any opportunities.

✤Jack King: Get out in bars, disco, and meet others.

✤Stefan LeDude: Amateur shows or competitions, or help other people in the business with numbers, doing walk on parts or back up.

✤Bailey Saint James: Join a troupe and get involved.

❀**Clark Kunt:** Go to shows and show respect. Talking to folks after, tipping, just being there consistently until you are noticed. Offer to assist with things like stage kittening, lighting, what have you. Take advantage of any open/new talent/competitions in your area, and see if any groups exist, you could join for information or assistance.

❀**Jamel Knight:** Talent shows and competitions are a great way to start. Contact show directors and be willing to offer to fill-in any spots they may have open. You may not be compensated for those fill-in spots but the fact that you are willing to work and help when needed can help you secure more bookings with the show director.

❀**Master Cameron Eric Leon:** Work your butt off. Go to everything, meet everyone, and start to make sense of the different shows, vibes and venues.

❀**Bruno Diaz:** This is what worked for me. I start doing small parts with Queens, a couple verses here and there to get the stage feel. Then I did a talent show, and I won a booking, the place where I perform is exclusive, so in order to work in other local bars, I had to earn a Title, when I became Mr. Blue Ridge Pride King, I start performing in other venues in my city and around my state, to promote our pride.

❀**Welland Dowd:** Join a troupe, do a number with other people, or organize your own amateur DRAG night in someone's basement or living room. Just because you start small does not mean you would not hit the big time!

❀**Michael Christian:** I suggest open mic nights. There are many benefits everywhere. Volunteer. Most times, experienced people are donating their time as well. Get in a dressing room to meet people. Start learning to network. Get up on the stages and show your hunger and dedication. You never know who is in the audience or behind the actual production of the show.

❀**MaXx Decco:** I took theater, vocal lessons, I went to every audition, performed at every open mic, co-founded a DRAG crew, branched out, started doing back up parts, then performing at open shows and fundraisers, I won a pageant title, then I was experienced and known enough to put together my own shows. I was determined and now I am always on stage, there are a million ways to get there for anyone who wants to be on stage; as long as you are persistently passionate, you will make it.

❀**Julius M. SeizeHer:** I started with Pride. It is big, and many venues go there. Start with smaller stuff, working with local bars and what not… contact DRAG friends, participate in their shows. See where it goes from there.

❀**Lyle Love-it:** Make yourself seen; go to shows, talk with performers; keep at it.

🎨**Hawk Stuart:** Talent nights. Ask other entertainers tips.

🎨**Jonah Godfather of DRAG:** The best bet for a new performer is to work amateur shows and fundraisers. Get your face and name out there. Always bring your "A" game and show them what you got. If you show people how entertaining you can be, people will remember your name and face. When people take notice, the bar owners/show directors will too.

🎨**Howie Feltersnatch:** Go to shows, talk to people. Post things on Facebook.

🎨**Jack E. Dickinson:** If there is a thriving DRAG culture already, ask around about opportunities to do numbers in mixed cabarets, or as a guest act in a DRAG show put on by an existing troupe. Alternatively, find out if they are taking newbies. If you want to remain a solo performer, pitch yourself all over the place: cabarets, burlesque shows, etc. Going out a lot helps because you get to meet people and if they like you as a person, they are more likely to want to include you in events.

🎨**Jake Bastard:** One word: networking! Being respectful and friendly is a big plus, also being open to new opportunities. Do not focus on being paid because although it is nice to be given money after performances, the main goal should be to interact and get to know your surroundings while being positive and encouraging of other performers.

🎨**Xavier Bottoms:** Amateur nights. Show interest in cameo numbers. Find a great mentor, one who is booked regularly in a show to become a part of a DRAG family.

🎨**Emilio:** Amateur Shows, pageants, contests, Join troops, make YouTube videos.

🎨**Juan Kerr:** Be good. Hone your craft. Work at it. Get yourself to the DRAG nights that are around. Get to know other performers. Be friendly.

🎨**Howie Feltersnatch: B**eing a new performer is scary and that nerves are just normal, but use those nerves to your advantage. Be cocky, but not too cocky.

🎨**Trey C. Michaels: I** started with a local talent DRAG show in Phoenix, AZ USA for a few months. After going to different shows I began meeting different performers. I would ask if they would give me a shot by letting me perform one number. Being new can be nerve wracking but if you do not ask you will never know. I am starting over in New Mexico, USA. I have been performing for 2.5 years, but to them I am still the new kid and have to prove myself as a performer worthy of being booked.

🎨**Aaron Phoenix:** Talent shows, amateur nights, and benefits. As many as possible. Work hard on improving your performance and costuming and stage presence, etc. every time you perform. Soak in feedback and criticism and learn with each show.

🎨**Devin G. Dame:** Open stages in your area, do not waste stage time, do your best every time and you will get booked sooner than later!

❀**Thug Passion:** Take advantage of everything you can. Amateur competition, back up for other people, duets, just being supportive of others in the craft, and networking which is the biggest thing in this craft.

❀**Soco Dupree:** Perform on Open Stage nights. Always introduce yourself to other performers and promoters. Attend other shows and pageants. Be social. Present yourself professional hand out business cards to promoters, show host, and ask them if they have openings that is how I started out it worked.

❀**E. M. Shaun:** Talent shows, benefit shows. Contact DRAG coordinators from different bars or venues. Promote yourself with fliers and business cards. Be willing to do a duet to get you on stage and build your confidence as well.

❀**Jensen C. Dean:** Open mic and amateur nights are a great way to get in the door. Create a Facebook page as your DRAG persona is a good way to start to get yourself out there. Friend request known performers and show hosts in your area to know when they have events, so you can introduce yourself in in face to do that. Facebook will also give you a chance to volunteer for fundraiser shows; I see so many posts on my news feed if people looking for performers to do a number or two at a benefit show.

❀**B J Armani Venues:** Venues do not contact around here, show directors do. I did hundreds of shows for free or nothing to get my name out there. I worked my butt off on costumes and never did the same number twice. Any song or genre not being done, I did. Any costume totally ridiculous, I wore. A decade later I still have friends in other shows that have gone on to other venues that I can contact if a spot opens up. NEVER be mean to anyone in a show, trust me they could be the next show director. ALWAYS take pictures and have time for your fans. They are the ones that bug the show to put you in it!

❀**Smitty O'Toole:** Take advantage of every open-call show. Perform at benefits and volunteer charity shows. Market yourself. Get to know show directors. Support DRAG shows, mingle, and let people know you are in business.

❀**Spacee Kadett:** Open stage nights abound. Many college GSAs also offer opportunities for students at their annual DRAG shows (this was how I got my start.) Benefit shows are huge too, showcasing new and seasoned talent alike for good causes. Use social media to get in touch with the individuals who run these things. Alternatively, just inquire at the venue. After that, start setting your sights on local pageants. Allow yourself enough time to prepare a package and network with the right mentors. In most cases, bar pageants are open contests that provide a stage, good exposure, and expert feedback to all competitors...plus one lucky winner gets a title, a crown, and a year of bookings! Who knows? It could be you!

❀**King Kline:** Seek out open talent nights at the local clubs.

Chapter Six
"What stage names did you have since the beginning? How did you get them? Why did you change it?"

🌸🌸🌸

🌸**Vinnie Marconi:** Always the same name. Vinnie for my girlfriend's last name. Marconi because I was a communications technician in the Navy. I am Italian, so it fit!

🌸**K'ne Cole:** My name came from the collaboration of many people helping me. K'NE are my initials and Cole for my wife's name "Nicole."

🌸**Luke Ateraz:** I have always been Luke Ateraz. Bunches of us were hanging out on a friend's porch throwing names around, someone said it, and here I am. It is been mispronounced a lot. I have been called Luke Alcatraz, Alvarez, and even Atari.

🌸**Gus Magendor:** The debonair Robin Erhart. My family and I were discussing my future performances and they wanted a part in it. Since they could not travel with me, they wanted to help with my name. I was going to use my actual name and did my first four performances. I go by Gus Magendor. Because my family stated that whenever we go out in public people usually, mistake me for either.

🌸**William Vanity Matrix:** Will DelVante was my first name until I was accepted into the Vanity household (Zoey Vanity-Matrix). Vanity-Matrix or just Matrix. I give my DRAG children the name DelVante still because like my now sister Zoey, she cannot pass down Matrix unless Damian Matrix-Gritte does it. I kept Vanity and dropped my original name in honor of Zoey.

🌸**Chandler J Hart:** Chandler was an infant my girlfriend once baby sat. J for my father's middle name and for a friend. Hart is the last name of a friend.

🌸**Ayden Layne:** First performance, they needed a name quickly. It was the first name I liked; Layne is my dad's middle name. Added y's to be unique

🌸**Dakota Rain:** only have this name and got it sitting around the pool at my apartment complex in Las Vegas, USA. I am Native American so it fit perfect, plus that's what I wanted to name my son if I ever had one.

🌸**Aaron Phoenix:** The Phoenix (as in the mythological bird) has been my favorite creature of myth since I was a little kid and always identified with them. My first tattoo was a Phoenix and it seemed like a no brainer it would be part of my name. The person who first asked me to do a king show put me on the flyer as Phoenix - "The Kid" (I was the youngest, probably the youngest-looking, and brand new). I rather liked the ring of it so I tried out Kid Phoenix as a name for the first 6 months or so. The more I worked on my character the more he seemed to "outgrow" the Kid persona, so I replaced it with my actual first name, Aaron. I see Aaron

Phoenix as an exaggeration or 'caricature' of myself, so it made sense that I am Aaron on or off the stage, but the Phoenix part comes out when I perform.

❀**Davion Summers:** My DRAG mother gave me Kam'Ron as my first name. Davion came later. It sounded better and Summers came from my mother.

❀**Viciouse Slick:** I used a name generator to get both parts of my name.

❀**Jonah Godfather of DRAG:** Jonah is just a name that I liked and picked. The Godfather of DRAG came from my best friend at a show as we were talking on stage about how long I had been performing.

❀**Teddy Michael:** My friends gave me the nickname of "T Diddy," which I used for the first two years. I have been Teddy Michael in homage to my transition, since 2006.

❀**Spacee Kadett:** I was Manhattan Tails when I debuted at my college. The name died with my career after one show. I picked it up again years later, as Brownideboi (Brown Eyed Boy), after my wildly successful Live Journal screen name from long ago. Everybody hated it. So five years ago I settled on the name Spacee Kadett. At the time, I performed regularly as a girl too - I liked that it was unique, androgynous, and a good excuse for occasionally being an airhead... (Still is). When I started doing pageants, I came under fire for having a name that was not "manly" enough..."You cannot hold a king title with that name!" Therefore, I tried Kaptain Kadett and Sargentt Spacee, both of which failed miserably, and went on to win six titles (including a national one) under my "girlie" name. It reminds me all the time how important it is to trust your gut when you create your DRAG persona.

❀**Kameo Dupree:** I have always been Kameo Dupree. My DRAG mom helped seal the deal on the name. I was playing around and sent her a pic of me in full face and her response was "it is time for your cameo appearance... hey, that should be your name" I changed it from "C" to "K" but every time I hit any stage, it feels like the first time and will always be a "Kameo Appearance"

❀**Romeo Sanchez:** I began DRAG ten years ago. Someone asked me my stage name. I blurted "Romeo Sanchez." I was told Sanchez was already taken and I needed to be adopted. I dropped the Sanchez but could never come up with anything different. Lucky for me that I was later adopted by the Sanchez family.

❀**Coti Blayne:** I was Coti Blayne Van De Kamp. I dropped Van De Kamp because I did not want to rely on someone else's name and fame to get me known. I wanted to be known for myself. Coti is the main character's name in my only published novel. I wanted something different as far as spelling goes and yet still semi gender neutral. Blayne was a friend's little brother and they helped me come up with that.

❧**Trigger Montgomery:** I got mine when I was 17. Trigger since I was quick to the trigger for someone in need. My last name Montgomery because I am proud of where I come from. I refuse to change my name to be a part of a group or any other reason.

❧**Shook ByNature:** I started in San Diego, California, USA as Dixon Dandridge since I was from below the Mason-Dixon Line. Dandridge because it was old Hollywood. I was not performing how I wanted when my DRAG family chose everything. I quit when I returned south. When I started, I chose Shook ByNature because Shook was my nickname growing up. I am naturally myself and it has been that way since.

❧**Freddy Prinze Charming:** Always Freddy Prinze Charming. It took me days of brainstorming to come up with it. My ex- partner always said I was a Prince Charming. Others described me as charming. I decided to take the Prince Charming, and play off Freddie Prinze Jr, and Freddy Prinze Charming was born.

❧**Kruz Mhee:** Kruz Mhee was born in 2007. I sat down with a friend and discussed male actors I liked; I liked Tom Cruise. I changed the spelling of his last name and since I was single added the last name Mhee. Kind of a play on words.

❧**Atown:** I have always had Atown. My biological name starts with an "A." I love Usher and in his song "Yeah." He sings "peace up, Atown down." It is a nickname for Atlanta, Georgia. In high school I had a friend whose name started with a "V." She said her nickname was "V-Town," so mine was "Atown" (no hyphen). It just stuck with me.

❧**Alexander Cameron:** My first performance was intended to be my only performance, I went generic with my name. I performed as Alexander DeKing for three months. Once I got more serious, I wanted to have a name that contributed to the illusion. Alexander is a combination of my first and last names and Cameron is my sister's name (though spelled differently).

❧**Ryder Long:** I originally was Ryder Gently because it was funny sounding and I wanted to be humorous, but sexy. The night after I won my University's DRAG show I got a DRAG parent and became Ryder Gently Michaels. I kind of evolved and my DRAG mom was not particularly right for me. I needed a DRAG dad, so on Christmas last year I asked my idol and DRAG role model to be his one and only son and he generously said yes so I took the last name Long. I have been Ryder Long ever since.

❧**Johnnie Blackheart:** I was going for Mister Spanks but could not get a page started because apparently many people have that name so I went with Johnnie Blackheart.

❧**Adam All:** Trevor. I quickly abandoned for lack of originality, then Adam Hall, then dropped the 'H' so more of my audience would get the joke.

✽**D-Luv Saviyon :** My name originally started as D-luv, which was taken from my Dj name, DJ D-luv Saviyon was added in 2006 when myself and a group of entertainers I performed with started the House of Saviyon.

✽**Clint Torres:** Clint Torres has been my name from the beginning. I choose it because I wanted my name to sound like an actual guy's name well still having that sexual innuendo that a lot of kings are famous for

✽**B J Armani:** The name B J Armani was born on a cocktail napkin. It was a collaboration between myself and my best friend Raquel Smith. I wanted a funny, classy, kitschy, and funny name. What can I say? It is memorable.

✽**Koomah:** (Kuma) came about as a nickname that was easier for people to pronounce than my actual name. The phonetic spelling was to make it easier for people to pronounce and to add an artistic twist to it. Most people call me Koomah every day. I never really created a solid DRAG name or persona. I am a character actor and present as many different characters onstage. Often other folks will name certain recurring characters that I do for me: Johnny Tsunami, Francisco Fiori, Bear Akuda, Jerry Hattrick, etc. I also perform as a Queen (also as different characters: Apiza Rogue-Glitter, Nana Puddin, Pariah Prism, T'aint Purdy, etc). The only solid performer name is my queer/DRAG burlesque persona Mallé FeMallé the genderfuck royale. Another burlesque performer gave that name to me.

✽**Ben Eaten:** I always had my name since sitting down with my girlfriend coming up with clever names. Added a last name for my DRAG family.

✽**Orion Blaze Browne:** It was Orion Blaze. Orion after the constellation I have been obsessed with since childhood, and Blaze from the dare devil Johnny Blaze, my friend had his jacket. I thought it would give me a "Billy badass" last name since I started as a hard rock king. Browne is a family name, which I took 4 months into DRAG when my DRAG mother adopted me. Since being adopted, I have also been announced as just my initials OBB. It was a catch phrase introduction when I was in a DRAG troupe.

✽**Wulf Von Monroe:** LOW- was a nickname since I was a kid. Also were my initials   Wulf Von Axe. I have a wolf obsession and needed a new name to go with my style of performing. I am Wulf Von Monroe since joining the Monroe family. They treat me like family since I have met them. I hated the idea a DRAG family but with them I just fit in so well that I could not turn down the offer of being Jak'kays husband.

✽**Diseal Tanks Roberts:** I was always Diesel Tanks. My best friend and now DRAG mother Natasha Roberts said it joking one night and it stuck.

✽**Rasta Boi Punany:** This has been my name since I began performing. My wife decided the name: Rasta- because I love reggae, Jamaica (12x); Boi- because I am a Tom Boi; Punany-well, because I love it!

✽**Rocky Valentino:** I have had the same DRAG name. I was named by my Co DRAG dads. Rocky Valentino because I knock all the girls hearts out.

❈**Brandon KC Young-Taylor:** I started my career as Brandon Young. I knew for my first name I wanted a B because that rather ran in my family. Brandon was chosen because I always felt like every Brandon I knew in school was the guy I would have been. My last name I choose because I look so young. It fit from the beginning and I have never changed it. I have added to my name over the years to show respect to individuals in the community that have helped me along in my career and my personal life. The K was added first for my brother Xander Kinidy. I choose to go with the initial because I never wanted my career to be built off the fame my brother had established for himself. A few years later, I had the privilege of spending some time with Bob Taylor. He had yet to adopt and King into the Taylor family and he felt like I fit in perfect. I hyphenate Taylor because I am proud of the family I now belong to! This year, after many years together, I wanted to acknowledge a person that has helped me through several pageants and person trials during my career. C was added to my middle initial acknowledging a best friend, brother and sister, Richard Cranium! Every part of my name has a special meaning to me. I have been poked at for adding so much to it but I am thank for the small way I am able to say thank you to these people that have contributed to my success!

❈**Chance Wise:** I was always Chance. I added the last name of someone I thought would be a good DRAG parent, which did not work out very well with that person. For a while I went back to just Chance and about a year later I added the Wise cos I had learned a lot about the people in the scene and how to better be involved. I have always loved the word chance as a name because it is a word full of possibility.

❈**Travis Hard:** Gregory Swallows because I thought it was clever. In reality, I chose this name because my very first song was Go Getter Greg by Ludo. I realized that name was not me and opted for a different name. While looking at my first photo in DRAG before performing, I looked at myself and thought; "Wow I am trying to be Hard." My last name was born. I always loved the name Travis. It went well together.

❈**Jack King:** I have always had this name on stage.

❈**Campbell Reid Andrews:** I started as Lyric. I was young and did not know what to do so I made something up. I just wanted to dance. I took a break to go to the military and started back up and decided to show people I was serious coming back into the scene so I saw a sign on a trip to Abilene for a town called Campbell. I was baby-generating names for my unborn child. Reid stuck out to me. My DRAG mother Erica Andrews passed her last name down to me. I love my name and am proud of it now

❈**D-Rex:** My first DRAG name because my family is Italian was Deangelo Rexini. Yeah try to have a drunk host say that all night long. D-Rex is better.

❈**Owlejandro Monroe:** My first name was Tom Sauy. Thai for beautiful butch. I am Androgynous. Changed to Owlejandro Lust. Owlejandro, pronounced "Alejandro." I have an obsession with owls. Lust, because I am a Scorpio and fits my DRAG persona.

🍀**Kenneth J. Squires:** I started out as Kountry KJ. I did a lot of Country music. I knew I needed to change my name when I started to branch out to do other types of music. My initials are KJS, so I took my Grandfather's Name, Kenneth. My middle initial is J and I took Squires as my last name, I liked that last name.

🍀**Adam DoEve:** I started with Adam since my real first name is Amee. I was told that I should have a last name and I could not think of one so I had a contest at my place of work to see who could come up with something good. It took about a week and some really bad ones but my head housekeeper came up with a good one. She was sitting there doing her paper work and all of a sudden she stood up and said "DoEve". We both had a good giggle about it, Adam DoEve, that was it and I bought her a six pack.

🍀**B J Bottoms:** I was always B J Bottoms. Four months into performing I was adopted by the Bottoms a well-known DRAG family in the DC area. They watched me perform often and saw something in me they felt worth investing in. I have been a part of my family four years now and could not imagine having any other people to call family.

🍀**Ashton The Adorable Lover:** Only this name. I came up with Ashton. All my friends used adorable to describe me, so it was taken to show love a element of myself that was always hard to see while growing up

🍀**Pierce Gabriel:** I have always been Pierce Gabriel .

🍀**Alec Allnight:** I was always Alec Allnight. I wanted something with humor, a little naughty, but not obscene. I thought about Mathew Broaddick before settling on Alec.

🍀**Hawk Stuart:** I changed my last name because of the family did not want to have their name anymore because people would think bad of me, I wanted to be better.

🍀**Silk Steele Prince:** I was Ms.Silky. I added an alter ego Prince Silk. When I was thirteen my best friends were trying to find a boy name for me, because they believed I looked like a pretty boy and I had long silky hair. The name Silk or Silky was born. When I began performing as an exotic dancer Ms.Silky stuck and I carried it on in the DRAG world. When I became confident, I performed as Prince Silk, a male illusionist.

🍀**Flex Jonez:** First three years I used Donvito Lopez. Then when began to travel I was given a more Vegas type show name with a catch "Flex Jonez."

🍀**SirMandingo Thatis:** I have always been SirMandingo Thatis and that is only because I wear a HUGE Mandingo (Dick) on my pants when I perform.

🍀**Cody Wellch Klondyke:** I have Always Been Cody Wellch Klondyke my DRAG Mom gave me my name. I love her to death and I would never change it

❈**George De Micheal:** I have always been George De Micheal. I created the name because when I looked in the mirror I focused on what my DRAG get up my image reminded me of. I never have changed it since.

❈**Thug Passion:** I have only had one name and one point I think it was about my sixth year I was thinking about changing the spelling from Thug Passion to Thug Pashión or Pashion. I decided not to. How my name came about was at the time that I started I was wearing baggy clothes as if society perceives thugs wear their clothes, but I was not a thug. That is where the Thug comes in. In reality I am a very passionate, loving, giving person so this where the Passion comes in. I have two first names no last name.

❈**Bootzy Edwards Collynz:** Originally Bootzy Collynz, because many Kings around me had suggestive names. Bootzy Collynz, sounded a little like "booty callin." Added Edwards as my middle name after my DRAG Mom passed.

❈**Colin Grey:** I have always been Colin Grey.

❈**J Breezy St James:** It was Breezy from the song Deuces by Chris Brown. A local DRAG King started calling me J Breezy. I met my DRAG mother during my third show and became part of the House of St. James.

❈**E. M. Shaun:** I have always been E. M. Shaun. When I first started DRAG I was a paramedic (EMS) my stud name is Shaun. I would introduce myself to women when I met them. I could not think of any names to stand for the EM so I went with those letters as an abbreviation like a famous writer.

❈**Sam Masterson:** Boomer CravenMorehead and Pimp Daddy.

❈**Bruno Diaz:** I knew my stage name when I saw myself at the mirror, I had a hero when I was six, in the USA he is known as Bruce Wayne, but in Mexico, Bruno Diaz is Batman. My DRAG Mama liked it and the story behind it.

❈**DeVery Bess:** I started as with Jack Oliver but I had to change it because the troupe did not want two people with the first name of Jack. I came up with Devery Wellson, but I never really liked it, then in my sleep, I came up with DeVery Bess. I have not looked back since; it fits the most and it unique, like my ego, and me

❈**Jack King:** I have Jack King from the beginning and still have

❈**Xavier Bottoms:** Always been Xavier Bottoms. My brother, Ophelia gave me the name. Xavier was not popular. He wanted my name to stand out. Plus he said the name Xavier just sounded sexy but classy.

❈**Stefan LeDude:** I have always been Stefan LeDude. I came up with it before I even started performing; I just wanted to make a Facebook profile for my male persona. Stefan was just a play on my real name, Stefanie, and then I wanted something to say I was a guy, so I thought of "LeDude".

🌸**Jamel Knight:** I just went by Mel. However, as I more serious about the craft, I changed my name to Jamel Knight. It is a combination of my real middle name and what my character truly believes in which is chivalry.

🌸**Clark Kunt:** The first time I did my makeup, I put on my glasses and my partner at the time just screamed it. My first performance was Kryptonite by 3 Doors Down with a little Superman gimmick into shows here and there.

🌸**Howie Feltersnatch:** Howie Feltersnatch since the beginning. I am known for my flashy balls and cock, and pulling things out of my pants.

🌸**Master Cameron Eric Leon:** I originally performed as "Cam E. Leon," but there was already a burlesque dancer in my town that performed as "Kamie Lyann." When my DRAG mama first invited me to perform, we sat at a corner of the bar laughing and discussing names, and that's what we came up with. I knew that I wanted a name that let me do a bit of everything. It has sophistication.

🌸**Welland Dowd:** I have been Welland Dowd from the start.

🌸**Harry Pi:** Started with Jim Maxwell, the name I was living under, but it sounded boring to me. I changed it to Harry Pi in December of 2012.

🌸**Dionysus W Khaos:** It always has been Dionysus Khaos.

🌸**Julius M. SeizeHer:** Julius M. SeizeHer is the only name I use It ws easy enough as Julius is the male version of Julie, and the only famous Julius I know of is Julius Caesar, change it, and voila! Julius SeizeHer!

🌸**Jack E. Dickinson:** In 2006, I started as Gary Dickinson. I liked the ruggedness of the name Gary. My plumber dad had a friend with that name who worked with him. He was rugged, but kind. Dickinson was to honor one of my inspirations, Bruce Dickinson of Iron Maiden. I decided to transition to socially male and do more gender fuck, I changed it to Duchess Jack. Duchess because the troupe I had co-founded was The Dukes of DRAG. Jack combined with Duchess made for a gender fuck name. I went with Jack E. Dickinson because the prior name made everyone think I was a DRAG Queen. Jack E. because, when you say it fast, it sounds like Jacky, which is my chosen name in "real life." I revived the Dickinson from my first stage name.

🌸**Emilio:** It has always been Emilio. Emilio - Latin DRAG King. It represents my Latin culture, as I grew up in Argentina.

🌸**Juan Kerr:** I have always been Juan. My name was actually thought up for me by a cabaret singer and good friend of mine, Eva Fox, and it just stuck. I sometimes think a more 'family friendly' name would be appropriate, but it is probably a bit late for that now four years on. In addition, not even all adults 'get it' straight away.

🌸**Santana Romero**: I was always Santana. It was the name that a member of my troupe and I agreed since I was the "S" in "BOIS w/Outskirts." I added Romero for a little Latin flair shortly afterward since I am from South America in my mind ha-ha.

🍀**Stefon Royce Iman:** I started at Stefon Royce. I change my name in 2009 to Stefon Royce Iman when I found my DRAG mother Tyria Iman. My name was a ladies' man name. I took off the PH; it was supposed to be Stephon. Added the F sound better and sexy. Royce,from the car I love Rolls Royce.

🍀**Soco Dupree:** It has always been a DRAG name. Soco is the abbreviation for Southern comfort, which is my favorite shot.

🍀**Dominic:** Always stayed Dominic. Became part of the Demornay family. I since have stayed Dominic Demornay.

🍀**Jensen C. Dean:** Always been Jensen Dean, a name born from the love my wife and I share of the show Supernatural. My last name Dean is one of the main characters and Jensen is the name of the actor that plays Dean.

🍀**Smitty O'Toole:** I have, and always will be referred to as Smitty O'Toole on stage. My friends call me Smitty because my last name is Smith. I am Irish, so I came up with the last name O'Toole. My stage character is a bit of a tool.

🍀**Papi Chulo Doll:** Lil' Monster, Kaos King, Tha Illist Studd.

🍀**Boi Wonder:** I always had Boi Wonder, an ex-partner of mine had a fascination with comic book characters and the name stuck.

🍀**Dixon Heat:** It has always been Dixon Heat. It just came to me one day.

Place Faces Without Peeking At The Answer Key In Book Two

Name the performers without checking on DRAG411.com

Chapter Seven
"How do you get a venue to appreciate you enough as an entertainer to actually book you? How do you catch their attention? What tricks will help someone find bookings into new venues?"

❀❀❀

❀Campbell Reid Andrews: I hold myself in a very professional manner all the time when at a booking or in the scene. I also put on one hell of a performance something new and fresh every show so I always stand out in their minds. By doing this the entertainment directors think of me first when looking for entertainment.

❀Freddy Prinze Charming: I show venues, bar owners and show directors that I make an effort when it comes to costuming and creativity. When it comes to a venue booking my own show, like Spotlight, I proved that we weren't a "typical" bar show, by having a different theme every show, never seeing the same numbers twice, and holding my cast to the highest standard when it came to costuming, etc. The trick is not to prove yourself once and stop for the day. Show the bar, and everyone else, that you continue to grow as an entertainer. Give them new reasons to appreciate you.

❀Travis Luvermore: I give respect to the regular performers. I put my best effort on the stage wanting to leave a lasting impression. I tread lightly and respectful in the dressing area making sure I am not stepping on anyone's toes. Take time to watch the regulars and give them respect. Engage the audience to leave them wanting more.

❀Dakota Rain: I usually try to be me. Show respect to all that is there, I make appoint to thank everyone for letting me show them what I can do

❀Ashton The Adorable Lover: I just be myself, act professionally, keep drama free, and do best I can do if they like me they will come to me because they respect me and the way I hold myself and my craft.

❀Clint Torres: Promotion. If you promote them and enough people come, they will know and will want you to keep coming back with business.

❀Rasta Boi Punany: Be professional, give respect to all, staying to myself.

❀Spacee Kadett: If you are just starting out, it can be crazy hard to get a booking of any sort. On top of doing what the above comments recommend (and I totally agree with) try to remain visible. Give a great performance at benefit shows. Participate in open mics and contests. Go out for pageants, if they are open to you in your community, regardless of who your competition will be. No matter how you place, the experience and exposure will be priceless. If you win, it will be much easier to secure bookings at the host venue and other venues you approach.

🎭**Adam All:** Depends on the venue but I have found in the United Kingdom its best to attend a venue, find out who books the acts, and who has most influence over how the acts get booked (not always the same person) and find a way of getting your information to them. It is best not to be pushy, arrogant, play yourself down, or grovel too much. Just present your advertising or information and ask gently if you could be considered for a future event. Make sure they know you are keen without scaring the shit out of them and how loyalty to their venue; publically praising the night you attended, bringing more people with you, liking and following their social media... It can be hard to get the balance between keen and bloody annoying right, and networking can be a massive and difficult task but, as they say, that is the way to do it. Also just plain old asking nicely works. Waiting for venues to contact you is relatively fruitless even with a high profile or good reputation.

🎭**Kenneth J. Squires:** Show respect to regular performers and the back stage dressing area. Clean up after yourself. Try not to get into any of the "Drama." Do what you do best, and make the show something that people would like to come back and see.

🎭**Kruz Mhee:** Always be respectful to the staff and management. The staff includes the current entertainers as well as security staff and bartenders. Treat it like a business and engage the crowd. If the crowd loves you then you will be asked back. If the management loves you then you will be booked again and paid. If you trip up and lose your demeanor then you lose respect. A great entertainer can and will lose bookings over a self-righteous attitude.

🎭**Flex Jonez:** Promotion and allowing them to know I am available. Keeping in touch with the booking promoter.

🎭**Silk Steele Prince:** In my small town no one books Kings only Queens. Therefore, I get it where I fit in and I stay professional, gracious, and humble.

🎭**Stormm:** Being professional, and respectful, keeping in touch with other kings and Queens and other venues letting them know when you are free.

🎭**SirMandingo Thatis:** As a title holder, I am booked but I stay professional and respectful staying in contact with the owners and show directors.

🎭**E. M. Shaun:** It is hard for those of us that are not in active DRAG families. I went to many venues talked with the owners of the clubs, or the heads of their performer contacts. Some clubs had me do an physical audition others had amateur nights. I also had some connections with popular Kings and Queens in my area.

🎭**D-Luv Saviyon:** By always being professional, approachable, giving respect to the venue/bar owners, the venue crowds, other entertainers, and promoters. Always show versatility and consistency in growth as an entertainer and titleholder. If you are new, get on every stage you can...amateur night, open stage, whatever. Exposure is a vital key to being booked. If you are seen and liked, you can build on that and possibly obtain future bookings. Word of mouth bookings can also come from exposure.

❊**Shane Rebel Caine:** Being professional is a first step, but also having stage presence with or without a big crowd. Once you get a booking though the best way to keep getting them is to show that you can bring in a crowd, the more people you can bring in the better your chances of continued bookings and could even get you a cast spot.

❊**DeVery Bess:** We book the venue, and take the door cover, rather than the opposite.

❊**Welland Dowd:** The Bromantics strive to be professional and respectful, so venues know we are worth their time and money. We started performing numbers in other peoples' shows. Soon people were asking us to perform in other places. It is all about doing your best on stage, making an impression, and passing out business cards!

❊**Julius M. SeizeHer:** It is always good to know the owners. Also, get in on other shows from other performers.

❊**Lyle Love-It:** National, State and local titles will help...make a POSITIVE first impression...support...and be prepared and professional.

❊**Jonah Godfather of DRAG:** Come prepared and professional. Nothing worse than making a bad impression. Do your best to leave the audience wanting more.

❊**Jack E. Dickinson:** I describe some of my acts and express how these acts would add to their show or venue. I behave in a cordial but friendly manner so they see I am someone they would enjoy having back.

❊**Clark Kunt:** I have asked to use the venue space to rehearse and where our main venue is a bar that opens in the afternoon - there is usually no one around for the first few hours of operation. The owner and bar manager let us use the space when we want, they know we are rehearsing to give the best performance we can to their patrons, and they get to see our numbers to determine how well we fit with their venue. In addition, I make sure to support the venue where I can, talk with the owners about what they are looking for from our shows and what we would like to bring.

❊**Bailey Saint James:** Make or get yourself a press kit and a preview video.

❊**Xavier Bottoms:** Go to their DRAG shows regularly. You have to earn their respect. Talk to some of the entertainers after the show. Start coming in DRAG. Show them you appreciate their DRAG. Once you feel comfortable, ask for a cameo spot.

❈**Aaron Phoenix:** Prove it. Put your money where your mouth is. Attend benefits, talent shows, amateur nights, etc. and put on a SHOW every single time. Make them pay attention to you. Wow them with your costuming; with your energy on stage. Get them to look your way, ask for a free guest spot, and use it as an opportunity to really prove yourself. Improve with every performance. Treat every booking like it was paid.

❈**Thug Passion:** I agree with all the comments above. Being professional in and out of DRAG. Networking is big. Getting bookings with other kings or Queens or even just simply asking if they can help you get a booking. Once you do, do the best you can to put on a great show so the venue will ask you back. Also, do benefit shows if possible. You give back to the community and the community will give back to you.

❈**Thug Passion:** Promote yourself with internet videos and business cards.

❈**MaXx Decco:** To start out get involved in the community, do fundraisers, open shows, auditions, promote, promote, promote yourself, if that doesn't get you an invitation inspire one by a simple introduction and conversation with whoever's in charge of booking, once you've landed it promote the venue, and if you want to be invited back CLEAN UP AFTER YOURSELF.

❈**Stefon Royce Iman:** Press Kit, YouTube and business cards.

❈**Jensen C. Dean:** Remain professional. Do not get sloppy drunk at potential venues. I make it a point to get to know the people in charge of booking performers along with owners or other venue staff. In this business it really is who you know sometimes so getting out and meeting people and networking goes a long way.

❈**Cody Wellch Klondyke:** I go to different venues and I show love and support to other performers. I also make sure that I have videos of my performance that way others can see what type of performer I am. I also enjoy doing duet performances with other kings and Queens. I am open to anything. Rather it is a duet or fills in.

❈**Santana Romero:** I always come into any venue I am performing at with a cheerful and approachable disposition so people are not hesitant to talk to me. Not to cheery though because I would not want to come off loony. I also introduce myself to all the other performers that I am sharing the stage with, tip them and buy drinks. When venues see that you are supporting their bar, they will usually support you back. I also bring my BEST the stage every time I perform, especially at a new establishment. At the end of the night, I always approach the owner, shake his or her hand, and thank them for allowing me to grace their stage. Grace and humility are 2 if the most important things if you are looking to get booked anywhere so make sure you keep them in mind at all times. Also, never be afraid to reach out to show directors on Facebook or via e-mail. You never know what kind of entertainer they are looking for at any given time. Taking calculated risks are all a part of the business.

❀**Mike Oxready:** That is a tricky one, because in Vermont we have producers who are booking the venue as opposed to venues scouting performers. So, in that regard, earning the trust and respect of the community producers, and showing them that I can engage the audience and put on a great act.

❀**Smitty O'Toole:** You earn respect and trust by giving it, first. I network myself and have never had an issue booking at a venue in my city. it helps to win a contest or race or pageant, but not required.

❀**LoUis CYfer:** You need to really focus on your target market and your marketing. Make sure u spread the word if your persona as far and wide as possible! Trust others and they will do the same

❀**Luke Ateraz:** It is not the venues you have to impress, it is the host/hostess you need to catch the eye of. A lot of places depend on the host/hostess to fill their own line ups.

❀**Papi Chulo:** I get a venue to see me as an asset to their business. I note my followers that will also be their patrons. I try to catch their attention with my charm and my "past performances"" to make them feel comfortable that I will "" bring it"" to the table! The "trick"" for me is to visit their establishment as often as possible, engage, and support in events they are producing to show my commitment.

❀**Jack Inman:** Start off by doing fundraisers for charities.

❀**Ox Ready:** In Vermont USA, we do not have designated venues with DRAG shows, but several promoters and producers who put together shows, or add on performers to a dance party. Catching their attention happens slowly, oftentimes. Putting yourself out there, performing at amateur nights, and asking to perform at fundraisers. The crucial thing is to be respectful, and not assume that you will get to perform.

❀**Papa Cherry:** From USA and Singapore. I am polite and professional when working with venues. I send them a reel and offer suggestions on how I will help promote their event and improve sales and guest counts. Great tricks are to have a following that you can commit to attending the event. Have many social media sites that allow you to market to more fans and bring in more attendees to the event etc. Often I find venues see me as a commodity because I am unique and interesting. I network with everyone and I am always kind to everyone, as you never know how he or she may affect your bookings. Never say something negative about anyone. See how all situations can be perceived in the positive.

Chapter Eight

"When did you become interested in dressing in the opposite sex? Explain the details including the reaction of your family and friends? When was the first time you took it to the next level as a performer?"

❀❀❀

Phantom: I remember the night I decided to do DRAG. I witnessed a DRAG show at local bar in Upland, California USA. I saw Glen Alen. She embodied everything DRAG stood for in my eyes. Her makeup, outfit for props, and her lip-sync was on point. I decided I could be as good as this person. I am so proud to say that he is my friend and a constant inspiration to my DRAG.

Vinnie Marconi: I was never "girly." I always wore slacks, vests, and jackets. I donned my first Tuxedo for a charity butch fashion show in August 2011. I went to a DRAG 101 class where I donned my first beard. A week later, I hit the stage for a USO charity show and the rest is still being written.

Gus Magendor: I never was interested. I did it because I always wanted to be a boy when I was little. I grew up being this way so most of my family was not surprised and almost all of my friends already knew. The next step I took in performing was to go to as many DRAG shows as I could and get to know the kings and Queens. Eventually they asked if I would like to perform and I took that as my time to shine.

Cage Masters: I was over at a friend's house and put on my guy friends clothes as a joke. I felt more comfortable. My ex-girlfriend got me interested in preforming and I have done it ever since. I am also on the male side of the royal family of the imperial court of Iowa, USA and do many charity shows and I love every minute of it.

William Vanity Matrix: I have always dressed rather tom-boyish. I never really had girl clothes until high school. I am an artist, so I had many characters I created. 'William' was a character I have had since I was thirteen years old and was a rock star. I always wanted to be him, and when I was twenty, I found out what a DRAG king was and ran with it. My parents of course disapproved and still do to this day to an extent.

Chandler J Hart: I dressed as the opposite since I could pick out my own clothing. I thought girl's clothes were uncomfortable. I was asked in school "are you a boy or a girl". Short hair and no chest to boot obviously gave ammunition for the question. As for the performer part of me. It thought it was to be a onetime deal ten years ago. A tribute to my passed away father.

Aaron Phoenix: I am transgender and have always felt male, but societal/family pressures and fear pushed me to go overboard with trying to look/dress/act "girly" to hide what I was feeling about myself. At around 20 I decided enough was enough and started dressing the way I was comfortable and coming out as a Trans male. When someone first asked me to perform as a king, I was not a stranger to the stage - I would been performing on a Rocky Horror cast as Brad Majors and had already started to learn the art of binding. I took DRAG as an opportunity to wear men's fashion that was far more showy and classy than anything I would just wear on the street. I have always admired the "Johnny Vegas" kind of look, with a little flamboyancy and attention to eye-catching detail, and that is what I strived for. I get to go overboard with fashion that makes me confident rather than uncomfortable.

Dakota Rain: I have been a tomboy and always like jeans and t-shirts. I am comfortable that way I am very shy but on stage helped me with that, I was asked by a friend to perform thought it would be a onetime thing, but once on stage I got hooked and love being there and making people smile.

Viciouse Slick: I was a theater geek in high school and with my college not having a theater group I went to see my DRAG Queen friend perform. The next week I went back again and saw two DRAG kings perform. I felt like it was something I could do, I went back the next Tuesday performed.

Jonah Godfather of DRAG: I had always dressed like a male even as a little kid. In school, I was often mistaken for male. I knew at a very early age that I was interested in females and knew that I was born in the wrong body. In college, my wife and I often went to DRAG shows and became very good friends with the Queens. After many years of just watching them, I finally joined them on stage and have been there ever since. During this time, I also began my transition.

Spacee Kadett: This is so awesome. I love reading everyone's stories! I love dresses and frills so much; coming to terms with my sexuality was EXTRA confusing as a teenager! I did not know that gender identity, expression, and sexuality were all distinct. What was a "lesbian?" How should she dress? Oh my God I had to cut off my hair and buy cargo shorts! At age 18, I did. I was awkward as hell. Yet I remember dressing in boys' clothing when I was 12 and accentuating my eyebrows with mascara from my dance recital in an attempt to convince my mother she had a third son. (She was NOT amused...) To me, it was not gender expression - it was THEATER. That was what I loved. The theater element of DRAG hooked me from day one, and continues to hook me to this day. I love portraying masculinity in art - and in doing so, I have found that my gender expression comes in two distinct halves. I live life as a girlie girl by day, and celebrate as a male illusionist by night - I feel like I am living all 360 degrees of life and it is amazing.

Teddy Michael: I tried all sorts of types of dress to fit in as a young person. I was super femme at one point in my attempts to fit in. However, dressing in a more masculine way allowed me to tap into the gender I felt I have always been. Going out in DRAG was the start of my mental transition and I finally felt comfortable.

🌸**Romeo Sanchez:** When I was around eight I started stealing my mother's eyeliner and lip liner pencils, making my eyebrows darker and drawing beards and mustaches on me. When I was around twelve, my mother would catch me "in DRAG" lip syncing usher into the mirror. Did not know it was a thing until I was about nineteen. I have always meant to do open stage night, and even signed up a few times, but could never muster up the courage to actually get on stage until a couple of months ago. My parents were actually pretty intrigued by the idea, and my father even came to my first real show outside of open stage night and has become my biggest fan.

🌸**Coti Blayne:** In college I met a DRAG Queen, who exposed me to what DRAG was. She ended up becoming a good friend of mine. I came with her to a few shows and saw my first DRAG King. I became obsessed. I have always been a big theatre junkie. I saw it as another form of theatre. Just a completely different world of it. I did one performance, to try it, not expecting to ever do it again. Almost 3 1/2 years later I am still just as addicted.

🌸**Luke Ateraz:** I have never been one to dress girly. When I was in elementary school, I would only wear jeans and a t-shirt. I felt I looked funny in dresses, skirt, and girly stuff. As I got older, I would only wear dresses to social events with my grandmother and when they were over, I would take them off and put on shorts and a t-shirt. Never wore make up until I became a king. I remember clearly, when I cut my hair off... I was 25. My grandfather was a retired chief master sergeant in the US Air Force. When I came home with a shaggy haircut, he told me it looked like shit. If that is what I wanted he would take me to the barber on base and have my hair done right. We went the next day and I got what was considered a marine cut. Five on top and zero on the sides and bottom with a high fade. He was perfectly fine with it. My grandmother however. Being very into how you are viewed by society was not. To her at first it was unacceptable. As time when by it grew on her. My grandfather told me I reminded him of one of the people in his crew.

🌸**Shook ByNature:** I started wearing men's clothing two days after I buried my Mother. I was 20, in the Navy, and I was tired of denying myself. I became a King after I realized Kings were hit on by a higher caliber of women than stud Strippers, which I was at the time. In North Carolina, USA it is not Kings you compete against. If you are not doing it like Queens as far as costuming and your craft, you are not booked.

🌸**Freddy Prinze Charming:** I have never been one for dresses and "girly" clothes. Even when I was, little you would find me in boys' shorts, knee socks, and no shirt. For my second grade school picture, I dressed myself in a blue button down shirt, dark blue sweater vest and a tie. With my fabulous 80s bowl cut, I looked just like a little boy. I loved it! My father hated it and did everything he could to keep me feminine. As an adult, the first time I shaved my head and dressed exclusively in men's clothes, my father just about had a fit. He would (and still does) tell me how pretty I would be if I grew my hair back out and wore more feminine clothes. In high school, I was cast as male roles in school plays often (the Lion in 'The Wiz', Riff in 'West Side Story', etc.), so it was not a huge jump for me to start doing DRAG. I made a name for myself in a top hat and tails, and after my first pageant back in 2008; I was able to see what other kings were doing around the country. That inspired me to really raise the bar in terms of costuming and performance. Later that year, I won my first title, and have challenged myself to keep evolving ever since.

❦**Atown:** As far back as I can remember, I have always wanted to dress like a boy, let alone, be one. One day, (when I was about ten years old), I stole my cousin's tighty-whities and stuffed them with an action figure toy to pretend I had a "package." Nobody knew about this, however, once I hit middle school, I started wearing Tommy Hilfiger overalls like every week, because they were the baggiest clothes anyone would buy for me. All other days were "sporty" wardrobe. I.e. Basketball shorts, t-shirts, hats, headbands, etc. Once I got a job and started making my own money, I could buy whatever I wanted! That is when my "swag" came in! The time I started taking it to the next level as a performer was when I discovered there was a thing as "DRAG kings" or "male impersonators/illusionists." I was 27 years old, and attended my first DRAG show. (I know, I was a late bloomer). In my head I said, "I can do that!" My vision was different. What I saw on stage, I wanted to intensify. I pictured my self-moving differently, dancing differently, interacting with the crowd and making them feel as if they were a part of the moment. Like attending a concert, so to speak. A friend, whom I would mentioned to, introduced my first half year of DRAG to me that I wanted in on the "DRAG world." The group I performed with showed me the whole "eyeliner thing." It was cool for a minute, you know, playing with make-up and what not, but it just did not look realistic enough. A few months later, a good friend of mine showed me how to apply "real facial hair." A few months after that, (about seven months into DRAG), I competed in a DRAG King/ MI pageant. Placing top two in California, USA led me to the national pageant, where I learned all kinds of things! I thought make-up was for chicks or Queens, but there is MAN make-up out there people! What? Little did I know, it intensifies your masculinity features, or creates them? I also learned how to tape my chest and apply make-up to make an illusion of pectorals and abs. In addition, there are kings out there who take it to the next level. Theatrical, so to speak, with incredible make-up, costuming, illusions that make you look twice. For the pageant, I had to create my eveningwear, so I learned to sew and stone. The DRAG king world is amazing! There is always something to learn, no matter how old you get or how experienced you are.

❀**Kameo Dupree:** I have always been different. My mom called me her "special baby." I walked like my dad, talked like my dad, even had his crazy style of dress. As I became older, my style of dress became bolder and ball caps became my best friend. Soon after I had conflicts within myself as far as sexually and who I was meant to be. After much praying, I came to realize I was not in the wrong body and it was ok to be a little different. During this time, I was a singer (local bars), comedian, and performer in a few plays. It was not until 2009 when I decided I wanted to take my talents to a new level. I started frequenting a few bars that had "DRAG shows" but could not find anyone quite like what I was searching for. It was not until 2010 when I ran across Princeton Makavelli-Valentino and he was what I aspired to be. I did not start until 2011 and everyday had been a new highlight in my life.

❀**Alexander Cameron:** I was always a tomboy, never dressing in particularly feminine clothing unless I was modeling. I cut my hair short in 2009 and went through a bit of a style transition in my clothing. I went out one night to a local DRAG bar and the king on cast told me that I should do DRAG. I would never even considered it. I decided to give it a shot. It was supposed to be a one-time thing but I fell in love with performing!

❀**Adam All:** I guess I was just a kid. I was always a 'boy' part in any game we played as kids, and I passed as a guy without trying most days. (Still do which is weird) I dressed intentionally in full DRAG for the first time aged 17 when I bought my first suit; it did not fit me at all. At 18, 19 I won a couple of local DRAG balls and at 20 got my first magazine cover. I did not start singing in character until I was 24. First gig was a half hour set in Southampton's most prominent cabaret bar. I never looked back.

❀**Clint Torres:** When I was a kid, I always felt there was a part of me missing or hiding. I dressed boyish when I was a kid and just never outgrew it. Dressing like that, it was comfort, I felt confident, and it just felt right. I took theater classes in middle and high school and discovered that I love to entertain, I love to act, take on the role of another person and lose myself in the character, that's kind of when I started to really dress up and the idea of Clint was born. By this time I had already came out as a lesbian so my family was used to the idea of me dressing in men's clothing. When I started to put on face that is when they became more anxious about the whole DRAG thing. My friends thought it was cool as shit. When I discovered the local DRAG scene ago 3 years ago, that is when I discovered what was missing, I started talking to my DRAG Dad, and the rest is history.

❀**D-Luv Saviyon :** I have always dressed as a boy since I was given free reign, with the exception of being forced to wear girls clothes when young, and while living with an aunt that was old fashioned (and very much like Madea). After I moved out, back to boy. My reason to do DRAG was not about dressing like a man, it was that I enjoyed being able to entertain people in a way I felt totally at home...with masculinity. My family did not understand at first, my friends were accepting, encouraging. I first took my DRAG to the next level by being a dancer, which where I lived was rare. I became known as a dancer, more upbeat than usual for Kings where I lived. I also began to more closely emulate looks of the artists I performed through mannerisms, dance, and costuming. I feel like if you can give the audience an association (does not have to be dead on look-alike) and balance your identity as an entertainer also, it gives you a happier crowd, and allows you much more flexibility than being one way or the other. Always TRY to make them wait to see what you are going to do, not know every time.

B J Armani: I am a straight woman that fell in love with this form of entertainment. I would been going to DRAG Shows for years. I went to a pageant with some friends and saw all Kings of all types and sizes. When my DRAG Dad Mik Andersen was asked "Why do you do DRAG?" He replied, "I want to prove we are not freaks" This shattered my heart that ANYONE would think of my friends as freaks. This is still as strong a statement as it was to me over a decade ago. If by entertaining as a male I can bring shows and sneak in a little more tolerance I will do it forever. My first performance was for our MC in Grand Forks, ND. She was moving to Minneapolis. I did the song "Cannot help falling in love with you" remake by UB40 complete with trumpets. You may say I had a flair for the stage back then, the costumes speak for themselves through the years. Every once in a while I will dust off that song and still perform it. I am ridiculous nostalgic! As for a next level, I constantly think I have peaked. I have my own show that I could NEVER do without the help of my friends and brothers. Dexter Maine-Love Kamen Cider-Love has driven down for it and LiquoRite Hipster my DRAG Son has grown up so much as a performer and an artist since he and I joined forces two years ago. EVERY show is a new level, EVERY person I meet is a new level, and EVERY audience brings us to a new level. That is why I constantly think I peaked and then I just realize NOPE we have much more work to do!

Ben Eaten: Unlike most kings, I never dressed like a boy or have ever really been a tomboy. I always wore dresses and skirts; I loved pink and had thousands of Barbie dolls. I always loved being on stage and performing I had been a dancer and a cheerleader since I was two years old. I went to DRAG shows and became friends with some of the show directors and started asking questions on how I could get started in this wonderful art. Most people looked at me as if I was crazy wanting to be a king since I am a total femme. They told me how to do with my hair, my girlish walk, and smile. I talked to my girlfriend about wanting to try DRAG and she was 100% supportive. Every one of my friends was supportive of me wanting to perform, many of them come to every show they can. My family was not as supportive. My mom did not like it so she thinks that I no longer do it. My sister in law is the only family who has wanted to come and see me perform and is excited for me. When I first started, I was doing amateur shows when they came up. During these shows, I met a king that traveled to perform in St. Louis, where I am from, and asked how I could start traveling. He got me in to another venue, which turned, into me getting booked in a "DRAG Off." This is like RuPaul's DRAG race with challenges and different themes, a lip sync for your life if you were in the bottom, and eliminations. This was where I really have to evolve as a performer. The competition lasted for 6 months and included kings, Queens, bio and burlesque performers. The judges would give you tips on how to improve and things that they recommend trying which greatly helped with my performances. I was the second runner up in this competition. Since then I have signed up to compete for a Pride King pageant and hope to continue to follow this journey to see where it takes me. Being a king to me is an outlet to express my inner creativity and to have fun, I do not do it to get money or to have the crowns, and my favorite shows are the tip shows and benefit shows.

Orion Blaze Browne: I dressed in male clothing since high school in 2001. I was always a tomboy. I hit the stage in 2010. I spent two years before following random DRAG kings on blogs and YouTube. My family and friends have always been supportive of me. My mother has even been to a few shows. I started DRAG for fun to bring out a side of myself I normally did not show. It was through DRAG that I realized I have been a boy my entire life inside myself. I started my transition 7 months after starting DRAG and now I love every moment of my life on and off stage.

Rasta Boi Punany: In College. I began as androgynous and found my comfort zone wearing men's clothing. My family accepted this because I was already out. I went to adding the masculine features as a DRAG King in 2011.

Chance Wise: Growing up I was mistaken as a boy. I got a kick out of it. When my mom gave up trying to put me in pretty dresses and putting bows in my hair (around 5 or 6 years old), I started wearing jeans and comfortable shoes and I never looked back. In 1992 I cut 20 inches of hair off and I came out officially as a lesbian. Coming out was kind of a letdown for me because everyone already knew. I watch DRAG shows just about every weekend and was always extremely intrigued; it just felt like I should be up there doing what the Queens were. It was a pretty long process of asking people how to do facial hair and binding before I figured it out for myself, I got mixed reactions from my friends ranging from really excited about the idea of me cross dressing to friends just being like, 'Ewww, you want to do what?' I am thinking it took about three years of cross-dressing and taking random pictures of myself playing around with facial hair before I ever got the nerve to do it in public. One night I met a Queen that wanted to help me out, and a month later, she put me in a benefit show she was doing. I honestly do not remember if I even lip synced the words I was so nervous, but Chance Wise was born that night in 2007, and even though I have taken about a year off the stage it is still deep in my blood and planning a reborn Chance, come back. My parents have always been supportive and even came to one of my shows. My mom brags to people that her daughter is a DRAG King.

Travis Hard: I became interested while watching a DRAG Queen show in Springfield, Missouri, USA. Kings were unheard of back then and I thought, I want to do that too, but as a guy. Two years later, Travis was born.

K'ne Cole: I cannot even think of a time where "girly" was really my thing. Always felt a bit odd or out of place. I however did not ever see or hear about the art form until I moved to FL. I went to a couple DRAG shows and loved them. It took a DRAG king at the time, Devon James, 3 years to convince me that I would be good at the art of Male Illusion. I finally gave in and went to a meeting for a group at the time that was the TNT Boi's and performed in the group number and a solo performance a couple weeks later. I loved it, entered the Mister Pasco Newcomer Pageant weeks later, and won. I still can remember the jitters I had the first time I walked onto the stage. My family is a bag of mixed emotions on the whole thing...my mom and dad still does not get it but my brother tells everyone he knows!

Jack King: I have always been boyish, so it was natural for me

Campbell Reid Andrews: My childhood was rough. From four to about six, my mother and I were living out of women's shelters in Virginia. Of course a single mom always has to make it work so we had our fun anyway we could. She would dress me up in all kinds of clothes from overalls to ruffle dresses and socks. Anything we could get our hands on to make the time go by. When we moved to Texas, USA we were stable but still did not have the funds to buy very nice clothes so I made due with cousin's hand me downs. During elementary through middle school I was in uniforms and weekends I would dress like "girls" were supposed to. Until I got into High school that is when the cat was out of the bag. I did not cut my hair quite yet my mother would have had a heart attack. That was my gangster phase haha. Even though I made the leap to start dressing more masculine, I still felt the need to dress womanly when I visited my family in Virginia, USA for some time. By my junior year, I ditched the women's clothes and started to express myself with men's clothes and continue to do so. Even the day's people I meet ask "why?" My mother did not really have any opinions about me dressing like a man. I guess my life choices and personality lead her to believe I was already planning on it. She helped me pick out clothes she always said, "Well at least I do not have to worry about you having kids at 15."

Lyle Love-It: The illusion of being a MALE came through a Halloween costume. I dress comfortable, but not male. My attire depends on the situation if I am going out on a date, I dress a bit more feminine, hell, I wear a bikini top and men's swim trunks, boi underwear, girl underwear, it all "depends", on who, what and where I am.

🎭Kenneth J. Squires: I saw my first DRAG show in 1999. I saw a DRAG King at the same show and knew it was something I wanted to get into. I was a huge Tom Boy when I was younger, so dressing in men's clothes did not bother me. I began changing my look for the better, trying different ways of putting facial hair on my face. I then won the 2002 "Falsie Award." I was hooked.

🎭Joshua Micheals: Started dressing in DRAG in my high school theatre department and was often cast in male roles. Performing at the club's I was invited to a DRAG show by a customer at the restaurant I waited tables at went with a group of friends from my theatre clears in college and was bet/dared to try and the rest is history

🎭Eddie C. Broadway: I always dressed like a boy at one time or another. Coming from a theater family and being a theater geek always pushed me in this direction. My family and friends were super supportive throughout it. I auditioned for Sisterzz twisted (DRAG troupe) and got in. I took my performing to the next level when I was adopted by Freddy Prinze Charming, and later adopted by Gunner Daimon Gatlyn. These two have been an integral part to my success, whether they know it or not

🎭Stormm: I was competing for songs with the Queens... and I sang live. I figured nobody was doing guy songs. That is when I started.

🎭Travis Luvermore: I was always comfortable in loose fitting and male clothes. I first dressed in DRAG on a dare. My partner at the time had performed at a local bar on talent night and gave me the challenge. I found the whole transformation amazing I had a new confidence in myself. I worked to enhance my look each new performance and developed my own stage style. Put always stayed myself of the stage.

🎭Kody Sky: My family tried to get me to be girly and honestly I did try for them. I always felt very uncomfortable in a dress and fake beyond girly makeup. As time went by, I felt like I was going to scream! I was tired of society telling me what I "should" do, what I should wear. As I entered high school, I promised myself I would wear what felt like ME. It was not a matter of dressing like a man or a woman; I wanted to dress like ME for ME. I realized I was dressing like a guy. I did not have a problem with it. I was comfortable finally in my own choice of clothes. My friends supported me through my change of clothes and were fine with it. My family had a hard time accepting that I am a lesbian and I wear guy clothing and accessories. I was lectured thousands of times by many people that I was going to burn for the choices I was making. I followed through my own beliefs and studies of God, as that was always the argument, and found that god loves us all and made us this way so we could learn to accept each other's differences and grow into our world of survival. As the years went by, I was introduced to the world of male impersonators and it clicked. As soon as I ended my first song ever on stage, I realized "this is what I am meant for"

AJ Menendez: I was part of a DRAG troupe called 100 Degrees Celsius and performing as a kitten (Diva). I used to watch my DRAG father Gage Gatlyn transform and it completely fascinated me from the very beginning. One night we did a turnabout show, I had to invent AJ, and it took off from there.

Rychard "Alpha" Le'Sabre: My ex-girlfriend thought I would make a "cute king" so I went to the nearest club she went to and checked it out. That was almost seven years ago and I have been doing it ever since. My family hates it still, but I grew up Mormon so that is completely to be expected.

Shane Rebel Caine: I dressed as a boy when I was a kid, tried to fit in through middle school and high school. After I graduated, I went right back to wearing guys clothes. When I was a kid, my mother took it, as I was a tomboy and would grow out of it, which she believed to be true until I was 18. My mom, dad, and brother are the only ones with a problem of me dressing as a boy and performing as a king. The rest of my family and my friends are supportive. When I turned 19 I would came out of my shell. I started having random people tell me I should try being a DRAG king. I thought about it but kept putting it off due to major stage freight. It was not until September 2012 when I spoke to a DRAG Queen that I greatly admired that I finally decided to do it simply because she told me how she had stage freight and what she did to overcome it. On Nov. 21, 2012 I stepped foot on stage for the first time and although I was scared to death I pushed through it and continued from then on and although my nerves still get the better of me from time to time there definitely is no better feeling that putting on a great performance and pleasing a crowd!

B J Bottoms: I became interested when I saw my first DRAG show. Watching the crowd react and entertainers having fun, made me want to be in stage. My life as an entertainer and my family is separate, besides my sister. It is two different lives for me. My sister supports me and loves coming to see me perform. I started pushing myself as an MI a year ago. I won my first title and really started to grow as an entertainer. My performances have become more elaborate and my outfits more detailed.

Stefon SanDiego: 17 years ago. I attended a local club in Port Huron Michigan named Seekers Show Bar owned by Mr. Arthur Payne. At a young age of 20 my dear friends Carmen SanDiego, Chelsea DelRay, Porsha DelRay and the many others exclaimed that my interest in the stage should be taken to the stage. A local owned benefit by Mr.Payne that organizes "Toys for Kids" seemed to me as a great cause to participate. Back in those days' ace bandages and clear plastic wrap was the medium of taking down. Most too many, entertainers would share different tips of advice and mediums to use backstage. Performances were that of great and many in those days, and to add families of DRAG were formed. The House of San Diego, The House of DelRay and many more. In our community, we were a tight nit family. As time marched on...so did the entertainment. Now, when it came to my family, I sent my mom a picture of Stefon SanDiego. For the world of her she had exclaimed that she could not understand, why I would sent this picture of this handsome young man. I kindly replied..."that's my mom as an entertainer." For a moment, there was blank air and she says this, "you grew a mustache, oh Lord." I replied, "no mom, it is glued on; that's entertainment"! She thanked God as she had worried. My mom had asked why I wanted to be a man, but simply I had explained the great causes and benefits I have had the opportunity to perform were well worth the illusion. Proud mom she is today of a daughter who was always willing to help and make that difference in this world.

Adam DoEve: I was brought up in a strict house and as the oldest of three girls, it was hard to please the dad that wanted a son and the mom that wanted me to act like a girl all the time. I was not permitted to wear pants let alone boy type clothing. My hair could not be above my shoulders and better be out on my face. I never really broke out of the always dressing like a girl until I met my second girlfriend in my early thirties. I had come out a few years before and was still trying to find out the real me. The big shock for my family and friends was when I cut ALL of my long blond hair off; it went well past my waist. The girl that cut it for me cried but I felt free. My dad was one of the first ones to see me. He was having a heart attack on the spot but he just got up and walked away and did not speak to me for about a week. I have not given up the girl clothing but now I know who I am and if there is a day, I feel like a girl that is what I put on for the day. The day I cut my hair is the day I realized I was playing dress up for the world because that is what they were telling me I had to do but I do not. I am I and that is what matters. Being a DRAG king was something I had been thinking about for a few years but because of something is that had gone on in my past I was afraid to go on stage. I had been a singer a good part of my life so it was nothing new to me but someone had stripped me of that, but when I saw my first DRAG king performer I knew I had to somehow get up there and do it too. My first few shows I used my reg. street clothing but as I started having more and more fun at it the clothing just exploded with a life of its own. See now I was dressing up for fun and making people smile and I was having fun doing it.

Pierce Gabriel: I always wore boy's clothes growing up; since I have never had a girly personality I was never interested in looking feminine. I have also always been an actor at heart, jumping at every chance to be on stage. The more challenging the character, the more eager I was to play it. The first time I ever saw a DRAG king show, I knew that was the next character I wanted to play. My family has watched the videos of my performances, and as far as I am aware, they only look at it as another character for me to play and it does not influence their feelings towards me.

❀Brandon KC Young-Taylor: I dressed in clothes of the opposite sex since being a kid. I never liked wearing girl clothes. My parents did not really mind but my mom always tried to put me in a special dress for Easter. Was not my favorite time of year!

❀Alec Allnight: My mom bought boys Levis for me as a kid. I hated it then because all the girls wore skinny-legged jeans. When I got older though, I only bought men's pants because they were just so much more comfortable. Then I had men's t-shirts and button up shirts. It was just more comfortable for me than trying to wear women's clothes. It was gradual I think for the most part. Family and friends just went with it. No one was horrified or anything. I called myself a Chap Stick lesbian in boy's clothes.

❀Ryder Knightly: About two years ago I came out but was still consider a "lipstick." It was not until last year. I said screw it. I am done with these skinny jeans. I had secretly wore my brother's clothes when no one was home singing, I will make a man out of you. My brother was supportive and gave me full access to his closet. No more hiding! I find myself doing more male costumes than just casual male wear for shows now.

❀Kruz Mhee: As a kid I always enjoyed entertaining my friends and family. Whether it was singing, which I did not do well, or dancing and acting silly. My idol at the time was Carol Burnett and my hero at the time was my dad. Therefore, my mom was okay with me impersonating my dad. At the age of nine, I was in my first talent show. When my mom asked me what I was going to do, I told her "Billy Jean." She argued at first, and then decided to let me do what I wanted to do. I had also gotten my first perm so it was easy to make my hair like a Jerry curl. My mom put my outfit together and my middle sister made me my first sequined Michael Jackson glove. I remember how excited I was for that performance and how proud my mom was. From then on, I mostly wore boys clothing with my mom's approval. That is, except for Sunday's going to church. Through the years, the male clothing became more prominent with my mom's disapproval. After I came to the realization that I was a Lesbian, I started going out to clubs. The first night I walked into a lesbian bar I witnessed my first show. It was a lesbian bar but that evening the special guest was a local DRAG Queen. She was Amazing! The next time I went out, I saw a beautiful thick Woman perform "Faux DRAG" and I was hooked! I took the steps to start performing. At the time, I did not know performing as a male was an option. The gay lesbian scene and shows were all completely new. After many years of performing as a female, I became bored and lost interest. After running into a few friends one night in 2007 I decided to start performing again. Still as a female. I won my local Ms. Her Gay Pride pageant and got back into the club scene. I met my partner Jennifer a.k.a Chynna Dohl in 2007. I had been performing for more than 15 years Faux DRAG. We had been together only a few months when she said, "You look uncomfortable in that." I was wearing a corset and go go boots. I said I had always thought performing as a male would fit me better. She suggested trying it and I never turned back. I love it and it suits me, or so I am told. I would not go back for anything. Within the first year, we started our own performing group "Generation NxXxT" and I have helped birth more than a handful of Kings and Faux DRAG entertainers. After the first year, most everyone in the community accepted me as a King and not just a female playing dress up. It is one of the most important decisions as an entertainer that I have ever made. It is because of a DRAG that I have met a number of influential people as well as made a number of friends I probably would not have made otherwise. DRAG has given me the creative outlet I have searched for my entire life. It is also given me an extended family that loves and accepts me no matter what I am wearing!

❀**Hawk Stuart:** I have always dressed the way I been, I am not a girly girl. I know my parents do not like the way I dress but they have to realize I am who I am I feel comfortable dressing as I do.

❀**Silk Steele Prince:** When I was about 10 years old I secretly would steal my older brother's clothes and sneak out the house in them. When my brother found out, he told my mom and she yelled at me and said I was a girl and I was going to dress like one. When I went to high school, I dressed more so like a boy and it was comfortable. When I was 18, I became an exotic dancer and my boss noticed that I did not dress like the other dancers outside the club and he told me I think we can find a way to work that in your stage performance. Shortly after Tuesday night's became Dyke Nite and I was the headliner. The first Stud performer. After that, I had private bookings and I started gender blending and doing DRAG.

❀**Flex Jonez:** 32 years ago at 16 my entertainment career in theater, TV and modeling began to bloom. I realized my desire to being a transvestite (cross dresser) during that time caused me to lose a contract with a NY agency that was not ready for a cross dresser at my age off and on stage. I was homeless at 17. I met my DRAG mother who assistant and encouraged me to use my entertainment skills to hustle in the clubs for survival and extra pocket change. It was then I became a performer and DJ. Traveled with a DRAG Queen troupe in and out of the USA for years.

❀**SirMandingo Thatis:** I started when I was twenty-four. When I came home my four year old son saw me and freaked out so I vowed to not do if again until he was older. He is nineteen and I am thirteen months into it with two bar titles and on to nationals. My family is supportive. I enjoy it because I get to make people smile and I love the music and I love the attention.

❀**Cody Wellch Klondyke:** I have never been a Girly Girl. I was a tomboy even when I was younger. I always wanted to be a DRAG King a Male Impersonator. One day talking with My DRAG Queen Mom, she ended talking to me about it. Then I went with it and ran she is the one that gave me my name also. After that then One day while I was living back In Monroe La I went to a club and give them Idea of Having a DRAG King Group Performing. There were eight of us in a group called Gurlzz II Men.

❀**George De Micheal:** I am transgendered and wanted a male form to exhibit my masculine role as a male impersonator as well as an entertainer. The first DRAG king competition I saw in vanilla in the gay village in Manchester in the United Kingdom of 2010 made me want to do DRAG as a male impersonator this is where I watched my mentor perform Valentino King.

❀**Bruno Diaz:** I was born and raised in Mexico so I grew up with limited resources. My mom sewed stuff for us. When I was five, I told her I did not want it to wear dresses anymore. I guess I kind of came out to her, the tomboy was taking over. When I was in elementary school, we had a class called Folkloric Dance. Boys do not participate so guess what, I got the male roll, and I danced with a girl. The first time I saw a DRAG show I was 18 and was fascinated by it, the males were also Queens in male DRAG, so I though I can do that part. I moved to the states when I was 25. A couple of years after that I came around the club scene and saw a DRAG King in 2000. It was not until 2011 I entered a talent search in the local bar and won a booking. I been in love with a stage and the feeling was back. All my families are friends with my Stage persona as well. I do not think anybody is surprised, maybe about how good looking I am! This is an art! Our job is to share it with the world.

❀**Santana Romero** I first became interested in DRAG an LGBT youth group I went to as a teenager. One day, we were watching a movie (for the life of me I cannot recall the title) that featured a DRAG show at the beginning. One of the adult volunteers informed me that there was a small clip of a "DRAG king" in the show and this immediately peeked my interest. Now, I had always been curious about DRAG kings actually existed but seeing one for myself on stage, performing with his Queen counterparts really gave me something tangible to hang onto. Like most of these others boys, I have been a tomboy for as long I can remember. I have always had a masculine strut to my walk and I have been dressing more androgynous since I was 15 or so. I have also had a passion for dance and entertaining since the age of 11. The prospect of being able to meld my love for the stage and my interest in gender bending through DRAG overwhelmed with excitement! My first opportunity to do DRAG came from a local DRAG troupe here in Toledo named the "Bois W/ Outskirts." I was only 17 years old. They were looking for a fourth member for their team and wanted me to audition. When they informed me that I made the cut, it was downhill from there.

Since then, I have only became more and more invested into my DRAG and I really took to the next level when I spoke with one my good Queen friends, National Holiday. Just out of curiosity when I asked her, what I could do to be a better King. She told me that I should grab a tube of E-6000 and some stones to really add flare to my clothing. I also starting speaking with more seasoned Kings through Facebook and received a lot of valuable advice about pageants and how to get my name out there. Studying other binding, and make up techniques really helped me step it up as well. My family and friends have always supported my career from the beginning. They were not at all surprised when they found out I was bouncing around the stage with a mustache wearing a tuxedo ha-ha. For the past three years, I have done pageants, had the opportunity to perform all over the Ohio and Michigan area, help my community and I am eagerly waiting to compete for my first national title. I love this art form and have truly been blessed with everything that has happened so far.

Colin Grey: I became interested in becoming an impersonator after seeing my first DRAG show. I was always enchanted with the theater and wanted to be an actress. Impersonating was like the ultimate performance and I get to do it each time I "get in face." My friends were all on board to include my *gasp* boyfriend at the time. My family never really knew about what I did until several years later and while the only family member to come see me perform has only been one of my sisters, my mother has shown her support in different little ways with sewing projects and the like. I have had several different breaks from performing for several different reasons and one of things I like to Pride myself on is coming back better each time. I like to see other kings/impersonators in action and truly love the art form.

J Breezy St James: When I saw my first DRAG Queens perform at the age of sixteen. I knew I wanted to do DRAG. I waited until I was 21. My mom and older sister are my biggest supporters they go to every show and pageant they even go to pride with me.

E. M. Shaun: I have ways been a tomboy growing up. As I matured and reached high school, I came out and knew that I was gay. I have been categorized in the group of being a stud so I guess I have always felt my inner man. After seeing my first DRAG king show, I fell in love with it. I have always loved and supported DRAG Queen shows. I am a dancer by heart so when I am in the club it is just natural for me to dance and be interactive with other people. When my father died 7 years ago to a brain tumor, it took a lot out of me. At 27 years old with father being a huge inspiration in my life and my parents being married for 35 years it was a major lost for us. My dad loved to perform in Community Theater and I loved watching him perform as various characters. The first time I drew on my face as E. M. Shaun, I saw my father staring back at me. It was my confirmation this is what I was supposed to do. I had studies my dad for years and now it was my time to follow his example.

🌸**Sam Masterson:** I always dress like a man it came easy.

🌸**Stefan LeDude:** I was dressing myself up as a man for years before I actually started performing. The first time was for a DRAG ball, and after that, just for fun and laughs occasionally. I think I started doing it at age 18 or 19. Then I started taking it to the stage when I was about 27 or 28. I have been performing for 5 or 6 years now.

🌸**Xavier Bottoms:** I wore boy's clothes as a tomboy growing up. I was the only girl out of many boy cousins, with hand-me-downs. My family never batted an eye. I have Double D breast and back then, nobody had heard of DRAG Kings

🌸**Jamel Knight:** I was always a tomboy and would wear my brothers clothing a lot when I was a kid. Therefore, it was not much of a surprise to my family or friends when I started dressing in men's clothes all the time. The first time I performed in DRAG was in 2004. I was begged repeatedly by a friend that had started a nightclub to come out and perform. She loved the way I would just dance in the club and thought I would be a good performer. After about 4 months of her begging, I finally gave in and agreed to perform in their Christmas Eve show. That show was crazy. It was packed and standing room only. Nervous does not describe what I felt that night. I have been on stage before quite a few times since the age of 3 but this was the first time I had ever performed in an LGBT establishment as a DRAG king and I really had no idea what I was doing. But, the funny thing is backstage I was officially introduced to my now girlfriend of 10 years and that kind of helped with the nervousness because at that point it was all about impressing her and I almost forgot about all the people out there. That was actually a great night.

🌸**Welland Dowd:** Since I was a little kid. Halloween was always my favorite holiday since it gave me an excuse to dress as a dude. Now I am trans-identified, so I get to dress all manly every day and it is AWESOME!

🌸**Julius M. SeizeHer:** Pride 2012: It was discussed with two of my close friends, and we even came up with my name. Pride 2013: One year later, I took the community Stage and rocked the House as Julius. It was amazing. No words can explain the rush of performing. My family does not know, but my friends are super supportive of me.

🌸**Jack E. Dickinson:** Back in 2004-ish, when I was still living as a woman. I began to experiment at home, then during outings in the village with friends, and dreamed up stage numbers. Since I already had a lot of facial fuzz, I simply applied mascara to it for a convincing beard and mustache. Binding was a bit more challenging because of a larger chest - eventually I discovered binders. I began to exclusively shop in the men's section. Alone at home, I would put on a "beard" almost every evening. When I started going out that way, some friends were supportive. Others were a bit incredulous and said things like: "Your hair is too long for you to look like a guy" or "you smile too much." It upset me because of the gender stereotypes that they, as queers, were continuing to propagate but some were supportive and understood that this was part of my gender exploration. 2 years later, my big chance came: there was a DRAG king competition at a local venue where they had a monthly cabaret show for "bent girls and their buddies." I actually won with my lip sync of Number of the Beast by Iron Maiden! I also met up with some other DRAG kings who were interested in working together, so we started doing group numbers and started a troupe a few months later.

🏵**Clark Kunt:** I never had an affiliation with the term 'female.' It was simply the box I was told I fit in. I have always worn clothing comfortable for my body, and as someone whose gender is very fluid. I have worn different styles of clothes, even within the same day. When I started DRAG, my first number involved ripping my shirt to reveal a superman shirt underneath; that made me nervous. Now I do full boylesque style stripping numbers where I get down to nothing but tape and boxers - and work superman logos into my duct tape. When I found a binding method (open bind with spray adhesive) that made me look flat and did not aggravate my disability by dislocating my ribs, I found a comfort in my gender identity that I never had before. Suddenly the audience seeing my chest was not a scary thought, and being able to feel comfortable in my body, in a safe space was such an inviting idea.

🏵**Lyle Love-it:** My first "male" dresses up was a Halloween costume and went from there into performing. I live life as A WOMAN I perform as a MALE ILLUSIONIST and work HARD at perfecting the ILLUSION have no desires to change gender.

🏵**Emilio:** I started performing in 2008 after I moved from California to the Pacific Northwest. I joined a DRAG King troop to meet new people, and push past my comfort zone. I quickly realized I was in love with performing, and became a solo act shortly after hitting the stage. Once I became a solo artist, I embraced my Argentine culture, and I now only perform Latin numbers. As much as I love being a male illusionist, I also very much love being a woman. I love the different personas I get to portray.

🏵**Juan Kerr:** I started 'DRAGging' as a Halloween costume. My two male friends who are straight and not Queens, decided to buy matching dresses, do their makeup the same, and wear LOVELY pink scarves. They did not wig up or anything and they both had facial hair so the resultant mess was a mess. This spurred me on to give being a boy a go. I drew on the old moustache and beard with a liquid eyeliner, got out my best blue man's shirt and whacked some braces on; VOILA. As I started to do it more and more my parents were questioning why I wanted to dress as a boy and what was wrong with being a girl etc. It freaked my brother out the first time he came to a burlesque show I was hosting in DRAG because, as the pictures can testify, I looked like a mini him! My dad's is not sure about it but my mum thinks it looks fun although I still do not like appearing in DRAG in front of her. I have been a singer in my 'normal' life since I was seven so performing was not new to me. Wearing the clothes of my character and building a male persona were new to my stage act. I still keep the two facets of my life separate, Beth is not Juan is not Beth and I like it that way.

Thug Passion: I become interested in being an entertainer when my girl at the time did a benefit DRAG show at Wichita State University. It was then I saw for the first time a DRAG king named Jae Luv. He did a song called sex you up by color me bad. Which was one of my all-time favorite songs. I remember she looked like the was having a great time up there being that person for that song. I add lays had stage fright when it came to speaking in front of people so I figured this would be a good way for me to overcome that fear. After the how I asked her how she put on her facial hair. I told her I wanted to do we hat she does. She said she would help me. I asked her if she would do a duet with me for my first number and she said yes. Therefore, we picked out a song and came up with a routine. My first day came and I went to her house and she put the facial hair on me. I told my friends at the time and Coworkers and they all could not believe I was doing it. They came out to support me and could not believe the transformation I had made. Several of them were straight and were very attracted to me. So they said " now I have to question my sexually because I know you are a girl but you look really good as a guy". Once I stepped on the stage, I knew I belonged there and just have not stopped.

Stefon Royce Iman: I was a female exotic dancer; it did not go so well. They thought I was a transgendered female. I have muscles so they said I was too masculine. I researched male impersonators and DRAG. I always enjoyed seeing DRAG Queens so I could be a DRAG king and keep my exotic dancing. My mom saw a picture of me in DRAG. I lied and said that was my twin brothet. She said, since when does he dress like that? I was lost for words. I said it was me and she said I knew it was because of your nose. I pulled out more pictures and showed her videos. She was impressed and when I have a show she says to me have fun and be safe. My mom took it well.

Dominic: I always dressed this way as far back as I can remember! My mom said she should have known I was gay because I woke up one day at the age of five, looked her dead in the eyes and REFUSED to put on my favorite sundress! She used to put my hair up in pigtails. I had the cutest little ringlets

LoUis CYfer: After I decided I was not comfortable with the binaries that life had to offer regarding gender I found my own way to play around … Thus was born LoUis CYfer and my family love him.

❀**Smitty O'Toole:** I have always dressed as a male, my parents said I started demanding not to wear dresses at age 3. My family has always seen me as a male, so they had no issues with me dressing as one or even transitioning. The first time I took it to the stage was in March of 2013 with the Gendermyn in Houston. They happened to be at an event I volunteered at, I chatted with them about DRAG and was put on stage two weeks later.

❀**Papi Chulo Doll:** Well as far as I can remember my mother was always fighting me as a very young child to stop wearing my brothers clothing. She was one of those strict ass Mexican mothers that tried to beat the boy out of me. My favorite uncle chewy was a breaker in 80s. We both just knew ... I. Won second place in first grade looking and feeling like Rob Base all Adidas out... man hearing that crowd feeling that love. I knew I loved this life. My mother never approved even after she passed. My father supported mi in anything I have done. My sisters and brother had been there as well. Too bad, they never saw any of my shows.

❀**Bootzy Edwards Collynz:** I was always a "Tomboy," so the transitioning from a dress was not so difficult. Mom had to come to terms over the years. As for performances, I find it difficult to change a style so often for being a "guy." Men's trends and are varied. My first outfits were lots of jeans, t-shirts, vests, and button-ups.

❀**Jensen C. Dean:** I have never been interested in the traditionally female clothing options so as I got older and started making my own money and buying my own clothes my wardrobe have gotten progressively more traditionally male. As for actually getting on stage and impersonating a man, the decision to do that came not long before it actually happened.

❀**Boi Wonder:** I was always a tomboy. I discovered DRAG kinging through American literature and TV. I stumbled on DRAG king Valentino King performing in my home city Manchester. We became friennds and DRAG Kings of Manchester was born.

❀**D-Rex:** Growing up on a ranch, dressing as a cowboy came naturally.

Chapter Nine
"Define the pros and cons in your relationship with dating or live in partners in regards performing."

❈❈❈

❈**Dominic:** I had a wife in the beginning. She was my most supportive and biggest fan! She taped me, helped backstage, song choices, dance moves, and helped promote!

❈**Freddy Prinze Charming:** I have had three partners since starting DRAG. The first was an alcoholic, jealous, discouraging. It made things difficult when putting together numbers with the troupe I was in; songs could be deemed too sexy, too misogynistic, etc., etc. It was stressful. The second partner was supportive, almost too supportive. She became a DRAG groupie, and pretty much embarrassed her and me throughout our relationship. The support was nice, as she would sit up with me and help me with costumes, but the rest of it made it hard to get excited about performing out in public. My third partner started out very supportive. She made sure she made it to every show, and was my biggest cheerleader and fan. Then she saw the drama and backbiting that happened. That left a sour taste in her mouth, and she began to withdraw from the scene. Eventually, she did not really support my DRAG at all, telling me she "wanted no part of it, didn't want to hear about it, and didn't want to see it." It made things difficult when trying to prepare for a show, as I had to time working on costumes for when she was not home or when she was sleeping. Finding a supportive partner is almost a must in this business. They do not have to be the typical "DRAG wife," but having that support makes things much easier.

❈**Adam All:** My previous partners have been supportive but distant from it. My current partner is part of my show. She rocks! We work together on everything and she is my mentor, my guide, and my manager. She teaches me so much. She is the one back stage telling me I can do it. She thinks I am the best and fiercely protects my image and me.

❈**Spacee Kadett:** Spacee was born about five years ago, very shortly after my wife, Kate Skarb-Hagemann, and I started dating. She has been incredibly supportive from day 1, and for that, I am SO fortunate. Brainstorming, shows, pictures, videos, props, luggage, travel...she has helped me with everything and put up with everything. Spacee has overrun our second bedroom since day 1. She has rearranged her work schedule to travel to out of town bookings with me, and even does almost all the driving. Without her tax return, I never could have competed at Nationals. Also, when I had the opportunity to move across three states for an amazing full time DRAG gig, she left her local family and her job to move with me. In fact, recognizing the opportunity, she was more encouraging of the idea than I was. I think it is important to note that Kat is NOT an entertainer and never desires to be. Work often prevents her from coming to shows or on trips. That is fine - in fact, it is better that way. DRAG is both my passion and my job. I do not follow her to her desk job, so it makes sense that she does not always follow me to the theater. I also reserve most of my DRAG talk for friends who are as passionate about it as I am. If I go to watch a pageant or to a special event, it will often be with them. Within our marriage, DRAG in moderation is key, as with anything, and I still know in my heart of hearts that without my amazing wife, Spacee would never be where he is today.

❀**Chance Wise:** It has never been easy to date while performing, but I finally found a lady that is really excited to be a part of my DRAG life. Since I have been off stage for a while, she is really inspiring me to get back on stage. She actually talked me into putting all my DRAG on a few nights ago. This just made me miss it 10 times more. I am much happier now.

❀**Davion Summers:** My partner has been amazing. She helps me get dressed, pick out songs that are out of my comfort zone and she even helps me clean off after I put my face on. I would say that the only con is that every once in a while she does not agree with my song choice and it causes me to second-guess myself. However, I have learned how to know what I feel comfortable with as a performer and to keep on doing it, if I feel strongly about it.

❀**Shook ByNature:** I have only cohabitated with one of my exes as an entertainer and when our relationship ended, she tried to destroy all my DRAG! I have had too many different experiences. I have had girlfriends who were only with me because of my DRAG persona, I have had girlfriends who want to control my career, girlfriends who demand I quit entertaining, but I have learned from each of them. I have known my partner, Coco Saní Addams-Davidson, for years and she is a FiFi/Femme Entertainer. We share everything (stones, fabric, etc.); we listen to each other's suggestions and make sure our relationship is equal on and off stage. Our relationship is based on mutual respect for our artistic styles, and if you can find someone that does not look for the conflict in your art, that is worth more than anything!

❀**Orion Blaze Browne:** I have had multiple partners since starting DRAG. My first partner helped me get into it. It caused jealousy issues when I would perform or talk to bar patrons after shows. My second partner was better with the jealousy and everything was ok. She even helped me make costumes. My third partner was a femme/burlesque performer so it was ideal when it came to performing. She understood everything I did and I understood what she did. We were also polyamorous so flirting with other people was never an issue. I was free to express my stage personae however, I wanted. Towards the end of that relationship, I became more attracted to men so we broke up. I was single for a while which gave me complete freedom on and off stage to do what I wanted. Now I am in love with a DRAG queen. He has some jealousy issues outside of DRAG but as for my craft, he is all about helping me go further with costuming, number ideas, and pageants. He is my biggest support and I am his. We have no problem telling each other when we look a mess or something is not for the stage.

❀Jonah Godfather of DRAG: I have been married 27 years. Of the 14 years that I have been performing, my wife has always been there for me. She does all of my alterations and stoning. I know she gets overwhelmed from time to time with all of the shows and DRAG related work, but she is always there. The only thing that gets to her is when an audience member gets a little "too excited" and takes things a little too far. She knows that there is nothing to worry about but she still has a problem when someone is touching what is hers.

❀Vinnie Marconi: I am blessed! My partner and I were together five years before I ever hit the stage and she is my biggest supporter! I cannot comment on the dating thing, but Lynn and I have one rule, NO kissing on the lips by fans. It is much easier for me to "play" with the audience when Lynn has a "bar buddy." She has NEVER missed a performance and if it is at a new venue where we really do not know anyone, I am more concerned with her sitting at a table alone than my performance. NOT good. If I believe she is ok, then I can concentrate better on my performance.

❀Clint Torres: A relationship, while doing DRAG, is a very fragile thing. It is like walking on eggshells because you do not want to do anything to upset your girlfriend when she is there, but you also do not want to play it too safe and lose your audience. That is the challenge I am facing right now. My girlfriend is very supportive but she can get pretty jealous when women will walk up and put their hands on me or try to get me to take the money out of their breasts. What I found works is communication. I tell my girl everything I plan to do while on stage and we prepare for what might happen. I have found that as long as we talk things out, everything is good.

❀Viciouse Slick: I was single before I was a king and still single. Being a DRAG king turns some people off for some reason but I have had some crushes on DRAG kings.

❀Koomah: I am happily single, I do not date or do relationships, and I do not hookup with fellow performers or people I consider friends to avoid drama. I would hate to lose a friend over a booty call.

❀Campbell Reid Andrews: My partner is so accepting and she knows the game. She is a networker and always has been. She talks to more people than I do. She also knows most of my tips come from flirting while on stage and touching others. No problems here. I do always tell new kings with possessive partners they should be careful with the touching and know their boundaries. Cons could be late nights, touchy audience members, not being able to realize when to checkout, getting wrapped up in drama, and becoming cocky. Pros could be gaining confidence, making new friends, becoming creative, and learning new skills.

❀**Coti Blayne:** I have had a few flings since I started performing. Most of them were only with me because I was an entertainer and they only cared about my DRAG persona, not the person I was off stage. That or they would get jealous about me being a cute DRAG king. The girls would hit on me so they tried to make me stop. Of course, that is never going to happen. My partner now though, is fantastic and I am very happy to call her my fiancé. She is another DRAG king, William Vanity Matrix, and we have been together about 2 1/2 years now. It was rough at the beginning because we both entered pageants and we tend to end up running against each other, so it puts a strain on the relationship, but we have worked through that and now she is my biggest critic but my biggest ally.

❀**William Vanity Matrix:** My fiancé, Coti Blayne, is a performer as well. I would say our worst fights have been about cross-dressing. There is no room in a relationship for jealousy, especially if one or both perform, male and female alike.

❀**Erick LaRue:** My wife supports me 100%. She has performed with me and has been in my talents in the pageantry/contest world.

❀**D-Rex:** My wife made or designed most of my costumes. She has been there through thick and thin. Plus she knows whom I go home with at the end of the night. She knows a good performer flirts but has boundaries.

❀**Rasta Boi Punany:** My wife, along with some friends, began this journey by encouraging me to get up on stage for the audience competition at the Mr. Philadelphia DRAG King/Mr. Philadelphia Gay Pride pageant held in Philadelphia, Pennsylvania, USA. She entered me into the competition the following year and I won. She became my manager, in my eyes, helping with choice of music and staying professional while being sexy, supporting me at shows in the area. Now I am on my own with her support as needed. There are boundaries of which I follow as a married woman. I keep my performances as respectful. We even performed together.

❀**B J Armani:** I could be with anyone that was less than 100% supportive. I have a very supportive husband that is also in the Air Force. The only thing that he ever said when I decided to do DRAG 11 years ago was, "Be as good as they are." Now he says, "See who they look up to?" when it comes to newer performers. He works the door at my shows and watches over the entire crowd. He is my linebacker.

❀**Lyle Love-It:** I had THE BEST support, but times change and now I am single.

❀**Kenneth J. Squires:** I have a partner who supports me. I thank God for her. She keeps me strong when I was weak. Having her out there cheering me on makes it so much better for me. I know I have got someone on my side who loves me. I have had others in my life that thought DRAG was not something they thought was ok or did not support me in. It was hard for me in times like those. I pushed on though.

✿**Joshua Micheals:** I have never had a negative experience with performing and dating. Almost everyone I dated I have met whilst in DRAG and were very supportive.

✿**Eddie C. Broadway:** My wife is the biggest fan I have. She is my harshest critic and keeps me on my toes. She keeps me going and helps me know what I need to improve on. She is talented herself and we keep pushing each other towards greatness.

✿**Jake Van Camp:** My partner is the only one I dated since I starting. She was the one that encouraged me the most. She is an artist herself and commonly helps me put my ideas into reality. She used to go to every show, but now her business has taken off and goes to them a little less frequently. I still consider her to be my biggest help. She is also my biggest critic and continues to help me grow and improve the craft.

✿**D-Luv Saviyon:** My partners have all been supportive, which is a blessing.

✿**Travis Luvermore:** Had a couple partners in my DRAG career. My first partner encouraged me to try, and it turned into a competition and was the downfall to the relationship. I am a lesbian and dress for the stage only. My one partner wanted me to be Travis 24 hours a day and it was not happening. My current partner has been very supportive helping me with song choice, outfit shopping and a respect and recognition that though I may flirt on stage, I go home to her.

✿**Gus Magendor:** My partner and I discussed the fact that I am FTM. She accepted me for that and then I mentioned performing as a king and she told me that no matter what, she supported me all the way.

✿**AJ Menendez:** I consider my wife to be the perfect DRAG wife; she is supportive, not have a jealous bone in her body, and encourages me to do the best I can possibly do.

✿**Atown:** I was about 6 years into my relationship before I became a DRAG king. The initial reaction from my partner was fear and mistrust. I do not think she fully trusted that nothing would happen to interfere with our relationship. She had to be my performance partner in every single number. When it was time to do a solo, it was very uncomfortable for me and nerve racking that I would do a certain look or movement that would cause an argument. Or someone would tip me and have some sort of physical interaction. After my partner saw that she could trust me and was assured that I am a professional and would not let anything get out of hand, she had full confidence in me and supported me to the fullest.

✿**Diseal Tanks Roberts::**My wife was very supportive at first, then after a while, she got bored with the whole DRAG scene and it caused some issues for a bit. Then we got her to perform as a femme and now she is totally into it again. She actually performs with me from time to time now.

❀MaXx Decco: Happily single, dating and relationships are a blurred lines in DRAG. It is a lifestyle and does not always fit with other people's lives, and it can be confusing. I have had women fawning and stuffing bills but as soon as the performance is over, they are buying a skirt a drink. It is hard to find dates and start relationships, and coming home at 3:00 am really does not fly in any relationship. It takes support and understanding and even then, people can get bored or tired of the scene. You learn who is not going to last real quick. It takes a true partner to stick it out, stay true to you. You will find one, you just have to recognize them and KEEP THEM.

❀Marcus Mayhem: Single was the best. Dating a king myself was fun and difficult at the same time. It started to be not just me getting ready, but now I had to get him ready too. It was no longer just making and stoning my clothes, I had to stone his too. I was doing all the clothes for the both of us and it was hard enough to just do mine.

❀Rychard "Alpha" Le'Sabre: My now ex-wife was never very fond of my DRAG career, but only because I was old enough to go to the bar, and she was not. She felt neglected and unwanted. It took a long time to heal those wounds. She is my best friend now, and she comes along to my shows as our company photographer and brings her girlfriend along, who is also a DRAG king in our community.

❀Shane Rebel Caine: Most of the girls I have dated since starting my DRAG career have all been supportive but I have only ever dated one person who was 100% supportive and came to as many shows as possible and even helped me with my makeup and costumes. Most other girlfriends supported in spirit, but they would rather sleep than come out and show their support. Also, jealousy has proven to be a big issue especially when a tipper gets a little too friendly, which in such cases I cannot really complain when whom I am with is not there, as it avoids conflict. Many people do not fully understand that it is part of the act and that is it. It is nice to have who you are with there to support you and cheer for you, but is less drama unless they fully comprehend the art of performing as well as trust you to keep it clean.

❀B J Bottoms: My girlfriends loved that I am an entertainer. It is something not many people do. Every girlfriend I have had over the last four years attended my shows. My last girlfriend I met through DRAG and was an entertain as well which is a hard thing to balance. The most important thing to remember when telling someone you are interested that you are an M.I is no matter what happens between you the stage will always love you and it will let you get everything out without judgement.

❀Dakota Rain: I have had one girlfriend during my DRAG entertainment. She fell more for the entertainer than the real person. I had to step away because we, Dakota and I, are the same person. Some people do not see it that way.

❋**Ashton The Adorable Lover:** Mine understood and not only supported, came to watch or performed with me if they were also an entertainer. The only negative I could say is due to my "Adorable" factor, I'm noticed a lot and tend to flirt, but as long as my partner was confident in me and my heart it never caused a problem. They date me, not my DRAG persona.

❋**Pierce Gabriel:** I have dated several people during the course of my DRAG career. The first one supported me as best she could, but she was not able to watch the shows. There were several issues at first as she felt like me being a DRAG king meant I was transgender. I went through a lot of detail to separate my personal life from my DRAG life. The next two girls were very active in my DRAG career, attending every show, helping me back stage or preparing for my numbers throughout the week. However, the problem I found there was that it caused problems with my fans. Girls did not feel comfortable tipping me or flirting with me because they did not want to cause drama with my girlfriend. The arrangement I have with the girl I am currently seeing is the best I have been in so far. She has no interest in DRAG shows, so she only comes to one or two a year. She supports the fact that it is something I want to do, but feels no need to be an active part of it. In this way, I am able to be fully Pierce Gabriel at the show, and drop the character to be who I really am at home.

❋**Alec Allnight:** I am engaged to a wonderful woman who supports anything I do. She actually runs the ladies night that I perform at through the Fresno Fresbians. She promotes, organizes, and manages the shows. She was doing that before I got bit with the DRAG bug. We can joke that her and I are engaged, but Alec is single. We can both separate our life and the performing life, which is rare, I think. It does not bother her if Alec strips on stage or flirts with the audience during a show. She knows it is part of the persona and that is what makes a good show. I am very fortunate.

❋**Brandon KC Young-Taylor:** I had three partners since I started performing.. It is not always easy if your partner is the jealous type. My experience has always been to be reassuring to my partner because the fans sometimes get really close and personal!

❋**Ryder Knightly:** When I first started, I had a girlfriend. The pros were that I had someone that was really pushing and helping me, whether it was getting ready or my dresser at times. It is also hard because you have to have a mutual understanding of what might happen on stage, and making sure jealousy does not become an issue.

❋**Kruz Mhee:** When I first started I was performing as a female and that for me was detrimental to relationships. Being hit on in front of your partner or significant other is not always handled very well. When I met my partner Jennifer a.k.a. Chynna, we had the discussion right off as to what she was going to have to deal with. I was very clear that these passes by girls or guys were for Kruz not Paula. Jealousy is not something you want to deal with while you are on stage and definitely not offstage. We had and still do have an agreement that if a pass goes too far I have one chance to clear it up, then It is all her. She gets to clear the air on my behalf. It takes two very strong personalities to be able to deal with the entertainment issues. Lucky for me, she is now also an entertainer and knows firsthand how to cope.

❀**Hawk Stuart::** When I was with someone, they loved that I did it. Now I am single. I want to find someone to love me doing it as well, though they can get jealous of me performing since you have people on you and touching you.

❀**Stormm:** My partner was very supportive about the whole thing.

❀**Silk Steele Prince:** In my past relationships, my partners who were in the industry said they could handle it, but they could not handle all the other women touching me or me touching other women. My current wife is perfectly secure and she looks at the other women as fans and nothing more. She knows I am leaving the show with her.

❀**Flex Jonez:** I am dating and my mate is aware and attends my gigs when she is able, it is not a requirement for her to be there.

❀**J Breezy St James:** One of my exes got very jealous and could not handle females coming up to me after shows knowing I was leaving with her. I have learned I need a partner that understands it is a job and will not get jealous.

❀**SirMandingo Thatis:** Well when I stared my craft, my wife was only my girlfriend and was cool, but as time went on, she experienced the desire to "try it out." I really feel that it is because I get too much attention and she does not, but I just smile, nod, and walk away. Hey, it is what it is.

❀**Kenneth J. Squires:** I have had a few relationships since I have been performing. Having a partner who does not support you is not a good idea. It was too much a problem if I wanted to perform. Now I have a partner who supports me all the way. She helps me the best she can and is my biggest fan.

❀**Cody Wellch Klondyke:** I have had one relationship partner and it was good. She was there to help me and she supported me. The con about it was when I performed and she was there, I felt that I could not give it my all because I know she was watching me. If I talked and danced, mingled with another female in the crowd, she got pissed and she was very jealous.

❀**George De Micheal:** I have had partners come and go but most have been accepting. Some have been jealous but at the end of the day, the one who backs you and accepts you for who you are, is the true person you should be with. My girlfriend at the moment accepts me as a person, artist, and DRAG performer and loves everything I am.

❦**Colin Grey:** Girlfriends have been supportive for the most part along the way. There was an ugly hiccup when one left me for someone else on the show. Best advice I can give is do not date your audience.

❦**Kameo Dupree:** I have been with my wife for about 13 years (married 8). She always knew I wanted to do DRAG but never thought this idea would come to light. Boy was she wrong! I hit the stage and fell in love with a new level of entertainment. We started having issues with trust when I started performing more and she could not make every show. She finally understood just because I flirt does not mean I am cheating. Now before I hit the stage, she checks to make sure I do not have my wedding ring on because (her words) "you messing up my money!" It took some time but she finally understood when I come off the stage she gets the money.

❦**Sam Masterson:** My wife backs me 200% and is my biggest fan.

❦**Stefan LeDude:** I met my last girlfriend not long after I started performing. I met her online and chatted with her. I met her in person for the first time when she came to see me perform. We started dating, and she would come to most of my shows, though in the end she started coming out less. Then we broke up and a couple of years later, I met my current girlfriend when she joined the DRAG king troupe I was in. Since then, she's been performing on and off, but she always comes to see me either way, and she is so supportive.

❦**Jamel Knight:** My relationship works well in regards to performing. We are both performers and have respect for the other's art. We have an understanding that in character, if you need to be single, it is about the art and nothing else. We never limit each other as performers. We have also both had our share of groupies and over the years have really learned not to let that bother us. We had to work to build that level of trust and understanding but it was definitely worth it and I can say that my relationship has been an asset to my performing career because of that.

❦**Master Cameron Eric Leon:** My mum asked me the same question. I am single and I think it actually makes things easier. Gender expression and sexuality are two parts of my life where my beliefs are unwavering, and DRAG is a great physical representation of that for me. If someone is uncomfortable with me in DRAG, it means they do not hold the same core values I do. I would not be able to date them. It helps to narrow things.

❦**Welland Dowd:** It is great that my partner is supportive of my art. The only friction is in the hours before a show when I am trying to focus. She knows now to keep her distance and let me get in the zone without distractions.

❦**DeVery Bess:** Well, performing was one of the reasons my partner fell in love with me. My partner is very supportive of my craft, always there to help build props and comes to at least one show a month. Some days she does wish I performed less so I may spend more time with her, but she respects that I love performing. She trusts me as I trust her, because you know what they say, everyone loves DRAG kings.

✿**Sam Masterson:** I am fortunate to have a wife that supports me in every step.

✿**Travis Hard:** My girlfriend appreciates my DRAG and supports when she can. I am very lucky that she is open-minded and inspires me every day.

✿**Bootzy Edwards Collynz:** Dating has been special. Certain women have a hard time with the "bending" of gender roles. I am an athletic looking female, which helps create my illusion. I have had girlfriends tell me they were worried about me "gaining a larger size" because they "didn't want to feel like they were dating a guy." I love my athletic look and love the sports and physical activities I choose to do. They keep me sane (because jail ain't a cute look at a certain age). I have learned to be more open and ok if a woman I would like to date is not comfortable with me as a DRAG performer, or as a muscular woman. Just do not disrespect or try to degrade me because of it. I try to make sure that the women I date now have a security within themselves that can deal with the security I have within me. It is not easy weeding through the BS. There are chasers out there for Kings just as much as there are for Queens. Just takes a little more time on the "questionnaire" to see who can hang and who cannot.

✿**Jack E. Dickinson:** I am polyamorous and queer, and would only date people who are accepting and celebratory about performance, DRAG, and gender expression. I live in a single-parent household and have no interest in living with a partner or any other adult at this time. If I ever did, they would have to be OK with at least a full closet being devoted to costumes and props.

✿**Xavier Bottoms:** When I started performing my girlfriend at that time hated it. It was not because of me performing, she hated the bar scene. So I stopped. Thank goodness that relationship did not work. Most of the woman I have been with since doing DRAG have no issues. I have been married for a while now and my wife is very supportive. Pros and cons? It is easier to pick up woman in DRAG for me. But it is not always the best way to start a relationship.

✿**Clark Kunt:** I have been through ups and downs with dating and DRAG. It can be dramatic. For someone who likes to leave the drama off the stage, it can be difficult to manage. If you find the right supportive people, dating and DRAG can go hand in hand.

✿**Emilio:** My wife is my biggest cheerleader when it comes to performing. I even call her my "wifeager" (manager). She books all of my jobs, and is front and center at every performance. She makes me confident, and I feel like I can conquer the world!

✿**Juan Kerr:** The girlfriends have always been turned on by it. I do not know why. Some girls just really dig it. My current partner loves Juan. She talks about him as if he is real. We are not the same person. Juan and her are having an affair. I love it!

❀**Trey C. Michaels:** My ex was not supportive at all. There were times she would ruin one of my outfits out of spite. Now any one I am dating I am up front about what I do and that if they have an issue with it then it might be best to remain friends. I am blessed to be dating a performer who is supportive and encourages me.

❀**Bailey Saint James:** Dating for me in the beginning was very sketchy. I was never quite sure if my partner was into me or just my craft. They always attended every show and pushed me to perform more, which is great, but whenever I took a hiatus from performing, it seemed like we would argue more. After the third girlfriend, I began dating people who did not follow the craft so closely, and it seemed like my home life was much more tolerable.

❀**Aaron Phoenix:** My partner is a DRAG queen. We support each other 100%. Whether she is helping me get ready for a show or vice versa, or we are lugging all the DRAG to a show together, we are constantly pushing each other to be the best we can be, to reach outside our comfort zones and put on dynamite shows, and to pursue new goals and endeavors. We live for the madness together and I cannot imagine it any other way.

❀**Thug Passion:** I do not have any problems with dating or live in partners when it comes to performing. They all understand what I do onstage is entertainment and at the end of the night, I am going home with them. When starting a new relationship I let them know that this is important to me. If there is something I do on stage they do not like we can discuss it, but if they cannot handle this life, it is best we stay friends. Being an entertainer is like being a celebrity in real life except it is in the LGBT community. There will be groupies and lots of people attracted to you, both men and women, and some people flirt. My best advice would be keeping open and honest communication with whomever you are seeing.

❀**Soco Dupree:** I have had a few relationships during my career. At first, they seemed to enjoy it, and then unfortunately the green-eyed monster called jealousy pokes it head. My current relationship is so supportive in my career from helping with music, to outfits, to props. She is amazing!

❀**Stefon Royce Iman:** Been with my girlfriend for three years. She supports my shows and attends my shows. She met me at a show and was amazed.

❀**E. M. Shaun:** I have had very supportive girlfriends since the start. A few of them met me in DRAG. I made it clear from the start that it was me that they were interested in and not just my alter ego. A few girlfriends have even performed with me. There has been a little jealousy at times, but once we cleared up that E. M. Shaun was a flirt and loved to be sexy on stage (and that is where I left it) because my heart belonged to them only and when the day was over, I only had eyes for them, we were good.

❦**Smitty O'Toole:** When I started DRAG, I was dating a woman who did not work in the industry. It was a bit taxing on her because I was entering DRAG races and spending 12-15 hours a day making costumes, prepping choreography, and learning lyrics. She came to most of my shows but was not interested in the scene. I now date a transwoman who has been a DRAG queen for 10 years and I find that we can bounce ideas off each other, perform together, and grow our art together.

❦**Jensen C. Dean:** When I started performing, I was in a relationship. We are married. My wife helps me in one way or another with every aspect of my performances. I could not do this without her; she is my biggest fan and manager all at the same time.

❦**Luke Ateraz:** My wife, Roxi, has been by my side since the beginning. I turned to her for everything. She started doing my makeup, costuming, everything. She became my manager. She was my go to, the one I would yell at when things were not right, for any and everything. Even when we split up for a while, she was my rock. She continued to manage my schedule. Now that she has started performing, she is a diva.

❦**Boi Wonder:** Good, all my partners have supported it (bar one who thought it was weird). After we split, she decided to give it a go herself.

❦**Miles Long:** Some people I dated got jealous when I performed. Currently I am involved with someone who is completely supportive in every area of DRAG and I do not know what I would do without her.

❦**Devin G. Dame:** Gage and I support each other as male illusionists. We have an agreement to not be in the same show together. One at a time works best for us.

Name the performers without checking on DRAG411.com

Chapter Ten
"What has a spouse/partner done for your craft? Positive. Negative? How did you handle the negative?"

❀❀❀

❀**D-Luv Saviyon:** I am single right now, but the worse thing I have encountered is although being supportive, I have had a few territorial girlfriends. I have had times where they made it so known (not that people were not already aware) that I was with them that it greatly affected my tips. Girls would catch me away from my girl and tip me, telling me that they were nervous to tip in front of her. That is NEVER okay.

❀**Adam All:** She kept very separate from it. Though she respected it, she did not want to intrude on my passion. Now she is not only my manager, advisor, and assistant, she is my on stage girlfriend and we present a double act, which is unique in our field. She is undoubtedly the single most wonderful woman I have ever met. We plan on world domination...or at least having fun with this show for as long as we get bookings!

❀**Travis Luvermore:** My partner has been extremely supportive. She does networking for me, helps me chose outfits, and assists me in binding and dressing during shows.

❀**Justin Cider:** I met my girlfriend because of DRAG. Johnnie Blackheart has been my hugest help. She helps me get ready, is crafty with facial hair, and as a king herself, knows what needs to be done. She takes pics of all variety of outfits. It is so much easier to bind with extra hands, too. She has sincerely brought my DRAG game way up in my opinion, and I am so grateful.

❀**Travis Hard:** My current girl was nervous because she never dated a king. Now she is that girl who comes to the show, tips every performer, and has the time of her life. She lets me do my DRAG on my own and supports me. It is wonderfully positive!

❀**Chance Wise:** My current girlfriend is excited to see me perform and doing everything in her power to get me on stage. Hopefully her excitement continues when I do get up there. The negative ex from 2010, super supportive as long as I did not actually perform. The day of a show would come around and I would be doing my normal getting everything ready for that night and doing touchups on costumes, and listening to my music. She would pout horribly and text me from 20 feet away asking why I was being so mean to her (I was not, I was just preparing). Every week that behavior would get worse, but she was super happy when I did not have a show and could not wait until the next show night. It started stressing me out when a show was coming because I knew the guilt trip/pouting would start up again. Knowing this would not work, I ended it before it got too serious.

❀**Coti Blayne:** My partner is also a DRAG king and my biggest supporter and my biggest critic. We compete in pageants against each other often, but it does not hurt our relationship because we keep it separate. We often joke that Sam and Steph are together but William hates Coti. Our relationship comes first. I know anything she says is meant to help me grow and not to spite me. We trust each other not to go do stupid things so neither of us gets jealous. Everyone knows we are together for the most part and if they do not know they are told very quickly, but it does not affect my tips or fans at all. If anything, it helps because everyone thinks we are such a cute couple.

❀**Clint Torres:** My girlfriend mixes my music, burns it on CDs, drives me to shows, is my designated driver, and supports me in any way that she can. She is great about it.

❀**Rasta Boi Punany:** My wife has helped me to begin this journey and now she has allowed me to flourish on my own. I try to keep this part of my life separate now. It keeps the peace in our marriage.

❀**Kenneth J. Squires:** My Girlfriend has helped me tremendously. She has supported me in everything I have done. I appreciate that from her, because it means so much to me. It all has been so positive.

❀**Spacee Kadett:** I could never be Spacee without the support, ideas, sacrifices, contributions, and inspiration of my amazing wife. She is also very protective of my public character, which can become a fine line to walk, but not necessarily a negative. One point of contention is the intimacy of accepting dollars in my mouth from patrons..., which, really, is fine. I do not like the taste of crack and feces anyway...

❀**Adam DoEve:** The person I am with now is the first one to say, "Ok, if that is what you want to do, then do it," but she does not like it. She does come to my shows but is not very supportive. She just lets me do my thing. I do have to tell her ahead of time if I am going to be doing a song that I know she will not like and then she has the choice of staying home that night so I do not have hear about it on the way home.

❀**Joshua Micheals:** My girl is my sounding board. She is the one who supports my crazy ideas or tells me to pull it back when I go a little too far out in left field. She is insanely creative, always positive, and my biggest fan.

❀**Phantom:** My Husband, Kevin Chatelain, and I are a team. He has been there since day one. My prop maker, video editor, music mixer, and all around support system. When something goes wrong, I keep going no matter what. If my prosthetic's fall off, rip it off and keep moving. Forget my music? Pick another song. Or my props breaking, tape or glue it back together. I bring all that I need with me just in case something goes bad. WE make a good team.

❀**Pierce Gabriel:** I had girlfriends assist me back stage, helping me bind, getting my next outfit ready, etc. I found it helpful, but never had problems doing it on my own. It generally caused problems for me with girlfriends getting jealous over a fan flirting with me, or requiring me to be physically affectionate with them all night so my fans felt like they couldn't approach me. So the positive was never really worth the negative in my opinion. I don't like arguing or fighting, and it always resulted in us just talking in circles. It is much less stressful if my partner is separate from my shows.

❀**Vinnie Marconi:** I would be LOST without Lynn. We were together 3 1/2 years before toying with the idea of doing DRAG, then another 2 years before I hit the stage. She helps with costuming, chooses music, keeps "Vinnie" classy, and listens to mixes for errors, is my sounding board, all of it. If I need a female (and sometimes male) back up, she is the first person I turn to. She was my dresser once for a pageant and was more nervous than I was! She now has a "bar buddy" so when I perform, she is not sitting there alone and I can concentrate on the performance. Rules: No kissing on lips of fans and no touching breasts or butts (but that is just respect!) She always was, and continues to be, my number one fan.

❀**Kruz Mhee:** My partner gave me the courage to try something new. Together we started our own performing troupe, Generation NxXxT. Together we had the longest running female show (5 years straight) at the top club in Birmingham, Alabama, USA. She encourages me to be the best person and entertainer that I can be. Whether it is putting on my makeup or helping choose the right music for each show, she gives of her time and talents to make mine better. She has stood beside me and helped me become the best entertainer and King I can be and I am still learning. Above all else, she LOVES me and in this day and age, that says a lot.

❀**Flex Jonez:** The women I dated have been honestly positive with the good and bad. Plus we video my work these days, to fix the mistakes.

❀**Silk Steele Prince:** My partner would help me get ready for performances by helping me get dressed or watching me rehearse and critiquing my performance. Most of all, just being there to support me.

❀**SirMandingo Thatis:** My wife is very supportive and even researches different parts of my art and brings her ideas to the table, and gives me the option to use it or not. Now of course there are negative issues, but I just let them go and eventually they will drop off. I try not to dwell on them because they will hurt your relationship.

❀**Stormm:** Usually she is supportive, but she does get mad when I do too many shows. I just tell her to stay home then. I enjoy doing it. Sometimes it is the only time I go out. Or maybe it is mid-life crisis. She does help with getting costumes together, and she videotapes my performances.

❀**Kenneth J. Squires:** My partner helps tremendously. She helps me dress and and bind, ensuring everything looks right. She helps with my makeup too, making sure that it is on right. I had a few partners in the past who did not support me, and it seemed like it was a huge hassle to want to perform.

❀**George De Micheal:** I deal with it and move on, as I do not do negativity in my life. It drains me so if I do find myself in that situation, I just perform my best even more.

❀**Chasin Love:** My partner is very encouraging, also helps supporting by coming to many of my shows. Family is now supportive. Before, they were amazed by the transformation but realize I do this for a job!

❀**DeVery Bess:** I dated someone who did not support my craft or even care...so I left them. I am passionate about what I do, and my passions come first. Now I have a partner who supports me by helping build costumes, sets, gives me constructive criticism, and keeps me humble.

❀**Eddie C. Broadway:** My wife is so amazing when it comes to DRAG. She has put up with so much and still is right there with me. She is my biggest fan and best critic. She pushes me to be better both on and off stage. She is also an amazing performer as well, and is extremely talented and creative.

❀**Colin Grey:** My partner has put up with a lot as far as me being an entertainer. I am fortunate to have her in my life.

❀**Xavier Bottoms:** My wife is extremely supportive. She helps make most of my outfits. She is a stoning fool. She loves to shop for Xavier's clothes. She also is a "femme" woman, so she knows what the ladies like to see. She has helped to create, build, and paint many sets for me. She is my biggest fan.

❀**B J Armani:** If I did not have the support of my family or my partner I don't believe that I would listen. Negativity can come from anywhere. It hurts when it is your family but I have seen jealousy take apart many a DRAG relationship. My straight and I married him May 27, 2005. He has helped DRAG my stuff inside when I am exhausted and worked the door when I've put on shows. He is a rock.

❀**Jamel Knight:** My partner is my inspiration, muse, back-up dancer, choreographer, biggest cheerleader, and my most honest critic. I wouldn't be were I am as an entertainer if it wasn't for her. The biggest negative that comes is when we disagree on the direction a number should take. At times that can cause arguments because we are both passionate about what we do. But, we always find a way to meet in the middle. And, that usually makes for a better show than what either of us wanted individually.

❀**Bruno Diaz:** My partner is a big supporter of the art. She has been around queens since she was nineteen, and helps me with Bruno's evolution. I need her as a partner to succeed, because it is time consuming.

She is my dresser. She does not like men, so when I am in DRAG I do not feel she sees me, she sees 'him.' She is a bit tougher on 'him' than she would be with me.

❀**Welland Dowd:** My partner is a big fan and always attends my shows. She respects my art. She keeps her distance on show days so I can focus and get in the zone.

❀**Michael Christian:** I am currently single, but my ex-girlfriend was supportive. She is an entertainer herself so she understood everything about it. We supported each other completely from song and costume concepts right through national pageants.

❀**Sam Masterson:** Supportive. Helps me with clothes and finding music.

❀**Jonah Godfather of DRAG:** My wife does so much to help me get onstage. She tailors my clothes. She makes costumes. She stones jackets. She helps me with song choices. She gets me to the shows, as I cannot drive any longer.

❀**Campbell Reid Andrews:** My fiancé is my rock. She handles all my bookings and helps with encouragement, emails, concept decisions, ass kissing... Without her, I would not be the performer I am today. We have a great balance because she is also a performer so she knows what it is like. I know I am completely blessed to have her in my life and for her to be so damn supportive. She pushes me to do the numbers I really want to do and the concepts I know are a little edgy for some crowds. She knows what will work and what will not, but she is also not afraid to tell me no.

❀**Howie Feltersnatch:** until recently, I have been single. I have only been seeing my current partner for a short while. So far, they seem really good with it. Next week I have three performances, they are willing to drive me to each one, and one is even out of town. So that is killer of them.

❀**Jack E. Dickinson:** I met my current partner after I began. She has been supportive as an audience member, and as a co-performer and organizer. Nothing negative at all!

❀**Clark Kunt:** My ex-partner helped me get courage to go on stage, and thought up my DRAG name! There were ups and downs, but a supportive chosen family helped act as my rock when the negatives flared up.

❀**Emilio:** My wife encourages, makes me better and stopped me from retiring.

❀**Juan Kerr:** Nothing negative. My girlfriend loves it.

❀**Trey C. Michaels:** My ex was supportive at first, but over time became very unsupportive. It caused me to take a break from DRAG because the constant fighting and negativity affected my performances. I now date a queen who pushes me to think outside of the box. We attend all of each other's show.

❀**Bailey Saint James:** My partner once decided to do DRAG herself and attempted to serenade me on stage. While it was adorable, it was very mocking. It made me and some entertainers upset. It seemed like she was trying to say that it is not an art and that just anyone can do it. We may seem to make this look easy, but it is still a craft.

❀**Aaron Phoenix:** My partner is also an entertainer, and we feed off each other to be our best. It gets stressful at times with both of us living the hectic life of an entertainer (do not know what we would do without two bathrooms), but we handle that with a lot of patience and working as a team.

❀**Mike Oxready:** My partner attends my shows, supports me in so many ways. She accepts before a big show I am rehearsing and unable to spend much time with her. She is so understanding and supportive.

❀**Thug Passion:** All of my partners have been supportive of my craft. My partner now helps with costumes, creativeness, comes to all of my shows, and gives constructive criticism. She lets me know that she always has my back.

❀**MaXx Decco:** Happily single. I need a creative partner who understands the passion, the crazy schedule, is extremely accepting and supportive of DRAG life.

❀**Soco Dupree:** My partner has been amazing from getting my bag ready, to downloading my music, stoning outfits, etc.

❀**Stefon Royce Iman:** My partner always videotapes my performance. She is always positive and supportive, never negative.

❀**Jensen C. Dean:** My wife is so amazingly supportive! She is my official costume designer and works hours on my outfits so that I look great on stage. She is also my ego check if my head gets a bit inflated, and my sounding board for ideas and any venting I need to do. I could not be Jensen without her constant help and support.

❀**Cody Wellch Klondyke:** My previous girlfriend helped me get ready and she made sure that I had everything together before a show. Now my new girlfriend thinks it is totally cool and it strikes her interest. She would like to know more about the DRAG king world. She is going to do some research in California, USA, to see what is out there and she is very supportive of me.

❀**E. M. Shaun:** My previous girlfriends have helped with music, costuming, promoting, and whatever I needed. A supportive partner is very important. Like the saying goes, behind every strong man there is a stronger woman!

❀**Smitty O'Toole:** My current partner is a prominent DRAG queen in the community, so she has opened doors for me in the business as well as given me tips. My last partner was great at supporting me in every way I needed.

❀**Luke Ateraz:** My wife has done more for me than she will ever know. She has helped make me who I am today!

❀**Dixon Heat:** My partner is supportive and usually does my beard for me.

❀**Kameo Dupree:** My partner allows me to be myself. When pageant season is in full swing, she is right by my side making sure I am where I should be at all times. When it comes to choosing music, she steps back and allows my creativity to come through. She is always there when a new costume needs glitter it rhinestones. She is amazing!

❀**Boi Wonder:** My partner is supportive about what I do. She stayed up until 2 A.M. re-sewing my new binder, as it was too small.

❀**William Vanity Matrix:** We help each other since she is also a DRAG king. We have been a little too honest and read a little too hard from time to time.

❀**Devin G. Dame:** Gage Gatlyn has done more for DRAG than any other single male illusionist. He paved the way for us across the country by getting into bars that never had kings before (The Masque Nightclub in Dayton, Ohio, USA being one of them). He was taught by 6pak (the very first to open shirt) and was the first to add makeup to the chest area for a more manly chest. He traveled across the country and still holds the record of the most traveled and booked king. He taught hundreds of kings across the country about makeup, open shirt binding, and costuming. He is the Original Master Male Illusionist.

Chapter Eleven
"How did you handle negative people in the beginning? How did they affect you? Looking back through today's eyes, how would have you handled it differently?"

❦Shook ByNature: I used to negative people coming for me. Looking back, I stayed in drama. Now I just focus on the entertainment. We all grow up!

❦B J Armani: Wow what a question, but hey, I kind of saw this one coming, and I think I have stalled a bit enough. I was so confused why a straight person had to shove that part of herself in the closet. I just let everyone assume I was a lesbian/bisexual in the beginning (elelven years ago mind you) and after doing it for a couple years I had to come out of the "closet" because I was getting married to a wonderful man and best friend of six years. Kind of obvious after that. Most backlash came from the fact I was such a different kind of performer. BIG costumes BIG numbers RIDICULOUS props. Hey, the audience was remembering me so I figured I was doing something right. Heck ANYTIME you do something right in this genre usually the haters come at you from all sides. Now I realize that taking every show I could for NO pay and building up my reputation only caused me to become more prepared for my own show. I wish I could say I would have handled it differently but all Kings know we have to pay our dues. I have been humbled by years of negativity towards kings, or even DRAG in general. BUT, it also keeps me on my toes as an advocate and a leader.

❦Brandon KC Young-Taylor: I got much negativity because I was good for a beginner. I tried to stay out of it, but I was young and got caught up a few times. Now I am blessed to travel, so I do not get involved in community drama. I am simply not there enough to really know what is going on!

❦Koomah: I am a pretty eclectic performer so I cover a range of performance styles from solos, group acts, DRAG cabaret, sideshow and novelty acts, burlesque, performance art, etc., and have heard some people say they link a certain type or style over other kinds. Some people prefer traditional DRAG numbers over narrative group acts, some like sociopolitical acts over traditional DRAG. It really depends on the audience and the performance space. One thing I learned was know your audience - what works in one bar may not work in a different bar or a club, or it may work better in an art space. I have encountered some confrontational performers and emcees backstage, sometimes folks behave arrogantly, sometimes-inappropriate behavior is a result of folks being drunk/under the influence, and a few times, I have had issues backstage in dressing rooms in regards to my intersex body. I have had people also hassle me about performing as both a king and queen among other things. It is inconvenient at times, but does not bother me much.

❀Clint Torres: I am still too new to the scene and have yet to deal with any negativity. I know it will probably come eventually and I will just deal with it the way I was taught. Haters are going to hate but you just got to keep doing you. Whatever makes you happy. That is all that matters in the end because your fans outweigh your haters

❀D-Luv Saviyon: I always been redistribute negative energy into determination and motivation. If you tell me I cannot accomplish something I want to do, it makes me hell bent on making you eat your words. I am equally passionate if I believe in a cause or need. I also had many people that keep pushing and believing in me to help in my weak times. People call the negative ones haters. There are no Real haters, they are either jealous because you have already accomplished something they wanted to or admirers who are afraid to be openly known for supporting you.

❀Vinnie Marconi: I think because of my age, a majority of people were encouraging to me. What you might call negativity, I call constructive criticism. The high school behavior does not bother me. I just shake my head and walk away muttering, "kids..."

❀Freddy Prinze Charming: My first experience with the negativity that comes along with all of this was my partner when I first started performing. She was an alcoholic, possessive, and jealous and was always discouraging. Had I listened to her, I probably would not still be doing this today.

❀Gus Magendor: Negative people were not really a problem but when anything was said, it only made me cocky, and I just blew them off because they could not dance better than me. Looking back I would have pulled them to the side and gave them a dance session 101 (free of charge)

❀Chance Wise: Drama always finds a way into my life. In the past, I let it frustrate me and almost win at one point when I thought about just quitting and never performing again. A wise person in my life got me through that and now I just ignore a lot of drama...and use it to inspire me to be better.

❀Starr Masters: I pushed the boundaries and limits, keep doing all Goth weird songs I could do! If they did not like it, they did not have to watch, but oh, how so they did! I would of done it all over again! I loved what I did for Colorado, USA, but we are far behind in male illusions and kinging.

❀Travis Hard: For years, I had a negative experience with another king who kept saying I was copying him, over the most ridiculous things. Because he wore a symbol often, when I wore it, he cried COPY. When he cut his hair and I cut mine (short but not the same style) I was copying him.

We had our difficulties over the years and I just dealt with it by being an adult and moving on to my next number.

❀**Dakota Rain:** I have learned way before I started this, that my life is different from others. You will have people that will always try to put you down and break you, but I as a person I have learned to be strong and take what they offer. Sometimes I give back (you can only push a person so far). I have a very strong willed family so that helps as well. I am who I am and always will be. As my dad use to say, "if you do not like me then walk away because I am happy being me and you can't change that."

❀**Rasta Boi Punany:** In the beginning, I stayed away from everyone. I was not on stage so I was Rochelle, the shy introvert, not very social around strangers. Today, I do pretty much the same unless I know you. I meditate a lot so I still get into my zone by staying to myself back stage.

❀**Adam All:** Negativity deeply hurts but I make a strategic plan to keep it at arm's length. I do not always succeed but for the most part now, I have my amazing partner to support me, and she can smell bullshit a mile away.

❀**Campbell Reid Andrews:** Wow, this is something that is always reoccurring. I use to try and prove they are wrong. Fight back because of my nature. Now I know how to be an adult and realize I cannot allow other to determine what I am or am not. I let the kids be kids and let my work speak for itself. Ain't nobody got time for that anyway.

❀**Diseal Tanks Roberts:** I do this just for fun and to entertain people, I do take it seriously enough, but negativity does not bother me one bit.

❀**D-Rex:** I was in the "Do not ask, Do not tell" Army when I started. I just had to hide who I was, what I did, and pray that they did not find out. Now I am retired from the Army so I must have done all right at hiding.

❀**Lyle Love-It:** I really never encountered any...all positive, so far.

❀**Spacee Kadett:** I used to be so impressionable. I doubted myself and took everyone's "constructive criticism" to heart. It left me confused and inauthentic. Today I have come to realize that everyone will have their two cents for you and your DRAG -- even when you are well established, but especially as you start out. The key is in recognizing whose two cents are worthless, and whose are worth a million bucks.

❀**Joshua Micheals:** I was lucky enough to be unaware of the negativity or to have enough positivity to make it not anything worth wasting energy on.

❀**Eddie C. Broadway:** People will always dislike you no matter how hard you try to remain positive or happy. I unfortunately had an incident that cost others and me the entire pageant (pageant was suspended for the year) and it took a lot out of me. I handled it by swallowing my pride, holding my head up high, and continuing to be me. The negativity faded. I am not sure how I would have handled it differently. It was a blessing in disguise because of the lessons I learned and it toughened my skin.

❀**Travis Luvermore:** Do not take comments to heart or affect your confidence on stage

❀**Kody Sky:** I took it as criticism for motivation to do better for myself.

❀**AJ Menendez:** To be completely honest, in the beginning, I dealt with it in the beginning by drinking and just about ruined all that I was striving for. I picked myself up out of that hole, got sober, and used all negativity as a stepping-stone into doing things in a positive manor.

❀**Romeo Sanchez:** I never really let the negativity affect me. If what they are saying is something I felt I needed to hear I address it within myself as a performer, otherwise I just take it with a grain of salt.

❀**Atown:** I focus on what I need to do as an entertainer; turn the negatives into positives. I have been blessed so far not to have to deal with anything too extreme.

❀**Rychard "Alpha" Le'Sabre:** I never really had a lot of Negative feedback. Constructive criticism at most, but that was all.

❀**Shane Rebel Caine:** I ignore negativity and not let it bother me. I learned growing up, you could not let people get to you and keep you from doing what you love to do.

❀**B J Bottoms:** I have been very blessed not to meet any negativity since my career started. Sure, you get the people who look down on MI's but I have not met any personal negativity towards me.

❀**Ashton The Adorable Lover:** They pretty much left me alone. I guess because I can have that, "I wish you would say something" kind of look when people think a bit much about themselves. I also let most slide off my back, I perform because it makes me happy and it lets me be a bit more outgoing and I enjoy entertaining people.

❀**Adam DoEve:** I try to hear people. Sometimes I do numbers that do not sit well with the one place I perform and that is because there is a big age range there. I do from country to grunge and I am not going to please everyone. If I see that there is not as many your people there I will sometimes change a song at the last min or go with it. Other than that, I have not really had any negativity other than family, but that was a different question. I have only been doing this for 2 years so I am sure I will run into this problem at some point. Everyone has their own thought processes and it is not always going to match mine, so the best thing is just to walk away from the ones that sling it and giggle to yourself. You know they are standing there looking like a fool with their mouth open because you didn't say a word but walked away with your head held high, and you know you love yourself.

❀**Stormm:** I really have not had any, but everybody has their views. I do listen, and can take criticism. If I am doing something wrong, it is nice to get the feedback so u can change something. Some people might not get into the music you are performing.

❀**Pierce Gabriel:** I have never really allowed negativity to affect me. I accept constructive criticism well, but if all someone is trying to do is put me down, I just let them roll off me like water.

❀**Ryder Knightly:** I actually took it very hard, and almost let it stop me from preforming. I was bullied a lot for being too feminine of a king, and not falling into a "butch" stereotype. I can't change the past nor do I want to, but I hope others understand it is okay to be yourself, and when in doubt turn to your other kings and queens that are close to you.

❀**Kruz Mhee:** Honestly, I ignored them. It was something new at least in my local community and people are normally afraid of or shy away from something they do not know or understand. I was made fun of, and by some entertainers, belittled. However, I chose not to let that stop me. After the first year or so, I guess I proved myself. I was not just a female putting on airs as a male. I was entertaining. I was dressed full out for every performance. That in itself made a number of lesbians in the community uncomfortable. I was told that I was trying to be a man and not be the beautiful lesbian creature that God had created. My response was "I have embraced myself completely, that includes the female side of my personality and the entertainer side of my personality." Now, it seems my local community has accepted DRAG Kings. I do like to think I helped a little with that.

❀**Alec Allnight:** I did not get much negativity, at least, not that I heard. I do not let that change anything in any aspect of my life anyway. I welcome constructive criticism always. That is how we grow as people and entertainers. Do not ever let anyone keep you from doing what you love!

❀**Silk Steele Prince:** In the beginning, I handled negative people from a distance. When people were negative towards me, it made me feel self-conscious and uncomfortable. This is what they were aiming for. I tried not to show it. I kept my distance. Looking back, I would not change a thing.

❀**Flex Jonez:** I am good for ignoring negative people and with a smile gracefully remove myself from their presence.

❀**SirMandingo Thatis:** I have not had to experience any negative comments or people in my journey of DRAG yet, but hey, I am sure it is coming!

❀**Kenneth J. Squires:** Needless to say, there are always going to be "Negative People." Sometimes it would really bother me, because I was doing the best I could with what I had. I came into my self, and realized, that no matter what, if I was giving my 100% best, then I got out there and did a good job.

❀**Cody Wellch Klondyke:** I ignore negative people, keep a graceful smile, remove myself from their presence, and continue to on. I do not let the negative things hold me back from what I enjoy.

❀**George De Micheal:** I took negativity personally at the start. It does not affect me now. I am an artist/entertainer and am professional in every way.

❀**Santana Romero:** I used to handle negativity terribly when it came to DRAG drama. When I first gained exposure through DRAG, I made a few critical mistakes that caused some to misunderstand who I really am. In trying to make the situation better, things only worsened and eventually, there was nothing that I could do to change it. This sent me into a downward spiral of depression. I felt like a failure, like everyone hated me and I would never be a success as a King. I harshly feared saying or doing the wrong things, which caused me to become insecure and closed off in most DRAG settings. I cared so much about what others thought about me that performing did not even feel the same. When I hit bottom, I knew something needed to change. It was a long, difficult process that required a lot of forgiving and love from my family, Rachel (my girlfriend), and my close friends. As I slowly began to recover, I learned a lot about others and myself. I learned that in some situations, you cannot change how others feel. You just have live and press on. I also learned that not everyone is going to like you for whatever their reasons are and some are not going to take time to understand where you are coming from. With that, you have to have enough confidence to say, "Hey, I know who I really am and I know that I am loved by the ones who really count." Today, I would have come at the situation from this perspective: letting one situation destroy all the success you have created will only bring you down and cause you to question whether you should continue with your passions. Let NO ONE or NOTHING define you and why you are doing what you do. Especially if you love it whole-heartedly. The only thing that matters are the ones you make and even more importantly, making yourself happy with what you love.

❀**DeVery Bess:** The only negativity I received while doing DRAG was from queens. Sadly, a portion of queens have this pre-conceived idea that DRAG kings are terrible performers. I overcame their negativity because I worked it, and put on a brilliant performance. Just do your thang, people gonna hate, people gonna love. Never mistake constructive criticism as negativity; they probably want you to do better. Give advice to become even stronger.

❀**Thug Passion:** I did not experience the negativity directly. I always heard it through he said, she said. I just let it be because eventually whatever problem that person had with me would go away once they got to know me. If it did not go away then that would be their loss. It is the teamwork through both female and male illusionists in the business as well as the individuality that helps it grow and making it fun.

❀**Bootzy Edwards Collynz:** I have not had any except from a few queens. I let people come around in their own time. They either will or will not. Not my issue, but theirs.

❀**Colin Grey:** I do not handle negativity well. Never have. I try to put on my best pageant smile remove myself from the situation as quickly as possible. In the early days I tended to let negativity rule whether I performed or not. If I wasn't feeling it, I wouldn't get up there. No longer the case. It doesn't matter what Melissa is going through, if Colin is booked somewhere, Melissa goes in a box when the face goes on and I go out there and give it my all.

❀**Sam Masterson:** I killed them with kindness.

❀**Jack King:** People were not negative as such; they have a little more difficulty figuring out what a King was, since I am the only one. So, after it was explained many times, everything was ok in the end.

❀**Kameo Dupree:** The negativity was really minimal, if any at all.

❀**Xavier Bottoms:** I taught myself to turn negativity around. For example, I receive some negativity because I am a male illusionist, not a real boy, when performing. I always ask that individual to stay until the show is over. So they can see me out of character, so they see it is about the art of transformation. I am still the same person they saw earlier, just with boobs and no facial hair. Then they respect me more. I have shown them you can be negative but you will respect me in the end for my art of illusion and to me, that's a positive. I teach the same to my DRAG children.

❀**Stefan LeDude:** Luckily, I did not really experience any negative people.

❀**Jamel Knight:** I used to le negative people get to me. Their opinions and thoughts limited what I did. If I handled things differently, I would have followed my heart on some key decisions regardless of their opinions.

❀**Welland Dowd:** I am lucky to be surrounded by positive people. Haters are going to hate, and I try to stay far, far away from negativity and drama.

❀**Julius M. SeizeHer:** I did not face much negativity; I still do not. Not everyone will agree with you. Be open to creative criticism, and hurtful words. Embrace who you are. You are you and no one can change that.

❀**Jonah Godfather of DRAG:** I never faced much negativity. I heard somebody say that they do not like kings. I know that it should be ok that everyone has his own opinion, but I hate the blanket statement of not liking kings. Each king should be judged on his own merit. I try to encourage doubters to give kings a chance to show them how entertaining we can be.

❀**Bruno Diaz:** I try to believe all people are good until they show me differently, sometimes it takes a while to see someone's, intentions if is other than a sincere friendship, we are only a few kings that perform in the same venue I do, we are brothers and the queens are very supportive of us, we are a family, so everywhere I go I take that spirit with me, I have face hostility out of town, not just from other fellow kings but also dressers and promoters, but you give someone power when you allow it to bother you, it hurts your feelings for sure, but, shake it off, keep moving, because alone the trail I've also meet incredible people that are in my life for the long run.

❀Howie Feltersnatch: I have been extremely lucky and have never experienced negativity from other people. The negativity I have faced has been strictly my own doing, and I get over that by improving each time I go on stage. I also like to surround myself with positive people.

❀Lyle Love-It: Not much of an issue. Ignore them and focus on positive ones.

❀Jack E. Dickinson: Ignore negative people and surrounded myself with the supportive ones.

❀Clark Kunt: I took negative people to heart at the beginning because I do not fit the typical checklist for what makes a DRAG King. I was concerned about losing any space I had in the community – but, once I found a few folks who I could relate to on and/or off-stage, it became a lot easier.

❀Juan Kerr: I nearly got battered by a cage fighter my first night as a DRAG king! Expanding on the Halloween story… We went out to a bar in Brighton, England, this was before I was strapping down my boobs, and some bloke poured a drink over my friends head so I gave him the v's (the English version of flipping the bird). I forgot I was dressed as a bloke and this guy grabbed my wrist and pulled me towards him. I could see his hand twitching by his side ready to punch me till he noticed my boobs. Lucky escape! He was apparently a cage fighter and so not responsible for his actions according to the friend who was with him. Still got him kicked out of the club. Being a man is no reason to act like an animal. It made me realize how dangerous being a bloke can be I suppose. Just having a penis can get you beaten up, that and giving someone v's I suppose. Otherwise the only, what could be called negativity, was the trepidation from my parents about their little girl becoming a boy, but that has chilled out a bit now so it is all cool.

❀J Breezy St James: When it comes to negative people, I have always ignored it and moved on, no point in dwelling on it.

❀Bailey Saint James: Negativity breeds negativity. I always try to follow the laws of attraction. Looking back, I probably could have smiled more and been nicer in the beginning, but DRAG kings were only found in troupes until myself and Travis Hard competed in a male born entertainer competition. We were the only competitors.

❀Aaron Phoenix: Negativity would discourage me here and there at first, but I ultimately used it as more motivation to really amp up my shows and 'prove a point,' so to speak. Without the negative feedback, I would not truly appreciate the positive feedback that I have worked so hard to gain.

❀Soco Dupree: I never paid attention really. If anything did cause me to have emotion, I used it to help channel my energy for the stage.

❀LoUis CYfer: I do not acknowledge negativity.

❀**Stefon Royce Iman:** I do not condone nor pay attention to it. I stand clear. ❀**E. M. Shaun:** I do not pay attention to negative people especially if it pertains to something that I believe in. A real friend or supporter will back you 100%. Everyone is entitled to their opinions, but if it is not helping me, then I do not need it in my life.

❀**Jensen C. Dean:** I never really dealt with a lot of negativity in the beginning, and if I did, it did not register on my radar.

❀**Boi Wonder:** It was more amazement than negativity; people just did not know DRAG kings existed. Fortunately, most people I know are open minded.

❀**Devin G. Dame:** I never let the negative people get to me; just kept positive and moving forward.

Chapter Twelve
"How do you handle anger in the dressing room? Explain what you determine as the biggest problem with bitter words exchanged amongst entertainers? What advice do you share to those dishing out the hurtful words and to those performers struggling to survive the bullying?"

❀**Jack King:** I smile and give them a hug…then it stops.

❀**Adam All:** It is a small DRAG world where I am. There are only a small handful of kings, we very, very rarely share changing rooms and for the most part are content to support each other as a family, and especially since I run a king night and most of them regard me as a sort of DRAG dad. The ones that do not, I keep away from me. Everyone is entitled to their opinion and I do not claim any superiority for any achievements long term. It is horrible dealing with coldness or bitching and can really cut you to the core, but leave the tears at home as best as you can, its work after all.

❀**Chance Wise:** I normally get very quiet when I am angry, unless something absolutely has to be said. Dealing with drama is a pick your battles moment, because I do not like to start issues in a dressing room. I will wait until after a show and pull someone aside. I have always been around performers joking and laughing and the usually friendly reading that goes on in dressing rooms.

❀**Shook ByNature:** I have seen all out brawls break out, but my policy is simple. Once my partner and our stuff is secure, I make the choice to step in and de-escalate the situation or we make the choice to leave. Sometimes anger is born of events outside of DRAG, so if that is the case there is not much I can do. My days of being a bouncer are over and unless a club owner or show director asks me to intervene, I will not.

❀**Vinnie Marconi:** I have NOT encountered this problem. The people I have been honored to work with remain respectful and professional. If there was a personality conflict, it did not show "on the clock."

❀**Campbell Reid Andrews:** I stick to myself and participate in small talk, but bitching and cattiness is something that is common in a queen's dressing room. I mind my business and concentrate on what I am paid to do, "entertain." If it got out of hand and physical, I would step in.

❀**Clint Torres:** If someone is upset, avoid them

❀**D-Rex:** MI entertainers need to be more adult rather than fight amongst ourselves. I believe in honesty is the best policy, I am not afraid to let you know how I feel about you. That way if someone ever says anything to you then you are not surprised, you already know what I said. In the end, we are a brotherhood, more family than most.

❀**Rasta Boi Punany:** I do not engage in any such confrontations.

❀**Freddy Prinze Charming:** I have seen entertainers throw temper tantrums and hissy fits in dressing rooms, and it is disgraceful. I have seen entertainers be rude to each other, attempt to start fights, and drama. Just like in real life, in a "real" job, you will inevitably have to work with people you do not like. Ignore them or be polite., Starting crap in the dressing room is just juvenile. If I witness behavior like this at a show I am running, neither individual would be asked back, and there is a good chance both would be asked to leave and their show pay would be forfeited. There is zero excuse for bad behavior.

❀**Travis Hard:** I have not really seen this. Is this a thing? If it were to occur, I mind my business and do what I am there for, entertain.

❀**B J Armani:** Most of the shade is from the Queens. NONE of my brothers have issues with me or each other. Even at competitions, we share and help each other. To all those that have faced it: consider it a compliment, or constructive criticism. I never got words of hate or anger until I really started working with bigger costumes and bigger ideas. The audience remembered me. When you start to get good, it is intimidating to veterans. That is why I promised myself that my show would never discriminate or hate. IF I hear of shade or drama, you are not booked, PERIOD.

❀**Spacee Kadett:** Our business is certainly full of "casting shade," although I would have to agree that most of these confrontations happen between queens - and I have noticed there is usually drinking involved. Just an observation. I'm extremely non-confrontational and tend to have fun no matter what, so on the rare occasion that a fight breaks out, I'm probably not involved and just keep to myself; which can also be a bad thing, because I'm often afraid to stick up for someone when I should. The good news is that I have never seen anything kill a career faster than a shady, argumentative reputation, no matter how talented an entertainer might be.

❀**Kenneth J. Squires:** As the saying goes, "Treat others as you would like to be treated." If there is conflict between people, leave it at the door. You are there for a show, and the audience likes to see a good show. If I see someone being bullied, I usually step in, and let them judge not, lest ye be judged!

❀**Adam DoEve:** I have not really heard this from the kings, but wow, the queens have some sharp teeth. One of the places that I perform, I have been the only king for almost a year and most the time I am the one standing between the queens to keep the peace. Sometimes it is like trying to get two 5 year olds to share a toy. I have heard some dishing on kings but never to their face. Most times, I know it is harmless talk, but I feel that no one is perfect and if you do not have anything nice to say, put a cork in it because you would not want someone talking about you like that.

❋**Koomah:** I have never really experienced this directly but I have seen it happen among others. The entertainers I surround myself with are usually community oriented and supportive of each other. I have been in some spaces with other performers who would bad mouth each other backstage, be confrontational, or need to be separated. As someone who performs as both a king and a queen in various different spaces, I have found this to be no different with anyone. It is the attitude of the individual performing not the type of performance. I am pretty nice to everyone and if anyone has an issue with me, I would always try to work it out calmly. If the other person is drunk, I usually encourage them to work it out with the other person when they are sober. When there is a situation, it is usually because someone is drunk or under the influence, this is a reason I perform sober shows.

❋**Joshua Micheals:** I do not get angry in the dressing room I always try to keep it positive and upbeat. I ignore and walk from the gossiping and browbeating. "This is supposed to be fun." In real life, when your hobby stops being all about the fun and starts being work it is time to walk away and take a break.

❋**Eddie C. Broadway:** I honestly have not seen anger in the dressing room from kings. I see it from queens. I stay back when that happens. Gossiping and bullying are an ongoing problem. I have had to deal with it since the beginning. Hold your head up high, keep doing you, be yourself, remain humble, stay out of it, and do not succumb to other people's drama.

❋**Stormm:** We do not have negativity in the dressing room. The only time I saw anything like that was from a queen about her ex. I just let her vent.

❋**Dominic: Von Strap:** Do not get angry. Let people say what they are going to say, brush it off your shoulders and get on that stage and prove their trivial bullshit wrong. To you that want to be "bullies"- stop being a dick and help your DRAG brothers and sisters out instead of being a negative douche bag. Ain't nobody got time for that!

❋**D-Luv Saviyon:** I have unfortunately/regretfully had a few heated discussions in dressing rooms, although the conversations were not vocal to the point that everyone could hear. I do not usually have an issue with backstage anger myself, but I am human and far from perfect. I have, from time to time over the years, had to intervene in some arguments and I always just try to refocus those involved that they have a job to do/entertainment to give. The crowd and show should be their focus, not drama.

❋**Travis Luvermore:** I try to stay out of the drama. We are all there for the same thing and should be brothers.

✤**AJ Menendez:** I have had to learn this the hard way but I DID find arguments and fights in the dressing room to be childish and unprofessional. The venues are NEVER the place to express either. Agree to disagree and walk away. We are supposed to be a brotherhood that helps each other, but on occasion, it does happen.

✤**Hurricane Savage:** I love what I do and have only had one issue that happened at a pageant that upset me. I would love to win but if I lose its not the end of the world. I just pick up and move on to the next one, but some of the others do not feel the same. As far as bullying, I do not think I have ever seen any and I have never had any pointed at me. Either way I am just the type to smile and keep going on about my day. I am not there to make every person like me. I am there to try and put a smile on the crowds face for the little time I am on stage because it makes me happy to be on stage.

✤**Marcus Mayhem:** I have not seen bullying by kings. Mostly just the queens bashing everyone and most of us just go on. I have seen kings come in angry but we all stop or semi-stop what we are doing to help our fellow man and see what is wrong.

✤**Rychard "Alpha" Le'Sabre:** Anger in the dressing room does not get anyone anywhere. The best thing to do is just put in some headphones, get dressed fast, and get out of the way of everyone else as soon as you can.

✤**Shane Rebel Caine:** I tend to keep my headphones in no matter what, especially if I am mad. The dressing room, nor the venue is the place to lose your temper, but it is also not the place to be bullying anyone. We are all of one community, no one person is better than any other is and no one has the right to put another performer down. We do not need negativity and bullying coming from people within our community, and you are also hurting yourself performance wise, as most venues will not continue to book you if you are bullying others. To those being bullied, keep your head up, ignore them, and keep performing.

✤**Ashton The Adorable Lover:** It is not as bad with kings, but some of us do have a tendency to get too big headed. Walk it off, and come back with a clearer head. That is not the time; you have a show to do.

✤**B J Bottoms:** As entertainers, we all have an ego, but at a venue or after a pageant is not the time to flex your muscles. People who argue in the dressing room are simply looking to blame someone for whatever did or did not happen. The best way to prevent this is just to keep yourself in check. Be mindful of your surrounding and of your emotions.

✤**Ben Eaten:** I have not had a personal experience with this yet but I have heard some things said that were hurtful to others. Just remember that being that "bitchy queen" only gets you known for being a bitch, not gaining wanted attention. Everyone is still human with feelings, if you have nothing nice to say then stay quiet!

❀**Pierce Gabriel:** Personally, I do not tolerate bullying of any sort, anywhere. When I hear it backstage, I always step in. In my opinion, it is the duty of the more experienced performer to help and teach the newer one. If you are not more experienced, you do not have the right to criticize the other one. Nothing good ever comes out of being hurtful.

❀**Ryder Knightly:** I have seen many arguments break out, and people lashing out at each other. I tend to stay quiet, and mind my own business; maybe throw in a few jokes here, and there. We are a brand, and need to remember we are not just representing ourselves on stage, but off stage too.

❀**Kruz Mhee:** If you have an issue and wait until after the show. You never probably tantrum inside the club for you perform and especially not in front of show directors or management. I have been a show director for more than seven years and I am not above putting someone out of the show or the club. Most arguments I have seen or heard in the dressing room are of no relation to what is going on currently.

❀**Hawk Stuart:** Walk away. If you hear someone bullying a performer, talk to them.

❀**Alec Allnight:** I have never heard or seen anything in a dressing room but passive aggressive shade on social media! I would really like to think that I would step in if I ever I ever came across any bullying in person.

❀**Silk Steele Prince:** When there is anger in the dressing room, I avoid it at all cost. It is not worth being unprofessional. However, bitter words between entertainers should not be happening and bullying is a definite no-no. We should not be embarrassing each other in our brotherhood.

❀**Flex Jonez:** I am an Elder King. I try to keep the moral standards and spirits high in a positive manner. We are all entertainers, and at the end of the day, we are all there for the stage, not for being butt holes to each other.

❀**E. M. Shaun:** I do not tolerate bullying of any sorts...but I had been at shows where some of the entertainers did not like each other. My advice to them was to stay away from one another, and go out and perform for the audience. Whatever personal issues they may have had with each other, needed to be resolved outside of the club.

❀**Cody Wellch Klondyke:** I do not like anger in a dressing room. I tend to stay away from that. If something is going on, I think it should be handled OUTSIDE of the Club.

❀**George De Micheal:** I keep calm and carry on. Staying focused!

❀**Colin Grey:** I bite my tongue until I am completely out of the bar and away from the situation. Nine times out of ten, it is just not worth it. If there is something that needs to be handled, I usually take it to the show director.

🍀**Kameo Dupree:** I am a loner. I love performing and I take criticism very well, but I had to learn that not everyone in this business is your friend. In fact, many of them friend you just to talk about you. I stay true to me and try not to let the words or actions of others dictate my life in and out of DRAG.

🍀**Phantom:** "We struggle every day for equality." Fighting helps no one. Helping each other improve our DRAG is important. We all started from the bottom. Guidance, showing respect and love for each other is the best way to grow as performers.

🍀**Sam Masterson:** I am the bigger person and do not get involved in the drama. I stay away from all the negativity.

🍀**Joshua K. Mann:** I keep to myself unless their drama is causing the show problems because then you are affecting other people's money as well. Fighting and drama have no place, but at the same time, sometimes people need to be put in their place.

🍀**Master Cameron Eric Leon:** I really have not encountered very much of this, and I have yet to find a way of dealing with it where I feel comfortable. I do not like talking about people, period. If I do actually have a serious issue with someone, I bring it up with the people in charge after trying to talk to that person directly. Any issues I have had at this point have been resolved with minimal stress, though. Just remember that two wrongs do not make a right. If someone is shit talking you, it does not mean you should go out and shit talk them. If you are a performer who is worth anything, you should be able to let your performances and track record speak for itself.

🍀**Bootzy Edwards Collynz:** I have never dealt with anger/anger issues in the dressing room... being that my cast/s are a majority queens, they do enough fighting amongst themselves. I have had to try to help diffuse certain situations in the dressing room. It does seem like most confrontations pop up after the show is over. I ask the individuals to handle the issue out of the dressing room out of respect for the other performers in the show. Take it out and away from everyone who is not involved and really does not care to be involved. If it is a close friend, depending on the situation, I will help still diffuse and help separate to get them calmed down, refocus, and maybe start to process a little bit. Everyone is going to get upset at some point in their career (we are all human and emotional, it is what happens at times), but knowing the appropriate time and place is what matters.

🍀**DeVery Bess:** I have been very lucky, I haven't had any issues with kings in the dressing room. I find they are generally quite professional . Sometimes entertainers like to poke fun not knowing that they are sound rude and hurtful. If you politely say I don't appreciate that, if they continue just focus on what you are there for. Kill the performance. If you do a good job on stage they will not have anything to say. Sometimes they just want to be funny.

❀**Welland Dowd:** Walk it off. Take a breather outside, or vent to someone sympathetic. I am pretty chill though so this is not much of a problem for me. I hate drama and try to stay the hell out of inflammatory situations.

❀**Michael Christian:** I think of DRAG as a business and work. You do not have to like everyone. You do not have to be entertained by everyone. You need to respect yourself, employer, and coworker for the night. If a fight ever happened, I would most likely stick to myself and head home. No need to get involved and leave a bad taste in anyone's mouth when they say my name.

❀**Howie Feltersnatch:** Everyone has always been so professional, and most of the issues that arise are from my own insecurities and butterflies. To get my mind set away from negative thinking, I go outside and listen to my song and practice. If that does not help, I surround myself with positive people that I know will get my mind off of things. I am my worst bully.

❀**Julius M. SeizeHer:** I do not notice anger. Just be prepared and having a backup plan in case something happens.

❀**Jonah Godfather of DRAG:** If you do not have anything nice to say then do not say anything at all." I promote this to other entertainers. Arguments happen because we are human. I was in a few, but always tried to go back to the other person and apologize for any hurtful words and try to talk about the issue in a calm manner.

❀**Jack E. Dickinson:** Tough one. I have had to perform after receiving bitter, angry words. Since I was one of the main organizers for our shows, conflicts often happened due to disagreements about organizational matters. Once on stage, I just brushed it off because my role is to give 150% of myself to the audience. Then I would try to have a conversation with the person at another time to make sure this would not happen again. Now I perform less and when I do, I am very careful about who I work with to avoid major personality conflicts and keep it fun and mutually supportive.

❀**Xavier Bottoms:** At the end of a pageant, ome people were upset they did not win or thought they were not judged fairly. There really is nothing you can say to them to calm them down. I feel talking to them just adds fuel to their fire. Telling them to brush it off or come back next year is a no-no.

❀**Clark Kunt:** I do my best not to get into much drama. If it impacts me, I take a breather outside, find a friend to play a round of pool, or if it is close to my next performance time I focus on every little detail ready to go. Throwing on a pair of headphones and blasting my next number usually helps me refocus on what I should be focusing on. At the end of the day my rule of thumb is if you're not having fun don't do it anymore, so I can't have had too much drama yet.

❀Emilio: I put my headphones on and keep to myself. I am a professional, and do not have time for the drama.

❀Juan Kerr: I have never encountered bullying. I have encountered bitchy episodes within scenes and I just do not think it is worth it. I hold no truth with those who want to be arseholes, not interested because they will not get far behaving like that. We should all be supporting each other not putting each other down. Share the love!

❀Trey C. Michaels: I witness queens because someone was in their "spot." When this happens I usually walk away. If you happen to be the person involved, I say apologize and move. Why have drama?

❀Aaron Phoenix: I have not experienced bitter hatefulness and anger in the dressing room. Of course, the occasional incident will happen anywhere you go, but in the places I have worked, the entertainers tend to get along, and those who do not get along can at least keep it professional. After all, a job.

❀Soco Dupree: Keep the ear buds in and stay focused on the show.

❀Stefon Royce Iman: Did not experienced it. I was always the only DRAG king in the dressing room, so queens would stop to flirt with me, and say wow. I was lucky never to experience it. I have seen fights and queens being hateful.

❀Smitty O'Toole: I have performed at many different venues with no issuee with anger, bullying, mean words, or attitudes. A few queens in Houston, Texas, USA, that think kings do not belong on stage. I beat their queen DRAG daughter's in an all-star DRAG race and changed their minds. My advice to those bullied is to take that and let it propel you to be bigger and better. Face adversity and shove your DRAG in its' face.

❀Jensen C. Dean: I try to avoid dressing room issues like the plague. It is not worth it to get involved, and it can really throw off the mood of the whole show. For the most part, what I have seen with entertainers getting into it with each other is mostly petty, almost to the point like siblings arguing. It might last a while and be bigger and more DRAG out longer than necessary, but it usually works itself out in time.

❀Luke Ateraz: My dressing room theory: Get in, get ready, and get out! Most dressing rooms are too small to be hanging out back there.

❀William Vanity Matrix: I am usually in the dressing room and out before a show so I can go enjoy a drink before we start. If things get hairy while I am back there getting ready, I finish up quickly and leave. If it got really bad, I have stepped in once and told both sides that we are all here to do a job and do it well and to keep personal vendettas out of the dressing room and show.

❀**Devin G. Dame:** It is a rare occasion on the nights I am booked for a show. I do not do drama and will put a stop to it immediately if it is my show.

Chapter Thirteen
"Do you currently have a DRAG parent or mentor? Who are they? Why are they your mentor? What do they do for you?"

❀**Jack King:** Nope I have myself; I am the only King over here.

❀**Adam All:** No one in DRAG but my partner helps me endlessly. Being Adam has become half of our lives. She plays my on stage girlfriend 'Apple,' and we plan everything together.

❀**Spacee Kadett:** I was born an orphan, and later adopted by queen Cheyenne Pepper and king Bryan Michaels. They gave me insight, support, and advice. Cheyenne was also integral in helping me develop my face-painting technique. (Bryan, of course, taught me facial hair!) Neither of them really performs anymore, but we remain long-distance friends and I still reference them as family. It is their type of supplementary support that I believe defines good DRAG parenting. I do not believe a DRAG parent should build someone from scratch, hold their hand, or tell them what to do. They should simply guide and enhance an entertainer's chosen path.

❀**Chance Wise:** I have always been on my own...I have a small chosen DRAG family and we encourage and help each other out a lot.

❀**Davion Summers:** My DRAG mother is Mystique Summers. She gives me makeup tips and taught me some different ways to put on facial hair. She encourages me to try new things and is a big part of my support system since I started. Alexander Cameron has also helped me. When I first started, he answered a lot of the questions I had, and still does. He is an awesome person and I am glad he has been there to help me.

❀**Shook ByNature:** I believe we call mentors in this Brotherhood of Entertainers. I am a DRAG stepparent to my partners DRAG children, but I learn from all artists I encounter!

❀**Orion Blaze Browne:** I have a DRAG mother, Kourtney Brown, who helps me when I need things. But my boyfriend, Gina Jordan, has also been a huge support. He is always picking up things for me when he goes out DRAG shopping for himself. Then I have my brothers. My brothers help to push me to be better every time I step on stage.

❀**Travis Hard:** I have neither DRAG parent nor a nearby mentor. I do admire Gunner and Gage Gatlyn, along with Landon Cider and Jordan Allen.

❀**Vinnie Marconi:** My Dad is Dr J and Mom is Nicolette T. Richards. Dad gave me the masculine moves, and mom taught me the DRAG ropes. Dr J made me seek out the best male impersonators. Nicolette made sure my costumes fit and shine on stage! My performances now have morphed into a combination of what I have learned AND CONTINUE to learn with each new song. I have Andrew Citino on SPEED DIAL!

❊**Clint Torres:** My DRAG dad is Atown. He is a very talented performer in our local community and he made the decision to take me on. We met after one of his performances and we got to talking about how I wanted to do DRAG, he said he would give me some pointers, and then a week later I had a DRAG dad. In the last six months he has helped me with dance routines, putting on face, stage presents, how to interact with the audience, costume ideas, and confidence. Every time I am going to perform, I think about what he says about how I need to be confident and have fun, because if you do not, then the audience will be able to pick up on that.

❊**Ben Eaten:** I was born an orphan and I searched to find a DRAG family that I could relate to and that was willing to help me with my hundreds of questions. I was adopted by Phoenixxx and gained a small family along with this. He helped me with my face and how to paint, he helped me with ideas I had for crazy talent pieces, he helped with costumes and songs, or anything I had a question about. He had an answer or one of my other relatives did. This was the best thing I could have found. Before this, I was totally lost. I did not know how to do pageants, or make-up, or costumes, but thanks to him and my family, I am learning some of the ropes.

❊**Viciouse Slick:** Not part of a DRAG family. I get advice from Gunner Gatlyn. Whether it is on what to post on facebook, how to do makeup, etc. He is also very supportive in the type of DRAG I do and it always made me push harder in this art form.

❊**Phantom:** I do not have a DRAG parent. I was self-taught and had plenty of inspiration all around me. With every show, I learn little by little the tricks of the trade. I gain the respect of my fellow queens and kings by working hard.

❊**Campbell Reid Andrews:** My fiancé helps me tremendously! She is the best thing to my DRAG career and me. As for other mentors, everyone I encounter in the entertainment industry is a mentor. I learn from everyone and everything. I see the world with open eyes, and will continue to do so.

❊**Zavier LuvanMuff:** Yes I do. I have the greatest DRAG dad named Alik Muff! He got me started and taught me makeup and costumes.

❊**Rasta Boi Punany::** Yes. I have a performance daddy and mentor. My performance daddy is Shizz Elegance.

❊**Freddy Prinze Charming:** Never had a DRAG parent or mentor. I learned with trial and error, and by bouncing ideas off of other entertainers.

❊**Ayden Layne:** My DRAG dad is Chandler J Hart. He taught me so much about being a great performer and a good person. He still continues to teach me new things and I share new things I have learned from others. He helped change me from a shy and awkward person into a much more confident and successful individual. He is a truly great entertainer and an amazing friend. I am so proud to call him family!

❃**Jonah Godfather of DRAG:** Candy James is my mentor. She was one of the queens who helped me get started in DRAG. She is always there for me with props and backdrops. She encourages me and pumps my confidence. She is the one who pushed me to step out of my box and try different things.

❃**B J Armani:** I started DRAG after watching Mik Andersen in a pageant. He is my DRAG dad. I will forever be grateful for all he has taught me. He does not get involved in drama and accepts me no matter how different I am from the norm. Another is Lyle Love-It who pushed me to enter a pageant and go for a title. I would not be where I am without these AMAZING performers!

❃**Lyle Love-It:** I had a DRAG queen, Holiday Rose. He was my nephew by my girlfriend, and help me get into shows in La Crosse, Wisconsin, USA. Along the way opened doors. I fly solo. I watch and learn from many, and perform from my heart, my passions, my creativeness, and style.

❃**Kenneth J. Squires:** I have a wonderful DRAG mother, Stratosphere. She was the only DRAG queen to help me and "take me under her wings." I did DRAG for a long time before I met her. I am proud to call her my DRAG mother.

❃**Adam DoEve:** I do not have a mentor. I have a group of performers that can help me out. I do not live close to anyone and drive an hour to be able to perform, so I am on my own most of the time.

❃**Koomah:** I do not have a DRAG parent or mentor per se, but I am involved with a DRAG troupe. We are all at different experience levels, have different performing styles, and focus on community and skill sharing; everyone can learn from each other and everyone has something they can teach others.

❃**Joshua Micheals:** I had a DRAG mother, Ashley Jacobs, when I started performing. About the same time I started to understand what it was to be gay and going through my coming out journey. She was great! I also loved to perform local band music when I started (with permission), and one of my favorite songs was written by my "grandmother," Amanda Jacobs.

❃**Eddie C. Broadway:** I am lucky to have numerous mentors. My DRAG dad is Freddy Prinze Charming. I have an uncle as a second dad, Gunner Daimon Gatlyn. Also have a DRAG mother, Celia Putty, and a father-in-law, Brandon Packer. All of these amazing performers taught me everything I know. I am who I am because of them. I am such a lucky king!

❃**Stormm:** My DRAG mother was the late and great Brandy Wells. I have a lot of DRAG sisters: Natasha Knight, BB Fox, and Roberta Norsha to name a few. They taught me a lot, like how to have fun, to dress, and to be a professional.

❀**D-Luv Saviyon:** My parents are Mac Productions, Queen mother Sapphire T. Mylan, and Bushra St. James. They all lent me their time, guidance, and support over the years to helped me grow into the entertainer. I have many mentors. I consider someone a mentor who takes the time to show/teach us to be better and also walks the walk/leads by example. It takes a village.

❀**Travis Luvermore:** I have had mentors in my past. Currently I have several supportive DRAG queens that help me find venues and shows.

❀**Gus Magendor:** So far, no. Surprisingly...

❀**Kody Sky:** I have a DRAG father Tre. Rick Oliver aka Lucy Pagenkopf, is my DRAG mom. I do not have a DRAG mother at this time. Tre, Rick, Spacee Kadett, and MANY OTHERS have been my mentors. I learn something new every day! They helped mold my image as Kody Sky and have supported me endlessly. Without them I would probably still look like a newbie.

❀**AJ Menendez:** I am blessed to have all of the above. My DRAG mama is Karrissa Wade, my DRAG father is Wolfie, and my mentor is Gage Gatlyn. But I learn from many other entertainers as well, even to this day.

❀**Hurricane Savage:** Well, yes and no. I do have someone I call my mom, Anita Richards. As far as a DRAG dad, it is more of a mentor at this point until I put my time in to be worthy of his family.

❀**Atown:** No.

❀**Kameo Dupree:** My DRAG mom is Ms. Portia Valentino Dupree. She is where my name comes from. I may not agree with her form of help, but I will say it made me the performer I am today. When I started to perform, I would call and ask things like "what you think about this song?" or, "what outfit do you think should be worn to portray this song?" Her answer would always be "I do not know." Her logic was to teach her kids to be original and think for themselves. She does not believe in "cookie cutter" kids. Her tools were no tools. Because of this, I have no limits within my craft.

❀**Rychard "Alpha" Le'Sabre:** My DRAG mother is Aphelia Bottom, and father was Michael Anthony, may he rest in peace. I have since been DRAG adopted by Randy Wolfe. My "mother" is one of my best friends, maintains a successful DRAG company in Tacoma, Washington, USA, the largest and most popular in the city, and has been running for several years now. She is a smash on the microphone and the audience loves it when we banter back and forth. She is my Aphie, and I am her Alpha!

❀**Shane Rebel Caine:** I was fortunate enough to be adopted just a few months ago. I have a DRAG mom and dad, though my dad is not a DRAG king himself. He has been around the business so long that he has his own stage name and takes DRAG kings and male impersonators under his wing. My brother and I are blessed enough to be his first, and by relation, got our DRAG mother who happens to be our dad's wife .PurrZsa Kytten Azrael and Devlin Caine are my amazing DRAG parents and mentors.

❀**Justin Cider:** I have a DRAG wife I admire and look up to but no official daddy. However, I do hope someday to be someone's daddy. It would be an honor knowing I helped someone get their start and major respect if they kept on the Cider tradition!

❀**B J Bottoms:** I have a DRAG father, Xavier Bottoms and DRAG mother, C.ITookher Bottoms. I also am blessed to have a huge family including eight brothers, one sister, grandparents, cousins, aunts, and uncles. Needless to say, I have a big family. My mentor is my DRAG father. He has not only been there for me professionally but personally. His guidance has helped me become the entertainer and helped me become a better person.

❀**Ben Doverr:** No DRAG mentor; DRAG brothers bouncing ideas off each other.

❀**Dakota Rain:** No DRAG parent, but I look up to SirStone Christopher Dwayne William. I call him Papi. He listens to me and helps me.

❀**Ashton The Adorable Lover:** Dillon MrDecardeza Dalton and Eva LeStrange. They both had different ways to entertain, knew me and what I could and could not do, and not only taught me many things, but also learned new things with me.

❀**Alec Allnight:** It takes a village! We have a small DRAG king community in Fresno, California, USA. We are supportive of each other with choices of songs, choreography, rehearsal, costumes, props, a group number; we know we can all count on each other. We also have some very supportive Aunties.

❀**Brandon KC Young-Taylor:** I have had several people act in the role of DRAG parents and mentors since I started performing. Bob Taylor adopted me a few years back. He is an amazing mentor and supporter. My other influencers include Richard Cranium, Xander CY Kinidy, Gage Gatlyn, and Justin King of Playboys. All of these people have had some influence, costuming, make up, etc., on my career as a male illusionist.

❀**Hawk Stuart:** I have both. My DRAG parents are Stephanie Stuart and Aaron Phoenix. I have many mentors such as Vinnie Marconi, Andrew Citino, and Brandon KC Young-Taylor; they all have helped me.

❀**J Estellado Knight:** My DRAG parents are Mahogany Knight and her partner Randy. They do everything parents should do. Support, encouragement always there to lend an ear or a helping hand. I am the baby boy of her children so I have older sisters that are always there to help, Jericha Knight, Deanna Knight, and Veronica.

❀**Ryder Knightly:** I was a part of a DRAG family in the start of my DRAG. Unfortunately, not all DRAG families work out, and you must part ways. I currently do not have a DRAG family, but have a few queens and kings that help guide me on this path. I do not think a DRAG family should make you, but guide you in some way.

✤Kruz Mhee: I do not have a mentor for DRAG. Most everything my partner and I have learned has been by reading or reaching out on social media with open questions. I mentored a number of kings and faux DRAG performers.

✤Flex Jonez: I have several. Ms. Jackson (DRAG Mother), many DRAG families in the New York, New Jersey, and North Carolina, USA, areas that are very supportive and encouraging toward my return.

✤Cody Wellch Klondyke: My DRAG Mother is CeCe Wellch. She is my supporter and she is there for me when I need her.

✤George De Micheal: My DRAG mentor is Valentino King. I was so inspired to do this because of the professionalism he showed. It got me hooked.

✤Colin Grey: I currently still look to Buttwiser for all things DRAG/pageant politics related. He has been doing it longer than me and is the emcee of the longest running king show in Kansas City, Missouri, USA. He is doing something right and I have always respected him as an entertainer.

✤Jack King: Myself.

✤DeVery Bess: Well I did not have a mentor per say, I learned from a collection of many people in the troupe, Dukes of DRAG (which is now retired). They helped me and I think I taught them a thing or two, so it was a give and take because we wanted to put on a kick ass show.

✤Corey James Caster: Yes, I have a DRAG parent but he does not perform anymore and my mentors are pretty much everyone in my eyes. Whatever advice they give to me, I take it and do the best I can and will keep doing my best until the very end.

✤Xavier Bottoms: I am lucky enough to have two DRAG dads. One is an old school (45 years) DRAG king and the other is a transgender male. Donna Gates and Michael Sanders. I also have an amazing mentor, Ophelia Bottoms, DRAG queen, who also happens to be my biological brother.

✤Stefan LeDude: Not really, but I learn things from my fellow performers.

✤Clark Kunt: I have developed a whole DRAG family. On the king side, a husband, brother and a few DRAG sons, while having the honor of being sister to one of my inspirations, Rouge Fatale. We see our group as a collection of brothers but these few, my family, are where I draw inspiration and support from, both on and off stage.

✤Jamel Knight: No DRAG parent or mentor. But I do learn from other, more seasoned entertainers and have a select few that I seek for advice.

✤Welland Dowd: All of my fellow performers are mentors, and I hope in some small way I also mentor them. I was super lucky to get my start with the Dukes of DRAG, so Jack E. Dickinson and Ian Poe Kerr were big inspirations.

❧**Michael Christian:** I do not have DRAG parents per se. I do have parents in the community. They have helped me in my day-to-day life and, of course, DRAG. My family is about far more than DRAG. We celebrate holidays, major life events, and simple Sunday bar-b-ques. I do, of course, have mentors, as anyone does. Somewhere along the way though, they too have become great friends. DRAG introduced us, but off stage, life took over. We sprinkle the rhinestones in there still though.

❧**Julius M. SeizeHer:** I did, but for now, I fly solo as a performer. I look up to all the DRAG kings and queens who have been doing this for a while.

❧**Howie Feltersnatch:** Everyone in the Fake Mustache DRAG Troupe.

❧**Emilio:** None for me.

❧**Juan Kerr:** Adam All, my newly adopted DRAG dad. Adam and his partner Apple are inspirations to me. They are so supportive and encourage new kings and the scene as a whole! I did not think I wanted a DRAG dad until I met these guys. Apple's my DRAG mum; she's a fantastic faux queen.

❧**Trey C. Michaels:** I am always learning from different performers but my mentor is Freddy Prinze Charming. He has always been honest with me and will tell me if I am doing good for me as a person and a performer. He is constantly teaching me different costuming and performing techniques.

❧**J Breezy St James:** DRAG mother is Alexandra St James who is originally from Chicago, Illinois, USA, and my late DRAG grandmother Tajma Hall.

❧**Bailey Saint James:** Ritchie Rich St. James is my DRAG father. He helps me learn how to take pride in my work and value my audience. My mentor is Leo Long of the Miltown Kings. He has taught me that having fun and being myself, is what the audience likes the most. I know I could call either one of these guys with any question and they would have my back.

❧**Aaron Phoenix:** Vinnie Marconi is my DRAG dad. I did not have a DRAG parent for the first year of performing. Vinnie did a lot to help me fine-tune the illusion and learn the details and "tricks of the trade" to take my DRAG to the next level. He saw the potential in me and really took the time to work with me and show me the ropes. It meant a lot, and his advice made a huge difference at my next pageant. It was *after* all of this that he asked me to be his DRAG son, and I accepted. A DRAG parent should never be for the purpose of gaining a name, it should be someone who supports you 100% in your dream as an entertainer, and strives to help you get where you want to be.

❧**Thug Passion:** I do have a mentor, her name is Adina Roneé. She has been my mentor since the first day I saw her step onto the stage. She is beautiful and very talented. She carries herself with pride, confidence, respect, and she always makes sure she looks her best when stepping on to the stage. She is always willing to help out or give advice to those who really want to be great in this business. That is the type of entertainer I want to be and continue to strive to be. I wanted her to adopt me as one of her children, but I got the best thing; I am her partner in crime. I get to stand side by side with her as her partner in life and try to be the best entertainers that we can be. Supporting each other every step of the way. Even though we are partners, she is still my mentor (even though she may not even know it).

❀Soco Dupree: My DRAG mother is Nicole Ellington Dupree in Nashville, Tennessee, USA who hosted amateur show years ago. She saw me and helped me ever since. She still performs and holds the family name with integrity.

❀Stefon Royce Iman: My DRAG mother, Harmonica Sunbeam, and Tyria Iman was my main support and are great friends as well. They always made sure I was professional and always looked out for my best interest. Their advice and me just learning from them, helped me be where I am today.

❀E. M. Shaun: My mentors have been other kings, my brothers. I believe in the brotherhood and that we need to stand behind each other so that we can be better at what we do, and help the future generation of kings.

❀King Ramsey: I have two of the BEST DRAG parents any son could ask for, Mr. Charlie Smith and Mrs. He^ven Smith. They have always been there for me since the very beginning of my DRAG career. They are there to help me with songs and outfits with any songs I do. They try to be at every show I am in and are the loudest of everyone to show they are proud of me. We are not only DRAG family, we are FAMILY outside as well. If I need anything or need to talk, they are always there with a listening ear. Then they always give the BEST advise a son needs. Loving my parents, MR. and MRS. CHARLIE SMITH.

❀Viciouse Slick: My mentor is Gunner Gatlyn. He helped me as a DRAG king and now that I am going into being a faux queen, he is even helping me with things that I do not understand with that art form.

❀Santana Romero: My main mentor is my DRAG father, Teddy Michael. He has supported me since Santana was born. He's helped me through hard times, encouraged me strive for the best and always goes out of his way to help me with anything I may need. I have learned A LOT about DRAG because of all of his experience and anytime I have question, I know I can go to him for an answer. I will always appreciate him being here for me.

❀Smitty O'Toole: I do not feel I need to be a DRAG son. I am part of a DRAG troupe called the Gendermyn. I also have the Blake family and my girlfriend. They have given me great advice. The rest I do on my own.

❀Jensen C. Dean: My mentor had always been Freddy Prinze Charming. He really helped me get going, especially since my "get going" involved two pageants in four months. He sifted through many long, LONG social media messages and got me through both pageants successfully.

✤Luke Ateraz: My mentors have always been queens. I can call Vanity Halston anytime with any problem, DRAG or not, and she would be there. She was one of the first Queens I have ever seen perform. I also have Delorian Chase in my corner. She helps to keep me grounded. Lately, I have been bouncing ideas for everything off Faleasha Savage.

✤Boi Wonder: The first king I saw, Valentino King. Always excitable and optimistic.

✤William Vanity Matrix: My main mentors are my DRAG parents, Damian and Jessica Matrix. They mean the world to me and we function as a family. I have learned so much from those two alone. There are many more, but those two are the main two.

✤Devin G. Dame: Gage Gatlyn was my biggest mentor. He taught me about costuming to the next level, packing, makeup, and being politically correct.

✤Dionysus W Khaos: Romeo White is my DRAG dad. I have a large extended DRAG family that has all given me tips on how to do things and grow.

Don't forget, Book 6 of The Ten Black Books is called, "DRAG Mother, DRAG Father;" Honoring your mentors.

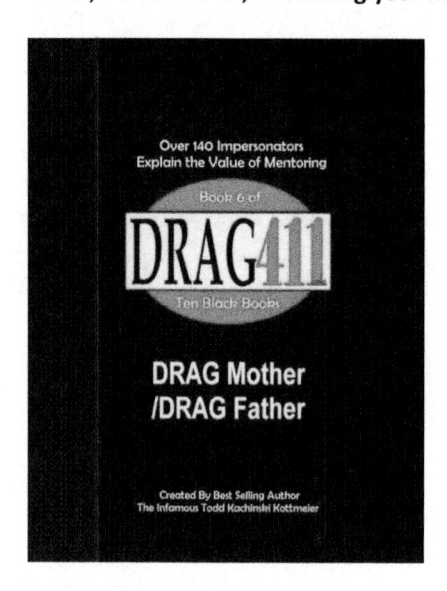

Chapter Fourteen
"Who did you look up to as you began your first number on stage?"

❀**Brandon KC Young-Taylor:** Eminem! He has never been one to not speak his mind or go after what he wants in life. My second number on stage was" Just Lose It." I even had the bleach blond hair!

❀**B J Armani:** I am the only impersonator in my family. I looked up to the Queens and Kings from all over that I was lucky enough to see. BUT, as far as costumes, one trip to Vegas led to the Liberace museum and I was DONE. Liberace influenced artists like Michael Jackson, Elvis, and Elton John. ALL Bob Mackie, who STILL does costumes for PINK, GAGA, and CHER, gets his inspiration for costumes from there. As for the attitude, well, I have to say I do not wear facial hair as an homage to Frank Sinatra, as he is a man's man, the gayness comes from the queens like Elton, and the "hey how's it going" lady lover comes from EVERY smooth operator I ever dated. Gentleman to Frat Boy happens many times during a show.

❀**Joshua Micheals:** I began on a dare from my theatre friends in college.

❀**Clint Torres:** I always looked up to my DRAG dad Atown, especially when I first took the stage. He was my DRAG inspiration along with Landon. My dad showed me how to own the stage and feel at home on it, whereas Landon showed me that being unique, you would be your own ticket to fame. My musical inspirations are Bruno Mars, Chris Brown, Drake, and Usher.

❀**D-Luv Saviyon:** When I began performing, I modeled myself after Bushra St. James, and then Atlanta, Georgia, USA male impersonators/male leads. As far as singers, I modeled myself after Usher and Ne-Yo in the beginning.

❀**Vinnie Marconi:** DRAG Daddy, Dr J, gave me my first "ear-flicks" as he was trying to break me of my 'girly' moves on stage. I am eternally grateful for the time and effort he put into training me. I am old school and do Sinatra; I am patriotic and do country, and I DO NOT dance, so I do emotion. I have some of the best mentors including Andrew Citino, aka 6-Pak, and AJ Menendez, Master Male Illusionist, with a few others that took the time to help me. If you want to do it right, LISTEN and LEARN from the BEST!

❀**Orion Blaze Browne:** I watched DRAG queens for years before I began DRAG. My inspiration came from them. I take the glitz and glam queens portray on stage and morph it to a male form. My first mentor was Caesar, who showed me the ropes. After that, I was adopted and taught by queens.

❀**Freddy Prinze Charming:** My inspiration to start doing DRAG was the movie 'Tipping the Velvet'. I wanted to keep it classy, and be a different type of king than the ones I had seen up until then. When I was little, I always wanted to be Gene Kelly, to emulate his style, his class, his charm. I figured DRAG was the perfect avenue to do that.

❀**Dominic:** Biggest influence is the music. Loved singing and pretending I was a star as a child, making dance moves to the popular songs on the radio!

❀**Gus Magendor:** My idols is Chris Brown, for his dance moves, Spikey van Dykey for his audience interactions, and Jimmy Skyy D'Stone for his style.

❀**Chance Wise:** I was inspired by queens and burlesque dancers I worked with since there were few DRAG kings. A couple years into performing I started looking at other kings and male illusionists for inspiration.

❀**Starr Masters:** Annie Lennox and Moby Dick from Casanova Kings.

❀**Jonah Godfather of DRAG:** I look up to the queens that helped me out. Miss Tracy was the First Lady of DRAG in St Louis, Missouri, USA. She taught me to have fun. She helped me with my confidence. She told me that I was good enough and pushed me to be better. Candy James started out in DRAG 45 years ago and is still on stage. I get to perform with her every month. She taught me to step out of my comfort zone. I also get to perform with Jennifer James each month. She showed me the importance of stage presence and lip-syncing. I model my performances after her.

❀**Travis Hard:** Landon Cider, Jordan Allen, Spacee Kadett, and DRAG wife, Mya Lynn.

❀**Dakota Rain:** Ivan Aycock, of the L-word, amazed me, and then I met JR Stallings and saw firsthand, an entertainer. I knew this is what I wanted to do. First time on stage, I guess I had Ivan in my head and went from there.

❀**Rasta Boi Punany:** I looked to Bob Marley for inspiration. I have a DRAG family now and I still have a lot of times where I am solo in my craft. Since doing more pageants, I have acquired guidance from my performance daddy and queen, and most recently from earning a title, in another family, I have been seriously mentored one on one.

❀**Jack King:** I am looking up to Adam Lambert, and still do.

❀**Adam All:** I had no one to emulate in 2008, I was all alone in the United Kingdom. I desperately needed support and found it in lovers and friends, but mostly in myself. It was a very hard few years.

❀**Viciouse Slick:** I looked up to Gunner Gatlyn and still do. He had such a stage presence and was so amazing that I wanted to be like him. Then after a year, I looked up to Adam Lambert, because he was a performer and was so different from everyone that I wanted to do that type of style as a DRAG king.

❀**Campbell Reid Andrews:** when I first started, I was not an Andrews, but when I saw my DRAG mother, Erica Andrews, on the stage for the first time, I knew I wanted to be a part of that family. She is exquisite, graceful, creative, and had the biggest heart. Everything I wanted to be a part of.

❊**Coti Blayne:** Damian Matrix and Landon Cider are my DRAG idols. Landon is unique. His style and humor are very similar to my own. It is great to see that I can go super crazy and it is okay because I am not the only one. Damian is a local king here and was current royalty at the club where I started. I looked up to him as a role model and had some great discussions with him. I am happy to say he is a very, very good friend of mine and I admire him now for many more reasons than just on stage.

❊**D-Rex:** I fashioned myself after George Michael, but in the end I am a combo of him and a few others, but still me!

❊**Lyle Love-It:** I surfed pageant photos.

❊**Spacee Kadett:** Detroit, Michigan, USA queens DeAngela Show Shannon and Trixie Deluxxe (now of Florida) inspired me with their theatricality and amazing presence years before I ever hit the stage, on those rare occasions when I was able to sneak out of my closet and into the LGBT community. As I began dipping my toe in DRAG, I found myself also aspiring to have a career like Sabin, Natalie Cole, Hershae Chocolatae, or Cheyenne Pepper (later became my DRAG mother). They drew crowds and commanded their performances as well as the microphone. They appeared at a bunch of venues and competed in *pageants.* I wanted to be like them. I did not realize at the time how little interaction I had with fellow kings, or how limited my opportunities would be because I was a king. I was not thinking along gender lines. To me, it was all DRAG. Today, my list of inspirations has grown, but I continue to look up to all of the individuals I mentioned here.

❊**Koomah:** I have always been inspired by character actors and seeing how body language and movement, even with minimal costuming, can create entirely different 'people'. Lily Tomlin, Carol Burnett, Jerry Lewis, Red Skelton, etc. have all been pretty influential in my performing career.

❊**Kenneth J. Squires:** I looked to all my peers. They all had something that I wanted to take away and use for my own. However, my favorite is Hunter Hayes, the DRAG King/Male Illusionist. All of the people back stage that helped me out, and my DRAG mother, Stratosphere Johnson, who helped me tremendously. As for my blood family, I am the only one who does DRAG. However, I have a DRAG son and my DRAG mother.

❊**Eddie C. Broadway:** I looked to my biological family. They are all theater people and I wanted to find my niche. I felt like this was a great outlet for my creativity.

❊**Dominic: Von Strap:** It was not really a person but an idea of a personality that a person dear to my heart and I had envisioned. I am the only impersonator in my family...but I am not supposed to be.

❊**Stormm:** I looked up to the DRAG family I was part of, but they were all DRAG queens. I was the first DRAG king at the bar and I taught myself everything.

✿**Ben Eaten:** I looked up to the St. Louis, Missouri, USA, DRAG performers. I adored Butterscotch and Robyn Hearts. The first king I idolized was Phoenixxx; he later became my DRAG father. I loved their energy on stage and stage presence. I look up to them and love watching them on stage.

✿**AJ Menendez:** In the beginning, it was my DRAG father Wolfie and Gage Gatlyn. Over the years, also Gunner Daimon Gatlyn, Spacee Kadett, and many more inspired me. In spite of how many years I have been doing this, I never stop learning.

✿**Adam DoEve:** I saw my first show, a pageant for Mr. Pittsburgh Pride in Pittsburg, Pennsylvania, USA. I saw Orion Blaze Browne do his number and win, I knew I had to get started somehow. The next year I was on that same stage going for the same title.

✿**Atown:** At the time of my first number on stage, I was not familiar with too many kings, besides local ones. I tried my best to bring out the person I was impersonating or performing as. Later on, I became familiar with Landon Cider and Ivory Onyx. I saw the lyric video for Lady Gaga's "Applause" and also watched the VH1 "Tough Love" DRAG king episode, which featured both Landon and Ivory. Ivory became my mentor and supporter for the preliminary pageant as well as nationals.

✿**Rychard "Alpha" Le'Sabre:** When I first started, it was Charlie Menace, another king from Tacoma, Washington, USA. He was always energetic, smiling, and friendly to every single person in the room. He answered questions and asked a few, and gave advice for improvement. His stage presence captivated the room, and it still does at the shows he hosts now.

✿**Sam Masterson:** Dion Martel, my DRAG mother, is from Dallas, Texas, USA.

✿**Shane Rebel Caine:** I looked up to Anastasia Alexander, a popular DRAG queen in Knoxville, Tennessee, USA. She is the sole reason I worked up enough courage to get on stage and the person I have looked up to not only as a performer, but also as a person. She has helped me and given me more advice than anyone else around besides my adopted DRAG parents. She has definitely been the greatest inspiration in my DRAG career. Since about 6 months into my career I started looking up to PurrZsa Azrael, another DRAG queen in Knoxville, and her husband Devlin Caine, who is not a performer but has been around the DRAG scene for years helping PurrZsa in her career and making her costumes. After knowing them for almost a year, they adopted my brother and me, and we took on the Caine name.

✿**Justin Cider:** I was, and am, a huge Drake fan from his Degrassi days.I did a lot of him in the beginning, but my love has always been for the queens. I have been a huge fan of some of the local favorites. I turned to some of them when I realized this was something I enjoyed. They mess with my emotions every time, looking sexy and such.

❀**B J Bottoms:** Michael Jackson's "The Way You Make Me Feel" was the first number I ever performed. He has always been an icon to me and I harness his energy and passion for performing every time I step on stage.

❀**Ashton The Adorable Lover:** My brother Dillon MrDecardeza Dalton, the old ways of a true gentleman, and the many R&B entertainers from Luther to John Legend and the many before, in between and after.

❀**Kruz Mhee:** I fashioned my look after George Michael to be a pretty boi, so I went for a more effeminate male persona. My stage attitude came from 80's hair band front men; Mötley Crew's, Bret Michaels… In your face and sexual!

❀**Hawk Stuart:** I did not have one at the time. I did it for fun.

❀**Silk Steele Prince:** In the beginning, I looked up to Prince and Sisco. I choose to do Sisco because at the time that is who I resembled and his energy was high. Plus, he sang his songs with feeling, as I do. He was perfect for me.

❀**Flex Jonez:** When I was 2 lbs. soaking wet, I looked Prince, Michael Jackson, James Brown, and Sammy Davis Jr… My performances were taken from them.

❀**SirMandingo Thatis:** I always said I did not want to imitate anyone but my inspiration came from Motown!

❀**Cody Wellch Klondyke:** When I did my first number on stage, I did not look up to anyone. Then the second number I did, "Live Like You Were Dying," by Tim McGraw, I said to myself, "this is for you mom."

❀**George De Micheal:** The great king himself, Mr. Elvis Presley, his actions and big personality; what an icon. My first number was "Hotel California," by The Eagles.

❀**J Breezy St James:** Hip-hop and R&B artists and the Hollywood Undead. Two DRAG queens, Destiney and Skylar, who I saw perform when I was 16 at our Pride Prom.

❀**Colin Grey:** Too many to name… but I really wanted to be the best Billy Joel I could be. I love all music of all types and that is kind of my claim to fame.

❀**Kameo Dupree:** I have always had a special love for music and there are entirely too many influential artists just to name one. The first number I performed was Bruno Mars', "Just the Way You Are." I look for music with meaning that speaks to my soul. The way I see it is, if I do not believe in the performance and every word that crosses my lips, how could I expect someone who does not know me to believe?

❀**DeVery Bess:** When I first started, I looked up to this one king, Ian Poe Kerr. I really look up other performers within the same field because they gave me the chance to perform. They always had these elaborate ideas, that when you hear them, they sound crazy, but when performed, they are amazing. Everything they did was fantastic.

❀**Chris Mandingo:** My first number was for my wife's, Cookie, 21st birthday. At the time, the two main queens that I looked up to the most was, and still are, Raven and Morgan. They are not afraid to say fuck it and be themselves.

❀**Stefan LeDude:** I never looked up to anyone in the beginning, but later on I would say it was Nat King Pole, who is an awesome DRAG king and lyricist.

❀**Jamel Knight:** For me, I looked up to all the male entertainers that I loved from day one. They had their own singing and performing style, but each one of them could hold their own and brought something that was unique and missing in the music/entertainment world. My top two performers that I looked up to would definitely be Michael Jackson and Prince.

❀**Master Cameron Eric Leon:** Landon Cider and Spikey Van Dykey were huge inspirations. They are veteran DRAG kings and incredible artists. I watched many of their videos and tutorials the first few months. I learned much from them. I was just honestly inspired by everyone around me.

❀**Welland Dowd:** Nat King Pole, Jack E Dickingson, and Ian Poe Kerr.

❀**Julius M. SeizeHer:** Oh goodness, there are too many idols, The Beatles, Rolling Stones, and The Eagles, to name a few. I grew up listening to these men. It was always a great day when I could turn on 94.5 and listen to the Beatles and know it was a sunshiny day!

❀**Howie Feltersnatch:** I really looked up to Greenday, Elvis Presley, Cher, and later on, the Canadian indie singer Diamond Rings, who is so androgynistic that it made me fall in love. To this day, if I need some sort of inspiration, I turn on any song from those bands, get inspired, and start thinking of other bands and songs I should try out.

❀**Jack E. Dickinson:** My main influence, for my first act and my name was Bruce Dickinson of Iron Maiden. I seen Maiden many times in concert and loved his energy. He radiates something that just reaches out to everyone in the audience. Some kind of passion. I tried to emulate that as much as I could.

❀**Xavier Bottoms:** I have always looked up at my brother. He is an amazing DRAG queen, Ophelia Bottoms. The entertainment value he brings to the stage is always very high. He has the ability to make anyone smile while on stage.

❀**Clark Kunt:** Long before I worked up the nerve to get on stage, I looked up to DRAG queens in my city like Rouge Fatale and the late LuLu LaRude. But going out on stage the first time, it wasn't so much looking UP to, but looking OUT in the audience to - a boylesque performer and DRAG king who stopped my panic attack backstage and managed to convince me it was still a good idea to try. Without Ewan Love and Felix Static, I am not sure if I would have ever worked up the nerve to get out there. Now I get to perform with Felix and the rest of our group in some incredible shows.

❊Emilio: From the moment I started performing, and even now, 6 years later, I like to emulate Ricky Martin. He is an incredibly sexy performer!

❊Juan Kerr: My inspirations for my character, the first one I did was 'White trash' or 'chavvy'. He was not particularly white trash though, he just liked dressing in tracksuits and wife beater t-shirts, and he liked his Burberry cap. I used to tend to do different masculine stereotypes like fireman. Now I tend to just dress sharp, suited and booted. Music wise, I go for soul music and cheesy 80's, anything that I can work out a funny routine.

❊Trey C. Michaels: Bruno Mars, because I love his stage presence, Freddy Prinze Charming, Gunner Gatlyn, and Ayden Lane.

❊Bailey Saint James: I looked up to Antonio Punani of the Chicago Boi Toiz. Out of costume and off stage, she is very feminine. She proved to me and reminded me that it is okay to be yourself off stage; the transformation into character is something I admired very much!

❊Aaron Phoenix: I look to male artists like Elvis, Johnny Cash, Brian Setzer, George Michael, etc. for inspiration starting out, and many of the performers I have met along the way have become mentors or inspiration to me.

❊Santana Romero: Michael Jackson, Usher, Justin Timberlake, and Prince are my biggest celebrity inspirations. I take what they do on stage, make it my own, and incorporate it into my numbers, especially their movement and stage presence. If it had not been for them, I would probably have no idea what I am doing on stage. Actual DRAG entertainers that have inspired me include Dred, Diane Torr, Mystikal Jackson, Spacee Kadett, Deja D. (an amazing local queen from Toledo, Ohio, USA), my DRAG father, Teddy Michael, and a host of other kings and queens. The list goes on and on and it continues to grow every time I watch another show.

❊Dominic: I really did not have ANYONE to look up to because when I started male illusion in 2005, it was not very popular at all! I had seen DRAG queens perform over and over and I thought, "Wow, I can do this. It has always been a dream of mine to be a singer/performer." Once I was approached by Jill, a bar manager at the old Sports Page, and was asked if a couple of us would like to form a group and be the house performers once a month. I was in...after a little freaking out of course!

❊Soco Dupree: Biggest inspiration stage wise has always been my DRAG mother, but any entertainers can be inspirational in their own way.

❊E. M. Shaun: I have always loved Michael Jackson, how he would grace the stage and put on the show of a lifetime every time. So I have shadowed behind him and also Justin Timberlake and Ne-Yo. I have taken a little bit of all these performers to make me. But at the end of the day, I still have my own style that suits my personality and me.

❀**Stefon Royce Iman:** Harmonica Sunbeam as a performer I watched her show and stage performance. After that, I ask her to be my mother.

❀**Smitty O'Toole:** As far as kings, I really had not seen a king show before I stepped on stage. I looked up to performers like Justin Timberlake, Madonna, Mark Wahlberg, and Jim Carey for their presentation skills.

❀**Jensen C. Dean:** I do not think I looked up to anyone specific.

❀**Luke Ateraz:** All I could think about when I took the stage for the very first time was, "God, please keep me from vomiting all over everyone!"

❀**Boi Wonder:** Valentino King and Sexy Galexy.

❀**Devin G. Dame:** Two DRAG queens, Jenuwine Beauté and Miss Moments.

❀**Dionysus W Khaos:** A large group of friends supporting me.

Chapter Fifteen
"How do you handle your anger with a venue no longer interested in you?"

❀**Eddie C. Broadway:** I do not know if I have really experienced that, other than moving a show to a new bar due to various issues. I just take it as, "it is their loss." But I have not had to deal with that really.

❀**Koomah:** Never really experienced this much. Usually gigs are a onetime appearance or a certain number of shows. The real emotion from venues has been because the space was closing. That has happened twice; a well-known lesbian bar closed (formerly the oldest lesbian bar in the city) and recently a gay community bar had their final show because they were closing. It is always sad when that happens.

❀**Travis Luvermore:** Only in the beginning. I was not the only one; the club manager had her favorites week to week. I not take it personally.

❀**Campbell Reid Andrews:** Email the director or manager what I would need to do better for the next club I am hired at. If you email them, might not get answer, but you will look and stay professional trying to better your craft. There is always room to learn. "You can't learn if you do not ask."

❀**Gus Magendor:** Move on, I was not what they were looking for. I have not had this happen, but would handle the situation professionally.

❀**Freddy Prinze Charming:** I have really only experienced this once, and I really was not angry about it. The bar owner thought that another show would do better, and I knew that they were making a huge mistake. Turns out, moving my show to a different bar was the BEST move I could have made. We have a packed house every time, and always draw in a great crowd. The other bar owner missed out.

❀**Adam All:** This has only happened with one venue and that was my first. Not after my first gig there, but my second, when I was trying a new idea that did not work. I just went out and worked elsewhere as much as I could. I look forward to the day they ask me back, but that bar is somewhat not so big a deal for me now. It can be really, really hard dealing with rejection, feeling that people just do not understand what you do. Sometimes that can mean you need to change your and show sometimes that can mean you need to aim for a different audience. I think about what I want from this and how it makes me feel when a crowd really goes with me. That helps me decide whether the venue is right for me.

❀**AJ Menendez:** I call it my "Puffer fish mode." I get mad as a human reaction and I puff up, but then I think of all the things I stand to lose if I flip out and decide it is not worth it. I Whoooo Saaaa, then I deflate. I can choose not to return to a venue if the situations get out of hand, but I cannot un-ring a bell if I allow myself to get stupid.

❋**Chance Wise:** All you can really do is move on, angry or not, even if there is some drama. Learn from it and move on.

❋**Travis Hard:** This will happen. Take it with a grain of salt, move on to the next venue, prove yourself and the previous venue will come calling again!

❋**Rychard "Alpha" Le'Sabre:** The best thing to do is just take it in stride and find somewhere else. Fighting about it is never worth the drama it can cause. Save your reputation, keep your head high, and just find somewhere new.

❋**Shane Rebel Caine:** I do not really see a venue no longer being interested as anything to be mad about. If I was a big hit with the audience, then I see only the venue hurting them. If it is because of something I did myself, then I can only be mad at myself not the venue. To me, if you are going to call yourself a KING, then you need to act like one and that means keeping your composure, staying level headed, keeping your chin up, and walking away without fighting.

❋**Rasta Boi Punany:** Move on. I have faith in my skills another venue will be interested in. I now chose who I want to perform with, and most times, I do it everywhere, out of state, and have a blast meeting new people.

❋**Dakota Rain:** I do not take it to heart. It is a business and if they do not want me, I am sure I can find someone that does.

❋**Ashton The Adorable Lover:** In that situation, I continue to do what I do, if they do not want me then someone else will.

❋**Spacee Kadett:** I feel like the first thing to do is a bit of introspection: "Why is this venue no longer interested in me? Was it something I did personally? If so, what can I do to change my performance/attitude/behavior?" More often than not, a venue does not lose interest in a performer, it overlooks him. Show directors are crazy busy people. Many of them book whoever is pounding down their door the loudest and for the lowest booking fee. If you know there was no direct break between you and the venue, just remind them you exist. Express your interest in bookings, and they may rekindle their interest in you, too. Most of all, do not burn bridges. Our community is political and budgets are tight. I have been personally and directly cut from two venues in two different states because of this. I cried untold numbers of tears and suffered tremendous anxiety behind closed doors, but I maintained a good attitude outside and went on with my life. My community backed me up. Both venues eventually re-opened their doors to me, and my return shows were better than ever.

❋**Adam DoEve:** I am still too new to all of this but have not had any problems as of yet. I am not sure how I would handle it, other than there will always be some other place to go that would like to have me.

❋**Kenneth J. Squires:** I have not encountered this yet. Maybe changing your performance or looking more the part of a DRAG king or male illusionist. Go to the director and ask if you did something wrong, and how you can fix it.

❦**Pierce Gabriel:** I have never been an emcee or host, so the decision was always passed down to me second hand. I will vent with the person telling me, talk about finding another place to perform, but I know there is no point in taking it much further. Business is business.

❦**Vinnie Marconi:** What anger? If they are not interested in your style of performance, move on. Maybe you do not fit with the clientele. If it is personal towards you, do a hot spot at the competition and draw their crowd from them. No anger, just solutions.

❦**Kruz Mhee:** Never really had that problem. Once when I felt that was an issue, I just changed venues. There was another club wanting me to perform.

❦**Hawk Stuart:** What anger? Do not let it bother you. Move on.

❦**Silk Steele Prince:** I do not. I find somewhere else to go. I do not want to be anywhere I am not wanted.

❦**Flex Jonez:** No issues in the past or present, I stay very much a businessman always, so if there is an issue, it is handled professionally.

❦**Atown:** This happened once and it was because they did not want to pay us after we had a business meeting about how much we were going to get to continue working at their venue. We did one free show, made them a butt load of money and it just did not work out with them. I look at it as their loss. I do not have a problem performing for free. I do it for fun, as a hobby. But when someone is using you, now that is different.

❦**DeVery Bess:** Suffered from venues not wanting me because they have never seen a show, but not wanting me anymore has never been an issue.

❦**Xavier Bottoms:** Not an issue. I was taught never to repeat a "number," always make is different, and wait a month before repeating it.

❦**Jamel Knight:** You cannot really be upset when a venue does not want to book you. It is their business and their choice. If you are only being booked at one place you always run the risk of having nowhere to perform. Diversity is the key. Get your name out to different audiences and helping build longevity in entertainment.

❦**Master Cameron Eric Leon:** I would probably start re-evaluating myself. There has to be a reason they did not book me- what can I do better?

❦**Bruno Diaz:** I am usually a pretty laid back individual, and I understand I cannot be everyone's cup of tea. I rather be a shot of tequila anyways.

❦**Lyle Love-It:** This has not happened, but "their loss."

❦**MaXx Decco:** Venues have reneged on the money arrangements and made scheduling mistakes, but it is just part of what entertainers deal with. I am handling it by looking for a manager.

❦**Jonah Godfather of DRAG:** You have to remember venues change things to keep fresh. Just pick yourself up, dust yourself off, and move on to bigger and better things.

❦**Howie Feltersnatch:** Within the three years, we have had two venues close on us. As a troupe, we were all collectively sad, but thank goodness for Dickens Pub who took us in to let us perform. Without a queer friendly venue, we would not be where we are today. Calgary, Canada, only has one gay bar, which is mostly about the queens and are not interested in letting us perform to raise money for our charity.

❦**Jack E. Dickinson:** In my beginning years as a DRAG king, I was occasionally invited to do an act at a local DRAG queen bar. When I started doing gender fuck more than straight up DRAG kinging, they stopped inviting me. I wasn't that surprised, because it's a very binary thinking environment, but I was a bit hurt and angry. I just kept doing my own thing outside of that location and reminded myself that it wasn't really my crowd anyway. People went there to see queens and 75% of the crowd had a lukewarm reaction to kings anyway.

❦**Clark Kunt:** I do not get angry at venues. I had times of being frustrated when it was hard to find space to perform, but that just pushed me to grow and have something new to offer, and to create my own spaces.

❦**Trey C. Michaels:** I have never had a venue no longer want to work with me. I have had other performers not want to work with me and I now try to talk it out with them. People will hear or see the anger and I think it puts a damper on the king community when people see that stuff.

❦**Stefon Royce Iman:** I have never experienced it. If I do, I will just be humble. I will still support their events, and come and bring friends.

❦**E. M. Shaun:** That has not happen to me but if it did, I would not bash the venue. I would say maybe there were some disagreeable opinions about some things and that we both decide on splitting ways.

❦**B J Armani:** It has happened to me and I just took it in stride. Many venues do not realize the income that is involved until you walk away from their establishment. Money always talks and DRAG shows are a wonderful income with a crowd that does not cause issues. I was dropped from a venue only to find a home at a bar that needs the sales and the advertising. It is a win-win situation when that happens!

❦**LoUis CYfer:** I never get angry at a venue for not being booked. That is obviously my responsibility to make myself high in demand, and if I am not, then only I am to blame for my staleness.

❦**Jensen C. Dean:** I never had this happen, but I like to think I would do so with professionalism and grace if I ever faced something like this.

❦**Luke Ateraz:** I have not been in a situation where a venue is not interested in me anymore. I have had a venue close without so much as giving the performers a heads up, but we just kept on moving. Found another venue and got to work packing the new location with our friends, fans, and family.

❀**William Vanity Matrix:** I have never had it happen. I would do my best to have myself more wanted by different venues and step up my game.

❀**Devin G. Dame:** It usually is not that the venue does not want to book you anymore…it usually had to do with money, the venue being under new management or the venue closing its doors.

Don't forget, Book 1 of The Ten Black Books is called, "DRAG Bully, A Survivor's Guide.

Thousands of words of wisdom from Male, Female, and Androgynous DRAG Impersonators from Around the World

Book 1 of

DRAG411

Ten Black Books

**DRAG Bully
A Survivor's Guide**

From Best Selling Author
The Infamous Todd Kachinski Kottmeier with Vinnie Marconi

Chapter Sixteen
"Which key people in your life are oblivious to the fact, you perform as an impersonator? Why?"

❀**Adam All:** Probably no one. Everyone knows but some know more. To others, it is just my hobby. I do not mind keeping the intense stuff from them. My partner is my main mentor and coach. I could not do it without her, now especially, in the competitive environment of cabaret performers.

❀**Spacee Kadett:** I have been fortunate enough to reach a place in my life where I am incredibly open with everyone close to me. When I started doing DRAG, only my wife (then girlfriend) knew. My parents had vehemently rejected my sexuality for years. I still lived under their roof, so they had no idea I performed. I remember hand sewing a space suit in my bedroom and sneaking off to gigs with my DRAG strategically packed. My life evolved dramatically. I believe DRAG helped. My parents are NOT my fans. They do not advertise to anyone that I perform (or that I am gay AND married.) But they recognize my passion and have helped me with my DRAG here and there, and have even been to a show. Everyone else in my life surprised me with their support when I was certain they would reject me: extended family, friends, co-workers, even my former boss. They all went to my shows and many are on my DRAG social network.

❀**Chance Wise:** I am pretty open about performing and my sexuality...people in my life either accepts it or does not. I will still do it.

❀**Davion Summers:** My parents and grandparents have no clue. My father is a minister at a church and would not understand. He does not know I am in a relationship with a woman. I did not tell my mother because I am not sure she could handle it. She accepts my partner but I think DRAG would be too much for her. My grandparents are old school. I do not want arguments or the lectures from me telling them anything about my lifestyle.

❀**Orion Blaze Browne:** My entire family knows I do DRAG. It was a little weird at first, but they have accepted it as something that makes me happy.

❀**Travis Hard:.** Everyone in my life knows. That is how I like it.

❀**Vinnie Marconi:** EVERYONE in my inner circle knows who I am, what I stand for, and what I do! Otherwise, they are NOT in my circle.

❀**Clint Torres:** My grandmother. She refuses to believe that I am gay/lesbian so the idea of me impersonating a man is something she will never understand. I tried to explain but she has made herself oblivious to the fact.

❀**Ben Eaten:** My entire family does not know other than my one sister-in-law. Most of my girlfriend's entire family comes to my shows and cheers me on but my family does not support it so they have no idea.

❀**Viciouse Slick:** The only my mom's family in Germany. Some of them are old fashion in their ways and some I do not think would understand, but everyone else knows, friends and family.

❀**Koomah:** Nobody who is actively involved in my life is oblivious to the fact that I am a performer. There are folks not in my life, and they know who I am and what I do as well, regardless if they support or acknowledge it.

❀**Campbell Reid Andrews:** Everyone knows! They love it. I am so blessed to be able to express myself freely and I am accepted for what I do.

❀**Coti Blayne:** My dad's side of the family, himself included, does not know about me being lesbian, engaged to a female, or that I do DRAG. They are very backwards minded and are still not even open to dating outside your race (someone was disowned for it). I do not tell them, though I hardly talk to them, so it is no big deal. I do not really want them a part of my life. Now my mom is amazing and she knows as well as a few of her family knows, she is super supportive and has even come to pageants.

❀**Rasta Boi Punany:** No one. If they are on social media, they know. If not, they have heard it from others in my circle and/or have seen me perform, i.e. my mother and father. No shame, no secrecy, no harm.

❀**Freddy Prinze Charming:** Everyone knows what I do. I do not know what they all think about it, but I do not hide it. If they do not like it, they do not have to come to a show. If they REALLY do not like it, they can suck it.

❀**B J Armani:** My workplace but I was in inter-office memo and a ton of them showed up to my last show. That proves nurses, psychologists, doctors, and med techs all rock if you give them a chance. If I meet someone I do not know, it does not take long for another friend to bring it up (they are quite proud of me), so I'm pretty open. Maybe my dentist?

❀**Lyle Love-It:** NO ONE, I am, LOUD AND PROUD.

❀**Kenneth J. Squires:** Many people at my work place do not know. I am out at work, but not when it comes to my DRAG life.

❀**Eddie C. Broadway:** I am super out and proud in every aspect and am heavily involved in the LGBTQ community, so I think anyone and everyone knows I am a performer, unless they have not met me yet!

❀**Dominic: Von Strap:** Nobody. If not, I have not gotten to tell them yet.

❀**Stormm:** Everybody knows.

❀**Travis Luvermore:** Only my immediate family, my grandmother never knew. I feel that if she did, she would have been very supportive.

❀**Gus Magendor:** Only people who do not go to gay clubs or people do not know me.

❀**Kody Sky:** The key people would be some of those in my family. They are still uncomfortable with my choices.

❀**AJ Menendez:** All the key people know, much like when I came out of the closet. With DRAG, I did not tip toe out, I leaped. My choices were mine and they could either accept it or reject it but I was going to follow my dream.

❀**Hurricane Savage:** I am 100% open with what I do and who I am so my family knows and my work knows.

❀**Rychard "Alpha" Le'Sabre:** My whole family and all my friends know. I hide nothing from anyone. This is a part of me.

❀**Atown:** I am thankful everyone has been very open minded for me.

❀**Ashton The Adorable Lover:** Key people? My extended family mostly, but that is because they do not talk to me to know what I do.

❀**Dakota Rain:** Everyone knows I perform, from family to friends to coworkers, everyone.

❀**Pierce Gabriel:** I do not tell my mom, because she has a difficult time accepting my personal life as a lesbian. She lives out of state and is unable to attend shows herself, I feel it is pointless to tell her when she will not be able to know what it is really all about. Aside from that, whenever I start a new job, I always keep that bit of information to myself for a while, so I can test the waters of my boss and coworkers to see how they feel about it. Once I know they are cool, I fill them in.

❀**Kruz Mhee:** Mostly coworkers, and the bulk of my family. I was raised in the "Church of God" faith and there are some strict rules. Women are women, women are to present themselves as such. My short hair and I dress mostly like a man does not fit into my upbringing. I have several family members that know I am a DRAG King and although they do not condone they do not reject me as family. They do give their opinions openly and try to lead me away from my "lifestyle." The people that matter most in my life unconditionally accept me (Paula) and Kruz.

❀**Flex Jonez:** None. Everyone I know, I love fans.

❀**Cody Wellch Klondyke:** Everyone. I love my family, friends, and my fans.

❀**J Breezy St James:** My dad has never really understood it and does not care to even though the rest of his side of the family supports it.

❀**George De Micheal:** My mum, my dad, and family. I also present myself as a transgendered FTM to represent this in my community.

❀**Colin Grey:** No one really.

❀**Stefan LeDude:** No one, I am completely open about it.

❀**Jamel Knight:** Most of my extended family does not know. I do not hide anything from anyone but I just have not felt the need to "announce" it to them.

❀**Master Cameron Eric Leon:** Only my work does not know. The immediate people I work with know, but I am not out about it with the head office.

❀**Bruno Diaz:** None. I volunteer at a summer camp with kids from 6 to 15 and sometimes I lip-sync to them, which helps me to know my words. They also help me to materialize my ideas in crafts. Some of the parents know also.

❀**Shane Rebel Caine:** Anyone who knows me or is a part of my life knows that I am an impersonator. I have refused to hide who I am and being a king is a part of me. If someone cannot accept that, then they are not important to me. I have made it clear to anyone who does not like it that I do not care for their opinion. I am me and I'm not going to pretend to be someone or something I'm not.

❀**DeVery Bess:** never stop talking about DRAG to everyone, if someone did not know or did not realize it, I would find it hard to believe.

❀**Welland Dowd:** Everyone knows I am a king. I have nothing to hide!

❀**Julius M. SeizeHer:** My family, because I choose to keep it from them.

❀**Adam DoEve:** Everyone in my life day to day knows. I have many in my family that do not, and that is not all my doing but that is a different question. I work in a hotel so I am carful when I talk to my guests, but you would be very surprised how many people ask me all kinds of questions, and I enjoy spreading the word about kings.

❀**Lyle Love-It:** LOUD AND PROUD.

❀**Jonah Godfather of DRAG:** My dad is the only key person in my life with no idea of my DRAG career. He is distant from all of his children. Do not get me wrong, he loves all of us, but he is very uninvolved with our lives. I chose not to let him in on this because he is very conservative and opinionated.

❀**Dionysus W Khaos:** Although I am open with the fact I am an entertainer, my family is not accepting for the most part. My mother especially hates it. It is not something I can truly discuss without making her visibly upset.

❀**Howie Feltersnatch:** I think my grandparents are. They know I dance in a troupe, but I do not think they know I am an impersonator.

❀**Jack E. Dickinson:** Most of my blood family is relatively oblivious. They vaguely know about it, but not the details. The same for most of my colleagues, they do not know, except for the queer or queer friendly ones.

❀**Xavier Bottoms:** Everyone knows I am an impersonator. My license plate on my truck says MRGUSMI. Mr. Gay United Sates Male Impersonator. People always ask and I am very proud to be who I am. My wife wears a shirt with a picture of Angel on the front, it says, "My Wife." The back of the shirt is a picture of Xavier, it says, "My Husband." Our DRAG kids go to my biological family reunion. No secrets here.

❀**Clark Kunt:** I do not hide from key people in my life. Performing is a part of who I am, and it is important to me that the people in my life know who I am.

❀**Emilio:** I am open even to my 3-year-old daughter. I am proud of it.

❀**Juan Kerr:** None of them, I have just 'come out', as it were, to my workmates as a DRAG performer but there has been no backlash so far.

❀**Trey C. Michaels:** The only person in my family who does not know is my mom. We do not have a relationship though so I have never felt the need to tell her. Everyone else in my life knows because it is something I am proud of.

❀**Bailey Saint James:** Until recently, my therapist was unaware of my stage persona. I thought she would think I had a gender identity crisis. When I finally told her, her first question to me was, "do you feel more like a boy?" I wish I could take back telling her. That was the longest session ever!

❀**Aaron Phoenix:** Everyone in my life knows I am an entertainer, including my coworkers and bosses in my "day job." I have been very lucky to live a completely open life. With how much time outside of work that is devoted to DRAG, though, it would be hard for me to hide it if I wanted to.

❀**Thug Passion:** No one. Everyone who is important to me in my life knows and is very supportive of me.

❀**MaXx Decco:** Until recently, my family and work were unaware.

❀**Santana Romero:** I think the only person who does not know that I am a DRAG performer is my granddad. He's really old school so I am not sure if he would really understand what "DRAG" really entails but I think he would support me either way if I were, eventually, to tell him. Everyone else knows and has been very supportive in regard to my career choice.

❀**Soco Dupree:** No one now, but for the longest time, my mother was. She would see tagged photos of me on social media and ask who the guy was and why he was tagged. Then one day, I decided to take her to dinner and reveal my second life, per se. I figured she could not yell at me in public, but she actually reacted amazingly and is a huge supporter now.

❀**Stefon Royce Iman:** My close friends and my mother support me, so they know and respect what I do.

❀**Viciouse Slick:** The people who do not know about me performing are my mom's side of the family. That side is a bit old school with life and so I feel that they may not understand what DRAG is or why I do it.

❀**Cody Wellch Klondyke:** Everyone knows but some people know more. To others, it is just a hobby I have and a form of art. I do not mind keeping the intense stuff from them. I love expressing myself from the music. Music tells a lot about someone.

❀**E. M. Shaun:** My closet friends and family members are supportive of me.

❀**Mike Oxready:** Most folks in my life know, but my extended family does not. I am relatively open about being a performer at work, and all of my friends know and are supportive.

❀**Smitty O'Toole:** Everyone knows I am a performer and is supportive.

❀**Jensen C. Dean:** The only important person in my family not knowing is my grandma. It is not that she would not approve, but would not understand. She has dementia and I have tried to tell her about it, but it just confuses her.

❀**Luke Ateraz:** I see no reason to hide the fact I am a performer. My grandmother has been to see me perform. It is a part of me, of who I am.

❀**William Vanity Matrix:** My extended family but that is only because I hardly ever see them and have not seem them since I have started. Not intentional in the least, just the way that it has fallen.

❀**Devin G. Dame:** I think everyone in my life knows I perform.

Name the performers without checking on DRAG411.com

Chapter Seventeen
"How did your family handle you performing by cross dressing in the beginning of your craft? How do they handle it now?
Are you the only impersonator in your family?"

❀**Joshua Micheals:** My family did not know about it until I had been doing it for a long time. They do not understand but they support it now

❀**B J Armani:** My immediate family was split. My sister is a lesbian but thinks it is weird STILL after a decade. My mom is SUPER supportive unless it is an election year (recently an issue to my surprise) and my dad hasn't met my alter ego, but gives me props on facebook the past two months. My grandmother was the kicker. My mom's mom, LaVern Anderson, wife of my grandfather, Ed Anderson (he was Police Chief of Fargo, North Dakota, USA, for 17 years and Potentate at the El Zagel Shrine), NEVER missed a performance if she could help it. I did "Beauty School Dropout" from Grease because it was her favorite character. She was my star and my Matriarch. My dad's dad grew up in New York, playing piano for Broadway and entertainers. Originally the fedora was (and still is) an homage to him.

❀**Shook ByNature:** I swear my mom thinks I am a stripper. If I say I have a show or pageant and she goes into shut down mode. My 4 yr. old son helps design costumes, pick songs, and he tells me when I look good! I know it is a good night when he says, "Mommy you look like a Rock star!" or "Mommy you look like a Gentleman!"

❀**Joshua Micheals:** I am the only impersonator. However, my brother is an actor and played "Edna Turnblat" in 'Hair Spray.' He is my biggest fan.

❀**Brandon KC Young-Taylor:** My family has been supportive from the beginning. My mom, dad, sister, aunts, uncles, and cousins have all been to see my shows. Before my grandmother passed, she donated money every time I ran in a pageant.

❀**D-Luv Saviyon:** I am the only one in my family. In the beginning, my mom thought I was just dancing with groups. I kept DRAG separate from my family (my mother was adjusting to me coming out at that time). My mom became unhappily aware of how involved I was in DRAG when I did pageants. She has expressed her opinion on the subject over the years, although she has come to respect me as an entertainer and loves the costuming I have created over the years. My mother feels my design talents have been sadly wasted on a time-consuming, life-intruding hobby that has not been even remotely lucrative for all my time and effort, except my most recent title.

❀**Sammy Silver:** I have been extremely fortunate that my family has been very supportive! My mum especially adores my DRAG king alter ego, sometimes more so than my actual girl self! The family always comes to see my shows and really have thrown themselves into the DRAG world.

❀**Clint Torres:** I dressed in guys clothes since I was a kid so it is easier for my family. The hard part was putting on face and taking on a new persona, a new name. Over time though, Clint seems like he has always been there.

❀**Nanette D'angelo Sylvan:** My father knew and was very supportive but he unfortunately passed the first year I started impersonating. I have still never said anything to my mother about it because she hates my lifestyle. Even though I am in a relationship with a man now, she still is not happy, so I just choose to keep that part of my life separate!

❀**Anjie Swidergal:** As a straight woman, my family did not really understand, but I grew up connected to the theatre, so I simply explained that I am portraying a character on stage. Yes, it is a gay dominated art form, but I still live my daily life as a straight woman So far, so good!

❀**Vinnie Marconi:** I am the only DRAG performer in my family and the only family memeber to see me perform has been Lynn, my partner.

❀**Freddy Prinze Charming:** I am the only DRAG entertainer in my family, but I am not the only performer. No one was surprised when I found another performing outlet, but I think it took them a little bit to really understand what I was doing. Almost everyone was familiar with DRAG queens and female impersonators (I had even gone to the famous Alcazar club with my parents when we lived in Thailand), but male impersonators were new. My dad, step-mom, uncle, aunt, and cousins have all seen at least one of my shows, and seemed to enjoy themselves.

❀**Gus Magendor:** Everything but the facial hair. They now support me and are excited to see where I go. As far as I know, I am the only one in my family and have ever been.

❀**Chance Wise:** My sister was a cross dresser for years before she realized that she is a transgender woman. She performed as a live singer for a number of years, but right now I am the only cross dressing performer in my family that I know of. My family has been amazing in support of my craft and me. Surprisingly supportive, being old school Brooklyn Italians...they even came to see me perform once. My mom, after a few drinks, jumped up on stage with me and danced around with me. It still makes me smile to think about.

❀**Travis Hard:** My mom thinks I look like Elvis, all the time, and is constantly sharing my DRAG photos. She thinks it is awesome, yet has not come to a single show.

❀**Dakota Rain:** The only entertainer in my family, and they have all been very supportive and still are. My sister said, one time, when she helped me get ready for Salisbury Pride in North Carolina, USA that she actually saw me transform from her sister to her brother and it was interesting. My niece has also helped me transform, very supportive family.

❦**Rasta Boi Punany:** My Mother and Father came to my crowning ceremony to watch their daughter crowned as a KING, pretty awesome. My son, grandchildren, and heir have performed with me, my daughters support me, and my wife started this whole thing. My family supports me, then and now. I am the only one in my family that I know of and I love it!

❦**Jack King:** Father is cool with it. I am the only impersonator in my family.

❦**Adam All:** To begin with, my family wanted nothing to do with it. They blamed themselves and made me keep it a secret from the wider family. I do not give a fuck though, I was on to something, and I loved it. Now both my parents and my sister share my videos and crow to their friends about my shows. I just recently did the main stage at London pride and my mum shoed my aunt and uncle, who both loved it.

❦**Viciouse Slick:** My mom loves it, if she lived in Phoenix, Arizona, USA, I would not doubt that she would have gone to every single show I was in. She absolutely loves DRAG shows and everything about them, even the pageants!

❦**Campbell Reid Andrews:** In my biological family, I am the only performer. In my DRAG family I am the only Male illusionist, and proud of it. My family has been supportive of everything I set my sights on. When I wanted to play football, become a swimmer, singer, dancer, and an impersonator, my mother has always been my #1 fan. She screams it at the top of any mountain she is proud of me. My fiancé and I are like the same person destined to be together. She dances, loves to sing, and is a faux queen so we fit like a glove. She also believes in my DRAG career one billion percent.

❦**Lyle Love-It:** Everyone is awesome. My mom is 82 years old, and loves my shows.

❦**Spacee Kadett:** Although I am (to my knowledge!) the only cross dresser in my family, I havebeen surprised and blessed that most everyone in my life has found my cross-dressing rather fascinating, and they've been supportive ever since I told them. My parents are a different story. They are not jumping up and down about my shows, but have always been far more accepting of my DRAG than they have of my lesbianism. I think because they (A) do not perceive DRAG as sinful and (B) recognize that I have been enamored with dressing up my entire life. My DRAG is very theatrical, so it makes sense to them. I have long hair and wear dresses by day, they are still convinced I am confused about being gay.

❦**Adam DoEve:** I took my time telling my family. The only one that is supportive is my son, he even comes to my shows when he is not working and brings his girlfriend and friends. I love him for this even more, but the rest of the family does not even want to talk about my life style let alone about me performing. I did try to explain it to them once, brick wall talk is what it was, but after that, I just gave up. I look at it this way, as long as I am having fun, I am going to do it. Just because someone does not understand why, it is not a reason to give up something this fun and freeing.

❈Ben Eaten: My mom told me not to do it, so I stopped telling her about it. My sister-in-law found out and asked when she could come see me perform. I am the only person in my family who does this amazing craft, although my girlfriend's cousin was a queen, so I am able to get a lot of help from him.

❈Eddie C. Broadway: My mom wanted me to do more gender bending stuff. I did not want to at first. She was concerned about me transitioning, which is funny because I AM transitioning. I am actually NOT the only one in my family. My uncle used to do DRAG in Palm Springs, Florida, USA!

❈Stormm: It did not bother my family. I am the only person who does this.

❈Dominic: Von Strap: They have been supportive. My mom wants to see a show but her health does not quite allow it. At first there were questions regarding if I were thinking of transitioning, which I am not, but they would not really care if I did, not as long as I am happy and staying true to myself.

❈Koomah: My biological family does not know or care, my legal family is very much against it, my chosen family is super supportive!

❈Travis Luvermore: I'm the only one in my family performing DRAG. They acknowledge but not totally keen on the idea. My mother sometimes helps with artwork. At first, they were worried that it was more than just performing. My stepdaughter was afraid I would dress in DRAG, other than on stage, and asked if she would recognize me on the street.

❈Kody Sky: I am the only impersonator in my family and it is still an uncomfortable conversation for most in the family.

❈AJ Menendez: Okay, so I was not sure how to tell my mother what I was doing, she was still having a hard time with my coming out. I waited until I won my first National title and I wrote her a letter. In that letter I sent her a picture of me in full DRAG with crown and sash, I did not tell her who the person was. She called me about a week later and the conversation went as followed: MOM: I got your letter today, thank you it was very sweet. But why are you sending me pictures of strange men? ME: Mom, that is me... Dead silence. Then blood curdling tears. MOM: What did I do wrong? Then it hit me. She thought I had a sex change! Once I explained it to her, she was somewhat easier with it and today she is proud.

❈Romeo Sanchez: By the time I told my parents that I was a DRAG king, they had opened their minds a bit already. My father actually came to my very first show outside of an open stage night.

❈King Dante: I have great support. My family is all on my social media sites.

❈Justin Cider: My mom and sister come to almost every show, they call them Mama Cider and Baby Cider (even though my sister is older than me). They are my rocks and number one fans. I am such a lucky person because of them. My mom really does not even see how much it means to me, and really, to all the kings, that she is there supporting us night after night.

❀Atown: I was already dressing as males typically dress before I became a DRAG king. It was the facial hair that really threw them off. I introduced them to it when I was fundraising for the Mister California USofA MI pageant in California, USA. Showing them pictures, they were like, "what is that on your face?" or "who is that?" It just took some getting used to. And yes, I am the only impersonator in my family.

❀King Dante: I am the only "man" in my family.

❀Rychard "Alpha" Le'Sabre: I have wanted to dress like a boy since I was a little kid, and being Mormon, that is completely not allowed. I turned 20, went to a club, and it felt natural. My family still hates it though.

❀Shane Rebel Caine: All except four members of my family have been supportive from the beginning and have accepted me for me. My mom, dad, papaw, and brother are the only ones who complained and still to this day complain about it and try to discourage me. In the beginning, I would wait until everyone went to bed, then I would get ready and leave the house. Now I either wait until I am at the club, or I just go ahead and get ready whether they have gone to bed or not. I have told my mom from the beginning that I enjoy doing it and I am good at it. I am not going to stop doing something that I have a passion for and I am not going to stop being myself just to please her or anyone else. I am the only impersonator in my family. However, I have a cousin on my mother's side who looks and dresses like a guy, except she does not do the makeup, bind, or pack, but she does sing live.

❀B J Bottoms: My mom has been supportive as well as my sister. They have taken an interest in my career and my sister attends shows and pageants. She is my biggest fan.

❀Ashton The Adorable Lover: I started while was away from my family so I was years into it. My parents cannot understand why I do it, but they also do not know me well, so it is what is. My little sister actually just saw me perform for first time this year July 2014. It is great that she fully supports me.

❀Stefon SanDiego: Being away from my family for so many years, since the age if twelve, they never knew. After some time, I finally told my mom and dad whom seemed a little confused by the image they had placed within their own minds. My dad, being an entertainer in the music world, was my inspiration for music. At first, my father's support was invalid, as well as to this day. Now my mom, on the other hand, being a professional showgirl in her years, found it odd, yet intriguing. Her support is amazing. At first, her reaction to Stefon SanDiego's picture was almost a heart attack due to the facial hair. I simply explained that it was a mere illusion and technique used to form that illusion. Today, my mom could not be more proud. Now my dad, there is no conversation to be spoken.

❦**Pierce Gabriel:** I am the only impersonator in my family. My dad was excited that I was trying something so challenging. He gave me many helpful tips about the body language and hand gestures. My sister thinks it is cool and often shows my videos to her friends. The rest of my family knows that I perform in costume on a stage once a week... But I do not think they have figured out that it is DRAG.

❦**Ryder Knightly:** I would love to see my brother cross dress, I am the only impersonator in my family. I actually got busted one night as I was getting ready to leave for the show, and my family came back early from a dinner. I believe, "umm, what are you doing?" with crazy stares followed. That was a moment to remember. Now they fully support me, and help me at times, too.

❦**Kruz Mhee:** To my knowledge, I am the only impersonator in my family. Of course, my parents are not too keen on the idea but my mother accepts that I am trying to better my community by participating in local benefits and so forth. Most importantly, I have the support of my partner.

❦**Kenneth J. Squires:** My blood family does not know I do DRAG. My DRAG family and extended family, I believe, support me in what I am doing. I am slowly getting better at my craft, but need more help in this process. I look up to all the DRAG kings and male impersonators who have been there before me. I thank my partner, who has supported me through all this. I also thank my DRAG mother, Stratosphere Johnson, who also supports me. I hope to build my brotherhood.

❦**Hawk Stuart:** My family does not know. My adoptive family loves it.

❦**Silk Steele Prince:** In the beginning of my craft, I hid the fact that I was performing and cross dressing, because my family spoke negatively about people who did it. One day I was getting ready before leaving for a show and my family saw me as I was leaving. They thought I had lost my mind. They were speechless. I just explained that I had a performance and I would be back. Today, my family is my biggest supporters. I have two daughters who are looking forward to performing as well.

❦**Flex Jonez:** My brother and father came to my shows whenever able. Once in a while, my brother will sneak in behind stage.

❦**SirMandingo Thatis:** My dad thought it was awesome but my mom was like, I must see this, and once she came and saw a show, she then became a fan. She even has her own favorite DRAG queen that she is very close friends with. She later mentioned to me that her uncle, who passed away before I was born, was a DRAG queen. My siblings think it is great because it makes me happy and proud to be me!

❦**Kenneth J. Squires:** My blood family does not know I do this. My extended family, they are happy that I am still learning and growing in the art of DRAG. I am the only person in my blood family that does this. I have a DRAG mother and a DRAG son.

❀**Mike Oxready:** I am the only performer in the family, and I kept it a secret for a while. Now, my immediate family knows, and we just do not talk about it very much. My chosen family has been supportive since day 1.

❀**Cody Wellch Klondyke:** My sister supports me. She has been with me to shows here in Houston, Texas, USA. My daughter loves it. She loves the kings and queens. As far as my mom, she is watching me from Heaven and my dad does not know.

❀**George De Micheal:** Family supports me in anything I put my mind and will to do.

❀**Thug Passion:** I did not know how to tell my mother so my woman at the time, did it for me. My mom could not believe it because I was shy growing up and did not really do too much dancing at school dances. The day she found out, she wanted me to demonstrate a little of what I do, without the facial hair and my chest being tied down. So I did, and she could not wait to see the full effect. Ever since then, she has been very supportive of me. She had recently remarried and my stepfather and new stepsiblings are also very supportive.

❀**Bootzy Edwards Collynz:** My Mom was not too happy, but knew I loved to perform. As long as it keeps my butt out of jail, and it is legal, they are cool.

❀**Colin Grey:** My dad and sisters ignores it. My mom helps sew projects. I have a very supportive family as far as my girlfriend and children, who all enjoy it and help me with my craft, when and where they can.

❀**E. M. Shaun:** My sister is supportive of all I do in life. I have cousins that know I perform. My mother does not know yet, but I do not think she would be too surprised.

❀**Sam Masterson:** My family is against my life style, they are very religious.

❀**DeVery Bess:** I am not the only impersonator in my family. My mother always told me to do what makes me happy. My mother did not really understand what it was at first, because DRAG kings are not mainstream, like queens are, but after a show, she loved it, and my mother did impersonations of Marilyn Monroe, if that counts.

❀**Kameo Dupree:** First response from my mother was, "So now you want to be a boy?" She still asks questions every now and then, but she became the proud parent of a king! She came to one of my pageants and found a better understanding of the craft. I think she talks about DRAG more than I do now.

❀**Xavier Bottoms:** I guess I had it easy. My brother is a DRAG queen. He started doing DRAG before me, so he kind of broke the ice. Our whole family is supportive. They come to shows, pageants, or fundraisers as much as possible. I have one biological brother and we are nine years apart, but we look like twins. Our parents have a picture of Angel and Chuck on one side of the hutch, and on the other, a picture of Xavier and Ophelia. People always ask, "Oh, you have two sets of twins?" My mom's answer, "Nope, we had a son and a daughter that switch gender from time to time."

❀**Jamel Knight:** I am the only impersonator in my family. My brothers and sisters find it interesting saying, "makes sense" for me to do. They have not been to any show because of scheduling. All of us living in different areas, but we are planning on them all coming to one of my shows one day. My mom does not really talk about it much, but she says as long as I am happy and being productive, she is good.

❀**Master Cameron Eric Leon:** I told my mum the day before my first show, because she asked what I was doing for my birthday. She was a little confused at first, but I think that when I came out as bisexual to my parents, which was the bigger thing they had to grapple with, DRAG was not really a big deal. It took them a few days to process, I think, but after that, they were fine. They have been really supportive and have come to every show I have done in Toronto, Canada, so far. I even got my mum up to dance with me during one of my numbers, once. My dad is an opera singer, so performing was in the family, but DRAG or impersonation was not.

❀**Welland Dowd:** I think my parents were a little confused at first, although now I am out to them as a transgender guy, so to them it is perfectly normal.

❀**Howie Feltersnatch:** I am the only impersonator in the family. My mom is ok with it and sometimes helps me with costuming, but does not want to come to any of the shows. My big sister, though, has been to a few shows, and tries to come when she is available and has a baby sitter.

❀**MaXx Decco:** I am the only entertainer in my family. My little sister knows, but has not been to a show. My mom has an idea, though it is never discussed. She is like Martha Stewart with a bible. I love her but we are not ready this conversation. My dad lives in a different state, but I am sure he would be cool, he wanted a son.

❀**Julius M. SeizeHer:** My family does not know. I do not plan to tell them since they have differing views from me, so I just keep them sane

❀**Stefan LeDude:** My family is fine with it. I am the only one in the family.

❀**Nolan Southwood:** My mom and brother try to come to every single show I have. My brother is definitely my biggest fan, he texts me to recommend songs all the time. My dad does not know too much about it, but has no problem with me dressing more masculine in my personal life and knows I perform DRAG. I am the only impersonator in my family, though.

Jonah Godfather of DRAG: My wife, kids, mother, and my sisters are very supportive of everything I do. It did take some time to come to terms with DRAG and transgender, but now it is just another part of me.

Jensen C. Dean: I am the only performer in my family. We do not talk about DRAG. My mom hates me doing DRAG now as much as she did when I started, refering to it as, "that thing you do that I hate," and will not talk to me if I am in face. As much as she does not like it, she always votes for me when I am nominated for community awards and wants me to be successful.

Dionysus W Khaos: I am the only impersonator in my family. My mom went to one show and walked out on me. I was raised very, very strict Catholic. That was a year ago and to this day, she is still vehemently opposed to the craft. My brothers know I do it but have never seen me perform.

Jack E. Dickinson: I am the only one in my blood family. They know about it vaguely. I live far from them, and they are not involved in my life. I keep it that way intentionally. They are open about me being queer and trans, but I do not think they could handle some of the stuff I do on stage. Some of it is very sexual. I am not comfortable sharing it with them.

Travis Hard: My family is completely okay with me doing this. My mom shares pictures of me in face all the time. I am the only performer of this kind in my family that I know of. They all accept it and listen to my stories eagerly.

Jake Bastard: I am transmasculine so my family was used to seeing me "cross dress" as it is just a part of my every daywear [only using a different style]. I just get to be more flamboyant while on stage. I am pre op and pre t, which makes things a bit more interesting. It is nice to be known throughout a certain social group as a persona much closer to how I identify, but with humor and glitz thrown in, and focusing more on masculine traits in place of a more androgynous appearance. My father seems to be proud of me for pursuing a long-sought dream, and my sister shows very little interest in my craft. Neither have been to see a single performance and that is kind of depressing to me, but it is their choice.
I come from a French Catholic family and am the only DRAG performer.

Clark Kunt: My family had a much harder time understanding I identify as gender fluid than they did understanding I wanted to perform with gender on stage. I think it surprised them that I got out in front of a big crowd of people and danced, because I am ridiculously shy in my non-DRAG life. It was less impersonation and more gender exploration in front of an audience. I am certainly the only one in my family who performs.

Emilio: I am the only impersonator in my family, but they are incredibly supportive. My dad even helps me tie my ties and even lets me borrow his!

❋**Juan Kerr:** I am the only impersonator. They were a bit freaked out, but now I think they are just like, 'Oh, it is just Beth'. It is just fun for me. I think even if I did identify as transgender, they would understand and get used to it eventually, but it does not go that deep for me.

❋**Trey C. Michaels:** My family was not surprised at all. In fact, they said they could always see me performing as a king.

❋**Bailey Saint James:** My family is very supportive. I explained to them a few times why I do what I do and how it is not the same as being transgender. My performing has helped my brother the most to become aware of the LGBT community and change his mind on homophobia. I am very proud of him, and the fact that I have helped just one person realize we are all the same inside; well, that is what it is all about to me.

❋**Soco Dupree:** Mom and dad highly disliked it. My sisters however, went to the bar to see me perform.

❋**LoUis CYfer:** At the DRAG idol final, there was a picture taken of my mum grabbing my 'cous-cous' balls ... Safe to say they support me.

❋**Stefon Royce Iman:** I am the only impersonator in my family. My mom took it very well. She does not mind.

❋**King Ramsey:** Most of my family took it pretty well. My family on my dad's side is very supportive when it comes to me. My older brother is a DRAG queen, so it was not much of a surprise with me being a king.

❋**Santana Romero:** My family was not surprised at all when they found out I became a male impersonator. We all are a bunch of artists and practice our respective art forms. Everyone has been extraordinarily supportive and as far as I know, I am the only one in my family who does DRAG.

❋**Smitty O'Toole:** My family supports me 100%. My grandmother loves to watch my shows. I am the only impersonator in my family.

❋**Luke Ateraz:** My family has always been supportive! Much of my family has seen me perform at least once. My family now has myself, my son, Cody Ateraz, and my wife is a diva, Roxi Ateraz.

❋**Boi Wonder:** They had several years to get used to it. I was very butch when I was about 16, I became more feminine since and do DRAG on occasion. I think my family prefers me to look less butch in general, so they are happy that DRAG is a temporary fixture.

❋**Devin G. Dame:** I am the only performer in my family. They did not understand it at first, but accepted who I am.

Chapter Eighteen
"Explain your inner circle."

❀**Freddy Prinze Charming:** There are quite a few people I have in my "circle." I feel I can bounce ideas off, get their opinions, ask for help, get suggestions, etc., they are Eddie C. Broadway, Gunner Daimon Gatlyn, Dominic Von Strap, Felicia Minor, Romeo White, and Teddy Michael.

❀**Kody Sky:** I would not call it an inner circle for me. I have many people that I interact with. I try to give everyone the upmost respect and treat them equally. It is only the times where I might think I cannot trust a person that I either avoid them or just simply stay civilized in an impersonal manner.

❀**Adam All:** I have some worthy of discussing, but would not want to single people out, except maybe Rogue DRAG King, who is epic.

❀**Travis Luvermore:** I am in an area where there are limited DRAG kings. I have been blessed to find a former Las Vegas, Nevada, USA, DRAG queen that is a Judy Garland/Liza Minnelli impersonator and has given me awesome advice that has expanded my craft and improve my performances.

❀**AJ Menendez:** The person who comes to mind with regard to this question has been my mentor since I first started performing as an illusionist. He is not exactly in my "circle," he has become more like "family" to me. Gage Gatlyn is famous for his Tim McGraw impersonations. Not only does his physical illusion resemble the singer, but Gage's moves and mannerism are the same as well, which is no easy task at all. I tried to do an actual impersonation once as AJ McLean, whom I physically resemble, but found it to be extremely difficult. Gage makes it look so realistic and easy, and to say I admire his craft and ability to do it would be an understatement.

❀**Joshua Micheals:** I have a great group of friends, performers and other wise, who fully support me. I love the Haus of Jadore.

❀**Orion Blaze Browne:** I have multiple brothers on stage and off. I am also close with a few queens. We all push each other to grow on stage. It is also great to have people to bounce number, costume, or pageant ideas off.

❀**Chance Wise:** My DRAG sister, Rachel, is the one person who always had my back, even when having my back was not the popular. We relate to each other on a deep level and support each other to no end. She's also great at finding good songs that are popular that suit me really well.

❀**Cody Wellch Klondyke:** Unfortunately, in Wisconsin, USA, there are not many kings. Competitions and titles are more important than friendships, so we keep our distance from one another. I get my advice from Ravyn Entertainment Troupe or my DRAG mom, Candi Stratton.

❀**Marcus Mayhem:** I have a few; I call them family. They are just as crazy and crafty as I am, King Mykal Kristen and Prince Blaze Kristen, to name two. We all hear music in a different way than most and put so much humor in what we do, we always try to make our crowds laugh until they cry. Even on a song like "Sail" by AWOL, to which Blaze heard the word sale not sail. He was the only person who had a garage on stage.

❀**D-Luv Saviyon:** The USofA brotherhood in the USA, Shon Franklin Thomas, Xander Kinidy, Ivory Onyx, Damian Matrix-Gritte, Teddy Michael, Sybastian Sr. Kennedy Armani, Asten Marten, Syr Kamron are the closest. They give me both DRAG and personal advice. They also are there whenever I need them. I am a lucky guy.

❀**Marty Brown:** Many brothers. Macximus, Shook ByNature, and kids, Firewalker Mi, Cory Stone, and Beth Williamson. We are close and helpful to each other. Even I, performing for over 33 years, has something to offer.

❀**Travis Hard:** I have a DRAG family. It is very random and split up along the country. I like to think everyone I meet and compete with, becomes family and part of my circle.

❀**King Dante:** Spiky van Dykey is awesome as both female and male.

❀**Justin Cider:** Leilani Price is my goddess! My DRAG wife's and mine go to person on anything DRAG. I love her so much and admire everything she does and continues to do both on stage and off. She is the kind of performer I hope to be. She helps with whatever, and whenever I need it. I do not know where I would be if it were not for her sexy, all be it, sort of fake ass.

❀**Clint Torres:** My inner circle is my dad's parents, the Fresno Fresbians, my DRAG wife, and my best bro. These people encouraged me to keep doing me, keep performing both on and off the stage. They mean the world to me.

❀**Hurricane Savage:** I know many kings, but do not socialize outside DRAG. My DRAG mom, sister, and son are the only ones that I see outside the bar.

❀**Stormm:** I would have to say my good friends and sisters, Monica Divine and Mer Cedes. They will be honest and straightforward with you. I look up to both these wonderful gals, but anybody I perform with throughout the years I consider family.

❀**Rychard "Alpha" Le'Sabre:** My DRAG family from AB Pure Entertainment.

❀**Shane Rebel Caine:** My best friend, who I consider to be my actual brother, is also a DRAG king. We share the same last name for a DRAG family that we started together and we were both "adopted" by the same DRAG parents at the same exact time. I started DRAG a year before him. I have been able to help him get a better start. Having my best friend performing alongside me makes the shows more fun. It allows me to have that person to perform in my songs with me, should I need a second person. I personally struggle with rap, so when I do a song that has a spot in it; he usually has it covered with no problem. I also have several close friends that are DRAG queens. It really just makes the "DRAG world" a lot more fun when you can all be like one big family.

❀**Rasta Boi Punany:** My brothers from Pittsburgh, Pennsylvania, USA, have been extraordinaire to me. I have my performance daddy and his queen who guidelined my professional craft. I have since acquired a mentor.

❀**Dakota Rain:** I have my queen, Nadia Rain, Xander Lee Rain, Cascade Paqure Rain, Ked Black Rain, Irish Rose Rain, and Stone Parque. They all offer a little something, but most importantly, lots of support for each other.

❀**Ashton The Adorable Lover:** I do not have an inner circle. I have a few DRAG friends to bounce music or talents off of, to get music mixes or mixed, can help with a costume or design, and knows where to get stones.

❀**Spacee Kadett:** Too many to name names. I am so appreciative of my genuine friendships with fellow performers. Mentorships are important in both directions, but a peer is just as invaluable. Someone in shoes like yours so you can vent to each other without being judged, encourage each other from similar perspectives, laugh and swap stories that you feel. Because sometimes it is not about make-up and costumes, it is just about life.

❀**Vinnie Marconi:** I am blessed to spend time with OUTSIDE of DRAG; Andrew Citino, AJ Menendez, Rico M Taylor, and my DRAG son, Aaron Phoenix. They help me with ideas, moves, advice, and to help keep it fresh. When I am too old to do DRAG, these people will still be my FRIENDS!

❀**Kenneth J. Squires:** Not have many in Lexington, Kentucky, USA. There are others in Louisville, Kentucky, that gave me pointers and are willing to help. I have many DRAG kings/male impersonators I look up to and would like to become like them when it comes to entertaining.

❀**Rico M Taylor:** AJ Menendez, Vinnie Marconi, Chance Wise, Aiden Taylor, Justice Darnell, and Ken Dartanyan, to name a few great friends and inspirations. They have always kept it real and have been there for me when I was not there for myself, but Florida, USA, all around, has always had my back. All the kings here are amazing.

❀**Adam DoEve:** In my town, it just me, but in the city an hour away, I consider the people there my DRAG family. I can bounce ideas of them about music and costumes. I also like it that we can give each other points.

❀**Kruz Mhee:** Chynna Dohl, K'hia Campbell, Solitaire, Blac Jac, Stacie Storme, and a new entertainer Kharris.

❀**Hawk Stuart:** Vinnie Marconi, Aaron Phoenix, Persian Prince, and Rico M Taylor. All I know outside of the DRAG world, and all amazing people.

❈B J Bottoms: My DRAG family. We all have a personal relationship with one another. For us, we are not just a DRAG family, we ARE a family.

❈Silk Steele Prince: Unfortunately, I never had that. I had to fend for myself. I am currently looking for a DRAG family as I speak…

❈SirMandingo Thatis: A DRAG queen and my very best friend, I call her my baby momma, and I am her baby daddy. She inspires me to go the next level in my art and to continue to inspire new kings as they come onto the scene because that is where I receive my drive to keep giving the crowd more.

❈Flex Jonez: We are scattered in our state. Most are DRAG queens in my personal circle. They are great with wigs, makeup, and costumes. We share ideas, and more, with each other regarding performance.

❈Atown: The USofA brotherhood in the USA has to be the best idea. Although we do not see these bois day to day, I feel like I know them personally. There is also so much inspiration from my local brothers and friends inside and outside of DRAG.

❈Cody Wellch Klondyke: USofA MI brothers in the USA are the best. Not only are they my brothers, but they are my inner circle.

❈George De Micheal: The DRAG Kings of Manchester, United Kingdom.

❈Chasin Love: My best friend is a queen. She inspires me by helping me see inside of the person, working on myself, and looking at this is a job. I play to the crowd that is there, even if there are only a few people there. Perform as if the room was packed.

❈Colin Grey: A good friend of mine is the entertainer, Mr. Logan Rider. He won Mr. Gay Kansas City in Kansas City, Missouri, USA, the first year we had it, and I was his first alternate. Logan is very passionate about the craft and I am better for having him in my circle of friends. He offers plenty of knowledgeable experience and advice.

❈Eddie C. Broadway: I have many in my inner circle, Freddy Prinze Charming, Gunner Daimon Gatlyn, Brandon Packer, Ayden Layne, and Dominic Von Strap, to name a few I can communicate with on numbers, shows, etc. and provide support.

❈Dominic: Von Strap: Mainly, Eddie C. Broadway and Freddy Prinze Charming, we can talk about concepts and costuming ideas. They taught me everything I know about the craft and continue to help me be a better performer and person in general.

❈Phantom: There were not very many kings around, just queens. Halfway through my journey, I made a couple of friends that became family. I asked one who performs as a DRAG king, Chris Mandingo, to be my DRAG son. We have been helped each other improve our DRAG. I am grateful to him and his wife, Chantell Cookie Turpin.

❈Sam Masterson: I have a friend that does DRAG as a woman and I guess they offer me the chance to do duets. I feel I do much better solo.

❀**Chris Mandingo:** My DRAG dad Phantom. He is always given me the drive to show my art the way I want to show it, and not to be ashamed of who I am. My big brother, Miles Long, and I do not always talk as much as I wish we could or are as connected as we used to be, but I always hear him in the back of my mind motivating me to do better, harder, stronger. I love them both because without them, I do not think I would have pushed myself to be the king I am becoming today. Thank you both.

❀**Jack King:** NO one. I am the only king here in Copenhagen, Denmark.

❀**Kameo Dupree:** My circle does not include performers.

❀**Xavier Bottoms:** My inner circle? I currently mentor 12 DRAG children. All of them but two are impersonators. I have numerous DRAG nieces and nephews. Some of them have or has had national titles. The Bottoms family is always encouraging each other to be better. We help each other. Whether it is building props, stoning outfits, making mixes or coming up with new talent ideas, we do it together. Family motto: Bottoms Up!

❀**Stefan LeDude:** Back in Montreal, Canada, I was in a troupe that is pretty tight. I just moved to Halifax, but I am already making some great friends with the other DRAG kings out here. As I mentioned before, my girlfriend is an on and off DRAG king, and she helps me out a lot creatively and such.

❀**Jamel Knight:** I have a few people in my DRAG circle. I have known Ryder Knightly and Macximus for over a year now and we are pretty close to them. I have also connected with several other kings such as Mr. Charlie Smith and Shook ByNature that have encouraged and inspired me to continue growing in this craft. It is all about building a brotherhood of strength and unity and helping each other to achieve the individual goals we have set.

❀**Howie Feltersnatch:** The Fake Mustache Troupe is more like a second family to me. We grow together as performers and as individuals. Without the other performers, I do not know where I would be today.

❀**Welland Dowd:** The Bromantics Montreal DRAG Kings in Canada are my DRAG brothers and very good friends.

❀**Michael Christian:** I have a few people I am beyond thankful for. While it all started with the common bond of entertaining, we have become more about life. They help build props, create costumes, and encourage everything. Then you can grill dinner, have a bon fire, and laugh all night about random things.

❀**Julius M. SeizeHer:** Blaire Phoenix and Jesse Mackonme showed me the ropes and give me advice.

❀**Jonah Godfather of DRAG:** Clitt Black is my DRAG brother. Even though our lives are very different, we have so much in common. The others in my inner circle are Candy James and Jennifer James. I have known them for over twenty years and they were both very instrumental in helping me onstage and still do to this day.

❀**Jack E. Dickinson:** I have extensively worked with Ian Poe Kerr as a co-organizer and performer. We think alike and have an awesome synergy on stage and off. We became close friends through the years as well.

❀**Clark Kunt:** Members of The Halifax DRAG Kings and Haus of are my inner circle. Many of my other close friends no longer live in the same city and within DRAG I've found a group of folks who share similar gender identities and have similar interests, so naturally we have bonded. My DRAG family pushes and inspires me in my craft - whether through watching their evolution on stage, performing alongside in group numbers, organizing shows and bringing new concepts to the stage, or just through sitting around hot glueing glitter and studs on our latest costumes and props.

❀**Emilio:** Ceasar Hart in Seattle, Washington, USA, has been an awesome collaborator! There is no rivalry; we just bring each other up.

❀**Juan Kerr:** Currently working on a short routine with Adam and Apple. I have tried to work with other kings before but it does not always pull off. Anyone who is open to ideas and easy going whilst still being productive.

❀**Brandon KC Young-Taylor:** I have several kings that are in my inner circle but I know many kings across the USA that have influenced me in one way or another. So many worth mentioning that I could never name them all!

❀**Trey C. Michaels:** I have my DRAG family in Phoenix who I try to talk to on a daily basis, whether through messages or comments to let them know I am thinking of them. My DRAG dad, Freddy Prinze Charming, has been so supportive and has taught me so much. I am in Albuquerque, New Mexico, USA now and I am finally meeting people and creating an inner circle here.

❀**Bailey Saint James:** I do not have an "inner circle" but my outer circle includes most of the kings in the state of Wisconsin and Chicago, Illinois, USA. I would discuss anything DRAG with any of them.

❀**Aaron Phoenix:** My entire "inner circle" consists of entertainers-impersonators. Some of them have become my family, and they offer a lot more to me than just people to bounce DRAG ideas off - they are my support group and cheerleaders in life, too.

❀**Persian Prince:** When I first started DRAG I looked to those in my inner circle for DRAG just for DRAG advice. Now I look to them for anything and everything because they aren't apart of just my DRAG life they are part of my everyday life! We laugh and have fun... they are my mentors my friends and my family.... and its fun when we all come up with different ideas and to see how excited each one gets and I have to say I love spending time with these mentors and friends because they want me to the best king I can be and nothing beats seeing how proud they are at the end of the day when they see how their advice and teachings help me grow

❀**Stefon Royce Iman:** Ivory Onyx, Gage Gatlyn, AJ Menendez, Romance St James, and Anson Reign are my brothers. We help each other.

❀**Soco Dupree:** I have quite a few from other kings, to queens, to divas, and even GQ. I value their opinion and their critique. It is the only way to grow. An entertainer should never quit learning.

❀**Mike Oxready:** I no longer have performers in my inner circle. For years, I was in a troupe with my then-partner, and a good friend.

❀**B J Armani:** I would not be anywhere without all the amazing performers and people I have met. There are those performers that push you and I would like to give a shout out to Lyle Love-It. Without you, I would have never received a crown! DJ Skittles it was your idea for my own show and you kept at me until I said yes. A year and a half later we are still going.

❀**Smitty O'Toole:** I am dating an amazing DRAG queen, Vivica Perry. There are many performers in my city. We have ab inner circle of DRAG here. They are sisters and brothers; we treat each other that way, as family.

❀**Jensen C. Dean:** I would have to say that my inner circle is rather small, but someone that is very close to me and has been in my inner circle is the queen that I refer to as 'My Queen.' She was my Miss in 2012 when I was Mister Phoenix Gay Pride 2012 in Phoenix, Arizona, USA. Her name is Grecia Montes D'Occa and she amazing. Been my rock for the past 2 years, she was even a bridesmaid in my wedding.

❀**Luke Ateraz:** It keeps shrinking. I have my wife, son, and mother-in-law.

❀**E. M. Shaun:** I have a very good group of kings that I admire and have supported me over the years...here are a few names: Shook ByNature, King Ramsey, Mr. Charlie Smith, Dakota Rain, and Montana Madness.

❀**Devin G. Dame:** In my inner circle, I have several. Just to name two, Gage Gatlyn and Gunner Gatlyn, we always swap ideas and creative ways to make our things better.

Place Faces Without Peeking At The Answer Key In Book Two

Name the performers without checking on DRAG411.com

Chapter Nineteen
"Who was your support group in the beginning for you as an entertainer? What did they offer?"

✿**Shook ByNature:** My support group at the beginning of my DRAG career has been my brothers of the stage and more recently my extended DRAG family, the Davidsons! It is hard when you are trying to figure out how you want your persona to evolve, but it pays to have someone to bounce ideas off and you also grow paying it forward. Thanks to social media I can hit up kings all over and ask questions and vice versa.

✿**B J Armani:** As a straight woman, there were many thoughts on my ability to do DRAG. It was not that I did not have the outgoing persona, just the thought of a "straight" person doing DRAG. My best friend of more than a decade, Raquel Smith, was more than supportive. She helped sew my costumes no matter how nuts they got. My husband, who is in the Air Force, told me to "be as good as they are." There was no hesitation in my inner circle of friends. The hesitation came mostly from the fellow performers. They thought I was doing this as a joke. That thought did not last long. I got tips and ideas from kings and queens but mostly I had to find my own path. I became a hybrid between the two, not because I am straight but because EVERY king needs some sparkle and zazz!

✿**Koomah:** I was (and still am) part of a DRAG troupe. They have always been supportive and community based. No hierarchy, no DRAG daddies, no competition; it was always more about skill shares and acknowledging that everyone had some things they could teach others and some things they can learn from others. We support each other as a group and as solo performers. We create numbers with each other as a group and help each other's solo acts. We focus on giving back to the community and fundraisers. The troupe was also performing at the same top surgery fundraiser where I did my first ever performance and invited me to perform in one of their shows the next weekend. Then I was invited to get more involved and do group numbers, I was encouraged to be creative and try new things. They offered me a stage to try things out, suggestions, encouragement, and friendship.

✿**D-Luv Saviyon:** At first it was Bushra St. James, Anonymous Men, Josephyn Edwards, China Charles, and Deshay Campbell, just to name a few. They offered encouragement, the basics of DRAG etiquette (do's and don'ts), tips, tricks, brutally honest critiques, and a sense of family.

✿**Brandon KC Young-Taylor:** My support in the beginning was a DRAG king group, Momma's Boys. I was fortunate enough to be a part of the group. We also had a very supportive community behind us!

🍀**Clint Torres:** In the beginning, my DRAG dad, Atown. He taught me how to look, dress, and act the part. The most important thing he taught me was confidence. Without him, I never would have had the guts to make it.

🍀**Vinnie Marconi:** My support group is the same as it was then, but larger. My friends encouraged me to be an illusionist, and still send me songs to perform. They inspire me. I could not do costuming without the help of other performers. They are the tailors and E-6000 (adhesive) junkies!

🍀**Freddy Prinze Charming:** At first my support came from DRAGstar Cabaret in Tucson, Arizona, USA. With them, I explored my creativity and be a part of a group with incredibly talented individuals.

🍀**Gus Magendor:** My mother, Rickie Martin, was my support. Yes, my mother's name is Rickie Martin. She told me how silly I was but was there to help me if I needed it. As well as my friends were at my shows to cheer me on and make me more confident.

🍀**Chance Wise:** My support group when I started were the other members of Twisted Entertainment, which is no longer together and the group has scattered into the wind... My support group is so small right now I can count them on one hand, but they are amazing and honest and inspire me.

🍀**Travis Hard:** My DRAG wife, Mya Lynn. You will see photos of us together. She was always there when I needed her went above and beyond for me. Unfortunately DRAG for her is on hold, but she is out doing the sisters of perpetual indulgence thing and I think that totally rocks!

🍀**Dakota Rain:** My support group are good friends from the Rainbow Inn (now closed but they own the Hide-A-Way) in Lake Wylie, South Carolina, USA. Tammy Black, Yvonne Crowder, Mrs. Margie Reid, and the list could go on and on, but most importantly my family; my mom was my biggest supporter; he passed before she saw perform. They offered all kinds of support and help, from picking out songs, picking out clothes, how to dress and so on. They still do.

🍀**Rasta Boi Punany:** My wife is my manager. She offers me guidance on music, how to be equally professional and sexy, and gave me the freedom to be me on stage.

🍀**Adam All:** My DRAG mum, Lucinda Lashes, gave me advice and some backing tracks, set me up with three gigs, before abandoning me to my fate. I had friends come see my show, but I was alone in it for the first year.

🍀**Campbell Reid Andrews:** I did not have support when I first started; I kind of just went with the flow. When I became an Andrews, my family and my fiancé became my support. They help whenever they can with industry advice. As far as male illusion, I am the only one in my family so I use a lot of my theatre, dance, and performance knowledge and skills. Research and such and practice, practice, practice.

🍀**Lyle Love-It:** Partner.

🍀**Eddie C. Broadway:** My wife and Sisterzz Twisted!

❦**Dominic: Von Strap:** So much support, mostly from Eddie C. Broadway and Freddy Prinze Charming. Eddie had been my mentor from the beginning and taught me how to bypass my allergy to adhesive. If it were not for him, I never would have started. Freddy helped me with tips and tricks for binding and makeup. They both have been there to help me with the pageant I was in as well as other performances. I am forever grateful for all they have done for me not only in DRAG, but in life in general.

❦**Stormm:** My partner.

❦**Coti Blayne:** Some friends are my support group with my then roommate coming to my shows, helping me with ideas, and DRAG shopping.

❦**Travis Luvermore:** I had a great group of DRAG kings and queens at our local bar that helped me with so much advice. How to dress, the lip-syncing, the many ways they did facial and chest hair, and how to bind. We would kid around and go DRAG shopping together at the thrift stores.

❦**Ben Eaten:** My support group was my girlfriend and friends. They all would answer my thousands of questions about songs and costumes along with listening to my performance songs on repeat for weeks. They helped me with my painting and making sure my facial hair was even, they did everything they could to help me.

❦**AJ Menendez:** Wolfie, Remmington Steel, and Gage Gatlyn.

❦**Adam DoEve:** Orion Blaze Browne answers questions I may have had and to give me a pointers, but I also have to say that the performers from Hot Metal Hardware has help a lot over the past year by first letting me perform with them as a guest performer and also pointers here and there.

❦**Atown:** My support group was made up of the crew (DRAG brothers) and my fiancée. She was a little hesitant at first, for the fear of other people "touching me." I assured her it did not work that way. Not even strippers are allowed to be touched. She wanted an inside look, so she actually joined the group as a "faux queen." After that, most of my family and friends came out to support at the shows. Two particular friends from Michigan, USA, Rita Gross (Boots) and Chloe Tarnowski, showed me exactly what I needed to do, as they had experience helping with the Motor City DRAG Kings. They were with me every step of the way and traveled with me to my first pageant. Mister California USofA MI held in California, USA.

❦**Orion Blaze Browne:** In the beginning, my support came from my partner at the time and two kings, Kevaughn and DJ. Shortly after my mother, Kourtney adopted me who has been a huge support and mentor in helping me grow and the troupe I was a founding member. I have had much support over the years from DRAG brothers, my DRAG mother, my partners, my friends, and the community.

❀**Hurricane Savage:** I was alone in it all. I did have other kings (Jimmy Skyy D'Stone, William Vanity Matrix, Coti Blayne, and Damian Matrix-Gritte) to ask questions, but for the most part, it was just me at first.

❀**Marcus Mayhem:** King Mykal Khrystian for inspiring me to be better, Blaze for showing me I can be crazy, Shannon for helping with songs (even if I did not always listen), myself, for not giving up on myself when I tried a new place and only made a dollar even if I did three songs.

❀**Rychard "Alpha" Le'Sabre:** I did not have much in the way of support, outside of my girlfriend at the time. But as I went along I gained friends in the DRAG scene that have I have to this day, 7 years later. Some of them the best friends I have ever had.

❀**Scorpio:** My friends are definitely my support in the beginning and still are now. I have gained support from people I did not know when I started just by talking to people after shows. I do believe it would have been harder to start out without the few friends who have always been there. My girlfriend has definitely been a great supporter, helping me with any and everything.

❀**Shane Rebel Caine:** My best friend who now performs alongside me was my main support group in the beginning. He was the only one who came to all of my performances for the first four months. He is still my best support person. I also have a couple of friends and two of my aunts who supported from the beginning but did not show up to many performances. But they all kept encouraging me and said they loved my videos, my best friend kept pushing me forward even when my nerves would get the best of me.

❀**B J Bottoms:** My biggest support group is my DRAG family. My DRAG father, Xavier Bottoms, has guided me from the start, along with the other members of my family. They help me with pageants, shows, anything and everything.

❀**Ashton The Adorable Lover:** Mostly my brother, Dillon MrDecardeza Dalton, and performers such as Ashley Adams, Bunny Flingus, Milton Laycock, Eva LeStrange, Coda Fatts. I probably forgotten to mention a few.

❀**Stefon SanDiego:** Truly, 20 years ago, "Kings" were still struggling to set foot upon those stages as the diversity came with the queens and the spotlight. Carmen SanDiego, my DRAG mother, was always insightful in all I was as a performer. Chelsea DelRay, Porsha DelRay, Damien Chase, Raven Cicconi, and many more included, finally emerged into a family. A family is united through the bindings of that stage floor, and even more so in the dressing rooms. I cannot express the importance of a quality support network when it comes to the entertainment industry in our communities. Not only does the support include binding and such, but also a higher level of emotional support as well as ambitions. Our families would often gather to design costumes, themes, ideas, venues, benefits, as well as confidence talks that included critiquing each other. In all, as an entertainer, any and all support is greatly appreciated, no matter the source!

✤Pierce Gabriel: The other kings and queens on the show were a big help. A couple took me under their wing to give me pointers on improving. There were a few non-performing members of the Bash helping a great deal from the audience perspective. I was what I call a "Village Child." Instead of having one or two DRAG parents to raise and shape me, I was raised by the entire cast.

✤Alec Allnight: Everyone was super supportive. I had a built in DRAG family. My older, straight, and married fire-fighter brother even came to a couple of shows! I think I have been fortunate in that regard. All my DRAG brothers share what works and does not work and we all try to help whenever we can, whether it is makeup tips, props, or backing each other up in performances.

✤Brandon KC Young-Taylor: My support group is my family, partner, DRAG king troupe, and our local bar. Over the years, the DRAG king group and our home bar has dispersed but I have gained so much support from other areas in the community!

✤Kruz Mhee: My partner Jennifer, aka Chynna Dohl. I had been performing for more than 15 years faux DRAG. We had been together only a few months when she said, "you look uncomfortable in that." I was wearing a corset and go-go boots. I said I had always thought performing as a male would fit me better. She suggested giving it a try and I never turned back. I love it and it suits me…or so I am told. I would not go back for anything. Within the first year, we started our own performing group, "Generation NxXxT," and I have helped birth more than a handful of kings and faux DRAG entertainers. After the first year, most everyone in the community accepted me as a king and not just a female playing dress up.

✤Hawk Stuart: My friends and adoptive family have always been there helping me out. Not just with the little things, but other things from outfits to wear to music, helping me make sure I look good.

✤Ryder Knightly: My DRAG brothers really pushed me to become better, even when I doubted myself. Later on started to network, and became friends with a bunch of DRAG queens that help me take on a whole new look.

✤Kruz Mhee: I began performing thanks to Lady Ace Von Costa. She's the reason my first performance went well. My partner made all the difference. She is in no way an average woman. She has been loving and supportive since I decided to perform as a male. When everyone I knew said it was a silly idea and or it would not go over she still pushed me to do what I wanted to do and felt would be right for me. Lucky for me she was right. Jennifer a.k.a. Chynna has never faltered by my side and my decision to perform as a male.

❀**Silk Steele Prince:** My support group was my immediate friends and partner. They kept me motivated. They came to all my performances, helped me with my routines and getting dressed before a show.

❀**Flex Jonez:** My DRAG family helped with suggestions, skill, and truth.

❀**SirMandingo Thatis:** My now wife was my biggest supporter and fan and she continues to help me enhance my art. She always gives me that extra boost in a positive manner that keeps me going further in the art of DRAG.

❀**Kenneth J. Squires:** My partner at the beginning of my DRAG career helped me a lot, but through the years, I had other partners. This one partner did not help much, so I had to rely on my extended DRAG family. I asked questions to people I know that would help me. My partner now helps me a lot, is my biggest fan, and makes a huge difference in my doing DRAG.

❀**Cody Wellch Klondyke:** In the beginning was my partner I was with, and also my daughter, my DRAG family, and the Corner Bar. My partner I had at the time would help me get ready, and also help me pick out my outfits. Now it is just my DRAG brothers and me when I have questions I ask.

❀**George De Micheal:** The persons that have been there for me from the start are Valentino King, Lydia Rullow, Boi Wonder, and the DRAG kings of Manchester. Mr. Tony Cooper has always backed us and gave us a place to call home at VIA on Canal St. in Manchester, United Kingdom.

❀**Thug Passion:** My first girlfriend, friends, and coworkers. They offered me a comfort zone on stage. I knew as long as they were out there, somebody was going to like me, whether I was the worst or the best one. I knew they would tell me if I needed to loosen up or if there was something I should do or not do again. They were my critics. I knew for them it was not about how cute or sexy I was, it was about being the best I could be.

❀**Bootzy Edwards Collynz:** I had awesome support from my dance team, DRAG mom Tracy Edwards, and a few queens that I had worked with.

❀**Colin Grey:** In the beginning, it was my boyfriend, Jim, and my best friend, Spence, who were there for every show. The queens also kept me going.

❀**E. M. Shaun:** When I began, I was single. It was my best friend and some of my other close friends who supported me. Over the first year, my girlfriend at the time was very encouraging and supportive as well.

❀**Jack King:** My dad helps with money for my costumes and cheers for me.

❀**Kameo Dupree:** Biggest supporter, from day one, is my wife's grandmother! She would find me old jackets or shirts. She still gives me jewelry. My support system was not that big but my sisters, mom, spouse, and granny have always been by my side.

❀**Stefan LeDude:** A couple of friends, and my friend Mimz, who encouraged me from the beginning. Now she has started doing DRAG, about a year ago.

❀**Xavier Bottoms:** My support group was The Academy of Washington, District of Columbia, USA. It is a group organization for all types of entertainers (queens, kings, transgender, straight, and bio) in the community. The group began over 52 years ago and is still going strong. It really taught me to be a well-rounded entertainer. I am currently still a member as well.

❀**Jamel Knight:** My support group was the house cast for "Jump Off Thursdays." We would have regular meetings and rehearsals to discuss the previous shows, ideas for new shows, and ways we could improve our performances. They really helped me to learn a lot in a short amount of time.

❀**Clark Kunt:** My partner at the time helped me with my first show. Two kings and a queen pushed me on stage. They were in the audience cheering for me, their 'competition', and even as my knees got weak and my throat got dry, I knew I could do it with them there. Now one of them is my DRAG husband, Felix Static. He offers encouragement, a duet/trio partner, a meaningful friendship, ongoing support and an understanding of what family meant in this community. If it were not for him, I would not still be doing this and having the amazing opportunities I have had.

❀**Master Cameron Eric Leon:** I have been very lucky. I have an amazing friend group, and I got into the burlesque scene very quickly. They were, and are, an amazing support network for new performers.

❀**Bruno Diaz:** My support system was my DRAG family. I have been involved with them for years. We support shows, learn, and have a good time. The HART family started in 1993. We do not share the last name, but they brought to the table friendship, encouragement, experience, and support. From genuine people, is priceless.

❀**DeVery Bess:** The DRAG king troupe I joined was really supportive. They listened and gave feedback, and always positively encouraging every one.

❀**Welland Dowd:** I got started as part of the Dukes of DRAG, and Jack E Dickinson and Ian Poe Kerr were big inspirations for me.

❀**Julius M. SeizeHer:** OneNTen Phoenix USA, Jesse Mackonme, and my college buddies, offering encouragement and advice.

❀**Jonah Godfather of DRAG:** My biggest supporter has always been my wife. She gets me to shows, makes costumes, stones jackets, takes pictures, and is always there for all of the performers. My kids also have been very supportive. My son, who is now 15, used to come in when he was a lot younger and "help" me practice. I have a certain circle of queens that encourage me to keep going even when the times get tough.

❀**Howie Feltersnatch:** My first few shows I was really shy and knew few people in the troupe. My friends were my biggest support by coming to every show I performed for the first six months. As I performed more and more, I got to know the other performers and they became my biggest support group.

✽**Lyle Love-It:** Family, friends, and partner.

✽**Jack E. Dickinson:** The people I met at the first gig I performed at and a few others we worked with before founding a troupe. We shared tips for make-up, hair, binding, packing, and performing masculinity. We helped each other fulfill our ideas for acts. We also went out together in DRAG.

✽**Clark Kunt:** My partner, and a few family and friends offer encouragement and an audience. Once I found a group of performers, they too became influential supports.

✽**Emilio:** My family offers support, encouragement & came to my shows.

✽**Juan Kerr:** The friends in the cabaret scene, little as it was. The friends involved in the setting up of 'Cherry on Top' burlesque in my hometown. I never had a DRAG family. I recently adopted a DRAG dad, Adam All, because he is fantastic, inspirational, and great fun to be around. I was involved in a DRAG king scene in Manchester and am still friends with them, but I was always 'just visiting' and generally just got on with things on my own until I moved to London, England, United Kingdom.

✽**Trey C. Michaels:** My family and friends were very supportive.

✽**Bailey Saint James:** Gia, Sebastion Cock Las Vegas, Harmony Breeze, Windy Breeze, Ritchie Rich, Sid Deucer and Leo Long of the Miltown Kings. They helped perfect my approach and style. My mother, Suzanne Garduno, and my brother, Thomas Klitzka, helped me to achieve success through continuing to push me during difficult times.

✽**Aaron Phoenix:** The queens in my area honestly were the biggest support and source of advice to me starting out. It may be a different kind of DRAG, but kings and queens can be a huge asset to one another.

✽**Soco Dupree:** My friends at the time.

✽**LoUis CYfer:** The male gay community of London, England, United Kingdom. My family supported me in this fabuLoUis venture to win DRAG Idol United Kingdom 2014, the first female to win since it began in 2004.

✽**Stefon Royce Iman:** My gay mother, Tyria Iman, and Harmonica Sunbeam along with the gay community. They always offered encouragement; they help coordinate benefit shows and events. They always help me develop my craft. They gave me a chance and booked me on their shows and events.

✽**Santana Romero:** My girlfriend Rachel and my mom were, and still are, my main supporters. Rachel could probably count the shows she HAS missed on her fingers. She always makes sure everything is together throughout every show, she takes photos and videos of most of my performances, and she gives me tough love when I am feeling unsure about something. If it had not been for her having my back, keeping track of all the little things, I would be a hot DRAG mess. My mom is always full of ideas I use for performances and she also gives me that motherly kick in the pants I need at times. I can always count on her to give me critiques on something that could be better. Having that eye for detail really helps, especially for pageants.

✤Viciouse Slick: The kings that performed in the same bar as me. My biggest supporter is Gunner Gatlyn. He made sure I was a professional entertainer. He would tell when I did not know my words or an outfit looked horrible. When I do well, he tells me how proud he is of me and it makes me strive to do better in the art form.

✤Smitty O'Toole: My number one support was and will always be my DRAG troupe, the "Houston Gendermyn." They offered advice, wardrobes when needed, friendship, everything a DRAG family should and more. Lana Blake and Dessie Love-Blake were also huge supporters of mine from the beginning. The best advice I have gotten was from Dessie, she said, "Get off the stage and in their face, they will either tip you to stay or tip you to leave," and more times than not, they tip for me to stay.

✤Jensen C. Dean: in the beginning, it was my wife (girlfriend at the time) and a few close friends. I kept my performing under wraps for a while so very few non-performers knew at the time even knew what I was doing.

✤Justin Cider: Mine is and always has been my family. Mama Cider attends practically all my shows along with my sister, cousin, and even aunt these days. They are my rocks and loudest cheering section. I love them and all the amazing support there giving from the start

✤Luke Ateraz: It has always been my wife, Roxi Ateraz, my son Cody Ateraz, my mother-in-law Laura Daugherty, and my friends and family.

✤Spacee Kadett: I started as a lone ranger at my university DRAG show. All I knew was that I loved performing. When my girlfriend (now wife) entered the picture two years later with my open mic nightclub debut, she wholeheartedly supported me, but did not aid in the creative process until a long while later. Over months, I was "adopted" by DRAG parents but did not take anyone's name. I waded through advice, both good and bad, before I found my truth. Over years, countless friends and fellow entertainers helped me in the development of my character, and still do. I cannot even begin to express my gratitu9de toward them. But truly, in the beginning, I just dove into this thing alone with a blind hunger to entertain, and I continue to pride myself in being a largely self-sufficient entertainer.

✤Boi Wonder: Valentino King, my friend Emma (now Ethan), Lydia, and the original DRAG Kings of Manchester Troupe (United Kingdom).

✤Dixon Heat: Partner, mum, friends.

✤Miles Long: My friends and family gave me support.

✤Mike Oxready: In the beginning, it was my then-partner, and my friends who formed a troupe, we were support for each other.

❀**Devin G. Dame:** I had two DRAG queens put me in DRAG for the first time. But quickly became part of the show cast at the bar and they all helped me by giving me tips and advice on my performances. Gage Gatlyn stepped in about six years into my career and showed me about packing, makeup, and taking my costumes to the next level.

Chapter Twenty
"What tricks with tape should every performer learn before heading on stage? What are the biggest mistakes with binding?
Any experiences you wish to share?"

❀**Adam All:** Arrogance will destroy your career. You only need innovation, not a massive budget to pull off amazing. It is all in the way you sell your product, emote your songs, and give of yourself. Do not try to use a she-wee when packing. Unless the two gadgets are one of the same, it can be a disastrous exercise.

❀**Travis Luvermore:** I have large breasts. Many newbies are afraid of tape. My first mistake was taping all around; I had no one to teach me. I hurt fiercely, and they had to cut it after my first song. I started with gray duct tape and moved to the beige color. I use the circle makeup wipes from the dollar store to cover my nipples, only one incident of having any skin tear. Make sure your tape is lying flat, no creases.

❀**Trey C. Michaels**: Never rip tape off! I was taught to use WD-40, and to take your time removing the tape. You will smell like a mechanic, but at least you will not have chunks of flesh missing.

❀**Freddy Prinze Charming:** If you tape and are wearing a tank top or sleeveless shirt, make sure you cannot see the tape under your armpits. Make sure it is low enough not to be seen, or add a layer of medical tape that you can put makeup on to blend it in with your skin. Do the same with any tape you may be able to see on your chest. It kills the illusion to see a bunch of silver/black/etc. tape sticking out all over the place. Use WD-40 to get the tape off, never rip! Know your limits, if you have raw skin, sores, etc., back off and use a binder. Take a break from performing until you heal.

❀**Travis Hard:** I do not work with tape myself, but I do help others with it. When using tape, DO NOT put it directly over your nipple; put some tissue over that area before you tape. I have also heard horror stories about people binding with saran wrap. This is definitely not safe for any entertainer, as it cannot breathe and I have heard of people passing out due to this. No Good.

❀**Chance Wise:** Never bind all the way around your chest. This is a mistake I did for a long time, and I nearly passed out on stage, and actually had chest pains after that performance. It scared the crap out of me and I immediately found a way to bind only going half way around. You can also jump into a hot shower and soak the tape off slowly, taking a bit of it off at a time. It is time consuming, but it beats having scars from ripping skin off.

❀**Rychard "Alpha" Le'Sabre:** Put a piece of tissue over the nipple. The tape comes off easy with alcohol wipes and hot water. Do not kill yourself.

❀**Stormm:** I only go around half way, which works the best. I can breathe. I have used binders, but they do not flatten enough. Ace bandages do not work either.

❀**Shane Rebel Caine:** Do not go cheap with the kind of tape you use, especially if you are heavy chested! Skip using an ace bandage, you will fight with it more to keep it from rolling up or down especially if you are doing a lot of dancing and moving around on stage. I would also suggest always placing some sort of tissue or cloth over your nipples before you go to tape, take into consideration what costumes you will be wearing and make sure that you bind yourself to where the tape will not be seen. Sometimes having a friend or someone who knows what they are doing tape you is a good idea as they may be able to get you flatter. Find a method of taping that you like and are comfortable with but that also flattens and holds well. If you do not like taping than it can be a good idea to invest in a binder. Decent binders for low prices on eBay, but keep in mind a binder does not always look good with every costume.

❀**Coti Blayne:** Do not tape all the way around and definitely invest in a binder. I almost never tape because it is so uncomfortable for me and with my size it is hard to tape me flat enough to where I can still breathe. I got my binder from underworks.com. It was a double front, I am a 32F and it gets me just about flat. I am going to eventually get a triple front. Tape will never be comfortable but if you are getting dizzy and you cannot breathe without pain, please get someone to cut you out immediately. Do not risk hurting yourself.

❀**Campbell Reid Andrews:** Biggest mistake is not supporting the pull and connecting in the back. Tape all the way around, using clear tape, not asking someone backstage, "hey, does my tape look shitty?" Tips: binders are great for a costume you do not plan to take off. Try underworks.com. They last, and suck in those other areas, too. Use a tape that sticks. Spray adhesive works for extra hold, Use Goo Gone to help with removal. I used it for years and have yet to grow another nipple. Another tip is to lift and pull so you do not look like you have a droopy chest. It is ok if you have larger breast, contour a little and you will look like you have buff pectoral muscles.

❀**Rasta Boi Punany:** I do not use tape directly. I have bound by using three small sports bras, ace bandages, taped that so it will not come loose, and a binder shirt.

❀**Dakota Rain:** I use binders from underworks.com. It works great. I also use duct tape if I want to do open shirt, still learning different ways for this, I have learned not to leave it on for too long and to cover the nipples with a Band-Aid.

❀**Ashton The Adorable Lover:** Shave; do not tape all the way around. Start with a nipple strap to anchor, and go top to bottom for a smoother look. Spanks are not just for the queens, it can smooth you out. Work up a sweat or jump in hot shower to remove tape. Do not rip it off, it can have long-term effects and remove skin.

❀**Clint Torres:** The only tape trick I know so far is the side tape trick. The one where you tape your breast to the sides of your body in order to obtain a realistic man chest complete with pectorals and a six-pack. Just make sure to use something like a non-stick adhesive, before the tape, to not cause injury your breasts.

❀**Adam DoEve:** When I first started, I got bad advice on YouTube and used the plastic wrap and duct tape around it, to try to get as flat as I could. I barely finished my number when I grabbed my girlfriend and my knife, went to the bathroom, and she had to cut me out of it before I passed out. I learned my lesson the hard way.

❀**Spacee Kadett:** I have never done an open chest, but I have sure used tape. The first time I did, I did not think to inhale before wrapping my chest with approximately 847 yards of duct tape, essentially binding my lungs shut, then running around the stage singing live as a half-cracked Superman. I was something else when I started. Tape pops and slips. Sweat is a beast. Gorilla Tape is much more reliable than even good duct tape. If you are doing something revealing, try to match your tape to your skin-tone just in case it does peek through. Then there are the occasions when you do not sweat enough and the tape rips off your skin. I suffered many a mark and scar before I started using a binder, and even that can be harsh.

❀**Pierce Gabriel:** Do NOT use duct tape if you are sweating. Whether it is the temperature being too hot, your last number was too physically active or you are stressed out about something. If you are sweating, the tape will not stick right and you will risk it coming off completely. If you absolutely have to use duct tape, wear a loose-fitting shirt so it will not be as obvious if it the binding loosens.

❀**Koomah**: Duct tape binding works for some and does not work for others. I recommend experimenting with other uses for tape too. I have assisted some kings with a complete shirtless look by binding using black duct tape and then using Sharpie/airbrush/latex body paint to create a wraparound tribal tattoo and adding fake male nipples. Carpet tape (double sided tape used to adhere rugs to floors; made of paper, cloth, or fiberglass) is great for 'flash tape' for large areas and it is also useful for adhering things to your body for creative costuming. If you side bind using tape and are small chested, look into DRAG queen chest tape (used to create cleavage/waistline on queens) it is flesh tone and can be used to side bind small breasts or can be used over duct tape/carpet tape to better blend with tan skin.

✤**Vinnie Marconi:** I bind with duct tape for open shirt but prefer binders. My best advice is not to bind too tightly! I have asthma and if you are not careful, you could will have a hard time breathing. Be careful when taking off tape, use WD-40 and SLOWLY take it off in the shower letting the WD-40 do all the work for you.

✤**Ben Eaten:** I personally do not tape unless it is an open shirt number. If you tape, do one breast at a time, cover nipples with something that is not tape first. Start in the middle and pull back under your armpits. Do not go all the way around and always leave a gap in the back so you can breathe. When taking tape off go slow. If you can wait until you are in the shower, the steam will help get the tape off.

✤**Hawk Stuart:** I normally tape because the binder I have makes it hard to breath. I have become un-taped once before but that is because of the tape, I now use the silver duct tape and spray adhesive to make it stay. Always make sure you stay cool because we all sweat and the tape can become undone.

✤**Kruz Mhee:** I have seen quite a few DRAG kings that were seasoned pass out from binding incorrectly. Always keep in mind when binding, do not exhale, and empty your lungs. You fill your lungs then tape. You must have room to breathe. As for me, I wear a binding bodysuit. It is costly; however, I do not pass out.

✤**B J Bottoms:** Binders are a godsend to entertaining but if you must tape, do not sacrifice your ability to breath. Yes, you want to have a good illusion but you are useless if you pass out in the middle of your number. If it is too tight, take a deep breath and push your chest out. If you still cannot breathe, than re-tape and inhale before you start, and exhale after so you have some room.

✤**Silk Steele Prince:** I would suggest that you bind before a show and wear it to test it out in your daily life to see how it works out with your movement, skin reaction, and breathing. Second, when using duct tape, use a spray adhesive to assure that when you sweat it does come apart. Then, I use tissue, cotton pad, or small piece of fabric over the nipple before I put the first piece of tape on, to assure I do not rip the delicate skin off the nipple. Then I bind for open chest one side at a time. I do not overlap because I do not want my breathing restricted. When I am ready to remove, I use Goo Gone or baby oil with peroxide and baking soda mix. I jump in a hot shower so it will peal right off, then I moisturize my skin.

✤**SirMandingo Thatis:** Well I have learned that with larger breasts, one should lay down while being taped because it makes your breasts fall to the side. Also if you sweat a lot like I do, use spray adhesive then Gorilla Tape. Now please do not just pull this off because you will rip skin off (as I did). However, use WD-40 and spray inside the tape where it may already be coming off and it will peel off with ease!

❀**Flex Jonez:** Duct tape and a hot shower to take off the tape.

❀**Atown:** I use Gorilla Tape and follow the same responses as everyone else was saying about how to remove it. I am top heavy so I need to use tape plus a binder. If that constricts too much for me, I will use either/or.

❀**Kenneth J. Squires:** I use Ace bandages sometimes, but I found a great binder from underworks.com. I use duct tape as well, but if you do use duct tape, be really careful taking it off. Use an old bra and then put Duct tape over it. Make sure it is tight. Hold your breath and stick your chest out while taping. This will help you breath better when you are done.

❀**Cody Wellch Klondyke:** When I first started out I was using the waist trimmer things you can purchase at Walmart then I went to using duct tape. When using duct tape make sure you do not apply deodorant because it will not stick and you will come undone. Now I am using a binder.

❀**George De Micheal:** Make sure you can breathe.

❀**J Breezy St James:** I used ace bandages but they never stayed. I started using spray adhesive and duct tape, which has worked a lot better for me.

❀**Colin Grey:** Find what works for you and stick with it. Open shirt binding takes time to get used to and can be painful. Sometimes it is about finding the right kind of tape to use to bind. I do not use spray adhesive because of the extra chemicals. We use skin so soft baby oil to get the extra adhesive off left behind at the end of the night.

❀**Eddie C. Broadway:** Tape your chest on days you do not have shows. It helps stretch them out. Only use taping method if you know what you are doing. Different tape methods work on different bodies. My method may not work for everyone. I use as little tape as possible; do not bind across the back, and use spray adhesive.

❀ **Joshua Grobelnik:** Take the time to learn your craft and your body. Tape is not for everyone and open shirt does not equal a better entertainer. If you tape open shirt, use your makeup! Shading, contour, blending. If you got a belly do not try a six-pack.

❀**Jack King:** I use a binder from underworks.com.

❀**Kameo Dupree:** If you can avoid it, do not tape to skin. Tape over sports bra or some type of sleeveless shirt.

❀**DeVery Bess:** I really dislike taping to be honest, but always cover the nipple before taping, because that hurts! I heard some kings in Halifax, Nova Scotia used spray adhesive before taping, for better results and easier time taking it off.

❀**B J Armani:** THE BIGGEST MISTAKE OF BINDING is only using duct tape. It is horrible watching my fellow performers take chunks out of their skin! If you cannot find a male waist cincher, a compression binder, or I have even seen a back stabilizer used, you can always use a tank top and tape THE TANK TOP and cut the side off. This can also be reused and NOT take pieces of you with it. I use a compression binder that is just very thick and stretchy nylon and pull my breasts to the side.

❋Stefan LeDude: The best thing to do is buy a binder. A friend recently found that you can order them from China for like five dollars.

❋Clark Kunt: If you choose to open bind with duct tape, get nice tape. Beige, or fancy, cut designs before putting the last pieces on, etc. Have an adhesive remover such as coconut oil. Also, learn contouring for your chest and abdomen.

❋Jamel Knight: Baby oil has is my best friend since I first started binding.

❋Welland Dowd: Johnny Depth is great create a 'naked' six-pack chest with tape.

❋Julius M. SeizeHer: Having an adhesive remover helps. The scarring from tape sucks. No one wants that. Binders help too.

❋Jonah Godfather of DRAG: I have seen a few kings make the mistake of putting tape over nipples. Make sure to cover nipples with a tissue or gauze before taping over. I never used tape. Before my chest surgery, I used a Velcro back brace.

❋MaXx Decco: If using duct tape I recommend exfoliating the chest first and LIGHTLY applying baby powder. Separate and side tape them. HOWEVER, an underworks.com binder would be preferable as opposed to duct tape. It is more comfortable and durable, bigger sized cups might benefit by combining the two.

❋Howie Feltersnatch: I do not normally tape, but the few times I did, I learned that toilet paper on your nipple is a blessing. Especially if you have nipple rings.

❋Jack E. Dickinson: Before I could afford binders, I used saran wrap with duct tape over it to bind. Not sure how safe that was though. Got really sweaty but was easy to take off by having a friend CAREFULLY cutting up the middle of the entire thing. It might have been said, but ace bandages are not considered safe for binding. Camouflaging is an option if the required outfits allows for it (baggy vests, etc.). I have had fellow performers who could not bind and went with it.

❋Juan Kerr: Your boobs get really pissed off with you if you do not treat them right. Taking binding tape off bare skin after a few hours of wearing it is breathtaking in a couple of ways, good and bad, hence why I started putting normal bandages underneath to stop it sticking too hard.

❋Trey C. Michaels: If you struggle with taping or binders ask for help! I popped once on stage because I did not know how to properly tape. After that mishap of flashing the crowd, I asked kings I knew how I could tape and not pop.

❋Bailey Saint James: Do not pull off duct tape! Use WD-40.

❀**Aaron Phoenix:** The biggest mistake with duct tape is the REMOVAL. Do NOT remove tape from your skin without lubing it up first. I use oil sheen, some use WD-40, whatever it takes, that adhesive has to be loosened or you will end up with blisters bad enough to leave scars. I am speaking from direct experience.

❀**Thug Passion:** I started out using four ace bandages and safety pins. I tried tape but it kept sticking to my skin even when I taped on top of a shirt. I also tried taping on my skin with spray adhesive but I sweat too much so it did not stick. Now I use a binding tank top and a binding body suit, which you can purchase on underworks.com. One bad experience I had with my ace bandages is when I did not place my chest in the right place and wrap the bandages. Right after one song my bandages would have slid down and my chest would bulge out at the top. Also, if I were to wrap them to tight then it would be hard for me to breathe because my ribs could not expand fully, and sometimes at the end of the night, my rib muscles were sore because of them being tied down.

❀**Soco Dupree:** I use makeup pads to cover nips and duct tape from front of breast to the back. I place tape over the shoulder area to control the bulge from taping.

❀**Dominic:** Cover nops with cotton pads. Best to try taping a few times before you get out on stage for the first time because the tape can cause allergic reactions, and from past experience, it can RIP OFF YOUR SKIN.

❀**E. M. Shaun:** Always cover your nipples so they do not get ripped by the duct tape. Use a good strong tape that will withstand your heat and movement. Tape all around to help keep your breast in place. Make sure you can breathe with all that compression. I use a compression shirt from underworks.com and it works great. Then I can tape on top of that shirt if I need any additional taping.

❀**Stefon Royce Iman:** When you use adhesive on your tape, spray oil sheen to loosen the adhesive, or use baby oil. The best tape to use is Gorilla Tape. Pull your chest back and tuck your nips under your pits and make sure it is nice and flat.

❀**Mike Oxready:** The times I have taped, I found it best to protect nipples with cotton pads, use spray adhesive to keep the tape on, and practice my makeup. Then for removal, use baby oil in a hot shower!

❀**Smitty O'Toole:** Protect your nipples first off. When I bind with tape, I do so that the tape falls under my shoulder blades, as not to restrict my movement. To keep the tape from slipping, I place one strip of tape across my back to connect both sides. I use baby oil to help remove it, but sweat usually helps to remove the tape as well. Take it off slowly to avoid ripping your skin. I would only recommend taping if you are doing an open shirt performance as it causes breast tissue damage. I would recommend buying a binder; they are very cheap on EBay.

❀**LoUis CYfer:** Never place tape on naked skin! Ouch.

❀**Jensen C. Dean:** I do not tape often because of an adhesive allergy, but when learning to tape, get help from someone who knows how, yes it is awkward, but it is worth it. When you are done with tape, Goo Gone works wonders.

❀**Luke Ateraz:** Protect the nipples! Hurts like hell ripping duct or Gorilla Tape off your bare nipples! Use WD-40 to help remove the tape. Never use Ace bandages for binding. The first and only time I did, I had bruised ribs for 2 weeks! It basically hurt to breathe and move.

❀**Xavier Bottoms:** Taping sucks! I have double D breast. Ace bandages never worked for me either. My mom had gastric surgery when I was younger and she had this compression vest thing, I used that at first. Now I use a compression shirt by underworks.com. A little trick...have your spouse/partner rub your chest down after a show. It really helps, especially the muscles above your chest.

Chapter Twenty-One
"DRAG Boxes become DRAG Rooms, which eventually take over your home. How much space does your craft consume in your home, car, and venue? How much is it worth? Where do you go to retire it?"

❀**D-Luv Saviyon:** My DRAG takes up about half of my bedroom closet and corner in my room. I honestly need to make a room, but I have yet to do so. As for its worth, I think my DRAG is priceless because it is all sentimental. As far as where to retire my DRAG, I cannot honestly say I will ever at this point. I have gifted DRAG from time to time, as well as inherited some. There are some sell/swap groups on social media, and occasional DRAG sales in the Nashville, Tennessee USA, area by various people.

❀**Adam All:** A huge box under my bed, a large stack of props in the dining room, half my wardrobe, a whole double shelf of hats, a few things at the club we work in, a few boxes of notes and filing stuff on the shelves, and that is just my stuff. Apple, my girlfriend, has all hers too. I need more space… Just bought a new suit!

❀**Adam DoEve**: For me, I have taken over the dining room table and my girl is not very happy about it. I have a small closet and then part of another, a large suitcase on top of my desk has all my hats and shoes. I have only been doing this for almost two years so I have not passed on anything. I have made a few things for queens or let other kings borrow stuff.

❀**Travis Luvermore:** I have a box at the bottom of my closet, an additional craft box, my DRAG bag, and half of my closet and top shelf. I lost most of my stuff during hurricane Sandy and am still working on building my wardrobe back up.

❀**Justin Cider:** My DRAG bag became a DRAG closet and now a DRAG room. I swear Justin takes longer to get ready than I do. He now shares a room with his DRAG boifriend, Johnnie Blackheart. The room is totally a man cave too, with a dartboard, stripper pole, and mirrors along the wall! Any DRAG king's heaven, but all the credit goes to Johnnie for that.

❀**Freddy Prinze Charming:** Right now, I have got 3 large plastic tubs full of costumes, 2 large cardboard boxes full of costumes and costume materials, numerous costumes taking up one side of my closet, various hats, boots, shoes, etc. in a hall closet. And there are always a few stray pieces in the trunk of the car. All in all, if you were to add up the materials, stones, etc. it is all worth thousands of dollars. I rarely simply get rid of a costume, I am more likely to take it apart and recycle it, turn it into a completely new and different costume. I have given a few things away, sold a handful of things. And I am a fan of DRAG swap meets!

🎭**Travis Hard:** My entire closet is full of DRAG clothes, some that do not fit still! But I figure I can use them to make other outfits. My entire trunk is also full of DRAG outfits and makeup just in case someone needs a king at the last minute. My DRAG is worth everything to me, so I cannot put a price on my things.

🎭**Phantom:** With the very limited space I have at my apartment, my bedroom is my DRAG room. My outfits, makeup, props, wigs, hats, canes, etc., are all in one place. I keep the door locked because I have two very curious children. Try to pack light; I only take what I need to do a show. I sometimes do my makeup in the car, which is another challenge in itself. Most of the time, back-stage can feel like a janitor's closet. But it is all worth it in the end.

🎭**Chance Wise:** I had an extra room which became a DRAG lab, which is slowly becoming a gym-DRAG-lab-spare-room. I do not know if I could put a price on my DRAG, but I was offered a lot of money for a jacket I costumed. I turned him down because I knew he wouldn't appreciate all the heart that went into making it. Does that make me crazy? When I have DRAG with me in the truck, it takes up the entire back seat. My DRAG son has called me a diva on countless occasions for that.

🎭**Rychard "Alpha" Le'Sabre:** I am blessed with a five-bedroom house and one room is all DRAG!

🎭**AJ Menendez:** I have three bedrooms; one is an office, which is consumed with DRAG. I have recently started to spill over into the spare room.

🎭**Stormm:** I used to have a playroom for my son, since he no longer lives with me. I have taken it over and use it for my DRAG.

🎭**Shane Rebel Caine:** I am still young and currently reside with my mom, my DRAG clothes overfill my closet, have their own growing pile in a corner where they will not get messed up, almost fill up the trunk of my car and the back seat and even over flowing into my storage unit. I'd say I probably have around $200 in it all with only two costumes customized and one designer vest bought as it was. Everything else has been bargain shopping and my own creations. When I go to retire a costume, I try to take as much of it as I can to incorporate into a new costume, or I hand it down to another king who may have use for it.

🎭**Shana Nicole:** I have a three room shop dedicated to DRAG, sewing, creating, and storage. I try not to keep it in the house. I once had a locked dressing room at my home bar that had seven double closets full and two trunks and several shelves. It was mostly stolen when it was moved upstairs. With all the beaded gowns, dance outfits, jewelry, and crowns I would say that room was worth $20,000 or more. Now I probably have about $10-15,000 worth if you do not count raw fabric and stones, etc.

❀**Shook ByNature:** My dining room is my DRAG Lab, but I am thinking of renovating my guest bedroom into the new Ruthless Entertainment DRAG Lab after Nationals because it will not just be my DRAG, it will be my partners, too.

❀**Anson Reign:** An entire separate bedroom.

❀**Coti Blayne:** Every room in my apartment, both of our cars, the closets are entirely DRAG. We have dressers and stuff entirely devoted to DRAG, but there are two of us kings together.

❀**Gage Gatlyn:** We have a 10' x 15' extra living room, set up as a DRAG room, and an 8' x 12' extra dining room for my DRAG office. We also use an extra kitchen for storage of extra and older costumes or stuff that needs to be updated. Essentially, an extra house set aside and dedicated for just anything DRAG related.

❀**Dakota Rain:** My spare bedroom is where I keep things, and if and when I retire, I will offer them to future performers.

❀**Ashton The Adorable Lover:** I always have a case of music and a DRAG outfit bag in the car. At home, a current project is under the bed in a tote and the closet is about 70% DRAG. If I could, it would have a room. I have things in storage in the garage, also. DRAG is priceless, especially if you created it for a special reason. As of now, my most expensive things are probably my earrings. I have different size stones.

❀**Ben Eaten:** My spare room has become my DRAG room. I have a CD case with my songs that I have done, and ones that I want to do. I have all my clothes and shoes in the closet. After the shows are finished, I retire back to that room. When I have to pack it all up, it takes 2 large rolling suitcases, 2 hanging bags, duffle, and my make- up box. That is not including the accessories or special large costumes.

❀**Clint Torres:** Right now, because I am still so new to the game, I just have a small standard sized hall closet that houses all my gear over the past 6 months. After about a year or two I'll probably have to expand to a small bedroom.

❀**Johnnie Blackheart:** At first, it was my bag and then a box, which moved into the guest closet. I got my own "Johnnie Blackheart" bedroom that includes a red stripper pole and a wall of mirrors. Currently, my stuff is everywhere. When I left in December, my roommate boxed almost everything up or gave it away to the Gay Central Valley Organization.

❀**Rasta Boi Punany:** It consumes a lot of space. I have most of it in the hall closet of my home, which takes up half of the space with two suitcases and clothes. I use the back seat of my car or trunk if necessary. At a venue, I utilize very little space because I keep everything in one corner and I only bring what is necessary, I keep everything together, neat and organized.

❀**Spacee Kadett:** Since my wife and I acquired a "spare" room a few years ago, Spacee has always occupied it, so it was never really spare. The entire closet, bins, boxes, racks, drawers, this is also important crafting space that may or may not spill into other living areas. I am also incredibly fortunate in that I now also have a sizeable closet and makeup station of my own at my home bar, where my wigs, makeup, dozens of small props and my most important wardrobe all live. The total cost? Thousands of tangible dollars, as well as dollars borrowed from Visa and MasterCard that have yet to be repaid, and this is with the THRIFT STORE as my main supplier. I do not retire much. I either repurpose things or throw them away because they are just too old and ratty, or I donate items that are so darned wonky.

❀**Kenneth J. Squires:** Most of my DRAG is in my closet. When I am ready to go do a show, I pack all my things in a suit bag. I bring my "makeup bag." I am in the process of downsizing only because I have gained weight.

❀**Pierce Gabriel:** I actually do not have as many outfits as most entertainers do, but I am gradually working on increasing it. Right now it takes up about 3 feet in my closet and a duffel bag in the trunk of my car.

❀**Brandon KC Young-Taylor:** I have an entire bedroom for my DRAG! Everything is set up and functional so I can work when I am home but shut the door when I need to go. Nothing is worse than starting a project and having to pack it up before you are finished. Currently in my DRAG room I have upwards of $10,000. This includes one-of-a-kind suits and costumes, stones, fabrics, makeup, workstation supplies, etc. I have downsized a lot throughout the years as I have moved from a few different cities. I have probably given away an equal amount in donations including all of the above!

❀**Nanette D'angelo Sylvan:** I have a one bedroom apartment but I have a DRAG closet of my own and half of my walk in closet consists of DRAG, plus my wife has her own closet for her DRAG as well!

❀**Koomah:** I have two 10' x 10' storage buildings, one is all costuming, and the other is all props and set pieces. This collection has accumulated over several years from my involvement in DRAG, theater productions, and film. Most of the items have been donated to me and I frequently rent/loan them out to others. I have one small closet in my home that is items that I use frequently. I keep inventory of my items and if there is something I have not used in a long time I will donate it. It is priceless, I feel, I cherish my costumes and props; that is my hard-earned money.

❀**Campbell Reid Andrews:** Right now I have a DRAG closet in my closet. That is where it will stay. I try to keep it organized but, meh. When I retire I think I'll donate them to one of the community theatres I perform at. I think they'd look great in the live community theatre scene. It would put them to good use.

Vinnie Marconi: We have a small studio attached to the back of the house with a bathroom and kitchen, and it is JUST DRAG. "Vinnie" still manages to invade the house! There are a few small kings around here that I would give some of my favorites to, but with a size 14 1/2 neck and 30 slacks, it is hard to say what I would do with the rest. In the last 3 years, I am sure there is thousands of dollars in DRAG, including stones, fabric, props, paint, etc. I can tell you there are thousands of man-hours, lots of head banging, sweat, and tears in that studio, too!

Kruz Mhee: I have only lost a small room to the craft. However, there is always DRAG droppings in my car and bedroom. Over the years I have given away a lot of my costume pieces and thrown out some. There are a lot of craft hours that have been spent as well as a good bit of cash. I do not believe I can put a price on my collection but when I do retire it, I will be glad to give it to deserving, up and coming newbies.

Hawk Stuart: I started out with a small box, just with little things, but now it is a lot bigger. I do now have some things I leave in my car at all times.

Flex Jonez: My DRAG wear is in my walk-in DRAG closet, and downstairs in my home. When retiring my wear, I donate to a local performer, but that is rare.

Silk Steele Prince: I have racks in my basement where I keep my costumes. I have no clue what they are worth. When I am done with them, I will pack them away until someone else needs them.

SirMandingo Thatis: Well, I have a room my wife calls my MAN CAVE and in it, I have all my favorite things. DRAG takes up half the closet and all of the walls, and I have more shoes than I can even count.

Chasin Love: I use a makeup bag, usually have a duffle bag for my other things or hangers, my closet is separated by one side DRAG, one side regular clothes.

DeVery Bess: The spare bedroom was turned into a "craft" room, which is really DRAG stuff everywhere.

Eddie C. Broadway: DRAG takes over about half of my house. Granted my wife and I are in a studio and both of us are performers. I have a good chunk in storage right now until we move into a bigger place. It is getting a little out of hand lately.

Jonah Godfather of DRAG: DRAG takes up about 1/3 of our attic, with it spilling down into our closet. I have given some of my clothing to other performers. When something is retired, it goes into a box in the attic. I do not want to get rid of most things as they are special to me.

Colin Grey: DRAG covers about half of my walk-in closet. I go through my DRAG clothes and things that do not fit etc. They are handed down to other kings in my area.

Sam Masterson: I have one room for my king stuff.

❈**Kameo Dupree:** My DRAG started as a room! I built a solid basic wardrobe prior to ever hitting the stage. I always keep an emergency bag of DRAG in the car for last minute bookings.

❈**Jack King:** I have two wardrobes in a small room for all my DRAG clothes and accessories, as well as all my shoes. Too much money.

❈**B J Armani:** My DRAG used to take up a closet. Now it takes up a whole small bedroom and a few larger props are scattered about the house. If I am doing three or four numbers, I may fit in the car with all of my gear (Elton John coats and HUGE props). How much is it worth? Priceless, I have to make almost everything. I am sure my DRAG children will put it to use when I am in no need of it anymore. Hopefully that is a LONG time from now.

❈**Stefan LeDude:** I have a prop box, plus random garments hanging in the closet.

❈**Jamel Knight:** I have a DRAG box and it takes up about half of my closet right now. I need more space though, so I am thinking of building a storage closet.

❈**Howie Feltersnatch:** Roommate and I turned a spare room into a DRAG room.

❈**Michael Christian:** I currently have an entire basement for DRAG. One room is simply a closet and the rest of the basement houses a crafting and sewing area for my roommate and me. When my size changed drastically and I was relocating, I handed down a few things to my kids. Beyond that I rarely throw anything out. I am a big fan of remaking older pieces into something new again.

❈**Bruno Diaz:** I have a room. It used to be our office but my outfits, costumes, and accessories have pretty much taken over. Not allowed to leave anything anymore at the venue, so it all comes back home after shows. About how much is it worth? Some of my pieces, especially for pageants, are pretty expensive. Most of the things I have crafted are priceless for me and I have not yet gotten rid of anything.

❈**Welland Dowd:** I have a corner and a big box in my closet for costumes, and props are kind of all over the apartment.

❈**Bootzy Edwards Collynz:** I have a spare room of DRAG/prop stuff. I am working on moving downstairs where I have more closets to separate stuff a little easier.

❈**Julius M. SeizeHer:** A single corner in my bedroom. A few outfits lay in my closet.

❈**Lyle Love-It:** Lyle has his own bedroom, and he is MESSY, messy, messy. Props can be found in the outside shed, Santa's train has taken the loft over. When I travel, it has been kind of a JOKE how much I bring. I once used a U-Haul AND my truck.

❀**Jack E. Dickinson:** Even though I have been on hiatus for a year, I still have a full closet devoted to props and costumes. This does not include regular clothes that sometimes come in handy. I cannot calculate the worth of it over the years but most of it has come from thrift shops. I am guessing in the hundreds. If I do not need something, I offer it to other performers at a swap, at a rehearsal, or social get together. If no one wants it, I would take it wherever I would take any second hand clothes.

❀**Clark Kunt:** Right now, I have four DRAG bins, three suitcases, half a closet, and a good section of my storage room overflowing with clothing, props, and craft supplies. Oh, and a pantry of duct tape. I do not even want to guess what it is worth. Thankfully, I reinvent a lot of my own clothing and turn them into DRAG costumes so I save money where I can. Also, it helps that most of my DRAG family are similar in size so we can share and swap clothes, oh wait, I guess that means my DRAG closet tally should include all their DRAG piles, too!

❀**Juan Kerr:** My DRAG clothes now outweigh my normal clothes! I have two drawers and a half a wardrobe for my various accoutrements, although I am starting to need more. I also have a bag of newly bought items waiting for a home somewhere. Most of my props are cheap, but cheerful. My clothes are not expensive but they are nice.

❀**Trey C. Michaels:** In my old place, I had a corner of the living room for my DRAG desk/crafting table. I took over the coat closet to store costumes. I have a whole bedroom to store everything to keep the animals away from projects

❀**Xavier Bottoms:** My DRAG room is a 20' x 24' room above the two-car garage. It has six racks for hanging cloths, three racks for shoes, and four totes. Most of the walls are full of awards, sashes, and medallions. It also has a dresser that holds my binders, bike shorts, colored socks, and t-shirts. Props are taken apart and put in the barn. Once broken down, they do not take up a lot of space. Price? My DRAG is priceless. I have worked very hard to get what I have or made, and for me, that has no price tag. Once I retire, my DRAG kids may have whatever it is. They do that now, though. Instead of it being my DRAG room, it will become my kids' DRAG room.

❀**Aaron Phoenix:** We have a garage that was finished into a huge room which is now the DRAG room. Half of it is the king attire (mine), half is the queen attire (my partner's). We also have a guest bedroom that stores the more expensive DRAG (evening gowns, suits) as well as costumes that are "works-in-progress." The kitchen table tends to be half-covered in some kind of work-in-progress as well, and there is inevitably some DRAG overflow into the bedroom.

❀**Atown:** Atown has his own bedroom. I try to keep it as organized as possible. I also use that room to create, so I have a table set up with a sewing machine etc., two closets, one armoire, and one rolling closet. It also has areas to keep spikes/stones/fabric, etc. I do not think I can put a price tag on my stuff. The majority is handmade or added, some was donated for pageants, but I added to it, and the rest is stuff that I buy if I cannot make it myself.

❀**Thug Passion:** My DRAG takes over half of my closet. If my closet wasn't so big it would take over a spare bedroom. When I decide to retire, though I'll probably be doing this until my body says stop, I will hand everything down or pack it up in boxes and store it if I do not have anyone to give it to.

❀**MaXx Decco:** Why is there never enough room? It started with a suit, then consumed my wallet, my closet, an additional freestanding wardrobe, a carted storage box, two makeup bins, and has officially become a tornado in my room. I am now looking into rehearsal space/storage unit.

❀**Soco Dupree:** I have a DRAG room. My DRAG persona has more clothes then I do.

❀**Santana Romero:** My closet is currently divided between my normal clothing and my DRAG clothing, with DRAG clothing quickly taking over. Boxes of shoes litter the floor of my closet and hats fill the top shelf. When I ran out of storage space in my closet, I decided to start keeping all my props in the basement. There is at least a couple thousand dollars' worth of DRAG all put together, but all the work put into it makes them priceless in my eyes. When I am ready to retire it, I plan on archiving my prized costumes and giving away others to performers in need.

❀**Stefon Royce Iman:** I have one closet full of suits and costumes and I have storage containers full of DRAG wigs and accessories, no DRAG room yet.

❀**Jensen C. Dean:** Jensen used to have his own room, but he did not keep it organized so he lost that privilege when we moved. He now has half of a room, half of a closet, and a storage space to keep all of his stuff.

❀**Cody Wellch Klondyke:** Well, I kept my stuff in an area, but since I have recently moved from Houston, Texas, USA to New Albany, Indiana, USA, but some things are still in Houston. Before I moved, I had a walk- in closet and also another room. Now, since I live with my sister, it is spread between two states.

❀**Mike Oxready:** It is sprawling! I live in a one bedroom and have two large totes, plus closet space dedicated to DRAG.

❀**Smitty O'Toole:** I have an entire room dedicated to my DRAG. The contents of that room are priceless. I have not retired anything, as of yet.

❀**LoUis Cyfer:** All that belongs to me now is a few bras! Only because LoUis does not find them comfortable anymore.

❀**Dionysus W Khaos:** It has become more out of control since my boyfriend, who is also a performer, moved in. We have a DRAG room, DRAG stuff in the main closet, some in the garage and have spilled into the guest bedroom. My stuff alone is thousands and I have been doing this less than two years. The only person who has had any of my DRAG stuff has been my boyfriend. I am sentimental and a bit of a hoarder when it comes to DRAG so I am, at this point, reluctant to let any of it go.

❦**Luke Ateraz:** My DRAG started with part of the closet. When we moved to Arizona, USA, it got a whole bedroom. Now that there are three performers in our home, we have mostly turned the front formal living room into the DRAG area.

❦**E. M. Shaun:** I started with a closet and now it has become an entire room. My DRAG wear is very valuable to me. I have a portable stash of clothes, music, and makeup that I always keep in my car; you never know when you might have to be asked to stand in for a cancelled act. I am always ready to perform.

❦**Devin G. Dame:** We have one whole side of our house dedicated to DRAG.

Chapter Twenty-Two
"Where do you purchase wigs? How do you clean them? How are they stored? What do you do when you retire them from your own DRAG room?"

❀Adam All: My partner wears wigs. Her tips are; do not use hair spray, keep them in their packet or an individual zip lock bag, brush them out as little as possible, just before you use them. After they die, they are saved for a possible costume. It is a joint effort wig thing.

❀Travis Hard: As of now, I am expecting my first wig in the mail from overseas. I hope to catch some great ways to take care of it, via this question.

❀Coti Blayne: William Vanity Matrix buys any wigs; I just jack them, use them and make him wash them. That is the benefit of being with another performer.

❀Kenneth J. Squires: I have only bought one wig. I have not used it yet though.

❀Spacee Kadett: Let us be honest. Wigs are a queen thing. I remember when I was scared of them. Then my hair started getting long again and to change it up, I tried a high-quality short wig for fun. Now I own dozens of wigs and wear them every time I hit the stage. They are fun and dynamic, they enhance my illusion, and make my tiny girl head look more like a man's! My own experience will not hold true for every king, many of us have gorgeous and convincing fades that are perfect for kinging. But to mix it up, I recommend any king take some serious wigs for a spin. Serious wigs, DO NOT WASTE TIME AND MONEY ON A COSTUME WIG. They are overpriced yet insanely cheap, cannot be styled, and lose their shape after one show. Go to a bona fide wig and hair shop/beauty supply store. Check the clearance sale section (rule of thumb for ALL DRAG.) Better yet, ask your local queens. A girl on our cast is a Wig America rep, and she places bulk orders for us regularly. I bet you know some sort of hair representative, too. Short wigs will almost exclusively come in female styles, so look for androgynous styles or ones that can easily be modified into something more masculine. Do not hesitate to ask your queens for help with this. They'll be tickled by a king wearing a wig. I hang mine on wall hooks to store them. or tuck them neatly away. Flipping them inside out is tempting, but will ruin their style. I wash them regularly with shampoo; Woolite also works for synthetic wigs. They'll dry however they are left, so I either use a blow dryer to style them as desired, or leave them to air dry in a style that will be desirable to wear.

❀Koomah: I get wigs from beauty supply stores, wig shops, resale, and online. I rarely get them from costume shops unless they are high quality.

Sometimes I make my own wigs from cuts of other wigs, or from weaves. I almost always restyle or cut them. Some are safe to use with heat styling tools others are not. Hairspray and other products are used as needed. Wigs without set in styles are washed with soap and drip dried. Wigs with set in styles have the inner cap sprayed with no rinse shampoo foam or spray. Mine are stored in bags in a plastic bin except for those with set styles which are placed on wig heads. For wigs I plan to retire, I will often cut sections for use in another wig or trim the hair for use as facial/body hair. Sometimes I pass them on to other performers.

❀Justin Cider: I always have to use a wig because I have long curly thick hair and I never want to cut it! I have found the cheapest yet best quality men wigs come from oversees; Amazon is the best place for me to find them. I have bought them from party city and they have looked crappy, held up worse and were twice as expensive. As for storage I have them in my DRAG bag I'll wash and dry them in my bath tub if I need to but usually they are less than $20 so if I can I'll just buy a new one when necessary.

❀SirMandingo Thatis: All wigs are in the DRAG room on mannequins, they are washed just as if they were a real head of hair on a person. Once they are done for, I donate them to the cancer patients at the local hospital.

❀Ben Eaten: I have super long hair so I do use wigs. I go to Amazon or I have done costume wigs. I get them styled after I buy them. I wash them with shampoo and hang them upside down to dry.

❀Flex Jonez: I purchase from a wig company. They are all are made with human hair so they can be treated as that when washed and done up.

❀Silk Steele Prince: wigs.com, beauty supplies that sell wigs, costume shops, or party stores sell wigs. I make my own sometimes with a bundle of weave, needle, thread, glue, netting or wave cap. I use wig shampoo with cool water and let air dry or dry shampoo. A trick I learned to get oil out of hair is to use baby powder and brush it out. After I am done with them I give them to someone who needs them.

❀DeVery Bess: I generally keep them on Styrofoam heads in the DRAG room. I brush them like any other hair, and wash them, then air dry.

❀Eddie C. Broadway: I am just now starting to look into using wigs. I store them in their containers for now, and make sure they are safe and away from things.

❀Colin Grey: I have one that I pull out occasionally for hair band nights. It stays in a zippy bag in a drawer until I need it, then it comes out, gets brushed and used, then back to the bag and drawer.

❀Phantom: I work at Halloween Adventure in San Bernardino, California, USA, here every year, and I have a discount that I receive, which helps with the cost. I also go to Fun Corner located in San Bernardino. They have more of a selection. Storing my wigs is difficult because I have two children who like to get into everything. I have many damaged wigs that I reuse, cut up, style, and clean as best as possible. Depending on the wig, if its real hair I wash and condition it with normal products. The synthetic wigs do not seem to last very long so I'd spend more money on buying new wigs.

❀**Kameo Dupree:** I get simple wigs from a local costume shop and store in Ziploc bags. They are used maybe twice a year; they have so much time before they retire.

❀**Bootzy Edwards Collynz:** It depends on the performance for me. I have not needed a really expensive wig for a few years, and that is a pompadour. I will reuse wigs if possible. I do not get rid of them until they are beaten up and useless. I will store some Ziploc bags with sprayed with oil sheen. Others have form to them, so they need to be on wig heads. For cleaning them, I just use a cap full of Woolite with a bit of warm water in the tub. Swish it around a bit until it rinses clear. Let it dry and reset/set your style, and do your thing.

❀**Jack King:** I make my own hair to look like the person I am doing.

❀**B J Armani:** I have long blond hair down to my chest. I wear the main BJ wig and I had to purchase it online. I then took it to my hairdresser to cut it to my head. Same with any other wig I purchase. I have to spike them with spray or glue, and keep them on wig heads to keep them nice. They usually air out so I do not have to wash them. I am sure I will be buried with the BJ wig.

❀**Campbell Reid Andrews:** I love, love, love vinyl, foam, and prosthetic wigs. To find them are a different story. Google, once again, saves my life. You can also go to your local wig shop and they have a crazy amount of synthetic, real, or horse wigs in all styles and colors. You can also use these real hair wigs for facial hair.

❀**Howie Feltersnatch:** I purchased my wig from a hair salon. I do not have a fancy way of storing it except flat on a shelf. I wash it with regular shampoo and conditioner then brush it after.

❀**Jack E. Dickinson:** I only ever bought one from a discount wig store. The other one I have was given to me. Early on, I followed the instructions that came with it, which was to store it on one of those heads and some other stuff. Forgot now, actually have not been taking very good care of it. Fortunately, the acts I use it for usually call for a disheveled look.

❀**Clark Kunt:** I only have a few cheap wigs from Halloween stores. Typically, if I use a wig, I borrow one from my DRAG family, but I prefer to use my own hair and change the style between performances. I use a LOT of hair products to change the look, slick back, side swoop, spikes, hawk, and pompadour. I also add spray in color, and sometimes bleach or dye my hair so it will be different from the last show.

❀**Juan Kerr:** I do not wear a wig, but you have just reminded me I need to get some more of the hair gel I use, I get maybe five performances from one bottle because I slick my hair back with a ton of the stuff. Not all hair gels are equal though!

Brandon KC Young-Taylor: I have never done a wig before, but if I did I would definitely use one of the many DRAG sisters in my family's wigs!

Xavier Bottoms: My DRAG queen/brother uses them and he washes his wigs monthly, he soaks them in Fabulouso. He has retired some of them as wigs, but uses them to create outfits.

Stefon Royce Iman: Online or at a Halloween store or costume store, or have a DRAG queen make you one.

Cody Wellch Klondyke: Online or a Wig or Halloween Store, or I would simply ask my DRAG family or my DRAG mom. I have never worn a wig.

Soco Dupree: The only wig I have used is the afro style when I do some old school R&B. I hand wash that and air dry. Machine washing can damage some.

Smitty O'Toole: I make my own wigs. I have several of them. I store them on a shelf. I wash and style them as I would my own hair.

LoUis Cyfer: I do not use wigs. I shaved the sides of my head and use hats as a way to show masculinity, instead of assuming hair will suffice.

Jensen C. Dean: I have one wig that I have never used, it lives in the land of costumes that are for specific numbers that have not seen the stage, and possibly never will. It is in its container just waiting. When the time comes to use and clean a wig, I know some amazing queens that I will go to for help so I do not mess anything up.

E. M. Shaun: I do not use wigs but I would think a costume shop or wig store would be the best places to find them. I know many DRAG queens that will make them for you.

Name the performers without checking on DRAG411.com

Chapter Twenty-Three
"What rules apply for padding and binding?"

❀Coti Blayne: I use a compression shirt and shorts, and if I use padding that night, I put it under the compression items so it smooths out. I will use pads on my waist/sides to hide my hour glass and I'll use some on the back of my thighs under my behind to hide my bubble butt. It is a two-person job though to do, so I only pad if I am wearing a tighter outfit or body suit for my number. I hardly ever tape due to my size. It is difficult and painful and I rip my skin painfully every time, so I stick to my compression shirt and I am much more comfortable and just as flat.

❀Freddy Prinze Charming: When it comes to binding using a binder, it is not as easy as simply pulling on the binder and calling it a day. The "girls" need to be pushed down and to the sides, essentially under your armpits. Expect to have to readjust throughout the night, since there is nothing more off-putting than a king sporting cleavage. If you're doing open shirt and binding with tape, learn the safe methods to prevent injury. Understand your body type and what works and does not work. If you've got a belly (like me) and you're doing open shirt, you may not want to paint a 6-pack on. It is not all that realistic. One thing to remember is that, unless you've had top surgery, everyone needs to bind somehow. Even small breasts still look like breasts; they still look like a woman's chest, unless properly bound.

❀Koomah: There are many different ways to bind and pad, find what works best for your body to create the illusion you are going for, especially if you have a larger chest or if you are a person of size. Padding is great not just to build up areas you want to accentuate (shoulders/upper thighs) but also fill in negative space (waist) to even out the body and give it a more masculine shape. Compression wear is also great to reduce butt/hips. The main rule is: If you wheeze, rattle when you breathe, or feel sharp pains when you bind, you need to give your body a rest. Unbind for a few minutes or find a new binding technique.

❀Dominic Von Strap: I will leave you with my own hard-learned lesson: mind the nipples. I have managed to do some damage even with a binder. Future kings, I beg of you, be fully aware of your nipples!

❀Adam All: Ok for those who do not have use of a binder, I find the following perfectly adequate for an already masculine figure. I have only a small chest and I do not have a curvy waist. I am pretty muscular as I work out a lot so small adjustments are just fine. Wear a tight crop top or sports bra, use cohesive bandaging to flatten, a couple of longish lengths is plenty, pull a plain high neck t-shirt or vest over it, preferably to match in with your dress shirt so it does not show. Watch out for bulging; make sure you can still sing with it on. And the bandaging has a tendency to roll up if you over stretch in the wrong direction. For me, it stops me from moving or dancing in a feminine way and makes me more blocky and stiff.

❀Travis Luvermore: As a large breasted woman I have not found a binder that works, in addition, I love working with an open shirt concept. I find the audience loves that look. It also is more amazing to the most people who know how large I am to see me with an open shirt and chest hair.

❀Travis Hard: This subject is touchy. Every king or illusionist has their own ideas. I personally believe if you are impersonating a male, you must bind your chest. Packing to me is dependent on the outfit. If I wear tight pants, I will pack. That is my own opinion though. To bind, I use a chest binder because I am a bigger king. underworks.com is great for all types of binders!

❀Chance Wise: Padding, I personally, do not need. I am trying to make things look smaller on stage. As far as binding, I think it is a must if you're portraying yourself as male, unless you're very small chested and can pass without binding. I do not consider it DRAG if the illusion isn't complete. To me it is like a queen that hasn't shaved their chest hair and wears a low neckline, it just does not work for me.

❀Rychard "Alpha" Le'Sabre: Do not let it show!

❀Shane Rebel Caine: I do not pad, but I do pack, I have found that packing, whether it is tight pants or loose, tends to help me keep more of a manly walk with less effort especially since my brother and I found a way to make it look more natural. You do not want a huge bulge and you do not want it to look like its positioned funny or attached to your leg. A cheap silicone strap on dildo works best, if you pin it tightly into a pair of silk boxers it sits perfectly in your pants and looks legit. For binding, I am very heavy chested so I usually stick with my binder, but if I am wearing certain costuming or want a certain look, I use Gorilla Tape as it holds the best Biggest rule for taping when binding is do not let them see the tape! Also, make sure you make your chest look as much like natural pectorals as you can, you do not want one having a strange bulge or shape that can be noticed through the costume.

❀Campbell Reid Andrews: This all depends on how flat you want to be. I use duct tape and spray adhesive because I sweat a lot and I am usually on stage or in some shows for about one and half hours. If you can handle it, you can tape and wear a binder. I use the onesie shorts from underworks.com. I use this method when I want to get super flat. My binding method of choice is the anchor method connected in the back because I have a bigger chest and need more support. That allows me to be able to breathe normally and wear open shirts, or tear my shirt open if needed. You can do this on your own or with a friend to get a good pull. One big thing I have seen that is NOT good and I would not encourage, is to tape your chest all the way around your body. That will constrict your breathing and crush your lungs.

❀**Dakota Rain:** I do not know about the rules, I am still learning myself, but as far as padding, I do not, as binding, I use a binder or duct tape.

❀**Ashton The Adorable Lover:** I now use a binder but with taping trial and error.

❀**Ben Eaten:** I do not know any rules, but for me, I have a fake penis that I use to pack. As far as binding, I usually use a binder because it is easier and looks more natural I think. Since I am bigger, a completely flat chest would look weird. Now if I do something open shirt, I do tape, but I prefer not to.

❀**Clint Torres:** If you are going to wear a binder, do not wear it over 8 hours, tops. If you do, you will end up causing serious long-term effects to your breast tissue and lungs. If you are going to use an ace wrap or duct tape, put on some sort of protective layer like non-adhesive spray so that you do not end up injuring yourself by removing pieces of your skin, and do not wear longer than 6 hours. For ace bandages, if it feels tight, it is way too tight. I do not really ever pad.

❀**Rasta Boi Punany:** Do not let it look like you have breasts and to make it look like pectorals, do not allow the binding to show.

❀**Spacee Kadett:** Queens can easily add curves by padding, but we cannot do the same to take ours away. Therefore, the right costuming is a must for a king's illusion. Without it, his body is all too often a flat-chested, curvy female figure with a package. A good-fitting blazer gives a masculine frame, hides feminine shoulders, and squares off curvy hips, when fitted correctly, i.e. no bunching or pulling at the waist or hips. This may require going a size up for a smooth fit around the waist, then have the sleeves tailored down. WEAR MEN'S PANTS. Women's pants accentuate curves. So do pleats. Flat front is optimum, if not in costuming then at least in pageantry. Finally, be mindful of the open chest illusion, which inadvertently showcases the feminine physique that we all work so hard to hide. I have a fantastic respect for this incredibly difficult trick, because for every time I have seen it done right, I have seen it done wrong ten other times. It takes a certain body type that I do not feel I possess myself, so I have never done it, and it is never hurt my career.

❀**Adam DoEve:** I am a fluffy king so I do not need padding. I come with it, but the binding, that is a different story. I have a large chest so it makes it more of a challenge. I found that an exercise belt works well, the kind you put around your waist. It has different zippers on it to change the size if need be. I then have a light binder shirt that goes over that and then, just to be safe, I put a wife beater over that. I did try the duct tape and I am just one of those that cannot have it on my skin. As soon as the show is over and the callbacks have been done, the belt comes off so that I am not bound any longer than I need to be and my back thanks me.

❀**Pierce Gabriel:** SAFETY. So many things can go wrong with binding. I have heard of performers with broken ribs, ripped nipples, and even torn sternums. I have almost passed out on stage because the binding was too tight and too low, and restricted my breathing too much. Always make sure that you are able to take regular breaths and move around without feeling any pulling or pinching.

🌸Vinnie Marconi: Binding AND a girdle work for me, for I have been blessed with Italian hips. Make sure that your outfits COMPLIMENT your physique and do not show off all the wrong bulges. Larger kings CAN get away with larger pectorals and as long as the shirt does not have the shoulders around their biceps (pet peeve of mine), and CLOSES without pulling, they can pull off the look with style. We smaller kings have just the opposite problem with tiny waists. AGAIN, the fit of the shirt is essential to the illusion. If you wear a tight shirt that shows those hips off, use PADS under your binder to give a FULLER LOOK. The guys have a natural "V" shape to their backs, broader at the shoulder and smaller at the hips. Keep this in mind when costuming and PADS at the shoulders WILL give you a broader top.

🌸Kruz Mhee: I wear a full compression body suit. As for my pack, I wear an 8 1/2 inch Cyber Skin. I know a number of kings that wear a packed sock or have purchased a pack. I am known for being on the dirty side so a full sized cock is my preference. For me, the rule is to be comfortable in how you present yourself.

🌸Hawk Stuart: Make sure your binding is right and it is not too tight, so you can breathe.

🌸Alec Allnight: I do not pad, I pack on occasion for the number. I duct tape. I am the only king locally here who does open shirt. I use cotton rounds to cover the important bits, and tape my boobs in my armpits. For a little extra security, I put an extra strip to connect the left and right sides. The look I am going for depends on how tight I pull the tape back. As soon as the night is over, I get home and in a hot shower to melt the tape a little at a time as I pull it off. I have never had a problem with it unless I try to tape two days in a row. One weekend, it was twice in one day and once the following day. That was a little tender for a few days, but never ever tried to tape or wrap all the way around. No one wants to go to the ER in full DRAG wearing a dildo.

🌸Silk Steele Prince: Buy a chest binder in your size or compression shirt. If you do not have one, use Ace bandages. Do not bind too tightly. It can cause serious damage to the breast tissue and they will begin to sag over time. Your breathing can be restricted. I would not suggest that you wear it pass 4-5 hours, tops.

🌸Stormm: I tape those puppies under the arms. I do not pad, I feel I have enough of that. I leave the front without tape so I can do open shirt when I feel I can and with what I am wearing.

🌸E. M. Shaun: I am a thicker king and have a very muscular build. I use a compression tank top I bought online from underworks.com. They have a variety of compression shirts and full body wear. I started with duct tape and Ace bandages back in the day, but it would compress and suffocate me sometimes. Also if the duct tape moves it can cut into your skin. Since I am a 44DD, I cover my nipples with cotton squares, duct tape my breast towards my armpits then that allows for an open shirt look, but if I am not doing open shirt, I also put the chest binder on and it adds a broader, more masculine looking chest. As for packing, I also pack. My fans like to get an up close and personal dance from me so I give them what they want.

Kenneth J. Squires: I do not use any kind of padding, but I do pack. Binding at first can be difficult. I used Ace bandages at first, and then found a "Guarder" that I used. I sometimes bind with duct tape. You have to find what is best for you. I use a compression shirt as well.

George De Micheal: Personally, I use a compression vest. Sometimes I will tape, but for comfort of being big on top, I use a compression vest.

Chasin Love: I use a sports bra, wife beater shirt and 2 compression shirts.

Eddie C. Broadway: Make sure you get the right size binder for your chest. There is nothing worse than seeing a misshapen chest or boobs with a beard. It ruins the illusion every time.

Colin Grey: Duct tape, more often than not, is what I use to bind. I have used Ace bandages in the past, but find they are itchy. I still use them occasionally when I am not doing anything open shirt or low cut shirts but I do tape over them now in strips across the front. I think my big rule is do not use one continuous strand of tape wrapped around your torso over and over again. It is a good way to break a rib.

Phantom: For me, it is not too much of a task because I am very small chested. I do it every once in a while when the number calls for it. Otherwise, I just wear very tight wife beater binders. I have not used any padding.

Sam Masterson: I had a chest plate made so I would not have to use duct tape to tape myself down.

B J Armani: Hide the breasts and try to create an illusion of a package in your pants. You do not want a uni-boob and no bulge. Kind of hard to look like a guy that way!

Jamel Knight: There really are no rules because everyone uses a different technique. As long as the illusion comes across the way it is meant to, then do you. Although I will say, be careful with duct tape when binding. You definitely want to make sure you can move and breathe well. And always take your time taking it off. Ripping it off can cause pain that you will never forget.

Howie Feltersnatch: It depends on your character, and the shape of your body. I like to use a compression tank for my regular DRAG king numbers, but I also do a lot of gender bending burlesque, so I end up not binding for those numbers, just because I am bigger and it is not that sexy trying to do the binder wiggle dance on stage.

❀**Welland Dowd:** No rules do whatever makes you look/feel good.

❀**Michael Christian:** I personally use the open shirt method most of the time. Even when I wear a closed shirt or suit, I feel like I can create the shape of male chest better with spray adhesive and tape. I feel like clothes lay better on me this way. I have also recently started taping my hips/love handles/curves back. I wear a lot of tighter shirts and skinnier cut pants and suits, so this helps. I ALWAYS pack. No matter how big and baggy the pants, they will fall against your body and shift on stage making the fact you did not noticeable. At the end of the night, make sure whatever method you use is what works for you. Make sure you can breathe easily (especially if you are a dancer), do not break ribs, and remove any tape or adhesive safely. Take care of your nipples (cover them before taping) and skin. To avoid scarring or the inevitable stretch marks if you have a long career, go ahead and start adding vitamin E oil to your daily routine. After more than ten years of binding I have almost no damage to my skin.

❀**Julius M. SeizeHer:** Do not bind too far in advance, as it can be dangerous.

❀**Jensen C. Dean:** For me, personally, the rules are no tape and use a binder as I learned after a long day of DRAG that I am very allergic to the adhesive on tape. I have found that the "Ultimate Chest Binder Tank suit" from underworks.com worked well for this. The shorts part of this helped smooth out my girl butt and hips, and the tank top worked well to bind my chest. This one is also nice because it does not roll up like some of the other tank top only ones.

❀**Jonah Godfather of DRAG:** I think the key to binding is to do so as not to make bulges elsewhere on the body where you do not want them either. You want it to look as smooth as possible. Clothing can also cover up or distract the audience from seeing what you do not want them to see.

❀**Clark Kunt:** Find the right tension to keep you held in but not to create bulges!

❀**Lyle Love-It:** I use a flexible, easy to remove medical tape.

❀**Emilio:** I have used many different methods: duct tape, ace bandages, Saran Wrap, it all depends on what I am wearing.

❀**Juan Kerr:** I use bandages underneath bondage tape because it hurts less when you peel the tape off. I have used duct tape but I sweat it right off and then there are boobs hanging out everywhere. I may invest in a compression vest at some point.

❀**DeVery Bess:** I found this out recently; that guy's underwear have an extra pouch thing that one can use to put a packer in, wearing two pairs of underwear is smart, so the packer can be stuck between the two. When

- wearing a binder and having boobs, separate the boobs so it does not give you cleavage.

❀**Trey C. Michaels:** The rule I was taught is if you are going to be doing open shirt, make sure you hide your tape. If you want to show stomach chest or be topless you have to know how to do your makeup properly. If taping is not an option then you have to invest in good binders. Avoid ace wraps and sports bras.

❀**Xavier Bottoms:** If you do not have a butt, create one. They make butt pads. They even make the shorts to put them in. If you feel you must "pack" make sure it is proportionate to your body type? No one likes to see a watermelon hanging from a stick. Any type of "taping" is not good for your skin, especially if you intend on doing DRAG for years. Your skin will tell on you. Binders are the best. If you have asthma, do not get a full binder. I follow the "b" rule, binder, bike shorts, butt, and bulge.

❀**Stefon Royce Iman:** Gorilla Tape and cut it into strips. If you are doing open shirt, use double-sided tape.

❀**Soco Dupree:** Always double-check your tape, and you can never have enough tape for security. If it feels like it is going to pop, it probably will.

❀**Mike Oxready:** I use a chest binder or tape depending on the performance. I used to pack with a water snake, but have since graduated to a packer.

❀**Smitty O'Toole:** Take care of your binding practice, as well as making sure that you are securely bound. Make sure your packer is secure.

❀**LoUis Cyfer:** Crepe bandages, cling film, duct tape a small swimming cozy and a backwards sports bra. Boom, no boobs!

❀**Luke Ateraz:** I typically wear two binders on stage to hide my fat and my chest and my trusty packer (my wife has pierced my packer).

❀**Devin G. Dame:** I have worn binders for most of my career.

Chapter Twenty-Four
"What is the best procedure for applying makeup to include performers with acne?"

❀**D-Luv Saviyon:** You can use a sealer prior to putting makeup on to protect sensitive skin...also to set the makeup after applying.

❀**Freddy Prinze Charming:** Find a good hypo-allergenic base or foundation to put on first. Something that you know will not irritate your skin. Certain sealers can work too, as long as they are non-irritating. Then build on that.

❀**Coti Blayne:** I just wash my face right after and scrub it really well with palm olive dish soap. It cuts thru excess oil from my skin. I do not use any special foundation or anything (but probably should so I am going take notes).

❀**Koomah:** Use a spray primer/sealer first to protect the makeup from settling in pores and irritating the skin. Concealer/beard cover/glue stick can help cover stubborn acne. Make sure the makeup is removed well using a low oil/oil free makeup remover or a petroleum based cleanser (dish soap/Vaseline/Albolene) and then a cleansing scrub. Keep the pores clean, reduce oil, and be conscious of skin sensitivities.

❀**Adam All:** I found, and this is random non DRAG related amazingness, my acne cleared up completely when I spent an intensive week drinking loads of water. Otherwise, I am a decorator, so applying makeup is like painting a room. Start with your hair, get it out the way and fixed, then do your base coats, do your eyebrows or something while it dries, then deep shadows, then draw out beard (fine line the edges) while that dries, then do your highlights and blending, and while that is drying stick on your beard and give your final touches. Then you can dab and touch at it and it is pretty much ready all over. Time for a stiff drink or a last minute routine run through. It takes about forty minutes. The more hydrated I stayed the better my skin was, it did not matter what face wash I used or what moisturizer, makeup or makeup remover, it was all about what was coming out from inside my skin.

❀**Travis Hard:** I use a water based cover up and do not leave it on longer than needed. I clean my face right after with soap and water. Usually the hottest water I can stand helps get rid of any acne.

❀**Shane Rebel Caine:** I do not have much acne problems except for around my mouth and my chin. If you are breaking out badly and it is along your jaw-chin or even above your lip then a good way to cover it is with facial hair. It may not be the look you wanted but it may turn out to be a killer look if you design it right. As for preventing acne, use baby oil to get the spirit gum and makeup off your face. Wash your face with hot water and use a soap that has the grains or minerals.

❋**Dakota Rain:** I do not use makeup, as of right now. I have never used it so I really do not know the techniques of using makeup.

❋**Ashton The Adorable Lover:** Mine is just facial hair so, look at the males in your family and around you. Figure out what looks good to you, use eyeliner pencils to outline and make a base for the area your facial hair is going. Apply spirit gum and hair. Use edging clippers to trim the line hair so it is all even. Also, look at your face. We all have facial hair or fuzz, that is how your hair grows, natural pattern so use it.

❋**Ben Eaten:** I say start with a good foundation. This helps with the blending and smoother look. Play with different facial hair. I do a few different things depending on my set for the night.

❋**Clint Torres:** Because I usually break out before a show, I wash my face with some type of face cleaner like proactive and then put on two coats of foundation, first, a light base coat that conceals any acne and the other to start the process of darkening the face. The whole process takes about twenty minutes and it really works for me.

❋**Spacee Kadett:** Yes. A hypo-allergenic base or sealer is a must, along with a thorough face scrubbing with a good cleanser afterward. I am fortunate to have relatively resilient skin myself, and I still find it being crabby about all the makeup I wear. There are no guarantees, everyone's skin reacts differently, but there are steps you can take to minimize breakouts and reactions.

❋**Adam DoEve:** I know that some use stage makeup but I use every day, girl stuff so I am able to get all the hypoallergenic. Because I have very light skin, this works for me. I have not had any problems in the time I have used it and I found a brand that does not come off on my clothing (and that is a plus). I wash my face well with goat soap before I go and then again when I get home after taking off my facial hair with the spirit gum remover and baby wipes (also hypo-allergenic). It works very well and leaves my skin very clean.

❋**Kenneth J. Squires:** Hypoallergenic would be the best. I have been blessed and have not had any problems with acne. Cleaning your face well afterwards is a must. I have used baby wipes to take all my makeup off and Vaseline is good. Everyone is different, so trying different things may be the best for some.

❋**Pierce Gabriel:** I never really did anything different when I had a breakout or clear skin; guys have acne too, so I never worried about covering it up.

❋**Vinnie Marconi:** This old man no longer worries about acne. I use a BARE minimum of make-up as required for the intensity of the spotlight. Eyebrows need to be a little bushier, jaw lines defined, eye lashes need to be seen if getting up close and personal. PRACTICE applying make-up and facial hair at home! When you are getting ready for a show is NOT the time to experiment, you are "on the clock" and should have it down pat by then.

❀**Kruz Mhee:** Final Seal is awesome to set your makeup both before you apply and after. Practice at home as much as you can. As far as acne, you'll just have to try different things until you find what works for you personally. I prefer hypoallergenic base or foundation and eyeliner.

❀**Hawk Stuart:** Use something that is good for your skin and will not bother you, since everyone has different reactions to different products.

❀**Flex Jonez:** Use Vaseline mixed with a base.

❀**Silk Steele Prince:** Wash face with salicylic acid based products then apply witch hazel as an astringent to reduce redness, blemishes, and oiliness. Plus it locks in moisture and tightens the skin. Apply a moisturizer for oily or sensitive skin. then use a gel or cream based with benzoyl peroxide to treat the acne spots. After that, apply makeup that is labeled for oily skin, for sensitive skin or hypoallergenic. Make sure you highlight spots that need to be accentuated and use darker makeup where it needs to me reduced or hollowed. Men faces are chiseled and women are rounded. So with that said, chisel out the roundness in your face and make male features more prominent. Do not forget accentuating the Adam's apple and sides of neck. For open shirt, use darker makeup on torso and chest for the muscle illusion.

❀**Stormm:** I do not usually get the break outs any more. You need to practice at home putting on facial hair and makeup. I do not use a lot of makeup, but I try to scrub my face really good afterwards and I try not to leave it on any longer than needed.

❀**E. M. Shaun:** I do have sensitive skin and had to battle with acne in the past. I make sure I wash my face very well. I apply a hypoallergenic base and use hair gel to apply my facial hair. The gel is water-based so it less harsh than spirit gum and it washes off with water or a baby wipe.

❀**George De Micheal:** Again using wet wipes and moisturizing.

❀**Colin Grey:** Make sure you have an even base. Shading is a great way to add subtle effects like jawline, etc. I always seal with hairspray after I have finished applying makeup, shading, and facial hair. I think it helps the hair stay stuck to my face. Use products your face can handle and experiment before you take it to the stage.

❀**Eddie C. Broadway:** Add some of the primer before putting makeup on to save some of your pores. Maybe oil based isn't the best for all. Using a mixture of foundation and powders, including finishing powders helps.

❀**Phantom:** Keeping your face clean is very important; I use witch hazel. Before applying any makeup, a clean surface helps with any further breakouts or future breakouts. Try several brands of makeup before stepping out on stage.

❀**Joshua Grobelnik:** DRAG queens taught me dish soap to remove any oil or buildup from makeups and then an oil free lotion afterwards.

❀**Kameo Dupree:** I believe real men have blemishes and scars. Due to this, I do not wear any makeup besides mascara to thicken eyelashes and brows. I brush my face with baby powder for moisture control.

❀**Xavier Bottoms:** I do not wear makeup nor draw on face. But if you must, shadow your facial hair. If you sweat a lot, I highly recommend coating your face with Noxzema first. It helps keep your face dry.

❀**Jamel Knight:** I do not typically use makeup unless I am performing in front of a large audience in a more concert style venue. Then it may be necessary so that the full audience can see the illusion. For club performances, I usually will not use makeup unless it is being used to create a different character or persona. Either way with makeup or just applying facial hair, cleansing and moisturizing is very important before and afterwards.

❀**Welland Dowd:** I guess it would be up to the performer to decide what they are comfortable with, whether they want to cover up the acne or roll with it.

❀**Michael Christian:** Use a primer beforehand. Try to use as many hypoallergenic products as possible. Never sleep in your makeup! Take the time for a good face wash after the show. It is refreshing and healthy. Also stay hydrated. The body is mostly water. Keep yourself healthy and the skin helps clean itself. You'll find your skin looking more clear and younger... Which never hurt anyone.

❀**Julius M. SeizeHer:** Foundation and washing. Wash before, pat dry, and apply foundation. That is what I do.

❀**B J Armani:** For oily skin, I tend to go for powder based, and for dry skin, I tend to use a liquid base. Make sure you are washing your face and moisturizing it every day no matter what your skin condition. If you are acne prone, makeup and a beard can easily cover many blemishes but make sure you use a cover stick that is a shade lighter than your foundation in order to make an even skin tone. There are no rules as each performer does their makeup differently, but the end result should be masculine!

❀**Howie Feltersnatch:** I use a lot of makeup from Lush to help with my acne, but I also make sure to wash it off as soon as the show is over. When I get home, I will do a giant face scrub and shower.

❀**Clark Kunt:** Use natural removers like coconut oil, and I find liquid bases helpful in cutting down acne along the hairline.

❀**Santana Romero:** Making sure your skin is completely clean before applying any makeup is critical for people who suffer from acne (myself included). I usually use the method of wiping off my face with a makeup wipe before putting on foundation to make sure no dirt, oil or sweat gets trapped underneath. Using makeup for sensitive skin and avoiding heavily oiled makeup make a big difference as oily makeup can clog your pores and make your acne worsen. When taking off makeup, it is a lot easier to use a wipe first THEN wash thoroughly. It is a lot less scrubbing which can cause skin to dry out and become flaky, and who really wants that? Of course, washing your face of all impurities is the best way to prevent breakouts, but avoid using normal bar soap. I have heard from a professional makeup artist that it can cause acne scars to darken and become more prominent. Instead, find a wash that works for you and wash faithfully after every performance.

❀**Stefon Royce Iman:** Clean your face and add moisturizer. Make sure it is hypoallergenic; always clean the makeup off fully so it is not in your pores.

❀**Soco Dupree:** Always wash your face first. I use a foundation and then eye shadow to accentuate my jaw and nose. I also darken my eyebrows a little with eye shadow. Clean up is easy. Use makeup wipes and then use a face scrub afterwards to make sure I am 100% free from makeup.

❀**Cody Wellch Klondyke:** Wash your face to make sure it is good and clean. Then I would apply a foundation and then a powder if need to do so. After you are done, make sure you wash your face and remove makeup. If your face is oily, make sure you avoid the oil-based makeups. Note: if you have sensitive skin, Sea Breeze afterwards is not a good thing.

❀**Jensen C. Dean:** Obviously, as many people have suggested, hypoallergenic would probably be the best way to go, but sensitive skin types can vary and what works for one person **will not** necessarily work for another. I think this really could come down to trial and error to see what works best for you. It could be worth it to try to get sample sizes of products (even better if you can score free samples) and just trouble shoot it until you find what your skin likes best.

❀**Luke Ateraz:** Start with a clean face. Use Kryolan makeup. I use spirit gum for facial hair, mascara for eyelashes, eyeliner when needed, and eye shadow for contouring.

❀**Devin G. Dame:** Start with a blemish hider then a good foundation. You will then use contour colors and mascara to highlight eyelashes & brows...then blend, blend, blend with a top powder.

Chapter Twenty-Five
"What is the most effective way to remove makeup?"

❀**Kameo Dupree:** I remove facial hair with alcohol. I cannot say too much about makeup because I do not use it.

❀**Justin Cider:** Apricot scrubs and showers but be sure to have good plumbing or Drano. All that fake hair can clog up.

❀**Joshua Micheals:** I just use baby wipes then soap and water. Since I use hair glue to put on my beard, it is easy.

❀**Freddy Prinze Charming:** WD-40 is a great all-purpose tool. It will remove makeup, adhesive, spirit gum, etc. Baby oil works, too. Both are a lot gentler on the skin than other things, but I definitely recommend washing your face with a good cleanser once the makeup is all off.

❀**Adam DoEve:** I use baby wipes and the remover that is made for the spirit gum. I then use a goat soap to wash my face. Very good for the skin and cleans well. Whatever you do, do not leave the spirit gum on overnight. I did it once and learned my lesson, had burns on my face for over two weeks, all because I ran out of what I use to remove it.

❀**Dante Diamond:** Albolene, hands down.

❀**Coti Blayne:** I use soap, water, and some good scrubbing. By soap, I mean Palmolive dish soap. Sounds crazy but it works.

❀**Dominic Von Strap:** I use makeup remover wipes, but I cannot use spirit gum, so I really do not need anything too special or heavy duty.

❀**D-Luv Saviyon:** To remove facial hair/spirit gum easily, use baby oil or oil sheen spray…let it sit a bit. Noxzema makes great makeup remover wipes.

❀**Jack King:** I use baby wipes, it is easy to take with you.

❀**King Dante:** Lotion.

❀**Koomah:** I use a spray primer before putting on makeup that makes it easier to remove. Makeup remover wipes work great backstage. Oil-based removers work good for removing adhesives. At home I use a charcoal scrub for harder to remove makeup/makeup that covers large areas, and an amino acid wash. Grease based makeups remove well with dish soap (Dawn/Palmolive/etc.) or other petroleum based makeup removers (Vaseline/Albolene/etc.).

❀**Adam All:** Moisturizer or makeup wipes with moisturizer in them.

❀**Rocky Valentino:** I use alcohol wipes. It gets both the makeup and facial hair.

❀**Travis Hard:** Rubbing alcohol for spirit gum removal and baby wipes for makeup.

❀**Travis Luvermore:** I tried several removers for spirit gum, so many bother my skin. So I use simple soap and water, the same for my chest hair.

❀**Phantom:** Other than soap and water, witch hazel works best for me.

❀**Chance Wise:** I find baby wipes are great for makeup; nothing is good for spirit gum that I have found. I wind up using warm water and soap and slowly work it off.

❀**Gus Magendor:** Baby oil.

❀**AJ Menendez:** Makeup remover wipes.

❀**Shane Rebel Caine:** Baby oil removes spirit gum and all makeup with ease.

❀**Hurricane Savage:** Makeup remover wipes.

❀**Justin Seago:** I always use baby wipes, they are cheap, and work as well as makeup remover wipes, and they smell better.

❀**Rychard "Alpha" Le'Sabre:** Makeup remover and baby oil for the beard.

❀**Stormm:** Baby wipes and alcohol.

❀**Dakota Rain:** To remove my beard and mustache, I use Skin So Soft.

❀**Ben Eaten:** Makeup remover wipes. They take it all off including spirit gum.

❀**Clint Torres:** I use either adhesive remover or baby wipes to remove any makeup.

❀**Rasta Boi Punany:** I use baby wipes.

❀**Spacee Kadett:** The best makeup remover wipe is the Neutrogena wipe in the light blue package. A close second is the Pampers baby wipe (not Huggies! It has to be Pampers). Baby oil, oil sheen, and Albolene are also good with a washcloth. Goo Gone is second-to-none removing adhesive, but be careful on sensitive areas of the face (better for body adhesives). I wash off the rest with a good facial cleanser.

❀**Anson Reign:** A chainsaw.

❀**Kenneth J. Squires:** I use baby wipes, and sometimes I use Vaseline. There seems to be less pain when taking off the hair. Noxzema works well for an after cleansing.

❀**Pierce Gabriel:** I use baby wipes for the makeup and facial hair, and baby oil for the duct tape adhesive.

❀**Vinnie Marconi:** I keep a package of makeup wipes in my DRAG kit that has worked for me. Since I use hairspray for facial hair, soap and water does the rest.

❀**Brandon KC Young-Taylor:** Shower!

❀**Cherry Tyler Manhattan:** Rubbing alcohol.

❀**Corey James Caster:** With me, couple of paper towels, run it under some hot water and it removes my facial hair and makeup.

❁**Hawk Stuart:** Shower, but if you want to remove it before you leave, baby wipes or makeup wipes. Now with the duct tape, I use the oil sheen, it works.

❁**Kruz Mhee:** Jergens Lotion or Oil of Olay face wipes. I have extremely sensitive skin and these two items keep me from breaking out. If you are removing tape residue, use Goo Gone. It does not hurt sensitive skin and washing with soap after using it, will take off the greasy film. No pain!

❁**B J Bottoms:** Baby wipes.

❁**SirMandingo Thatis:** Well I do not wear much makeup, but when I do, I use makeup remover wipes. When I am removing my hair off my face, I use spirit gum remover and let if set for 5 minutes, then jump in the shower.

❁**Silk Steele Prince:** The most effective way to remove makeup is to use cold cream or a makeup remover pads. They are gentle on the skin and eyes. For hair, Goo Gone, 3D skin adhesive remover, or a mixture of alcohol and baby oil.

❁**Flex Jonez:** Noxzema and cold cream together in a hot shower.

❁**Dionysus W Khaos:** Remove all by Ben Nye is the best, castor oil a close second.

❁**George De Micheal:** Wet wipes.

❁**Chasin Love:** I use soap and water, or cold cream.

❁**Santana Romero:** I have found that Neutrogena wipes are excellent at removing makeup. They even have a grapefruit kind that easily removes spirit gum with a little effort. They smell great and keep my face clear of acne for the most part. I recommend them highly along with washing your face with mild cleanser that fits your skin type.

❁**DeVery Bess:** The makeup remover wipes. For getting off the mustaches with spirit gum, Bond Off, it is stronger than the remover is and it wipes right off!

❁**Colin Grey:** Walmart makeup remover wipes are great for at the bar. Then good old soap and water once home.

❁**Eddie C. Broadway:** Baby wipes, spirit gum remover, coconut oil, and water.

❁**Stefan LeDude:** For the spirit gum, I use spirit gum remover or Bond Off.

❁**Clark Kunt:** Coconut oil, it is also amazing for removing binding if you use duct tape/spray adhesive.

❁**J Breezy St James:** Makeup remover or baby oil has always worked for me.

❁**Jamel Knight:** Baby oil and makeup remover works wonders.

❁**Welland Dowd:** I do not use makeup but for removing facial hair, I use spirit gum remover or olive oil.

❀**Michael Christian:** I use makeup wipes for my face and chest makeup. Neutrogena brand is great for the skin. For the duct tape and spray adhesive, I use oil sheen or coconut oil. Then of course, when you get home, the after-DRAG shower is the best shower you will ever take.

❀**Julius M. SeizeHer:** Makeup wipes, I love them and swear by them.

❀**Jensen C. Dean:** Makeup removal is subjective to the type of makeup you use and your skin type. The best thing I was ever told was that you should exfoliate any area where you added hair to make sure you get it out of your pores. I also found that when you are removing Spirit Gum, if you first wet the cloth you are using to put the baby oil on, the oil does not get absorbed into the cloth and there is less scrubbing to get the Spirit Gum off.

❀**Jonah Godfather of DRAG:** Baby wipes and Noxzema.

❀**MaXx Decco:** I do a basic face wash first, and then exfoliate with St. Ives apricot scrub. Then I use makeup removing wipes.

❀**Campbell Reid Andrews:** I love Ponds; it takes off any kind of makeup and is very moisturizing. It smells like cabbage patch kids (well I like the smell at least). Great for sensitive skin. If you have never heard of it, ask your mom or grandmother they will tell you about it. Or baby oil, makeup remover wipes, lotion, and when you are on a budget, soap and water.

❀**Howie Feltersnatch:** After a show, the kings always have an abundance of baby wipes. I find it works pretty good for the stippling, but not always the best if you actually use facial hair.

❀**B J Armani:** A good face wash (Proactive, Philosophy, Neutrogena, etc.) that is for your skin type is good to use AFTER you have removed your beard. BABY WIPES are a staple, never pay for makeup wipes, and they are expensive. Baby wipes are cheap! If you have done thick costume makeup, a couple drops of baby oil and a baby wipe will work just fine, but make sure you wash with a facial cleanser and then moisturize.

❀**Lyle Love-It:** Baby wipes.

❀**Emilio:** My wife's makeup remover towelettes and spirit gum remover.

❀**Juan Kerr:** I use baby oil to get my beard glue off, it works.

❀**Brandon KC Young-Taylor:** Rubbing alcohol, baby wipes, warm water and soap... There are so many different ways; you just have to figure out what works best for you!

❀**Trey C. Michaels:** I use baby wipes right after the show and then when I get home I use facial items to deep clean my face. Hormones are causing me to be greasier so I have to remove makeup that night or run the risk of breaking out.

❀**Bailey Saint James:** Makeup remover.

❀**Xavier Bottoms:** Oil sheen and baby wipes.

❀**Aaron Phoenix:** OIL SHEEN.

❀**Thug Passion:** Soap and water has worked for me.

❀**Stefon Royce Iman:** Baby oil, makeup remover, oil sheen, baby wipes, makeup remover wipes, or cold cream.

❀**Soco Dupree:** Makeup wipes first and then Dawn dish soap and water.

❀**Cody Wellch Klondyke:** Makeup remover wipes, baby oil, warm water, and face wash.

❀**Smitty O'Toole:** Makeup remover or baby oil.

❀**LoUis CYfer:** Baby oil.

❀**E. M. Shaun:** I use makeup remover or baby oil.

❀**Luke Ateraz:** I use baby wipes to get most off, then when I get home, I use baby oil to remove the spirit gum, and face cleaner to get whatever is left.

❀**Mike Oxready:** Pond's Cold Cream!

❀**Devin G. Dame:** Makeup removal wipes...alcohol works great in a pinch. WD-40 to remove duct tape and/or spray adhesive.

Chapter Twenty-Six
"Where is the best place to find clever outfits for a production?"

✤D-Luv Saviyon: Thrift shop, your closet (stuff you no longer wear) or consignment shop for canvas, Jo-Ann Fabrics, Hobby Lobby, Michaels, and Wal-Mart for other material and embellishments. Richard Cranium does sickening stuff (if your budget permits), stones from Charles Brennan and lots of imagination. Learn to sew.

✤Coti Blayne: Thrift stores and clearance. Lots of coupons. I make a lot of my stuff. I cannot sew very well, but I can do some basic hand stitching. I can use glue, Velcro, and safety pins, and make some cool stuff.

✤Coti Blayne: As for ideas, I watch music videos of my favorite artists and use that to base some of my ideas off of.

✤Adam All: Honestly, my local Highstreet is amazing. We have a lot of Greek wedding shops on our street where I can by the most beautiful suits, really cheap, and some great shops with accessories.

✤Adam All: Try primark.com.

✤Travis Luvermore: Salvation Army and thrift stores, I landed a tuxedo for $15. I try to design my outfits toward the songs I choose and, on a limited budget, I check out the thrift stores as often as possible.

✤AJ Menendez: Salvation Army and thrift stores. With limited funds, I check out the thrift stores as often as possible.

✤Joshua Micheals: Thrift shops definitely. Also being creative with embellishing can save money. I use spray paint, paint, and stones. I get mine from China, on eBay, and the resin stones are great and are much cheaper. I have recently started beading, look up techniques for embellishing on YouTube and Pinterest, a lot of great ideas.

✤Michael Christian: I love thrift stores and my own closet. As I began my transition and my body grew and changed, I turned my old clothes into great costumes. You can go back and do a quick remake of old costumes. I watch concerts on YouTube and look at photos of red carpet for ideas to jump from. As you start to create and define your style you will find it easier to embellish and get inspired. EBay is wonderful for stones from China. studsandspikes.com is great for that kind of stuff. If you have local friends, you can get deals there for buying in bulk.

✤Gus Magendor: Thrift stores and Halloween shops.

✤Chance Wise: I buy from thrift stores and add to things. I have found many ways to make a basic pair of jeans look custom made and designs painted on them. But I do love having a sewing machine and I am getting pretty damn good at making a whole costume from a little fabric.

✤Marty Brown: Just normal stores and tweak them.

❊**Justin Cider:** Thrift stores! Also, if you need wigs like me, because I do not have short hair and do not want to cut it, check out Amazon. Way cheaper than Party City and a lot better quality.

❊**Hurricane Savage:** Thrift stores. I just get the basics and put my own spin on them.

❊**Marcus Mayhem:** Thrift stores or cloths given to me from friends to help in the arts.

❊**Stormm:** Thrift stores, also depends on the song.

❊**MaXx Decco:** Thrift stores and party supply stores work, but when I need something a little more specific or unique, I usually turn to Amazon or Google to find it.

❊**Kameo Dupree:** Any thrift stores. I am a fan of yard sales! There is always a treasure in someone else's trash. You can find unique items in the free section of Craig's List.

❊**Freddy Prinze Charming:** I find 98% of my costuming supplies at Goodwill and a local fabric store. I find the base (shirt, jacket, pants, etc.) at Goodwill and then look for embellishments in various thrift stores, fabric stores, and even yard sales.

❊**Dominic Von Strap:** Goodwill or Ross Dress for Less.

❊**Adam DoEve:** Goodwill is my best friend and yard sales. I also sew so I make a lot of my stuff. I will not pay big bucks for a suit when I can make one for about $50 - $60 and I know it will fit the right way the first time.

❊**Koomah:** Aside from the internet: In-kind donations, thrift stores, dollar stores, garage sales, closeout stores, art supply recycling centers, independent shops in International districts (Chinatown/Little India), and after Halloween sales are great. Do not just look for off the rack items! Find things you can alter, fabrics that you can use in other pieces, and clothing with embellishments to re-purpose. Get a sewing machine and learn to sew. get a good glue gun, and crafting adhesive like E-6000.

❊**Travis Hard:** Thrift stores do wonders for shopping for DRAG on a budget. It is what I use most often for my creative outfits. Another cheap option to go with are TJ Maxx and Burlington Coat Factory!

❊**Shane Rebel Caine:** Goodwill, thrift stores, and flea markets make excellent places to find wardrobe, and even things to make your own costuming. You can find decent items to put on your costumes at the dollar stores, you just have to be careful though, because you do not want you're costumes to look like they are just cheaply made.

❊**Rychard "Alpha" Le'Sabre:** In your own head make them then buy pieces to put something original together.

❊**Rasta Boi Punany:** I have been told the thrift store; there are some in my area.

❊**Dakota Rain:** I shop at Goodwill and any thrift store, but also go to Rue21; they have awesome sales sometimes.

❀**Ashton The Adorable Lover:** Goodwill, friends' closets, garage sales, and your local fabric/arts and crafts stores.

❀**Clint Torres:** Thrift store or my personal favorite is Amazon. You could also use clothes you no longer wear from your closet or go to yard sales.

❀**Pierce Gabriel:** Thrift stores are a great idea. That is how I got most of my outfits starting out. I also go to Wal-Mart, and I have been lucky enough for several more experienced performers, to gift me with hand-me-downs from their own DRAG closet.

❀**Vinnie Marconi:** Thrift stores and yard sales. Then you start to bling and paint with the savings from the clothes. One thing at a time and as money permits, have it grow.

❀**Ben Eaten:** Thrift stores, yard sales, and clearance racks. I will find something simple and make it into what I want it to be.

❀**Kruz Mhee:** Thrift stores every time! Surprisingly enough, a number of DRAG queens have a number of items most kings can use/borrow. Remember, it is a family affair!

❀**Alec Allnight:** Thrift stores are my friend, Ross is decent sometimes. I am always on the lookout for stuff though. Even if I do not have a plan for it yet, I know it will come in handy at some point. Even if I cannot use it, one of my brothers always can. And a little duct tape goes a long way people!

❀**B J Bottoms:** Thrift stores are great. If you are really strapped for cash, find things in your own closest that you can turn into outfits. You will be surprised what stones can do to a simple t-shirt.

❀**Silk Steele Prince:** For DRAG on a budget, I go to thrift stores, garage and estate sales, costume shops, dollar stores, and craft stores. I usually hit up the clearance racks at any local stores. You have to get creative. No imagination is too big. In addition, next day holiday clearance is the best time of year to shop for your costume needs. I love to revamp things and make it something great to wear.

❀**SirMandingo Thatis:** I find a lot of things at thrift stores and Goodwill here in Nebraska, USA. Our Goodwill stores have 10 for $10 twice a month, and boy do I hit them up. I also sew a lot of things because I really love to sew and see how original I can get. My friends call me a DRAG queen because I am always sewing.

❀**Flex Jonez:** Anywhere cheap, fabric stores, and DRAG queen closets.

❀**Atown:** Thrift stores, or buy some inexpensive additives to put on some clothes you may have laying around.

❀**Kenneth J. Squires:** Thrift stores, Goodwill, garage sales. Someone who can sew, is a plus! Adding stones to clothes can help as well.

❀**Cody Wellch Klondyke:** Goodwill, consignment shops, Salvation Army thrift stores, and friends.

❀**George De Micheal:** Charity shops and retro stores.

❀**Colin Grey:** Thrift stores are a DRAG king's best friend. I love finding different pieces and then taking them home and adding my own bits of flair, be it a few stones, some paint, or even Sharpie Stain marker designs.

❀**Eddie C. Broadway:** Thrift stores for sure. You can find some really crazy things there. Just add things, alter them, and make them your own.

❀**Stefan LeDude:** Thrift shops. Value Village is great!

❀**Howie Feltersnatch:** Value Village!

❀**Clark Kunt:** Thrift shops like Value Village, and rhinestones from the dollar store! I add chains from old jewelry or cheap chain from the store, old hockey or sports gear you can adapt, and many, many rolls of duct tape.

❀**Jamel Knight:** Thrift shops are awesome. It is also good to try sewing your own costumes. I want to learn to sew because I think it can save me a lot of money. Also, using pieces of old jewelry and other items can help take a costume from ordinary to something unique.

❀**Welland Dowd:** Thrift stores are the best. Costume shops are good too although tend to be more expensive.

❀**Sam Masterson:** A costume shop is the best place here in the Midwest.

❀**Julius M. SeizeHer:** Easley's Fun Shop. It is relatively cheap, and they have everything!

❀**Lyle Love-It:** Goodwill, rummage sales, flea markets, and estate sales.

❀**Jonah Godfather of DRAG:** Goodwill and Michael's. Or I have also raided my dad's closet for things he no longer wears.

❀**Campbell Reid Andrews:** A giant thrift shop would be the best place to shop if you are on budget. Then you can take it home and stone it, or put some glitter on it, or whatever you choose. You can also use hand me downs from family and friends. Amazon, eBay, etc. online are a definite place to look. There are a lot of DRAG resale groups on social media if you do not mind wearing someone else's costumes.

❀**B J Armani:** Goodwill, rummage sales, eBay, about anywhere cheap. Break out the hot glue gun! I make almost everything I wear. Find inspiration from fellow performers and artists that you are representing on stage.

❀**Crash Bandikok:** Goodwill and buffaloexchange.com.

❀**Bootzy Edwards Collynz:** In the beginning, I could find my costume pieces at thrift stores or vintage stores. Some of my ideas had to go with the budget I had, which was little to nothing. You do the best with what you have (glitter, wigs, glue gun, landscaping spikes, fake fur jackets, and LOTS of rhinestones). It is very important to have a game plan of what you want to do and to know your time frame to get this accomplished. Things can go wrong and you need to have plan b, c, d, e, f, g, h, i... just in case. The more I got to perform and the more money I was making, I got to create the bigger and better ideas, from bald caps to using a grinder for a routine. I will also hit the local costume shop to see what I can put together on my own. NEVER underestimate the power of your glue gun. Now I am able to look online for particular pieces that would work. It is EXTREMELY handy to have someone who can sew available too, especially if you cannot. Some outfits just need construction, but if you have someone you can barter with (who is reliable as well), it is helpful. Recycling old outfits to new is always a great time and cost saver as well.

❀**Jack E. Dickinson:** Thrift shops, clothes borrowed from friends. If you are handy with sewing and crafting, you can make a lot of your own special stuff that you cannot easily find (a knight's tabard comes to mind). Dollar Store is an underground performer's friend as well!

❀**Xavier Bottoms:** Material is cheap. Buy it, sew it. It is easy to learn.

❀**Emilio:** Emilio uses the same clothes Vanna uses. I shop in my own closet.

❀**Juan Kerr:** eBay. I am a massive eBay-er. Also charity shops.

❀**Trey C. Michaels:** eBay and thrift shops. Albuquerque, New Mexico, USA, has a thrift shop on every corner so I am always finding items. I also buy clothing I would never wear but can use the fabric to add to an outfit.

❀**Bailey Saint James:** Goodwill, Value Village, and raiding your male friends' closets.

❀**Aaron Phoenix:** Buying the pieces (fabric, stones, embellishments, accessories, etc.) and making the outfits/costumes yourself is always the best way to go.

❀**Thug Passion:** Thrift stores. My first stones were bought at a fabric store. Then I learned later there are different stones to purchase. Networking on where to find cheap good stones.

❀**Soco Dupree:** Thrift stores. Goodwill is amazing.

❀**Stefon Royce Iman:** The Goodwill, Salvation Army, other thrift stores, discount clothing stores, or online.

❀**Jensen C. Dean:** Thrift stores are great. eBay has good things too, for not too much money. The big trick is to find a way to make things look your own and not off the rack, a cheap way to do that can be to hit up the "scraps" section at fabric stores.

❀**Smitty O'Toole:** Thrift stores, vintage shops, resale shops, and eBay. I make all of my costumes.

❀**LoUis CYfer:** So High Soho in London, United Kingdom, is the best costume shop!

❀**E. M. Shaun:** I have gotten many, many outfits from thrift stores. Also borrowing someone else's clothing in the beginning will help with not spending so much money. Some of kings just have the skills and the talent to sew their own outfits.

❀**Luke Ateraz:** Goodwill! Thursday's is dollar day. Every other Saturday is 50% off.

❀**Spacee Kadett:** This is a great question not just for productions, but also for costuming in general! And probably the number one thing new entertainers and their partners have asked me. My rule of thumb is this: costumes are not bought. They are MADE. Avoid party stores and costume shops unless for accessories or inspiration. Their costumes, like their wigs, generally look cheap and are way over-priced.

❀**William Vanity Matrix:** Thrift stores and craft stores. Make it and build it from bases you find. It is much cheaper. And after Halloween sales.

❀**Devin G. Dame:** Thrift stores have many costume ideas waiting to be found.

❀**Dionysus W Khaos:** Thrift stores, eBay and local costume shops.

Name the performers without checking on DRAG411.com

Chapter Twenty-Seven
"Where are the best places to find perfect shoes? What are the biggest mistakes in purchasing foot wear as an impersonator? Any experiences you wish to share?"

❀**Coti Blayne:** Being small, I get everything from the little boys section. Wal-Mart, K&G, Amazon, anywhere and everywhere. Clearance is my best friend. Oh yeah, eBay! Lots of stuff from eBay.

❀**D-Luv Saviyon:** Wal-Mart, K&G, Amazon, and eBay

❀**Spacee Kadett:** My native Detroit, Michigan, USA, has these fabulous $10 shoe stores. I highly recommend Lizzy's in Madison Heights. Check out their men's AND women's sections for androgynous shoes. Alas, I am pretty sure they do not fulfill orders online. Otherwise, good shoes can be found in the wildest of places. And again, CHECK THE WOMEN'S SECTION. The craziest, coolest stuff is there. Thrift stores have always brought me random luck. Other good stores include (and, as my fellow kings here advise, check the CLEARANCE section) JC Penney, Burlington, Payless, Sears, TJ Maxx, Marshall's, K-Mart, Target, and sometimes DSW (Designer Shoe Warehouse) and Wal-Mart. Famous Footwear is expensive. So is Shoe Carnival. Unless it is a pageant or special event ($80-$100+), do not pay more than $30 for shoes! Most of mine were $20 and less. I have named physical locations here because of the weird try-before-you-buy nature of shoes...though I will readily acknowledge the good online suggestions of my fellow kings here. And, incidentally, while we're on the topic of shoes, my king mentors taught me that wearing a slightly large shoe will naturally force you to walk with a more masculine gait. IT IS SO TRUE. Fun fact to keep in mind, even if you straddle boy's and men's sizes as I do.

❀**Adam All:** Definitely Primark, but wear a size too big and pack them with socks. It is more masculine to have bigger feet.

❀**Travis Luvermore:** I search retail chains and thrift stores to find the right shoes for my outfits.

❀**Joshua Micheals:** I shop for shoes on sale. I got lucky at Ross a few times.

❀**Michael Christian:** Anywhere there is a clearance! I am lucky enough to be in the Detroit, Michigan, USA, area for the $10 store. I love it. Rue21 is also wonderful for $5 clearance shoes. Remember you can embellish shoes as well. Paint, stones, spikes, fabric. If you buy them on clearance, you can end up with a wonderfully bad ass looking shoe for $20 at the end of the day.

❀**Orion Blaze Browne:** I never pay more than $20 for shoes for stage. Clearance almost anywhere that sells shoes, you can find a deal. I have bigger feet so it is hard for me to find anything in the women's department. Advice for newbies would be always try them on. I have bought shoes before that were my size however, were small when I put them on. It is not comfortable to go on stage with shoes you have just squeezed your foot in. Also watch when buying shoes a size bigger. Even if you stuff them so they fit, I have seen performers trip over their toes. It is also good to walk around the house in new shoes to get comfortable with them.

❀**Alexander Cameron:** I have been blessed (or cursed) with very large feet so finding shoes is relatively easy for me. I usually go with Kohl's or stores like it. I hit the jackpot at a thrift store once and got a pair of leather Sperry wingtips for $8!

❀**Chance Wise:** Instyle at the Lake City Mall, Lake City, Florida, USA, has some amazing suits, and the shoes are to die for and both reasonably priced.

❀**Marty Brown:** Clearance racks work for me.

❀**Hurricane Savage:** I have a lot of older cowboy boots that I just shine up and put stones on, and they look great. But for anything else clearance is my best friend.

❀**Marcus Mayhem:** Thrift stores and then adding fabric to my shoes and stones. Everyone wants to steal my shiny shoes!

❀**Koomah:** I have big feet so buying men's shoes has never been difficult. Pointed and square-toed shoes give the illusion of bigger feet. Buying your shoes a bit too big can alter your gait so you walk with less hip action. Shoes can be altered with paint, dye, fabric, stones, etc.

❀**Travis Hard:** I find my shoes in a large array of places. Flea markets, eBay, Amazon, and thrift shops are all good for shoes. I once bought a pair two sizes too big and couldn't move as well as I had wished. This taught me to wear what fits rather than promoting a bigger foot image (men have bigger feet generally).

❀**Rychard "Alpha" Le'Sabre:** You can get shoes from anywhere and make them "you." Anything can be "blinged."

❀**Shane Rebel Caine:** eBay or Amazon. Or just get a typical pair from Wal-Mart of the kind of shoe you want, dress shoes, tennis shoes, boots etc., and decorate them yourself for your own designs and cool shoes. You do not want to buy shoes that are too big, yea they give you a better manly image, but it can prohibit you from moving on stage and cause you to stumble or fall.

❀**Campbell Reid Andrews:** I purchase most of my footwear online. Google what I need and sift through websites to find the best pair. eBay, Amazon, Stacey Adams, K&G, and sometimes Combat Boot Academy for $30. Any suit warehouse website will have shoes. I usually wear dress shoes. It is tedious but you have to find those deals.

❀**Rasta Boi Punany:** Payless and K&G.

❀**Dakota Rain:** Payless, Shoe Show, and Wal-Mart. I want them to be comfortable.

❀**Ashton The Adorable Lover:** Wal-Mart or a local suit shop. Also, the internet can have great sales and very unique styles you do not get anywhere else.

❀**Clint Torres:** For everyday wear, I am cheap and shop at Big 5 or Payless, but for my DRAG, I want him to always look good from head to toe, so I shop online or at places like Famous Footwear to ensure his look. The biggest mistake you can make is not knowing your male size or buying it in that size but it is still too big. You need to familiarize yourself with men's shoes. Sports shoes are typically always going to be in your size, the tick is the dress shoes. Men's dress shoes run smaller, so if you are a size 8 in men's you might have to get a 7 1/2. I have made that mistake plenty of times.

❀**Adam DoEve:** I always find good stuff at the Goodwill. I like the older looking stuff and you cannot get some of those styles any more. I do buy new stuff, but it has to feel good on my foot, not just look good. Also a good place is your local costume shop. They will sell the shoes that they have rented out for cheap and most time they just need a little tender loving care.

❀**Stormm:** It depends on the outfit, Wal-Mart, thrift stores, Target or Payless. I want something comfortable.

❀**Kenneth J. Squires:** Wal-Mart is good for shoes and is better when you can find them on sale. I have gone to Men's Warehouse as well. Never get any shoe that is too small for you. Your feet will feel it by the end of the night! I have been told that I needed to buy shoes that were a little bigger for me, and stuff the toe area. That way, you look more like a guy, because some women have small feet.

❀**Pierce Gabriel:** I always got my shoes at Wal-Mart, with the exception of a couple that were given to me as hand-me-downs from another entertainer.

❀**Freddy Prinze Charming:** Goodwill. I look for shoes a size or two too big, because I have tiny feet, which look weird in men's shoes. If you have small feet like me, I would recommend doing the same. That does not mean get shoes that are so big they are like clown shoes, but if you can wear them comfortably with two pairs of socks, you should be good. They should not flip flop around. And as a general rule of thumb... do not ruin a great outfit, be it evening wear or costume, with a pair of grungy shoes.

❀**Vinnie Marconi:** For pageants, I go to regular shoe stores, like Florsheim. Formal wear shoes come from tux shops. Regular performances, THRIFT STORES, so I can paint or bling to match a costume.

❀**Brandon KC Young-Taylor:** I found this store in Kansas City, Missouri, USA, called Viva Fashion. It is like a small flea market of clothing stores. I have found places like this in other cites but I cannot remember the names. Places like this have the flashy looking shoes for reasonable prices. But do not expect a lot of comfort as this shoes aren't made from the same materials as the high dollar Luxury Men's Shoes.

❀**Ben Eaten:** Clearance racks. I like thrift stores. Also stores like TJ Maxx and Ross. I have small feet and can fit in children's shoes so they usually have these on sale.

❀**Kruz Mhee:** If you have small feet like I do it's a bit of a problem. I generally purchase men's shoes from Payless shoe stores. They carry men's size 4 to 6, very hard-to-find sizes. I also tend to wear little boy shoes with shoe pads for comfort.

❀**Hawk Stuart:** I get my shoes at Wal-Mart, or online at shoe stores. But always make sure you break them in before you hit the stage.

❀**Silk Steele Prince:** The best place to find shoes is the thrift stores and clearance racks at your local shoe store. Check that they are clean and wearable. If they are a size too big add extra soles inside. If they need cleaning, spray disinfectant in them and tie them off in a bag for a few hours. Make sure the shoe you choose is comfortable and you can perform in them. I am very cautious.

❀**SirMandingo Thatis:** I find the best shoes online at "Wish." It is an application I have on my phone. They are original and you do not find others like them.

❀**Flex Jonez:** Shop, shop, and bargain shop. Get a shoe 1/2 size bigger than what you would wear. Your feet may swell a bit if dancing in the shoes and wear thick, dark socks as well, for cushion.

❀**Atown:** It depends on the type of shoe you are looking for. I do not like to order online too much because I do not know how they feel on me. I need to know that they are comfortable enough to perform in, dance in, walk in, jump in, model in, etc. So I would have to say various stores.

❀**George De Micheal:** Charity shops and old clothing shops have the best shoes. ❀**DeVery Bess:** Thrift stores are a king's best friend, and get a good pair that fit.

❀**Bootzy Edwards Collynz:** I buy from anywhere. There are some "mom n pop" shops that have nice dress shoes that I will buy. Everything else I go to the "outlet" stores or DSW like shoe places. Usually pretty inexpensive.

❀**Colin Grey:** Thrift stores are good, again, for stuff like this...make sure the shoes have insoles. I took a set of insoles out of a pair because I have bad feet and forgot that I had taken them out. Packed them. Took them to show and had to perform in them.

✤**Eddie C. Broadway:** I go anywhere; Goodwill, Target, order online. My nice stuff, i.e. my boots, I order online or get from a local store called Off Chute Too.

✤**Sam Masterson:** I always wear Stacey Adams shoes.

✤**Kameo Dupree:** I have child sized feet. I come out cheaper buying my boots from "Chuck's Boots." My size is always under $50. Now dress shoes, I will have to say "Stacy Adams." I shop the clearance section and get 5-7 pair for around $150 plus free shipping. Any shoes I decide to paint, stone, or reinvent are all shoes that have survived a long time, but I'm too cheap to throw them away.

✤**Jack King:** I have small feet, so I go in a boys shoe store.

✤**Stefan LeDude:** I mostly use shoes I already own. I would say thrift shops.

✤**Jamel Knight:** Finding shoes is difficult for me because I have small feet. This usually means ordering online or going a size or two bigger. Anytime I go with a bigger size, I have to make sure I stuff them so that I am not walking awkward and can dance with them on.

✤**Jamel Knight:** Occasionally I can find affordable shoes that fit in stores like Rugged Wearhouse and Burlington Coat Factory.

✤**Howie Feltersnatch:** Thrift stores are always awesome, but if you are worried about germs and stuff, try Wal-Mart. I suggest that you try the shoes on first before buying them. One time I was in such a hurry because I had forgot my shoes at home and had no time to go home and grab them, I went to Wal-Mart, grabbed what I thought were my size, paid for them, and went straight to the venue. When I got there, I realized my shoes were too big and had to go with it. Wearing a shoe that is a size to big made me dance like I had two left feet, and made me miss my timing for that number.

✤**Harry Pi:** I try Wal-Mart and Payless most of the time, especially for a pageant. But other times, I go to a large thrift store.

✤**Julius M. SeizeHer:** Payless is my go-to. I have to get a size larger or they are tight.

✤**Lyle Love-It:** Goodwill, rummage sales, and hand-me downs from my father.

✤**Jensen C. Dean:** I do not have a go-to shoe place, although eBay is always good for a deal. The big thing I have noticed is if you wear women's shoes it looks different, even if they are sneakers, because women typically have more narrow feet than men and showing off narrow feet can hinder the illusion.

✤**Jonah Godfather of DRAG:** I have bought a few inexpensive shoes from eBay stores. They look good but are not all that comfortable. I do have some nice shoes that I bought from Kohl's for pageants. They are not too high priced. They look great and are also comfortable. For boots, I always go for a higher price. They not only have to look good but be very comfortable as I wear them at other times and not just for shows.

✿**MaXx Decco:** I got some decently priced dress shoes from Kohl's. For me being a boys 6 ½, it is really hard. I recently ordered some from Amazon online. They arrived and do not fit properly, so I am going to try the outdoor mall downtown.

✿**B J Armani:** eBay, Wal-Mart, Target, rummage sales, good will, pretty much wherever you can find what you are looking for. I actually have as my main pair of stage shoes, a pair of Serve Safe shoes. These shoes are specifically non slip for greasy floors of restaurants so they are perfect for the many bar surfaces I have had to deal with. They have saved my life many times! For stoning shoes, E-6000 is the best.

✿**Jack E. Dickinson:** Thrift shops are good. Borrowing is good. But if you borrow someone's footwear, make sure it is not for an act that might damage the shoes somehow. It is also possible to add things like colored duct tape to footwear that you do not mind modifying (i.e.: you do not need them for other uses). Avoiding slippery shoes is a good thing to avoid hurting yourself! Also, it is important to practice your steps or dancing WITH the footwear you plan to wear well in advance of a show. It can really change your movement.

✿**Xavier Bottoms:** Wal-Mart, Payless, outlet mall. Adding stones or your own design to a shoe makes it your own. Biggest mistake is not practicing your dance moves in the new shoes. A helpful hint...I buy shoes that can be dyed or painted. I also buy shoes one size bigger and stuff the toes.

✿**Clark Kunt:** I tend to use a wide variety of footwear - army boots, sneakers, chucks, dress shoes, boots, and things with spikes or designs like zombie faces. There is no one spot to find all those things so really, I am always on the lookout for masculine or androgynous looking shoes in my size. I am also always adapting my footwear with duct tape covering, rhinestones, studs... anything to keep the look fresh.

✿**Emilio:** Again, Emilio shops in Vanna's closet.

✿**Juan Kerr:** Again, eBay or local markets.

✿**Trey C. Michaels:** eBay, Payless when they are having a sale, and honestly, local thrift shops. If I find a pair a size or two too big, I will wear extra socks or stuff a pair in the toe of the shoe.

✿**Aaron Phoenix:** I tend to shop online for shoes, or there is a place in Tampa, Florida, USA, that sells every piece of men's formal wear imaginable where I have found some great shoes. The easiest mistake to make in this area would probably be buying the wrong size.

✿**Thug Passion:** The internet is good place. Try eBay, thrift stores, and flea markets.

✿**Santana Romero:** I know many entertainers do not like to spend a lot of money on shoes but it is honestly a good long-term investment! Buying a quality pair of shoes will last you much longer, maintain their shape and color, and be a lot more comfortable to perform in. eBay and Amazon are gold mines for shoes of all styles, colors, and sizes, especially for us smaller guys. If you are on a tight budget, another good option would be places like Burlington, TJ Maxx, or Marshall's since they are discounted by a good percentage. For a good pair of sneakers, Finishline usually has an amazing sale rack selection of stylish kicks, same for DSW shoes. I personally do not recommend buying shoes from a thrift store because of health risks but if it works for you, go for it. One thing I see a lot of performers do with shoes is not keeping them clean! Make sure you take good care of your shoes just as you do with your costumes. I have seen an amazing outfit be ruined by unappealing looking footwear.

❀**Stefon Royce Iman:** The internet is the best place. Always buy men's shoes, not boy's shoes; your feet will look small. Or always look for sales like prom and wedding season.

❀**Soco Dupree:** eBay, Amazon or the local mall here.

❀**Mike Oxready:** I do not have any trouble finding shoes, but always buy men's shoes!

❀**Rychard "Alpha" Le'Sabre:** I usually get my shoes from any store, and add my own details, designs, or "bling" to them. King shoes do not just come straight off the shelf.

❀**Smitty O'Toole:** I have never had an issue buying shoes or performing in shoes. I would recommend wearing shoes that your feet do not slip in to avoid blisters or your shoes tripping you up.

❀**Luke Ateraz:** Do not be afraid to get shoes from Goodwill or thrift stores! Just clean and disinfect them. But I find a lot of good buys down on the garment district in Los Angeles, California USA.

❀**E. M. Shaun:** Goodwill or any good shoe store. Remember to practice in your new shoes so are comfortable with them when you decide to use them in a performance.

❀**Devin G. Dame:** Always buy shoes too big...they give the illusion you have bigger, manly feet. Thrift stores are normally my choice on where to buy my shoes for DRAG.

Chapter Twenty-Eight
"What do you say about shaving?"

✤**Adam All:** I just shave my legs and armpits as normal. Try not to leave a scruffy bikini line? Changing room reveals all...

✤**AJ Menendez:** I shave my legs and armpits as normal. The dressing room reveal all!

✤**Gus Magendor:** I do not shave except my face, so the facial hair grows thicker.

✤**Chance Wise:** I just try not to chop up my legs for once. Someone mentioned once about the peach fuzz that women get on their face, so I use an eyebrow trimmer on that since men do not have that hair from shaving their faces.

✤**D-Luv Saviyon:** I shave my face, pits, and chest (when wooly) for shows.

✤**Marty Brown:** I do not shave at all, well, except for the man-scaping.

✤**Coti Blayne:** I am lazy when it comes to shaving. I am a ginger so it is all clear blonde and I only shave my pits, legs, and mmhmmm area. I tend to break out with shaving cream so I usually use shampoo or body wash.

✤**Ryder Knightly:** In real life I do not have to shave much except the normal girl areas, however, when I put on a beard, I have to shave it to get different designs within the beard, and with that I just use a Venus double sided razor. It is small and easy to use for tiny areas along with marking with eyeliner.

✤**Hurricane Savage:** As far as shows go, I trim my facial hair. I do not take T but I do have facial hair (the Joys of getting old and having a kid). I do not have a full beard so it just looks cleaner if I shave it all and apply fake hair.

✤**Marcus Mayhem:** I trim my side burns so it looks better and just shave like I always do. Legs, (unless I am lazy that day), pits, and the no-no area.

✤**Travis Hard:** Seeing as I am physically a woman and intend to stay that way, I believe that everything should be shaved, in my personal opinion, for my own comfort. I have grown out my leg hair for a performance but nowadays, even guys shave their legs!

✤**Shane Rebel Caine:** I do not shave my legs or armpits. My hair there is blonde so it is not really noticeable but I have had many compliments and remarks regarding having armpit hair. Many say it just adds more to the "manly" look, and since I do a lot of sleeveless costumes, it works better for me and adds to my own illusion.

✤**Ashton The Adorable Lover:** I am simple. I use hair clippers and edger. They get head, face, pits, and trims sensitive areas fine.

✤**Ben Eaten:** I shave my legs, armpits and the no-nos. For my face, I do not shave that; I position my hair.

❀**Clint Torres:** I shave my legs, armpits, and around the bikini line and trim the rest.

❀**Kenneth J. Squires:** I only shave my legs and underarms. I have shaved my "Sideburns." Other than this, I do not shave!

❀**Pierce Gabriel:** When I am not dating someone, I do not shave my legs or arm pits so it is more realistic when I wear tank tops and shorts or jeans with holes. But when I am in a relationship, it bothers me too much to not be clean-shaven, so I just wear non-holy pants when I am on stage.

❀**Koomah:** Shaving is a planned thing for me, especially as someone who performs as a king and as a queen. If I know I'll be performing as a bear i will opt not to shave. I feel like it is easier to accentuate hair that is already there. I know of a couple kings who shave their temples/widows peak for a more masculine hairline (one who shaves their head so it appears to be a receding hairline) but my head is always shaved completely. Typically, I shave my head with clippers and save the hair for later use. I usually trim other areas (armpits & pubes) but do not save this hair!

❀**Campbell Reid Andrews:** To be honest, it depends on what type of "man" or character you are trying to emulate. Some characters are hairy, bear like, grizzly (woof), or metro.

❀**Vinnie Marconi:** Will not share anything except facial hair after I apply it.

❀**Kruz Mhee:** For me everything is shaved. The only hair I will try to accentuate is on my face with the makeup I use.

❀**Stormm:** Usually my head is shaved on the sides. That is what I use to make the beard and mustache. Otherwise my legs, I wear a lot of shorts.

❀**Silk Steele Prince:** I shave armpits, bikini area, and sometimes my head. Depends on the performance. I use a product called Coochie, made by Pure Romance, or Bump Off and a razor or clipper. I use these products because it is common for people with curly hair to get razor bumps.

❀**Flex Jonez:** I shave what needs to be shaved for the gig I have planned.

❀**Atown:** I sometimes shave to edge my beard, but I have gotten it down pretty good to where I do not really have to clean it up so much anymore. To me, it looks more realistic with leg hair and trimming the armpit hair.

❀**SirMandingo Thatis:** Everything, because whenever I am not in DRAG I am completely a female (heels and makeup). I shave as a woman.

❀**Colin Grey:** Out of DRAG, I am all woman, not transgender. I have tried letting the leg and armpits go for a while, just not my thing.

❀**Eddie C. Broadway:** I am transgender so I do not really shave much. I shave my face though, because I like knowing that my makeup is good.

❀**Welland Dowd:** I am transgender so I have not shaved my body hair in a long time.

❀**Michael Christian:** I personally do not care for body hair at all. Even though I am a transgender man, I still shave my legs. I fully have to think about this and let the hair grow for certain costumes or pride month. I try to wear shorts and sleeveless costumes to avoid heat stroke. I also really pay attention to any chest hair. No lazy days if there is a show duct tape and spray adhesive is super unpleasant no matter how you remove it if there is hair. My facial hair just pretty much goes with my life. Always cleaned up though. If I happen to have shaved and want a beard for a show I just use make up like everyone else. I don't let DRAG or my transition dictate my DRAG.

❀**Adam DoEve:** Most times I have long sleeves and pants, so it does not matter if I shave or not, but most times I really do not pay attention to it, but I probably should. I will have to take this into consideration for upcoming shows.

❀**Julius M. SeizeHer:** I wear my hair back, so I get the biker look. I also wear jeans like 99% of the time.

❀**Jonah Godfather of DRAG:** I will just say that I do not. I trim my beard into a mustache and goatee.

❀**Howie Feltersnatch:** I just shave my legs and armpits depending on the number. Sometimes I **will not** shave for weeks just to have that extra masculine feeling.

❀**B J Armani:** I just use any moisturizing shaving cream and a triple or quatro blade. Some costumes call for hair and that is when the prop hair comes out (kind of like nylons with hair attached). Facial shaving I do not know much about, but facial hair is always more course, so be careful and adjust products. Sephora is heaven sent for this! The people that work there are very knowledgeable!

❀**Bootzy Edwards Collynz:** I do not shave. I will use spirit gum and cut my hair into fine pieces into a glass bowl. Line my facial pattern and use a disposable mascara brush to apply the hair on. This way I don't have that much trimming down and clean-up of the hair to do. I do make sure I use a very good moisturizer and astringent (day and evening) for my face. Being all the glue and make-up that goes on my skin, it is really important to keep take care of your face clean and hydrated; after all, it is our "money maker." I have noticed it does help in removing some glues when my face is well moisturized. As for my body, I will do a shade/contour under my chin, the main muscles on my neck, clavicle, and line under my collarbone and the spilt for my pecks. I will use a white highlight to brighten make certain areas pop (like my chest). Spikey Van Dykey give an awesome tutorial on YouTube of body contouring/shading.

❀**Xavier Bottoms:** Shaving? Yep, the author of this book is a real boy, I can tell. It is not complicated. Either you do it or you do not. I live my life as a female; I shave my legs, armpits and keep my "area" high and tight.

❀**Clark Kunt:** I do not worry much about whether I have shaved recently or not. I am more concerned about keeping a clean line on my eyebrows and not letting the hairdresser buzz off my side burns!

Emilio: My shaving habits do not affect my performance habits.

Juan Kerr: I do not tend to show my legs, although I'll be doing a 'camp' routine in a full body leotard as a 90's British fitness instructor called Mr. Motivator, so I'll need to decide if to shave them or not for that.

Trey C. Michaels: I go to a barber every two weeks to have my hairlines cleaned up. I had him teach me how to do it at home so I can keep that look up. Being on hormones I am now getting patches of hair, but I shave every couple of days to keep the peach fuzz down and to not have the patches look weird.

Bailey Saint James: I do not grow hair anywhere but my head. Shaving does not apply. Putting on a beard or mustache is a very tricky technique. Please, for the love of DRAG, stop using eyeliner, eyebrow pencils, and mascara to make your mustaches!

Aaron Phoenix: Shaving is irrelevant to my performing.

Thug Passion: I just shave my armpits and legs. I make sure I have a fresh haircut. Other than that, I do not shave anything.

Stefon Royce Iman: Shave your pits. Legs are ok, most men do not have shaved legs, but if you are a metrosexual than you may shave everything.

Soco Dupree: I only shave the feminine area religiously. I tend to be lazy with the legs and arms.

Santana Romero: My arms and legs are usually covered when I perform, so I do not bother with shaving. It is too much work unless I am performing as a woman.

Mike Oxready: I shave my neckline, but that is just because I like to keep it fresh, and is irrelevant to my performance.

Smitty O'Toole: I am a female-to-male transgender so I do not shave my legs or arm pits. I keep my hair and beard neat.

Jensen C. Dean: Shaving is not really relevant to my performances. I am ghostly white so I try not to subject audiences to the blinding light that is my legs in shorts. If I am doing a number with shorts though, I will skip shaving my legs right before the performance to help with the illusion if necessary.

E. M. Shaun: I just shave my armpits. I wear my hair in an afro or in twists so I do not shave my hairline.

Dionysus W Khaos: I identify as female in my day-to-day life, so I shave as a normal female does. When I do impersonations that require hair, I use fake hair and bald caps for when I need a baldhead.

Devin G. Dame: I have not shaved in years...helps me with my illusion on stage.

King Kline: My facial hair is skimpy, so if I want a mustache, side burns, and a beard, first I need to shave my facial hair, and then apply theatrical hair.

Chapter Twenty-Nine
"Make-up!"

❀**D-Luv Saviyon:** I buy mine at a local costume store called Performance Studios. Performance has their own line of makeup, spirit gum, crape hair, etc. I have a makeup bag in which I store my makeup. I do not wear much makeup unless I am doing a makeup-required performance, but I usually test it out at home to avoid issues during a show.

❀**Adam All:** I have a DRAG bag for makeup. I buy things as-and-when I need them in pound shops, savers and Superdrug. I do not hunt things down specifically, except spirit gum. But I use my own hair for my beard, going so far as to dye it before I cut it so that I maintain the color coordination (once I went purple).

❀**Travis Luvermore:** I do not wear much makeup, many of my tools of the trade for facial and chest hair can be found at the party store for spirit gum and accessories.

❀**Joshua Micheals:** I used to stock up when I went home to visit my parents at a costume shop, but they closed. I order on Amazon to get what I need and pick up things to get by at the drug store our Wal-Mart... I do not use spirit gum as I am allergic (went to work with a goatee shaped red face once). I use 'Got to be Glued.' Spider glue holds my hair well and is easy to wash off with my makeup wipes when washing off makeup.

❀**Michael Christian:** I use all kinds of makeup. Typically, I find most at a costume/theater store. The basic fill-ins I can find at Target or the local drug store. My makeup has recently started to expand in a different direction and I have been gifted with some lessons and cosmetics from a few girls who work for makeup companies. I will be honest; I really like to buy Cover Girl fill-in products. Mostly because I enjoy the way they support and advertise all types of beauty.

❀**Chance Wise:** I have really just started playing with using makeup, and learning how to make it look good. Right now, I have probably the cheapest no brand name makeup known to man...but when I get better at making it work, I will put some more money into better quality makeup.

❀**Coti Blayne:** I use standard brown pallets found at various stores including Walmart, Party Galaxy, Dollar Tree (they have cheap pencil liner and face glitter), Ebony Beauty Supplies, and Masquerades.

❀**Hurricane Savage:** Cheap! I always sweat and forget and wipe my face, then have to reapply, so buying the expensive stuff does not make since to me. Dollar Tree and Dollar General, for what I use, have the best deals.

❀**Hurricane Savage:** I have a toolbox to keep makeup and random things.

❀**Marcus Mayhem:** I keep everything in my caboodle. I have seen others use a tackle box. Cheapest makeup I can, but most of mine came from family, friends, and queens.

❀Kameo Dupree: Local costume shop. I have not set any limits as to what or when to buy. I buy 2-3 big bottles of spirit gum which lasts about 6 months. I cut and save my hair (no barber, no weave).

❀Freddy Prinze Charming: All of my makeup, brushes, colored paints, etc. are kept in a toolbox that I take with me to every show. I get the majority of my makeup from various costume shops, but I am a fan of Mardi Gras Costumes here in Scottsdale, Arizona, USA. I generally buy trusted brands like Ben Nye, Kryolan, and Mehron, because they do not irritate my skin as much and provide great coverage, especially with their foundations. Using cheap, sub-par products have caused some crazy skin irritation, which prevented me from performing for quite a while.

❀Dante Diamond: Raised by DRAG queens, I tend to follow their lead and mostly invest in the "good stuff" from the theatrical supply store here, simply because I just think it looks better; I "fill in the blanks" as needed. To store everything, I bought a makeup case for myself.

❀Koomah: Makeup comes from several different places: department stores/drug stores, specialty shops, costume/theatrical shops, internet, and I make some of my own. I have some items separated into smaller bags for certain characters that I can put in my larger makeup kit so everything is easier to keep track of.

❀Travis Hard: I buy Ben Nye. That makeup is amazing. I have an entire starter kit I got while taking a course in stage makeup (specifically to improve my art). I find other Ben Nye items in Chicago, Illinois, USA, at a crazy DRAG store called Beatnix that my girlfriend introduced me to. I walked in and literally had a DRAGasm! So phenomenal. I store all of my makeup in my DRAG bag. I use them and immediately return them to the same place so I do not lose them!

❀Rychard "Alpha" Le'Sabre: Make sure you get something that will not make you break out, follow your natural skin tones, and ask other performers who use makeup to help you find what you need based on your personal needs

❀Shane Rebel Caine: I get my main makeup such as the foundation from stores like Wal-Mart. I get the simpler items from the Dollar Store, like the different shades for my cheeks, mascara, eyeliner, and non-glittery eye shadow, which I use for my eyebrows and to underline my facial hair so it looks thicker. I get my spirit gum from Party City and use my own head hair for my facial hair. I try to stay cheap with the type of makeup I get and try not to go too dark with the shades, so that I get a shadow look and can blend it well, and not have black on my face. I keep all of my makeup in a makeup box that I have had since I was a kid, even has a mirror on the lid.

❀Dakota Rain: If I used it, makeup would probably be bought from Wal-Mart.

❀**Ashton The Adorable Lover:** The only makeup I used was a cheap black eyeliner pencil to draw and darken in my facial hair as a first step. I had a sharpener and Q-tips for blending. I made sure to wash face as I tend to sweat and look greasy in the face.

❀**Rasta Boi Punany:** I use Maybelline black eyeliner now to outline my beard, mustache, and sideburns to apply my own hair with Spirit Gum. I just recently began applying real hair in May. I had once just used the eyeliner as my complete facial transformation. I use my wife's makeup kit and bag to apply and store my stuff. I use baby wipes to remove the eyeliner, hair and gum. I apply Cocoa Butter to my face to ensure it remains soft and blemish free.

❀**Ben Eaten:** I use Ben Nye brand power for dark, and I eye shadow for light and dark for accent. I use spirit gum and real hair extensions for my beard. I use makeup wipes to get everything off after a show. I store everything in a big tackle box type case.

❀**Clint Torres:** I like Revlon. It iz expensive and I only get it when I have some extra money handy. I usually buy NYC make up at the local Rite Aid because its cheap and accessible. The way it works is that I set a budget for myself at the beginning of every month and then I plan out what I need and how much it'll be. Usually a little over 50. I store all of my make up in a make up baggie in my DRAG closet.

❀**Kenneth J. Squires:** I use Crape hair for facial hair and spirit. I put a good base down, eyeliner for my eyebrows, and eye shadow to darken areas.

❀**Vinnie Marconi:** I use Kryolan makeup from 6S Boutique in St. Petersburg, Florida, USA, and keep it in my DRAG box. It is theater makeup and I trust Andrew Citino with picking the colors. I have not tried any other makeup... "If it ain't broke, don't fix it!"

❀**Stormm:** I use a large tackle box for my makeup and hair and it holds my jewelry. I use my own hair and I use Nu Skin Liquid Band-Aid to put it on. The only bad thing about that is it smells. Use Revlon makeup.

❀**Hawk Stuart:** I use the Kryolan makeup from 6S Boutique in St. Petersburg, Florida, USA. You can order from him online to if you are not from the area. I used a different kind once and I just sweat it off, so I stuck with what I know is the best.

❀**Kruz Mhee:** All my makeup is from local pharmacies. The only stage makeup I purchase is called Final Seal. It keeps you from sweating off your makeup. You can also use it to set your makeup so you do not sweat it off outwardly.

❀**Silk Steele Prince:** I use a variety of makeup, mostly professional makeup. I have a cosmetology license to purchase. Other than that I use products for sensitive to normal skin. If you do not choose products for your skin type, you can have mild to severe breakouts and irritation. Always cleanse and moisturize before you apply makeup so that you have a barrier and you can prevent clogging pores. In addition, I use concealer/primer for highlights, compressed powder foundation (at least two shades), eye shadow, eyeliner, mascara, and pre-cut hair. The hair is usually my own.

❀**Flex Jonez:** I have a makeup handler and a personal makeup box. I have sensitive skin so I HAVE to make sure my box is ready at all times. I check it after each performance and the day before a performance.

❀**SirMandingo Thatis:** I do not wear makeup.

❀**George De Micheal:** Fancy dress shops.

❀**Santana Romero:** When it comes to buying makeup, the costume store is my ideal spot. Ben-Nye and Mehron are excellent, professional stage makeup that is a pretty decent price compared to other brands. Both can usually be found at most local costume shops in your area if you have one. Of course, if your budget is tight, drug store makeup works just as well and there are endless brands to choose from. Making sure I have adequate coverage to hide imperfections and having colors that fit my complexion when contouring are the most important for when I purchase makeup, so I try to find the best products for that. I have never had much of an issue with using the wrong products but sometimes spirit gum can break my face out when not cleaned properly. I remedy this by thoroughly cleaning my face of all residue with water and cleanser. I usually have to carry a lot of makeup with me when I perform, so a case is must have. I have a small makeup case from the Kaboodle brand that has a key lock and plenty of storage space. They are pricey, but worth it. However, I know a lot of queens who use a tackle box for theirs, which is a much cheaper alternative if you have a boatload of makeup.

❀**Colin Grey:** I have a case that I carry my makeup in and it was originally a soft side tackle box. I use Mehron spirit gum. I have purchased my facial hair pieces that I use at reputable theater shops in town such as A to Z Theatrical supply. Most of my base makeup is purchased from Walmart. Best advice I can give is make sure it matches your skin tone and looks good under stage lighting.

❀**Eddie C. Broadway:** I get most of my stuff from Boom Boom's and Easley's. I have gotten the wrong colors before and it has messed up my contouring. I keep them all in my DRAG box, ready to go at any moment.

❀**Jack King:** I get my stuff from Mata's and in a costume store.

❀**Stefan LeDude:** I mainly just use spirit gum and crepe wool to create facial hair, and eyeliner or mascara to thicken my brows.

❀**Jamel Knight:** I have a sister who is a make-up artist and also have friends who work in costume shops. They help me to pick the right make-up for me and show me how to apply. Right now, affordability is the biggest deciding factor for me. I have sensitive skin so I have to be careful of what I use. Most times it's trial and error and if I choose the wrong product I can have a serious breakout. I have a bag that I keep all of my make up in. It makes it easier to pack.

❀Howie Feltersnatch: I use stippling which is a cream based face makeup with a stippling brush. I usually buy it at Don's Hobby Shop. My favorite makeup tool I use is mascara. I try to get a color that is as close to my hair as possible and I'll use it for my eyebrows and any highlighting on my face.

❀Welland Dowd: I mostly do a beard (my own hair trimmings and spirit gum) and a bit of mascara to thicken the eyebrows. I buy supplies at a local costume shop, and the mascara at a pharmacy.

❀Julius M. SeizeHer: I use a mix of spirit gum and mascara. The hair is a base, and the mascara fills in empty spaces. I keep everything in a DRAG kit.

❀Jonah Godfather of DRAG: Makeup is not a normal part of my DRAG. I have used theatrical makeup for characters that I have performed. I have also used a liquid foundation to even out my skin tone. Just make sure to wash your face thoroughly afterwards. I have had problems with breakouts due to makeup and not getting it completely off after a show.

❀MaXx Decco: I wear more makeup in DRAG than out. I have a whole checklist for performances: primer, concealer, foundation, bronzer, eye brow kit, mascara, eye liner, lip gloss, make-up brush kit, and make up setter/hairspray I regularly use elf, Cover Girl, and Maybelline and shop at target, for theatrical make up I would go to Sephora, for facial hair I shop at Sally's beauty, use hair extensions and eyelash adhesive (a glue stick will work in a pinch)

❀Campbell Reid Andrews: I always hit the theatre world for makeup. I would suggest Ben Nye; they have a very big selection of makeup for all kinds of characters or looks you want to achieve. You can also Google 'Halloween wholesale websites' and they sell makeup as well, might not be as good, but it is budget friendly. For basic makeup, NYX cosmetics and Kryolan are great as well. Kryolan, I have heard, has a great flesh color, cream foundation for contouring. Any makeup store in your town should be sufficient like Ultra, Sephora, or Mac.

❀Adam DoEve: For me, I like to use Covergirl whipped cream clean foundation, but for everything else, I use whatever is the cheapest. I have light skin and light hair and brows, so I have to darken things some for the stage. I use different shades of brown eye shadows for shading, and eyeliner. When I have a show that has more than one number, I have makeup changes so, by using regular makeup and having baby wipes at hand, it is easy and quick to do. I also put on a beard most times and use crape and spirit gum, but I also have real hair and pre-made chin beards that match my hair.

❀B J Armani: I use AVON and BB cream from Neutrogena for foundations. I tend to darken my complexion for the stage as you need to stand out.

You do not need the most expensive, but make sure you experiment. I use liquid latex instead of spirit gum since the gum dries out my skin and is ridiculous to get off. Nail polish remover helps with the heavier adhesives like super glue when you do horns or larger pieces on your face. I recommend stronger glue for any area NOT around the eyes.

❊Lyle Love-It: I have never used makeup except for a mustache and for that, use many shades of eyeliner pencils. I am usually tan and have never seemed to have an issue of looking "pale." ALL NATURA'L.

❊Bootzy Edwards Collynz: I do not have a lot of makeup, but I will wear makeup depending on the show/theme. I have separate bags for costume/fashion makeup and for DRAG makeup. I never buy expensive makeup unless I am absolutely positive that I will use it more than three times in that year. I try to throw out any old makeup after 1 year. Old makeup can give you breakouts, plus it does get old and some will mold. The only bad makeup experience I had was using someone else's makeup and supplies (brushes and sponges), because I forgot mine. I had a really bad break out because they did not clean their utensils. That was my first and last time for that.

❊Jack E. Dickinson: When I started as a DRAG king, I only used mascara to highlight my facial hair. Over the years, I began to use regular makeup to help highlight facial features on stage. Just regular makeup from the pharmacy has worked for me. Without going into the super high end stuff, I have tried to get decent quality stuff that I could use for a while. I use a tackle box as a makeup kit.

❊Clark Kunt: I use a few different foundations to contour and highlight, then a selection of eye shadows and creams for shadowing, facial hair, chest, neck, and arm contouring. Mac has some great dark browns that I use for hairline, eyebrows, sideburns, and facial hair (when I choose to have facial hair). The key for me is in the brushes: using the same products with different brushes or sponges can drastically change the look you get. I prefer a small, hard bristled, sharp angled brush for anything hair related because it gives the most distinctive look.

❊Emilio: I use my wife's makeup and crepe wool with spirit gum for my facial hair.

❊Juan Kerr: I recently added a layer of pencil eyeliner to my list of perishables. I draw my beard shape on then apply the spirit gum. I use a technique learned from fellow king Flirty Bertie. It involves putting finely chopped crepe hair on a blusher brush and applying it to the glue on my face that way. The first spirit gum I used was rubbish it was called Snazaroo. It dried up and flaked off and the bits that did not turned pure white. The best one I used was called Rubies but I cannot find it anywhere now!

❊Trey C. Michaels: My ex-partner was a makeup artist and only used MAC products. Now that she and the makeup is gone, I shop with local queens to help me get my makeup kit started. I go to Target and the local costume store. I do not use any specific brand, but my goal is to get back up to using MAC only products.

❀**Xavier Bottoms:** I do not use it, but if I ever feel the need, I go to my brother's makeup box. He will apply it, I have no clue what this pencil or that brush is for.

❀**Aaron Phoenix:** I buy everything from 6S Boutique (owned and operated by a former DRAG king, 6-pak, and his wife Sasha, who are incredible people) in St. Petersburg, Florida, USA. I am a fan of LaFemme shadows/powders for contouring and Kryolan for anything colorful/artsy. I keep a makeup box with everything I need organized in it that comes with me to every show, and go to great lengths to ensure I do not leave it sit in the hot car.

❀**Atown:** I try to find a foundation closest to my color or one shade darker. For contouring my face and man chest/pectorals, I use eye shadow that is about two shades darker than my skin tone. As far as facial hair goes, I use straight up hairspray and finely buzzed hair extensions that I buy at Dollar Tree. So far, I have only tried Covergirl and it makes my face really shiny and oily, especially when I am sweating and performing, so I am going to get a different brand next time.

❀**Thug Passion:** Well at first, I did not use makeup. I always thought I looked fine without it. My partner now is the one who talked me into wearing makeup to help even out my skin tone. I do not buy the makeup; I leave it to my woman to get it for me. It is another way for her to be involved. She also had to teach me to put it on because I had no idea what to do. I just keep the makeup in my DRAG bag. I really do not have a special place for it.

❀**Stefon Royce Iman:** Always test your makeup before you buy it. I use foundation and you need to make sure it is the right color so I would use Sephora or Mac and have someone apply it as a test. I also use eyeliner. Some can be purchased online, once you find the right color.

❀**Soco Dupree:** Performance Studios in Nashville, Tennessee, USA.

❀**Cody Wellch Klondyke:** I wear more makeup in DRAG than out. I have a whole checklist for performances: Foundation, bronzer, mascara, eyeliner, makeup brush kit, and makeup setter/hairspray. I regularly use Covergirl and Maybelline, and shop at Target or Wal-Mart. For facial hair, I shop at Sally's Beauty Supply and use hair extensions. I use spirit gum or the Gorilla Snot gel, which is awesome.

❀**Smitty O'Toole:** I only use loose mineral powder. Before my transition, I used only powder, fake beard hair, and spirit gum. Take care of your skin while not "in face."

❀**Jensen C. Dean:** I keep all my makeup together in one kit, that way nothing gets lost or forgotten. I buy my stuff locally (Phoenix, Arizona, USA) at Easley's or Boom Boom's, these are the makeups that more designed for stage. I have used just regular, buy it anywhere makeup, when I first started, but the stuff designed to be under stage lighting just looks better for this.

❀E. M. Shaun: Always practice using different types of makeup until you find the right combination for you. Some people use spirit gum for their facial hair. I use hair gel since I have sensitive skin.

❀Spacee Kadett: Ben Nye and Mehron make excellent stage products that do not sweat off. They are amazing, affordable, and can be purchased online, at local theater shops, and novelty stores. Airspun powder is also great for the stage; it is kind of a strange phenomenon. The stuff goes on thick and smooth, and smells like grandma's perfume. But kings and queens alike swear by it across the USA, and it is available at your local drugstore. Facial hair can be adhered with spirit gum, hairspray, liquid latex, or even painted on with smart stippling techniques (no hair required...but note the word "smart!"). For all of it, the products and techniques depend on the individual and his own preferences/complexion. That said (and this took me awhile to learn), I would like to emphasize the IMPORTANCE of a king's makeup. The fascinating thing about our art form is that we paint our faces only to give the illusion that we are NOT wearing makeup, and it is one of the myriad of reasons why we are so underappreciated. But I do NOT believe that any stage face should consist of hair only. We kings have inherently feminine facial structures and this is theater, baby. We need to paint for the bright lights, so in addition to hair, we must thicken our brows, square off our jawlines and foreheads, create an eyebrow ridge, hollow our cheeks, adjust our hairline, etc. Yes, it sounds like a lot of work, because it is. But it is totally doable, worth it, and NECESSARY if we EVER want to command our arena the way our queens do. Talk to your seasoned kings and willing queens about it. Do some internet research. Take some time and play around with makeup. The quality of your illusion will increase dramatically, and along with it your respect, versatility, and probably even your booking fee.

❀Master Cameron Eric Leon: I am still trying to find a better makeup source. Currently I am just using a bunch of makeup that my friend gave me when she stopped being a salesperson.

❀Devin G. Dame: I buy my makeup from 6S Boutique in St. Petersburg, Florida, USA. It is a mixture of Kryolan, Ben-Nye, and Mehron products. I use either hair spray or spirit gum to apply my facial hair. It has taken practice to perfect the exact method of apply everything to make it look correct. If you use the wrong makeup, it can make your skin burn and/or breakout. I have a DRAG box that stores all my makeup, hair, and accessories.

Chapter Thirty
"What procedures do you have in place to ensure your belonging are safe in the dressing room? "

❊**Freddy Prinze Charming:** I try to keep everything compact, in one place. I have a combination lock for my toolkit/makeup that I use when I know I will be in and out of the dressing room. I can put my tips, jewelry, and other valuables in my toolbox for safety. If it is my show, I try to keep the people in the dressing room limited to performers only, as much as possible.

❊**Jack King:** I have my stuff in my pack all time, after I have used it.

❊**Adam all:** Generally, I have not had a problem with theft, as most gigs I do, are alongside other kinds of performers. We all chat and try to get on in the dressing room, so I tend to find a corner to discreetly tuck my suitcase.

❊**Chance Wise:** I have always performed around people I knew. If not, I give any valuables and tips to friends to hold for me during the show.

❊**Shook ByNature:** I am always investing in my DRAG, so my fellow entertainers know my stuff is one of a kind. If I see it "out of place," I am not afraid to address the situation. I have been blessed not have dealt with this issue in a long time, but if it really matters, it stays locked up and in my car!

❊**Orion Blaze Browne:** I keep my things in a small area and as soon as an outfit comes off, it goes right into my bag. My tips always get zipped into a pocket while I am performing and as soon as I get done with my last number, my money goes in my pocket when I walk around the bar. I am very good about packing my things up before I go out to mingle after a show. I have, luckily, never had problems with stealing, though I have heard lots of stories locally.

❊**Vinnie Marconi:** I have not encountered a problem but I DO use common sense. Keep your area small and everything tidy. Move things out of the way when you are done with them. Keep everything in suit bags and closed prop cases. I also use a makeup kit that was a photographer box with a lock.

❊**Koomah:** I suffer from the dreaded "DRAG Bag Explosion" and try my best to keep my items in a centralized location or in my bag. I rarely work in environments where tipping is a main source of income versus being paid at the end of my gig, so that is rarely an issue. I do have a old, non-smartphone, flip cellphone, It is humorous to leave it lying about on top of my bag, because nobody wants to steal that thing!

❊**Campbell Reid Andrews:** This is something I am super anal about, not that I feel people or other performers are thieves. However, I perform mostly out of my state and city, so I do not have the pleasures of being close with cast mates, so usually I make sure to stay in my own area. Keep it clean and neat. Make sure after each number I place my costumes either in my suitcase or on my hangers. I also **will not** leave the dressing room until after I am done performing. As soon as I am done, I place my belongings in the car and go back in to mingle.

❀**Diseal Tanks Roberts:** I never have to worry about my things; the people I work with are trustworthy and family. I do, however, keep all my things organized in a bag.

❀**Travis Hard:** I have learned to keep my things together, nice and neat and not to leave anything valuable in the dressing room. No matter what, my wallet and phone are always on my person or with my girlfriend. I have worked with untrustworthy people before, it is sad that it comes to this!

❀**Coti Blayne:** I keep my stuff in a corner out of the way. Theft is not a big issue. My stuff trends to be very different so even if someone did walk away with something, everyone would know it. As for my phone and wallet, I will either keep it at the front desk of the club, or with a good friend.

❀**Clint Torres:** I perform with people I know so I keep all my gear in my bag and have never had any problems with anything going missing or anything like that. The room is open to performers only, so that is also why I feel secure leaving my stuff back there.

❀**D-Rex:** I never worry about my stuff. Most of the time, one of my brothers forget to keep up with their stuff, and I to find her.

❀**Rasta Boi Punany:** I keep my stuff in one place, in a corner. I rarely leave the area for too long. I keep everything in my suitcase as I change and prepare. Neat and orderly. There are usually persons assigned to keep others out of the dressing room as well.

❀**B J Armani:** I do not bring performers to my show that I would ever have to worry about. Out of town, I keep all my stuff in the same area and, TRUST ME, there is no time someone can claim one of my sequin mania creations as their own.

❀**Jonah Godfather of DRAG:** I normally work with a group of performers that I fully trust. But when I am at a venue that I am not familiar with or with performers that I do not know well, I have a pad lock that I can use on my DRAG case.

❀**Lyle Love-It:** Organization and I have never had an issue.

❀**Spacee Kadett:** Well, if I shared my secret, then you would know how to steal my stuff! Just kidding. Staying compact is important (though challenging at times). I have been fortunate to work with people I know and trust, but that still is not necessarily enough. I also pay close attention to people's comments, attitudes, and mannerisms so I am especially in tune with what is going on around me. It also helps to have unique DRAG. Everyone will recognize it as yours.

❈**Kenneth J. Squires:** I keep all my belongings in one place. I do not mind lending items if asked first. Respect is a big part of everyone's DRAG life.

❈**Adam DoEve:** Right now, I only perform at two places. At the one place, I work with a great group of people and do not have to worry about it, and at the other, I have a private dressing room and my door opens right on stage. I do however, try to keep everything together in one spot and close my case when I am not in it.

❈**Joshua Micheals:** I keep my stuff put away, kept together, and do not leaving anything tempting lying around.

❈**Eddie C. Broadway:** I have a lock on my DRAG box and I constantly make sure I am keeping track of my stuff, cash, and everything. If I am at a pageant, I make sure my dresser has eyes like a hawk! But overall, I have not had any troubles.

❈**Stormm:** I have not had any problems, but I usually keep an eye out.

❈**Dominic Von Strap:** I work for a razor company. Touch my stuff and I will cut you. I only take the absolute necessities and keep it all together.

❈**D-Luv Saviyon:** I try to be as compact as possible. I do not leave my stuff everywhere. I repack when done and in one specific area. I have been stolen from a lot over the years, so I also usually take my things straight to the car when done, even if I am staying at a venue after performing. That lessens the chances greatly.

❈**Travis Luvermore:** Leave important things at home. I have a dresser who helps me andwatches things backstage. I give my tips to her and my partner.

❈**Gus Magendor:** I do not. I just have faith that as much as I pay it forward, people would not intentionally take my things.

❈**AJ Menendez:** I do not either; we should not have to lock our things up. I make it a point to let them know if they run out of something and I have it (duct tape, glue, spray adhesive etc.), they are welcome to use it.

❈**Hurricane Savage:** I lock it all in the car but really never had anything stolen. All the regulars that I have worked around have always asked if they needed something.

❈**Marcus Mayhem:** Had a shirt and bra disappear. I keep money on me or hidden when near others I don't know. Family does not take from family.

❈**Rychard "Alpha" Le'Sabre:** I do not have an issue with anyone on my cast or any worries things will go missing. I used to lock my stuff up in a tackle box, but the cast I am on now is my family and I trust them all completely.

❈**Shane Rebel Caine:** I try to make sure if I am not in the room, someone I know and trust is. I never leave my money with my stuff; it stays in my pocket until it goes into my wallet, which is always chained to my side. I also try to avoid having my stuff laid out or scattered, I keep it in as small a space as possible.

❀**Atown:** I bring my own mirror, DRAG bag, and clothes rack if I have to. I have never had a problem with anyone.

❀**Ashton The Adorable Lover:** I am very organized, pack and unpack as I finish. Also my military background and an "I wish you would" body stance are always a plus.

❀**Dakota Rain:** I have not had any issues so far, but I do have people I trust, so most personal belongings will go to them, or I leave it at home or in the truck.

❀**Ben Eaten:** I have not ever felt my things were not safe in the dressing room. I do not really keep anything that is too valuable in the dressing room.

❀**Pierce Gabriel:** My phone, wallet, and tips always stay in the pants that I am wearing when I am not on stage. When I am on stage those pants are folded up and in my bag. I have had a couple items go missing back stage, but it was not anything valuable, and it could have easily been a mistake, so I never worry about it too much.

❀**Alec Allnight:** I keep everything together. I have a DRAG bag I keep whatever I need in. Everyone is family so I do not worry about anyone taking anything. They all know if they need to use something, they can. And I always leave with everything I came with. Sometimes we end up with random stuff in our bags, but we always find their owner! Plus I do not leave anything important in there anyway.

❀**Brandon KC Young-Taylor:** It is not easy to make sure all of your things are safe when you travel to places you are not familiar with. The best thing is to always keep everything in a neat order so you know when things have been tampered with. Also, try not to put your money in your bag while other people are watching.

❀**Ryder Knightly:** I tend to perform with many queens, so my area is limited in space. I pack lightly and make sure I have everything in my one area. I usually do not have to worry about a queen taking my things, we tend of have different tastes!

❀**Kruz Mhee:** It is unfortunate but necessary. I usually have at least one "DRAG bitch" stay inside the dressing area. A "DRAG bitch" is simply a friend or family member that can dress and undress you and handle the timeline of the show and get you ready. Just to be clear "DRAG bitch" is not a derogatory term for me.

❀**Hawk Stuart:** It is not easy to make sure your things are safe. You can keep your things in order so you know if someone touches it.

❀**Silk Steele Prince:** To make sure that your belongings are safe, bring only what you need. Keep your things neatly together and a lock on your luggage.

❋**SirMandingo Thatis:** My wife, and when she is absent, the good Lord will watch over my things and I feel if they steal them, they must have really needed it.

❋**Flex Jonez:** I have handlers, people that travel with me to keep an eye on me, my items, any other needs I may have. Most of the time my valuable items are locked up.

❋**Mike Oxready:** I bring one bag or suitcase into the green room and find a space out of the way. I do not lock my belongings, but do try to keep the more valuable items out of sight.

❋**Cody Wellch Klondyke:** I only take one bag, which is a rolling backpack. Where I perform, I tend to keep my things together and not scattered out and about.

❋**Viciouse Slick:** I just take my bag and makeup with me and once I am done with a performance, I put all the stuff together and back in my bag. Once I am done with my makeup, it goes back in my bag to make sure that I do not misplace anything, and it is not easy for people to just take it off the makeup station.

❋**George De Micheal:** Locked suitcase.

❋**Colin Grey:** I have been fortunate enough to have performed in venues where I do not really have to worry about it. I also try to keep in mind, that if something gets jacked, it is just stuff. I always keep my tips on me or with my partner.

❋**Kameo Dupree:** All of my luggage has locks. Granted, I have not had to use them since I started, but I know they are there if I need them.

❋**Phantom:** Every show I pack light but I carry many props and more expensive items go in my DRAG box if the rolling giant makeup case. It comes in handy and lock. I take it to every show. I make sure I pack up everything right away because it is hard to trust people with your belongings. Many things need to change in DRAG trusting each other is one thing we should start with. Many people ruin and break that trust.

❋**Sam Masterson:** I always take my big black bag and have been lucky no one is shady like that.

❋**Stefan LeDude:** I always just leave my stuff around. I trust my fellow performers.

❋**Xavier Bottoms:** I have never had an issue. Most of the show directors have a dressing room attendant. They stay in the dressing room during the show. It is not that other performs cannot be trusted, but nine times out of ten, the dressing room is in the basement of some bar that anyone can get into.

❋**Jamel Knight:** I keep everything together and packed. Essentially, I only take out what I need for that number, so if you were to steal my things, you would have to take the time to go through everything to get what you want. And I would hope that during that time, someone backstage would notice.

❀**Welland Dowd:** There is a lot of trust, but also general rules regarding people backstage: unless you are in the show, or dating someone in the show, you probably should not be hanging around backstage. Everyone seems to keep an eye out for strangers wandering around. Also, I usually keep my wallet in my back pocket, just in case.

❀**Michael Christian:** I try to remain as organized as possible wherever I go. I always know what I brought and where it is. Everything has its place like a puzzle when I pack, so I know what is going on, partially for sanity on a busy night, and partially for security. For bigger events I try to keep my wallet on me at all times. If not possible, I hand it to another entertainer (friend) for my time on stage. If I am out of town alone, I bring simply my identification and very minimal money. I keep it in a strange place and try not to let anyone see where. Not to say I am not trusting, I think I was just raised to be safe and cautious in life.

❀**Julius M. SeizeHer:** No one is in my stuff unless I am present. You need something, ask.

❀**Howie Feltersnatch:** The Fake Mustache Troupe is so close, that I trust everyone with my stuff. We share stuff all the time, and there are so many people in and out, that I trust that no one is going to take my stuff. If I am performing at a show that is not part of the Troupe, I always make sure I have a friend in the audience to hold on to valuables, like my wallet and phone, so it does not get stolen.

❀**Jack E. Dickinson:** When we were just among us, we had signs up to make sure no one but us and the staff of the venue could come it. We looked after each other. When sharing dressing room space with other folks...well, that's a chance each person decides to take. Some people leave their valuables with friends in the audience. I used to just check on my stuff on a regular basis, between acts and such. Stuff my wallet way underneat other stuff, etc.

❀**Clark Kunt:** Our performers are the only ones allowed in the staging room. I move my things to the DJ booth or coat check for safekeeping.

❀**Emilio:** I leave my valuables with my wife. The venues we perform in are safe.

❀**Juan Kerr:** It depends on the venue. Sometimes I am close enough to my stuff to be able to keep an eye on it. Sometimes there is a non-public backstage area which you're told/hope is secure enough.

❀**Trey C. Michaels:** Depending on the venue, I will keep everything in my bag with a lock on it to prevent sticky fingers from looking through it

❀**J Breezy St James:** Only once something was stolen from me, and that was my facial hair at Pride last year. Now I triple check that I have everything before I leave a show.

❀**Bailey Saint James:** I always kept a personal assistant or dresser in the room.

❀**Aaron Phoenix:** I keep my stuff back stage in the dressing room and mostly just keep an eye on it throughout the night. I feel comfortable leaving my belongings around the entertainers I work with and have never had anything stolen. If I were in a new environment with people I did not know or at a benefit with a lot of entertainers I did not know, I would keep the valuable stuff tucked away somewhere, but it is never really come to needing any drastic measures.

❀**Thug Passion:** I do not really have a procedure. As stated, "the good Lord watches over my things." Mostly I try to keep everything together and I only take what I need, so if anything does come up missing, I know what it is.

❀**Soco Dupree:** At the bar I am on cast at now, everyone is well trusted, but I do have a key lock on my jewelry box. As for tips, I usually hand them to my partner; otherwise I would lose them myself.

❀**Santana Romero:** One procedure I use to make sure my things remain safe, are packing everything in one carrier. I have a huge suitcase that I use to pack clothes, accessories, and shoes all in one, so I can keep track of all my items. I also only take out things I need in that moment, and make sure I place them back when I am finished so they avoid getting lost or taken. I keep important things like tips, my wallet, and phone on my person or with a friend, so I always know where it is.

❀**Stefon Royce Iman:** I never had anything stolen from me. The queens do not use what I use and I just zip my bag up and tuck it under where it cannot be seen.

❀**E. M. Shaun:** I just keep an eye on it, but hope and pray as entertainers, that we can all be honest and not mess with other people's belongings. I know things go missing from time to time, and I feel it is disrespectful for someone to steal. My tip money and cell phone are always with me or with a friend. I leave my DRAG in the dressing room. If someone steals my DRAG, it would hurt, but I can replace it if necessary.

❀**Jensen C. Dean:** I make sure to keep my things mostly packed up and organized. Honestly, during a show, the only time I am not next to my stuff is when I am on stage, most of the time. As a show host, I do not like when you have to track down a performer mid show or when you have to stretch because someone was not paying attention and they are not ready in time, so to make sure I am that person, I am pretty much back stage ready to go at all times.

❀**Smitty O'Toole:** I keep things in one suitcase. I keep that suitcase zipped while I am on stage and not in the dressing area. I was a cast member for a year, so I have never had to worry about my things because we were like family.

❀**Dionysus W Khaos:** I have in general, always been trusting. I have had a few things taken from me before, I have learned around certain individuals, I need to keep my makeup case and luggage box closed, but in general, most performers have the decency not to steal.

❀**LoUis CYfer:** Always have a personal assistant you can trust to take care of you and your belongings.

❀**Luke Ateraz:** I keep my keys in a zipped pocket, my wallet and cell phone is always with my wife or on me. I do not leave valuables backstage.

❀**William Vanity Matrix:** Out of sight out of mind is my safest logic anywhere. Keep it together and organized.

❀**Devin G. Dame:** I keep everything together and have a lock on my DRAG box. I usually have one person in the dressing room watching my belongings if there is any question of safety.

DRAG411's DRAG Memorial page on DRAG411.com

Chapter Thirty-One
"What are the top three things a performer can do to impress an audience? Why are they important enough to be the top three on your list?"

❀**Travis Luvermore:** Relay the emotion and feeling from your song. Your look should grab their attention; know your song forward and backward.

❀**D-Luv Saviyon:** Know your words, do performances because you really enjoy or believe in them. Be approachable and get to know them when you are off stage. They are important to me because they are things that I have learned over the years I have entertained. I frequent a lot of shows and pageants; people who are in the audience are never afraid to tell you how they feel about shows and performers. Their opinion is VERY important to me.

❀**Holden Michael:** Eye contact with the audience. Know your words, and always remain open minded and teachable. Do not ever think you know it all; that was told to me by a great Male illusionist, to whom I look up to very much.

❀**Clint Torres:** Be confident, know your words, and be interactive and unique. These are important to me because it is what has helped my DRAG come from nothing to someone people want to actually see. If you are confident, then you can go up on stage and own anything you decide to do. If you know your words then that is a plus because you should. The audience loves it when you interact with them by pulling someone up on stage or just going into it and looking someone in the eye. If you are unique, well then they will remember you for a long time.

❀**Alexander Cameron:** Know your lyrics, connect with your audience, and REMAIN HUMBLE! To me, there is nothing worse than a cocky entertainer. Be gracious, talk to people, take pictures, and say thank you! It is our job as entertainers to deliver an experience to the audience that does not end when the song is over.

❀**Joshua Micheals:** Know your words. I know it has already been said but it is that important. Have fun, and of course be respectful, of yourself, other entertainers, the bar staff, and the audience. And one more: be on time and prepared.

❀**Shook ByNature:** Connect with the audience (that means more than picking a girl up and grinding). Know your words; forgetting is one thing but if you do not know the song, do not do it. Do not bring outside drama onstage unless you can detach enough to not kill the mood. The last one comes with experience and time: if you and your girl broke up it is probably not the best time to do a love ballad.

❧**Campbell Reid Andrews**: Energy, energy! Be entertaining! Give a great story or concept to your number. That is what people want to see. They want to be taken somewhere else. Cut loose, relax or whatever reason they are watching this show for, it needs to be worth their time.

❧**Gus Magendor**: Take yourself seriously but not to where you and the people you interact with are not having fun. Make your performance personal to every single individual and, last but not least, BE YOURSELF.

❧**Freddy Prinze Charming**: Know your words! Put effort into makeup and costuming. Be original.

❧**Kody Sky**: Interaction, eye contact and the ability to inspire. Without any of these, you might as well put a pink elephant on stage and call it a day.

❧**Coti Blayne**: Know your words. Do it for you and enjoy yourself; if I am not having fun no one else will be because my energy will not be where it needs to be. Lastly, wow them. Every time I step on stage I try to make it better than my last performance, I try to top myself. That way the crowd never gets bored of me. I try to continuously wow the crowd, that way they never know what I am going to do, but they can always expect a good show. Whether it be crazy shoulder pieces, or face makeup, or LEDs, or cool characters that no one else would have the guts or ideas to do.

❧**Adam All**: Great voice, great impersonation/costume and great humour (that does not have to be spoken jokes). The audience is interested in great entertainment, which they measure by things that they know.

❧**Spacee Kadett**: I feel like there is only one rule, and from there, everything else falls into place: ENTERTAIN THEM. Per recent studies, the average attention span today is only 8 SECONDS! Remember that your audience is out to have fun, is in a loud environment, and is probably intoxicated to some degree! So... 1) Bring the music they love or a mix they want, 2) Wear a FABULOUS costume (something they would NEVER see on the street!) and, 3) own your performance.

❧**AJ Menendez**: Connect with your audience and make them feel a part of your performance, know your lyrics as if you wrote the song, and perform the song, do not just stand there and lip sync the words. I feel this way because without the audience, we would be absolutely nothing. It is not about us, it is about them.

❧**Kenneth J. Squires**: Know your songs well, and lip sync as if you were really singing that song. Put emotion and energy into it. Move around the stage and give them a good show.

❧**Chance Wise**: Costuming is a big deal for me. I always went to DRAG shows because I knew I would see some outrageous costume, and that's what I want to give to an audience, that 'what are they going to wear tonight' appeal. Do not just walk in circles or back and forth, you have to entertain.

❧**Justin Cider**: Creativity, practice and knowing your stuff.

✤**Travis Hard**: KNOW YOUR WORDS, and energy. Yes, knowing your words is definitely something that should be mentioned twice. I get compliments while performing about actually knowing my lyrics. People pay attention! Also, keep your energy high. You can know all your words and have a blinged out outfit, but if you walk around looking blah, then people get bored!

✤**Rychard "Alpha" Le'Sabre:** Creative costuming can make a huge difference. Mastering a difficult song, and some kind of climactic moment in your choreography to dazzle the masses.

✤**Shane Rebel Caine**: KNOWING YOUR WORDS, creative costuming, and definitely energy. Knowing your words is the most important thing. Nobody wants to watch anyone on stage performing to a song they do not even know the words to. Creative costuming is a really good way to catch the audience's attention so they are more likely to start watching you to begin with. Energy is how you keep the audience's attention, that does not mean that you have to dance, but do more than just walking around, even if it is just jumping around the stage, put energy into your movement and your emotions and you're definitely going to keep the crowd's attention.

✤**Rasta Boi Punany**: For me, it is to look confident, know my words and moves, take off enough to look sexy and tease, respond to them.

✤**Ashton The Adorable Lover:** Know your words and the music, be professional, and make the song mean something to you/ connecting with it brings out many expressions that keep your audience entertained

✤**Adam DoEve**: Knowing your music is big but for me I cannot dance as much as others, so facial expressions, being confident and looking people in the eye make them feel like you are singing only to them in that moment.

✤**Stormm:** Know your words, connect audience, be grateful, have fun, be professional.

✤**Vinnie Marconi**: Lip-sync is #1! KNOW YOUR WORDS! Entertainment is #2. You have to draw a crowd in with your number. If they are texting on their phone while you perform, YOU need to AMP IT UP! Appearance is #3. Make sure you LOOK like a KING and can stand next to the Queens without being in the background! Our height is already a disadvantage with queens in heels, so your costume better stand up to their sequins, stones, glitter, and feathers!

✤**Brandon KC Young-Taylor**: Have an amazing costume, giving great stage presence and an impressive illusion can impress an audience enough that even if you miss a few words here and there they will not notice! However, if your audience is made up of a crowd of other entertainers you had better know your words to impress them!

✤**Kruz Mhee**: For me, music choice is the most important thing to keep in mind for a show. The feedback you get from the crowd when the music is right is amazing, it makes all the difference. Second is your persona or your stage presence. You have to connect with the crowd and for me, being charismatic and connected pays off every time. Even if the crowd is not into the overall show. And third, make the show about the crowd. They are paying to see you and I feel they truly want to be a part of it. It isn't easy, what we do, and not everyone can deal with the pressure. However, everyone can enjoy the show.

❦**Hawk Stuart**: 1. Know your words 2. Draw the crowd with your number. 3. Look the part, dress the right way.

❦**Alec Allnight**: KNOW YOUR WORDS! You have to know your audience and choose your song accordingly. My biggest pet peeve is performing at a themed show and not being anywhere close to the theme. It throws the vibe of the whole show off.

❦**Flex Jonez**: Make sure your makeup is correct, costumes, signature dance routine, stage presence and be a fan yourself of the audience. Show love to them off and on stage. Enjoy the fans, handle yourself as a celebrity.

❦**Atown**: Take something off. The audience LOVES when a performer removes something. It does not have to be sexual, it can be a pair of glasses, a wig, a jacket, break a ways, etc. Try to be different or stand out in your own unique way. Be entertaining, energetic, and confident.

❦**Cody Wellch Klondyke**: Be confident and energetic. Your stage presence and knowing the lyrics to your song. Interact with the crowd, get them involved.

❦**Viciouse Slick:** Know your words, one thing, as a audience member, if it looks like you are lost, confused or unaware of your words I will start to lose interest and do other things. Be confident in what you do, no matter if others think it looks weird or silly. And be interactive, show some people in the audience more attention and they will come back to see you perform

❦**George De Micheal:** Eye contact. Body language. Smiling

❦**DeVery Bess:** Eye contact, stripping, audience participation

❦**Bootzy Edwards Collynz:** Know your WORDS, understand the song (strong presentation, confidence) and KNOW YOUR WORDS.

❦**Colin Grey Costuming**: The art is in the illusion, if your face is good enough that they mistake you for a man and you have gay boys hitting on you, you're doing it right. Know your words! Have passion for what you are doing.

❦**Eddie C. Broadway**: Knowing your words is key. From there, making sure your makeup is well done and not just looking like a woman with sharpie on your face, and stage presence. Yes, costuming is extremely important, but that can be taught. Stage presence is a hard one to teach.

❦**Sam Masterson**: I think getting the people involved, and working the crowd, eye contact, and knowing your words are very important.

❀**Jack King**: Look like a man and have some cool dance steps, cool costume and a look in his eye. Lip syncing is top, the first thing on my list.

❀**Kameo Dupree**: Being believable is most important. Believability includes lip sync, creative costuming, emotion, and movement. Every song does not require an over-the-top costume. Be sure if you are portraying a butch male, your body movement reflects the same. If it is a heart wrenching song, or slap happy comedy, feel it! Do not be afraid to show emotion. Make it believable! Next would be know your patrons. Make them comfortable. By this I mean, come to the bar/lounge a little early hangout and talk to the crowd. Show them you care as much as you want them to care. At the end of the night go back to the same people and thank them for coming and show your appreciation. It does not matter if they tipped you or not. They took time out of their day to sit and watch you perform! My last one would have to be leave your drama at home. Performers often fail to realize when they are angry and have not let it go, the patrons and other performers can see it in your face and movement.

❀**Stefan LeDude**: Put a lot of attitude into your number, big facial expressions/body language, and if you are dancing, make your moves big and sharp. You to be noticed.

❀**Jamel Knight**: Confidence is first because if you do not believe what you are doing, no one else will. You also want to have eye contact. A little bit of eye contact can make a person feel you are there just for them during your performance.

❀**Howie Feltersnatch**: Confidence in yourself and your number. If you have it, the audience is going to feel that energy you feed to them. Eye contact. People love it when you look at them and flirt with them with your eyes. Facial expression, you may not be the best dancer in the troupe, but that's ok, as long as you have your facial expression down pat, you'll be an amazing performer.

❀**Welland Dowd**: Energy, swagger, hotness!

❀**Michael Christian**: Always, always know your words. Costuming: it is more than street clothes. Even a simple suit can be made a costume with a rhinestone shirt, collar, tie, or accessories. Entertain! Capture their attention and move them in some way.

❀**Julius M. SeizeHer**: Confidence is key. Without it, your performance will end up lacking the appeal. Know the audience: Choose songs that will keep their attention, and get the crowd going. Be prepared for anything: if the equipment stops working, sing it out! That's what I had do!

❀**Lyle Loves-It**: Confidence, a well-choreographed number, outfits.

❀**Jonah Godfather of DRAG**: Perform the song. Lip-syncing is very important. Just as important is showing the emotion of the song. Have a diverse wardrobe. The audience can be impressed by your look. They are looking for a king that has a male illusion.

❀**Jack E. Dickinson:** Engage with them somehow! Make them feel involved, like they are a part of the show. As an audience member, I like to be a part of the magic so I try to give that back too. Surprise them! I love to be surprised, so I try to offer that too.

❀**Clark Kunt**: Feel the music - emote with facial expressions and body language. Know your words! Make sure you enunciate the lyrics and make your mouth movements big enough for the audience to see. Do not always just wear street clothes on stage - costuming is an important, yet often overlooked, aspect to DRAG as a King.

❀**Emilio**: Your attire; look sexy at all times. Music selection; my case, Latin. Be a crowd pleaser. Stage presence (carry yourself like the awesome King you are!).

❀**Juan Kerr**: Make them laugh. Be confident in yourself. Work at your routine to make it the best it can be. I think these are important because it is about communicating and sharing experiences with people. People mirror each other, so if you are having a good time, so should they. Just enjoy yourself.

❀**Trey C. Michaels:** You have to have a costume, not street clothes, but an actual costume that will grab their eye. Music. I do not give off a rocker or Broadway vibe, so I stick with more pop and 50's. Personality, both on and off stage. If you have a good personality, both off and on, it will stick in people's minds

❀**Aaron Phoenix:** 1. Costuming - your look should be entertainment in itself. 2. Energy - Feel your performance, exert some emotion and passion, use facial expressions, move around, get into it - the audience is there to party and have fun, so your performance should encourage them to do so. 3. Confidence - the more swagger you have on stage, the more impressive you look. This includes knowing every word to your songs - you cannot look completely confident if you are not sure of the words you are lip-syncing.

❀**Thug Passion**: To believe in the song you are performing, as in make it come to life. Interact with the crowd and taking something off like a jacket, a belt, wig, glasses etc.

❀**MaXx Decco**: People are impressed by an amazing transformation, a good performance, and MOST of all, CONFIDENCE!

❀**Soco Dupree**: Say thank you and acknowledge everyone who tips and compliments you. They are not there for you, you are there for them.

❀**Stefon Royce Iman**: Stage performance and appearance. Make the audience feel special by thanking them when they tip or greeting them a hand shake, hug, or wink.

❀**E. M. Shaun**: Be confident in yourself, and what you are doing. Look the part costuming, facial expressions, appearance and stage presence is very important. Make eye contact, know your words, and be gracious to the audience for their attention

❀Jensen C. Dean: Knowing your words is very important. Next is confidence (confident not conceited), the third thing is your look, from top to bottom you want to look right for what you're performing

❀B J Armani: Know the words to a song, have an awesome costume, and look at the audience. Bring them into a number with acknowledgement and give them something to enjoy. If you do not know your words, that may end up being the only thing the audience remembers. Above all, have fun! Even if you are nervous just use your costume and your eye contact to make that connection!

❀Smitty O'Toole: Eye contact, confidence, and humility. Let them know you are performing to make them happy by your actions.

❀LoUis CYfer: Be unique, be confident, and be energetic!

❀Luke Ateraz: Know your words! Or at least look like you know your words! Keep the crowd entertained! Do not wander off and start performing only to one section of the crowd, know how to work the stage. Play to the crowd, make them feel important, and that you appreciate them taking the time to come see you perform.

❀William Vanity Matrix: Inspiration, entertainment, and kindness. Inspire with your costumes and life you bring to the stage. Entertain with the performance itself. Be kind and acknowledge your crowd and those who tip you.

❀Mike Oxready: Engage with the audience, own the stage (this includes knowing your words up and down!), and put something of yourself into your number. These are my top three because the audience does not have to pay attention to you, but they are there to be entertained, so make them know you appreciate them. Own the stage- there is nothing worse than seeing a performer who is meek and hasn't rehearsed enough. Practice and perform with all the confidence in the world! It makes such a difference. And be creative; this is an art, and if takes a lot more than just a good outfit, facial hair, and lip syncing to be great.

❀Devin G. Dame: Having costuming. If you can buy it at the store the way you wear it on stage, it is not a costume. You should do something to your clothing - rhinestones, chains, spikes, safety pins are all examples of what you can add to make the outfit a costume. Know all of your words at all times. Have fun entertaining your audience. Let them feel the song and feel you performing your heart out for them. The three of these things are the most important and are at the top of my list because this is what I have done all my career and has made my career very successful.

Chapter Thirty-Two
"How do you handle an aggressively affectionate or groping patron?"

❦Eddie C. Broadway: I usually give them a hug and, if I am performing, I whisper to them that I will talk to them afterwards and direct them to sit without embarrassing them. If it is after a performance or something, I tell them thank you and I appreciate it and usually go back to the dressingroom, or something like that.

❦D-Luv Saviyon: If performing, I usually get away with a hug on top of my usual cheek or hand kiss. If not performing, I give lots of hugs and I usually get bailed out by someone. I talk to them a bit, say it was nice meeting them and politely excuse myself to talk to someone else I see I know.

❦Shook ByNature: The first altercation gets a polite smile, a conversation explaining my disinterest, and explaining the behavior inappropriate. If it continues, I point out my 6ft 9inch girlfriend. I remind them, the show is the show. I am happily taken!

❦Campbell Reid Andrews: Aggressive audience members during my number are great. As long as they have tips, I am all for the extra fun. Usually I mess with them, give them the attention they are tipping for and be on my way. If they are drunk and obnoxious then I will give them tiny bit of fun and walk away most of the time they are just drunk. Once the crowd is focused on me they usually get the hint and sit down. Most of them just want the spotlight, I have noticed. If I am networking after show and a "handsey" person comes up, I will say my hellos, laugh, joke take pictures and tell them to buy me a drink.

❦Joshua Micheals: The polite hug and move on, or talk discreetly to whilst retiring to either the dressing room or company of my friends

❦Gus Magendor: As long as it is on stage, and only when they are paying my tip, I do not mind it or take it too seriously. It is entertainment.

❦Freddy Prinze Charming: I am not a fan of the aggressive, groping fan. Just because they are giving me a dollar does not give them leave to be inappropriate. I am not a stripper... do not try to take my clothes off. Do not grab my packy, and stop trying to touch my nipples. If faced with an overzealous patron, I will back away, and then avoid them the rest of the evening. Getting that extra dollar is not worth my comfort.

❦Spacee Kadett: Groping tends to associate itself with intoxication, so (as with others here) a smile, a nod, and a quick exit usually are not too challenging. My one exception: I was doing a silly Lumiere number with giant "candlesticks" on my head and hands. It is a fun gig because patrons slip dollars into my big, stretchy shirt collar. But one patron at the end of the crowded catwalk felt the need to also tug my jacket open, undoing the Velcro and revealing the hideous underworkings of my costume. This was especially cruel because I COULD NOT USE MY HANDS! His behavior was just plain rude. I really could not avoid him in my effort to collect tips. My advice? If nothing else, create costumes that permit the use of your hands...

❀Adam All: This happened to me the other night and it was really horrible. A couple of men thought I was actually a man and refused to believe otherwise so repeated grabbed my ass and at one point pinned me against a bar, rubbing his cock against me. I yelled for help at the bar but they did not understand the situation and threatened to kick us all out. I had to get away as quickly as possible. I tried to convince them they were being massively out of order and no matter if I was a man or woman, physically molesting someone is not on, and they eventually gave up. If it happens in a show then I humiliate them to the room. I do NOT like being man handled. It is not part of my show.

❀AJ Menendez: I have only had that happen twice. Both times I tried to maintain my professionalism yet be very firm with my convictions. I let the bouncer of the venue handle it rather than handling it myself.

❀Orion Blaze Browne: I am one that does not mind a patron getting handsy as long as they are tipping. I have had patrons try to dance up on me or get me to give them a lap dance and not tip me for it. If they dont pull out money then they need to be happy with the free lap dance and I avoid them. Off stage I spend a lot of my bar time with gay men and DRAG queens. As a gay identified transman, I am use to friends smacking or grabbing my ass so it does not even faze me anymore. If it is more than that a hug and a step to the side usually works to get away from the situation.

❀Chance Wise: I can deal with some groping, but if it is excessive, I stay away from them. I only had that happen once, and keeping my distance helped a lot.

❀Marty Brown: I do not mind this to an extent. If it is too excessive, I have people around that will take care of them.

❀Justin Cider: Bromance! Me and fellow performers just look out for one another. If all else fails I literally just twirl them off the stage that usually works.

❀Hurricane Savage: Had it happen once. I went with it until she started to unzip my pants. I just moved away to a different part of the stage. But a little is to be expected.

❀Marcus Mayhem: Happened once to me. For most the part, I do funny and hump people at times, but when the lady tried to put the dollar in my pants while I am trying to not have them ride my pony, I quickly grabbed her hand with the money and said thank you and hugged her, and the rest if the night hid back stage till almost closing, since at call backs they were screaming how much they loved me. Quick, fast and in a hurry I bolted when I thought they were gone so I could go home. Someone always tries to grope me when I do that song.

✿Stormm: Do not mind a little. If too aggressive, I dance away, laughing

✿Travis Hard: I had a woman reach down my pants while performing to give me a tip. Thankfully, I was packing this night, so she got a handful of fake penis! I just avoided her for the remainder of that number. It happens, it will always happen, it is a part of this life!

✿Rychard "Alpha" Le'Sabreim: Light on my feet, I just dance away from them and move to the other side of the room, try to avoid getting too close, or, if necessary, let someone from staff know there is an issue and have them removed.

✿Shane Rebel Caine: If I am single, I do not really mind as long as they do not try to kiss me or grab my "package". If I am in a relationship, though, then I may play a little but then find someone else to mess with that isn't going to try and be all up on me. I continue my performance without letting it affect my interaction with the crowd. Putting the dollar in my shirt, or even into my pants, does not bother me as I do not keep my pants loose enough for them to stick more than a few fingers into them and I always have a pair of boxers under the pair that my package is stuck into.

✿Rasta Boi Punany: I whisper in their ear, "I am married. Back off."

✿Dakota Rain: If I am in a relationship, I ask them to please respect my partner and if they continue, I ask them again and explain that I am happy with the person I am with, and I feel honored that they choose me to show their affection to but please show respect. If I am single, I do not mind but I will not let it go too far, I do not like the idea of leading people in a direction that I am not willing to go, I hate dishonesty.

✿Ashton: The Adorable Lover usually a quick hug, or dance, if it is a really clingy patron. If that does not work I just keep doing my performance and usually they get point or a fan/security tells them to sit down.

✿Adam DoEve: I let them have their fun for a bit, and then move on. You just wait for that moment in the music and do a spin to get away. If I have a second number, I keep that person in mind, and time it so that I am only near them for a minute, and move on. They are the reason you are there so you have to give them some attention even if they are not tipping and the next show they come to they just might bring that friend that tips better than they do.

✿Pierce Gabriel: A lot of that all depends on the situation, who it is, and if my girlfriend is watching. I am a lot more defensive with guys, and I will usually step back out of their reach, if not physically divert their hands. Girls I will tend to allow to do whatever they want to with me. My girlfriends have all known that it is just an act, and I never reciprocate the touching.

✿Flex Jonez: I use them as stage props.

❀**Vinnie Marconi:** I had that just this past week. This woman had already latched on to two performers before me. I saw her coming toward me, made a jazz hand gesture that she was hot, winked and moved on to the birthday boy and played to him. I acknowledged her but did not allow HER to cross any lines. It is a tricky situation and if you are in a bar that usually has an unruly crowd, security will be on hand.

❀**Kenneth J. Squires:** I haven't had too many times when a patron got unruly. If a woman gets a little too close, I back away just a little, smile, wait for the tip and get out of there. Part of the show is putting on a show! But if it gets to the point where there is too much groping going on, I back off after telling her that I am happily taken.

❀**Ben Eaten:** I generally dance away or go through the crowd on the other side of the room. If they are too bad, I will say in their ear to stop but that's usually not an issue.

❀**Kruz Mhee:** It has happened several times. If I cannot calm them down and get away, then my partner, or my DRAG bitch, normally clear the air for me. I have been injured by a fan more than once. I had a young female jump on me, we fell and landed on my elbow which cracked. And I had another young female do the same we landed and cracked my tailbone. But I did go on with the show!

❀**Silk Steele Prince:** I politely move along.

❀**SirMandingo Thatis:** I usually just go with it. I have never had one get harsh or anything with me, and it is all in fun anyways.

❀**Atown:** Do your best to be as professional as possible.

❀**George De Micheal:** Act professional and politely remove any physical contact; blow them a kiss with a wink.

❀**DeVery Bess:** Either make a joke, or get awkward about it. If it is uncomfortable they usually back off.

❀**Sam Masterson:** I have been touched myself, and I usually take their hand and with force ask them to keep their hands to themselves.

❀**Jack King:** I have not been exposed to this.

❀**Kameo Dupree:** Make them feel special, and whisper in his/her ear and say, "I need you to get of the stage. I will talk to you after my number." They usually smile and step down. Yes, I keep my word and go speak with them after my number.

❀**Xavier Bottoms:** Typically, the aggressively groping patron is my wife. I look at it this way: I am there to entertain you. My wedding ring stays on while performing. So for me, if someone wants to rub me down, do it. I know whom I go home to.

❀**Jamel Knight:** Overly aggressive can sometimes be a lot of fun, but when things start to go too far sometimes you just have to tell them they are doing too much, and that you will talk to them after the show.

❀**Dominic:** I allow the crowd to grope. I use it to my benefit, and it works.

❀**Welland Dowd:** I have not really had to deal with this. Typically, the drunker patrons do not try to get up on the stage unless they are invited.

❀**Michael Christian:** I generally smile and back away. Then try to stay away for the rest of the night. Of course, after the show, there are the hugs and pictures, but anything extreme on stage or off and I am out. I like my personal comfort bubble.

❀**Jonah Godfather of DRAG:** Just recently. A woman came up to dance with me. She wouldn't let me go and kept pulling me back by my chains. I kind of made it funny by mouthing to the audience to "HELP ME". I think it made the situation lighter for everyone. I knew she had too much to drink and understood that she probably wouldn't have acted that way sober. She came up to me the next week and apologized for her actions. I told her that it was totally fine, that things like that happen from time to time, and that I was flattered that she took so much interest in me.

❀**Howie Feltersnatch:** If it is on stage I will play with the situation and make it look planned, but if it is off stage I will usually walk away. I am not a touchy person when it comes to people I do not really know and I can get uncomfortable quickly

❀**Jack E. Dickinson**: This has never happened to me. Actually, after shows, people often seem too shy to talk to me. I have been told I am intimidating because I do crazy, absurd stuff on stage and people do not know quite what to make of me. That said, I had a drunk friend once grope me while I was on my way onto the stage from the stairs in front of the stage. I had to ignore them since I was actually in my role! But I was not happy with them!

❀**Clark Kunt:** When I am alone I am really awkward, so that usually takes care of itself. If I am with my DRAG brothers, we all sort of watch out for each other.

❀**Emilio**: I kindly step away from them, and spin them away from me, and I twirl them. Make it part of the show.

❀**Juan Kerr:** Sometimes I offer them a crotch to feel. I think my girlfriend would sort out anyone who got TOO handsy.

❀**Brandon KC Young-Taylor:** People like to get "friendly" sometimes, but that's part of the entertainment business. You just have to know that someone will eventually give a crotch squeeze and try to get a kiss, but the trick is to give them a little show, and quickly move on. You do not want to make your tippers feel like you aren't interested because that will stop them from coming back, but you do have to maintain your own limits. When I run into this off stage I always try to engage in a bit of conversation with the person then find a group of my friends to surround myself with, people that can help defuse a situation should one arise.

❀**Trey C. Michaels:** I usually ask to be place more in the middle or end of the sets. I like to go and watch the crowd to get an idea of the vibe and to see if there is a patron who is being more touchy feeling than I would like that way I can keep my interaction with them short and sweet. If I don't get that chance to I will usually walk away from them. if it continues to happen I will usually let security know that someone is making me uncomfortable so they can speak with that patron.

❦**Bailey Saint James**: Back up. Usually we have some kind of bouncers near our stages. If you do not feel comfortable amongst the crowd, there is no rule saying you have to go out there. Stay on stage.

❦**Aaron Phoenix:** There's usually a way to play it off when on stage - a "shame on you" look/gesture, a wink and then a spin off in the other direction, or just simply backing straight up and heading away can stop a situation while making it all look like part of the show. When it happens off stage, I back off and look for someone I know. The "buddy system" is great for these situations.

❦**Thug Passion:** I have not experienced an overly aggressive patron. If I were to, I would just politely let them know that they are over-stepping their boundaries.

❦**Santana Romero:** Well, here's an interesting one. I have actually had several run-ins with this, especially at my old home bar. What I usually do overly aggressive patrons is dance with them for a while, maybe give them a little grind with the hopes that they'll move away. If this does not work, and they get to handsy, I will dance with them, smile then slowly back away. They usually take a hint after that. It is always good to handle situations like this with gentle assertion, since the patrons are actually enjoying what you are doing, but are too drunk to know boundaries.

❦**MaXx Decco:** I usually acknowledge them, dance with them, if it goes with performance, and move on. Performances have ended and security has been called on some enthusiastic, but overzealous, audience members for being a little too hands-on.

❦**Soco Dupree:** I take their hand, spin them in a twirl like a dance move to get space between us, kiss their hand say thank you and slide away. Works every time.

❦**E. M. Shaun:** If I am performing and I have an aggressive fan, I will dance with them and then try and lead them away from the stage in a smooth way. If the fan does not get my gesture, I have some of my friends that can help with keeping them at bay. I try and give all my fans a little individual attention if I can, but sometimes I can miss someone because one individual might be a little pushy.

❦**Stefon Royce Iman:** I usually place their hand somewhere, and smile and dance with them, or if they are trying to tip inappropriately, I take their hand and show them where I want to be tipped and I dance with them and smile.

❦**Lyle Loves-It:** I do my best to be polite, distract if possible, and move on.

❦**LoUis CYfer:** I say, "Five pounds please," which does the trick.

✤Viciouse Slick: I try to just ignore them, or when they start to get to the point of too much contact, I just move away from them to go to someone else. After the number, if they have made me too uncomfortable I ask security or the show manager to have them leave, or talk to them about the situation

✤B J Armani: I am a comedy king. I also host a lot so I get away with a little more sometimes. I have spun a gal back to her chair, I have put the dollar back down their shirt/pants, and I have run away. Most of the shows are in bars so alcohol can whack out people. I take it as a compliment they get that excited!

✤Smitty O'Toole: I am a performer, not an object to be fondled. I do not allow patrons to fondle me. I grabbed a few hands and sternly advise them that I am a professional and that behavior isn't tolerated. I have not had anyone try to fondle me on stage.

✤Jensen C. Dean: This isn't something I have really been faced with, at least not as intense as the question words it more I just get the lingering tippers. And for them I normally make sure to find a way to kind of signal to them that it is time for them to go back to their seat.

✤Luke Ateraz: Oh boy... I have actually got experience with this one. I had competed in a little event hosted by Morgan McMicheals to gain a spot on her Saturday night cast at VIP Nightclub in Riverside CA. I decided to do a spoof of Sexy and I know it. I was wearing a fat suit that had tassles on the nipples and it had a thong on as well. I had a binder on underneath and boxer briefs. As I am walking through the crowd, a guy sitting there actually grabbed my crotch! I smacked his hand away and kept going. As I was walking up the side of the audience, I could already see him being escorted out by security. A few months ago, we were back in Riverside, back at VIP to see a show while we were in town. Standing there and who do we see? That same guy! He did not recognize me, but my wife sure knew who he was!

✤William Vanity Matrix: Well, besides people I know, I do not take kindly to being touched at all be random people. I grin and bear it, and find ways to leave the situation as soon as possible. Hugs for pictures, and such, are fine, and if people ask I usually do not mind them feeling my hair, but as far as that goes I have not had a really bad case yet. Anytime it gets anywhere near that, I have been lucky enough to find a reason to get away from them without offending the patron.

✤Mike Oxready: My character tends to be flirty, but if it gets uncomfortable, I find a reason to exit. The bathroom, my partner, and the green room are all escape routes.

✤Devin G. Dame: I play with them so they feel special, then move to another in their group to just make the rounds and keep it in small doses.

Chapter Thirty-Three
Music makes me dance!

❀**Freddy Prinze Charming:** Much of my music is suggestions by other entertainers, friends or fans. Then there are the songs that I hear and immediately a concept, costume, etc. appears in my mind. I generally mix my own music, using a program called Goldwave, but I have had mixes made for me by people like Richard Cranium.

❀**Mike Oxready:** I mainly go with music that moves me in one way or another, or if it is for a themed show I will mix in something to change it up a bit. I do not like to perform a single song, so I mix my own using Garage Band, integrating other auditory components to round out the show.

❀**D-Luv Saviyon:** I am always trolling the internet for new music. Over the years, I have found making mixes to be much more fun and a way to make up for music choices not being as good in current times. I faithfully use Audacity and PC DJ to make my mixes.

❀**Joshua Micheals:** My music comes from whatever moves me. I make my mixes using Adobe Audition Sounds, or from friends when I am lazy.

❀**Coti Blayne:** Many random YouTube searches. I do get many suggestions, too. I find songs I like, and download them and listen to them constantly. I have hundreds of songs on my phone as potential numbers, and I am constantly adding more. I make my own mixes when possible, unless I need something really, really, really cool, because I am not quite that skilled yet, but I am getting there.

❀**Kody Sky:** My music comes from Pandora, radio, suggestions and whatever song I hear that inspires me to share it with the audience.

❀**Spacee Kadett:** Top 40 from any decade works. Occasionally a random upbeat song connects with the audience, but any music must be catchy and relatable (or, if you are doing a theme number, fit with the theme). I use the free program Audacity to mix my music. It is just complex enough that it fulfills all my needs. If I ever need something beyond my scope (have not yet!) I will outsource to a reputable name.

❀**Adam All:** Mostly by listening to the radio or other people's music. You just hear something that's going to work, something you can twist or work with and go for it. I use Audacity to manipulate my music.

❀**Travis Luvermore:** Songs that touch me and I feel that have the ability to hold the audience attention and touch them. Local radio and YouTube. I check out my favorite artist's songs, and check out the Billboard top songs.

❀**AJ Menendez:** I find my music all over the place and mix my own 98% of the time using a program called "Wave Pad." I am very versatile and can perform to almost anything but if I had to choose, I had choose Alternative / Rock, Creed, Disturbed etc. I find I can be very theatrical, and it is fun to play with. I choose songs that touch me in one way or the other.

❦**Adam DoEve:** Well, right now I do two shows a month. One always has a theme to it, so after I find out what it is, I start going on YouTube to see what I can find. For my other show, I go with whatever mood I am in. I never stick to just one type of music; that is just too boring for me. I could be doing all country one night and the next time doing heavy metal. I have not started mixing yet but would like to start.

❦**Campbell Reid Andrews:** Of course, I would be excited about his one! Music is a big deal to me, and I feel it makes or breaks a performance. I was once told by the DRAG mommy to collect music rather than wait until you have a show. If I hear a song, I write it down. So, that is exactly what I do whenever I am anywhere or hear anything: movies, store, tv shows, commercials. I am collecting music and building characters and stories to go with them. Before you know it, you've collected enough music for 10 mixes. I do mix my own music with free music editor. Literally, that's what it is called. If I need something more formal I will use a DJ friend of mine. Music is very important, do not overlook it. It sets the tone, mood, story, emotion. Music is what make the world go 'round. It needs your thought and attention, if you take this seriously. "There's always 2 things in life: music and noise. At the end of the day it is all about the music, baby"

❦**Gus Magendor:** I choose music I know, and songs that hit me personally. I search YouTube as well.

❦**Chance Wise:** I use a lot of music that relates to me, but I also ask many people what they would want to see someone do on stage. Unless it is something I cannot feel, I will do something suggested to me. I use Audacity to make mixes.

❦**Justin Cider:** I was a huge Drake fan when I first started used a lot of his stuff, and knew a lot of it already. As I have grown, I have done all sorts of other performers and genres but he is always still my boy, even when he was Jimmy Brooks on Degrassi. I have done mixes but I usually ask a friend or DJ to help me with it, as they are more practiced. Like so many say, it is not what you know but whom you know.

❦**Clint Torres:** I pick my music off the Top 40 charts for R&B, Rap, or what I hear is popular around the time. For me, Bruno Mars never fails.

❦**Travis Hard:** I searched online for songs to perform to. I get mixes made, as well, from Cuntalicious remix. I scour YouTube! I can do this for hours! Or, if I hear a song I love on the radio, I try and put it together in my head and work on that!

❦**Rychard "Alpha" Le'Sabre:** Really depends on the mood I am in. Performers always, always do better when they can really FEEL the song they have picked.

❦**Shane Rebel Caine:** YouTube is the best place to find random songs, cover songs, or songs you otherwise would not hear on the radio. Otherwise, I like to keep my ear on the radio for new and old songs and to know what is popular. Every once in a while I may mix a song but usually it is just adding one song onto the end of another, otherwise I will do already mixed music from YouTube, if I choose that route.

Rasta Boi Punany: I find them on YouTube, the radio or I ask my Music Mixer to find songs for me depending on the theme.

Dakota Rain: I check out YouTube for ideas. I do not mix my own (wish I knew how). I do country, so I try to see what is hot at the time and sometimes throw in some old stuff. I cannot dance.school or mainstream songs, and YouTube artists that have remixed a song I like, especially if it is female. I have mixed many songs using a simple, free Mixcraft program downloaded from the internet.

Pierce Gabriel: I usually perform 90s rock or current pop songs. Passionate music, songs that have meaning behind them. If myself, or one of my friends, do not have a song I want to do on CD already, I download it and either put on a cd or a flash drive.

Koomah: I find music all over. Sometimes I find great songs after a fall down the YouTube rabbit hole, sometimes I will hear a song I like playing overhead at a store, other times it is a song that a musician friend of mine has created. I do mix music using Audacity or SoundForge, depending on what needs to be done to the track.

Vinnie Marconi: From friends' and fans' requests. I mix my own numbers using MixPad except pageants, and then I ask Delorian Chase!

Ben Eaten: I pick songs with a good beat or becoming popular on the radio or iTunes. Luckily, I have gotten my music mixed by my DRAG father because I cannot seem to get it to work on my computer. Sometimes when picking music, I will go to a certain year like 2000 and pick like a top song from then, the audience enjoys a throwback every now and then.

Kruz Mhee: I love dance music, however Kruz is known more so as a rocker. I do enjoy parodies and fun music. My music comes from pretty much everywhere. For example, in my last show I performed a song by Ray Jessel "What She's Got". I saw this guy on America's got talent, I thought he was amazing and the crowd at my last show was loved it! I prefer music with a rock 'n roll baseline, and normally my song choices are dirty. Give the crowd what they want! I have mixed some of my own music using wave pad but normally I employee a DJ.

Hawk Stuart: I get my music from what I know, I stick with some of the same music, and most of it comes from friends and family. I just started mixing my music and I get help from my family if I need it.

Alec Allnight: I like to branch out. I do not want anyone getting the same ol' same ol' at my show. I will start making my own mixes soon. I have to be 100% about my song selection; otherwise, I will not do it.

Flex Jonez: I am a DJ with a house full of music, and have DJ buddy that works with mixing my music to fit my skill and routine idea.

❀**B J Bottoms:** I listen to the radio a lot and talk to other MIs to see what is new out there. Music has always been a big part of my life so I am always keeping an ear out for songs I know I can perform and perform well.

❀**Silk Steele Prince:** I find music on the radio, YouTube, iTunes, Grooveshark and old CDs. I find songs that speak to my Inner Kings ego. I have to feel the song inside out, so the audience feels my passion. I am entertaining and fits the theme of the showcase. I mix songs so that the audience is not bored and detracted with other things like there phone. When I mix. I use WAVPad or Magix Music Maker and Studio.

❀**SirMandingo:** I stay true to myself when it comes to music. I do music that I grew up with and music that I listen to now. I am a hip hop and r&b guy at heart; if I can feel the music and the beat, it is all me. I have recently just gotten into mixing my own songs. It is super difficult, because you have to know where to break the song and start a new one or even change the beat, but I use Virtual DJ at home.

❀**Atown:** I make my own mixes, but when I do not, it depends on the theme. I search YouTube for the genres, and some of my favorite movie clips. I use Magix.

❀**Stormm:** I listen to all kinds of music. It depends on if there is a theme to the show, otherwise I try to do what is big out there. I either buy the CD or download it. I have not gotten into the mixes yet.

❀**Kenneth J. Squires:** If I hear a good song on the radio, I will find it on YouTube or go out and buy it. I do not know how to mix my own music, so if I have someone that knows how to do it, I will ask them if they wouldn't mind helping me out.

❀**Cody Wellch Klondyke:** I listen to all kinds of music. I love the beat of The Music. Music is my soul. Whatever I am feeling is what I will pick. It also depends on the theme of the show. I also reach out to my fans and ask for song preference, to get them involved .

❀**George De Micheal:** I am into all sorts of music. I love the meaning of words in music and the way you can perform them.

❀**DeVery Bess:** YouTube, usually have links to the songs on iTunes so you do not have to be a pirate. Also audacity is a good free program for adjusting pitch, and I like using virtually DJ for mixing songs, but there are some wicked mashups on YouTube.

❀**Bootzy Edwards Collynz:** I will find random goodness on the radio every once in a while. I will make a few mixes, just depends on the show. Anywhere I can hear it, and I like it, I just might perform it.

❀**Devin G. Dame:** I feel songs and music. If it moves me, and I think I can move someone else with it, I do it. I do not mix my own music.

❀**Dionysus W Khaos:** For simple mixing, I use Audacity. If it is more complicated, I have it made for me. I do a wide variety of things so I do not stay in one generation.

❀**Colin Grey:** Radio, albums, sometimes Muzak in department stores or restaurants, Sirius, Pandora. Basically any place you hear music. I do occasionally do my own mixes and I use Audacity.

❀**Eddie C. Broadway:** I use Spotify religiously. I am into hipster/alternative music so I try to dive deep into music that people may not know. Music is my passion. I also go to music festivals a lot, and look for new artists and music. I use Audacity, Abelton, Virtual DJ, e.t.c. to mix my music.

❀**Sam Masterson:** I search and make my mixes, I go outside the box to try new things.

❀**Jack King:** YouTube. I mix from Windows Movie Maker.

❀**Kameo Dupree:** My father was a DJ so I own much vinyl. Then my sister took after him, so I have downloaded all of her music and I just sit and listen. If it draws me in, I write it down for my favorites. I know how to cut music but have yet to mix my own.

❀**Corey James Caster:** I find my music through beemp3. I know it is made to download music to an mp3 player, but it is a good website to use to download music for your shows.

❀**Xavier Bottoms:** I do such a variety of songs: pop, country, and all kinds of parodies. Since I have been doing DRAG for so long, my cd collection has its own library. When making a "mix" or "mashup" I use Audacity.

❀**Stefan LeDude:** I just come up with ideas sometimes, like "oh, it would be fun to do THIS to such and such a song" Or sometimes I will hear a song and think, "THIS song would make a great DRAG king number."

❀**Jamel Knight:** I find music for performances everywhere. I have a vast music collection that ranges from the 1920s to 2014, so I can listen to music one day and a song will play that grabs my attention and makes me want to perform it. Music heads at work and in my family surround me, so they are always introducing me to new music. I like to make my own mixes and usually use Audacity or Soundtrack Pro to create the mixes.

❀**Howie Felterschnatch:** The songs I find sometimes come from nowhere. I could be in a coffee shop and a song comes on that inspires me. When I get home I look up the artist and I just keep getting inspired more and more.

❀**Welland Dowd:** I find music all over the place, but prefer rock music from the 1950s, 60, and 70s. I have happily done numbers to contemporary pop/dance music too.

❀**Michael Christian:** I have had some suggestions from other entertainers. Mostly though I stick to what moves me and I can convey well on stage. I like people to believe I wrote that song. For major events (prides or college shows) I search a little YouTube and look up the top 40 list. Make sure I can reach the entire audience of all ages. They do not know me, and my love of obscure country, after all.

❀**Emilio:** 95% of my numbers are Spanish numbers by Ricky Martin, most of which I already have in my library.

❀**Julius M. SeizeHer:** I use all kinds of music. I choose songs based on how well I know the words, and how easy it is to dance to them. Also, the appeal of it helps too!

❀**Lyle Loves-It:** Radio, friends, YouTube...

❀**MaXx Decco:** I am not big on dancing. I discover new things through friends, local radio stations, Slacker Radio, social media, and Shazam. I have been coming up with A LOT more mix ideas, I have the ejing and pocketband apps I am learning on, but the amazing Jessie Perales does the engineering of my mixes.

❀**Jonah Godfather of DRAG:** I do songs that I love, and I think it shows in my performances. I also take into consideration how well known the song is. If the audience does not know it, they will not listen and pay attention, so I try to pick songs that are loved by others as well. I have mixed a song or two in the past. I am not the greatest at it, so if I need a mix, I usually leave it to one of my friends to do for me.

❀**B J Armani:** Everywhere and anywhere. I find songs from friends or just go on YouTube and randomly watch videos until you find another wacky song. As far as mixing I tend to leave that to the professionals. I have tried, with not so much success.

❀**Crash Bandikok:** I use anything I like to move to, and mix my own music.

❀**Bootzy Edwards Collynz:** Anywhere and everywhere! Even did a song in Puerto Rican by Chayanne-Salome (loved that song for YEARS). Soundcloud, some radio, Pandora, Spotify, NewJams.net, RnBExclusives.net, Mzhiphop.net, Beatport, Datpiff.com. If I hear a good song out shopping, I will Shazam/Soundhound it in a second! I will also ask my friends what they are listening to at the moment. I will do concert versions of songs, because I like dance routines. Concerts have some of your best "mash-ups" of that artist's best/most popular song. I use Sony Acid to cut and edit music. I can add effects as well, but not often. I can do the mixes for concert versions together. (NEVER USE recorded album audio into concert audio version-sounds funky, be consistent in your sound and feel).

❀**Jack E. Dickinson:** All over the place! Sometimes I have a flash of inspiration while listening to something and I go with it. Not always songs that I am necessarily a huge fan of either, sometimes they just work with the idea I have in mind and then I wind up loving them. I have done touch ups to replace words or to make medleys using Gold Wave. I tried their free trial, loved it, and bought the "for life" version. Heard there are better options out there but I have this and am used to it, so it works for me.

❀**Clark Kunt:** Radio, old CDs, YouTube... I mix songs using Audacity.

❀**Juan Kerr:** I use music that I have known and loved all my life. I have a lot of soul songs that I love singing, plus I already know all the words to them. I started by miming but then moved on to singing. I am a music technology student as well so I can use Ableton, Pro Tools and Logic to do any mixing bits that need to be done.

Santana Romero: Typically, I stick to Top 40 singles from 2003 or so to now. This is music I have listened to faithfully, due to the fact that Pop music is so dance oriented. However, I do love R&B and hip-hop/rap. Usually, I find my music from YouTube or the radio. The only software I have used to make mixes are Audacity. I honestly think it is best if you are on a budget, because it is free and easy to work with.

Brandon KC Young-Taylor: YouTube! And I like to use cuBase to mix my music!

Trey C. Michaels: YouTube. I am dating who can make mixes for me.

Aaron Phoenix: I use things like YouTube, Pandora, and Spotify to find new music, as well as tapping into stuff I already knew and loved, nostalgic classics, and current hits. I mix my own music (I almost never do a single song on its own anymore) using a program called Magix.

Thug Passion: I get my music mostly from music videos, music on radio, when I mix music I have people do it for me.

Soco Dupree: I do a lot of my own mixes, but I get numbers from supporters wanting one done or listen to what may be popular, however I enjoy during older style music. I.e. Temptations, Def Leppard, White Snake, Marvin Gaye.

Dominic: My best song choices are always related to my current mood or situations taking place in my life!

E. M. Shaun: I mix my own music. I live in NC but originally from Washington, DC, so my mixes are old school songs with up-to-date music with a DC/Baltimore club feel. My mixes are themed and they tell a story from the first song until the end. It takes me weeks, sometimes, to create a new theme and then use the right songs use to create my story. It is extremely rare for me to perform a single song. I have a large music collection with various genres. I also use YouTube and Audacity for mixes.

Stefon Royce Iman: I always use the music from the top 40 on Billboard. I use YouTube, RealPlayer and Audacity to mix music.

Smitty O'Toole: I find my music all over life. TV, movies, radio, YouTube… I make my own mixes and record my own vocals using Audacity and FL10 to edit and mix.

Jensen C. Dean: I find my music pretty much anywhere, I am lucky to have my wife and my best friend who both really have an ear for music they frequently find hidden musical gems for me. For mixing I use a program called Acoustica Mix Craft (last time I checked, there was not a Mac download for it only PC). It is a free trial then like $20-ish for the full version after the trial ends.

Luke Ateraz: I mix my own stuff using Virtual DJ or I have it done for me.

William Vanity Matrix: YouTube, radio, clubs. Audacity is what I use.

Chapter Thirty-Four
"What is the most embarrassing mistake done on stage? What advice do you give the entertainers believing mistakes are career killers?"

❦**Freddy Prinze Charming**: It was not really MY mistake, but the fault of the DJ. During my talent number for the 2010 Phoenix Pride Pageant, my music mysteriously stopped. The CD had been tested earlier in the day and it worked fine, My dancers and I performed more than 2/3 of the number without music. I was accused of switching out CDs for one that purposefully stopped, to try and get the pity vote, etc. I believe it made me a stronger person and a better performer. Mistakes happen. Music stops. Costumes malfunction. Props break or fall over. Things do not go as planned. It is not the end of the world. How you handle it shows the community what kind of entertainer you are. If your CD will not play, do not throw a hissy fit. If your music stops, do not storm off stage in a huff. If your costume breaks, hold it up and keep going. One mistake will not kill your DRAG career, but your attitude in regards to the mistake might.

❦**Jack King:** If you do a misstep, do not stop just perform. Only you know it was not part of the plan.

❦**Adam All**: I guess for me, it would be forgetting the odd lyric when singing at full belt, but the audience are only behind that 4th wall, let it down and laugh with them, you'll win their hearts and they will help you through it.

❦**Spacee Kadett:** Harry Potter is jinxed! First, the crotch of my Harry Potter pants split wide open at the end of the catwalk in a PACKED house. All I had underneath was my "package" tucked into a jock strap! I finished the number with my legs close together, hoping no one had really noticed... Then a few months later, with my reluctantly-supportive parents in an even MORE packed audience, I obliviously performed almost the entire Harry Potter number with my seven inch fly unzipped. I have also, for the record, twice slipped in the middle of a cartwheel (should've worn grippier shoes), botched choreography, gotten trapped in tear-a-ways, forgotten my own lyrics singing live... Just last weekend my baton unintentionally flew out of my hand, nearly took someone's eye out, and popped about 10 feet in the air before landing. But the laughter that ensued at my shocked reaction actually made my night. The same thing happened when I zipped the fly of my Harry Potter costume. It is live theater. Stuff happens. Mistakes are the best opportunity to grow as an entertainer, laugh with your audience, or remind yourself that they were actually probably too drunk to even notice.

❦**Chance Wise:** I would say, know what you are physically capable of doing before you try to do it on stage especially since some costuming can be difficult to move in. Do a dress rehearsal. I had a costume that was pretty hard to move in, and I wanted to do a crawl across stage; did not turn out so well, but I hopped up and improvised quickly enough that I do not think anyone noticed. Also, know your surroundings. I did a faceplant during a Disturbed song and nearly cracked my head on a speaker on stage. So, as deeply passionate as I was into the song I could feel my hair bend against the speaker and thought, "Holy crap, that was almost really bad".

Vinnie Marconi: POOP HAPPENS!!! Even in a national competition! Things will be forgotten, batteries quit working at the worse time, material snags... Like Freddy Prinze Charming said, "One mistake will not kill your DRAG career, but your attitude in regards to the mistake might." I could not agree more!

Clint Torres: The most embarrassing thing that has happened to me on stage was at the very beginning of a play I was cast the lead of, I forgot the dance. I was four counts behind, and it took me a minute to catch up to the other dancers but once I did, it was fine. My DRAG dad told me that the audience did not mind my slip up because I kept going. I did not stop I kept dancing kept moving and in the end, the show and my DRAG have been a huge success.

Ben Eaten: I had been practicing some "basketball skills" for a Disney themed number I did, I knew what I was going to do with the ball etc. Well, live performing does not always go as planned, and I threw the ball and nailed a girl in the face! This was during a pageant and I was mortified. Do not let the little mistakes keep you from going on. I finished the number as planned then found the girl to apologize. But the way I reacted to the mistake when it happened kept the rest of the routine going.

Viciouse Slick: I have forgotten words to songs, and during a music break, I do not know what to do. In those moments just push forward, no one is perfect and we make mistakes or have issues with things. You will do better the next time.

Campbell Reid Andrews: This happens on a regular basis. Doing DRAG in live community theatre is dangerous for me. Very often, I perform, binding open shirt for 2 hours, and sometimes I do not tape well enough, and with my sweaty body my tits want to be famous and pop out. Not fun for a full house of blue-haired ladies.

Travis Hard: I have yet to have an embarrassing moment on stage, but I am due for one. I have had issues such as costumes falling apart before shows. I have lost a button on pants and had to wear a pair of regular jeans that was not cute. I have also fallen right before getting on stage but never on.

D-Rex: Got too drunk on my birthday and fell down.

❧**Rasta Boi Punany:** The one moment I was uncomfortable on stage while performing is when my lips got stuck to my gums and I had to turn away from the audience to pull them apart. I did it very smooth so no one really caught it. That is it. Everyone makes mistakes or has an awkward moment. Do not sweat it.

❧**Max Hardswell:** I have had a few mishaps where I forgot a prop, or my hat, or did not have my shirt buttoned. But my most embarrassing incident was at a club I had never performed at, in a town that I had never been to. The crowd was not getting into my song, and I started forgetting the lyrics because I had not practiced enough... And I froze. I turned to my king friend and mouthed, "I cannot do it" and he said, "get back out there!" I stumbled through the rest of the song trying to look like I was into it. Afterward I went back into the dressing room and cried my eyes out, thinking I was a failure. I never got booked by that show director again, but I learned my lesson on preparing. Do not get cocky because you think you're getting good, always drill your lyrics and do a run through before you get to the stage. And most importantly, do not let a bad audience affect your performance.

❧**Justin Sider:** One of my very first shows (approximately 6 years ago) I made the rookie mistake of not binding properly. Back then, I was using bandages as I hadn't yet purchased a binder. I was performing a cowboy act with another king and I heard the pop of the clip snapping that held my binding down. As I kept going through the show, which involved a lot of stomping, quick draw cowboy guns and hat tipping I could feel the bandages unravelling and eventually one end dropped down into my shirt. I did the remainder of the show slightly hunched and trying to keep it all together. Thankfully, my cowboy flannel made it not overly noticeable, but it definitely stirred my stage nerves enough. It definitely was not a career killer. Whilst it made me more cautious of the methods I chose for binding, I made sure I had another show the next week and the adrenaline and thrill of performing overtook any nerves and bad memories I had from that mishap. I have since gone on to run my own successful DRAG event, with the above-mentioned king I cowboyed with in Melbourne, Australia. Mistakes are made to be learned from, not feared. Take what you learn and use it to propel you into a better performer each time.

❧**B J Armani:** NO SUCH THING as a mistake, if you learn from it! With all my costumes, there was bound to be a whoopsie, and in using props like wigs, they tend to fly off. It happened and I stuffed it down the front of my pants like the world's WORST "man bush." Crowd DIED. Career killers come from performers that are rude, entitled, and steal (ideas or property). Anything else can be covered in sequins!

❧**Lyle Loves-It:** I tend to embarrass myself on purpose. WINK; a fly left open...

❧**Kenneth J. Squires:** I have had any yet, thank God and knock on wood.

❀**Joshua Micheals:** I was trying my first pair of tear-away pants, they did not tear away so much, and I spent half the number DRAGging a pair of pants behind me attached to my ankle.

❀**Eddie C. Broadway:** I have made numerous mistakes on stage, but kept going. One time I fell down some stairs and luckily caught myself. I kept going, and acted as if nothing happened. I joked around a bit about it later and it was fine. Besides that, I have had pageant numbers go wrong a bit, but I kept going through the entire thing. Nothing is a career killer if it is a mistake!

❀**Stormm:** Besides screwing up words, I just start smiling. I would have to say more or less a costume malfunction, and I always kept going.

❀**Dominic Von Strap:** I forgot my jock strap before a show and hoped to god my packy would not fall out of my boxer briefs. My wish did not come true. Half-way through my song, I had to run to where some friends were sitting, pull my dick out of my pant leg, and toss it behind a friend.

❀**D-Luv Saviyon:** I have fallen off a few stages, forgot the beginning of a song, had costume malfunctions, and messed up dance moves... you just have to keep it moving.

❀**Travis Luvermore:** I tripped up on stage, tried to jump up on a stage, and fell, and my package slid down my leg.

❀**Gus Magendor:** So far the only mistake I have made is choosing a chick's song, even though I asked specifically and my booking agent told me any song.

❀**AJ Menendez:** I slipped and fell on stage once. I wanted to run off and cry but instead, I played it off, laughed at myself, and kept going. That is my advice, if you mess up, just keep going.

❀**Adam DoEve:** I was doing a strip number (no, not all the way boxers and muscle shirt stay on), and had lost some weight. Well, I lost my pants and did not know it till I went to grab the tabs to give to a girl to rip them off, and couldn't find them.

Max Hardswell: I had forgotten a belt once after I had lost some weight, and my pants kept slipping and I got sick of pulling them up so I just dropped them, and kicked them to the side, and I did the rest of the song in my boxers.

❀**Justin Cider:** Eating it hard core. I was performing an Enrique Iglesis song, and as such wore much tighter pants then I usually do. When I went to jump on one of the stage boxes I missed it completely and took myself out at the shins. I face planted on the box, got up threw my hands up, and just kept going not knowing what else to do.

❀**Hurricane Savage:** It was my very first pageant. I was performing to the 'Lazy Song' by Bruno Mars, and at one point I was going to pull down my PJ bottoms to show my boxers BUT both my PJ's and my boxers went to my ankles leaving me standing there in my undies. Without missing a step, I just went with it and finished what I was doing. No one but a few people that had been helping my get ready knew that I messed up. Even judges thought it was all part of the set. Still waiting on when I fall.

❀Marcus Mayhem: I fell backwards once, and broke my bracelet and quickly kept singing while I sat there a few and got back up and finished my song. Even lost my hair props I had in my hair. A few times, while changing clothes on stage, getting stuck in a shirt here and there. Never understood why, when I practiced at home I never had trouble, but on stage... Blah. Never fails.

❀Atown: At the Mister California USofA MI pageant last year, my guitar strap popped off, and fell on the ground, and wrapped around the guitar. Thankfully, the judges said they did not notice it and that I played it off well.

❀Rychard "Alpha" Le'Sabre: Know your damn words. Falling happens, choreography mistakes happen, props break, wigs fall off... it all happens. But there is nothing more embarrassing in this craft than getting on that stage unprepared.

❀Shane Rebel Caine: The most embarrassing mistake I have made was trying to pull off a group performance when the people I asked to help never showed up to practice, and hardly knew their lines, and one of them had terrible stage freight. The performance wound up a complete disaster and a complete mess. I learned then that group performances are a really bad idea, or any performance where you have to rely on someone else, can be a bad idea. But you just have to brush off your mistakes, and get back on stage, and redeem yourself. Always keep your chin up.

❀B J Bottoms: I was performing in Charlottesville. I am known for jumping over and off things. I went to jump over a chair during the bridge of my number and stepped wrong. The chair slid out from under me and I fell flat on my back. For a split second looking up at the ceiling, I was like, "Well, I am going to lay here." I remembered things happen, and not only for myself, but also for the crowd, got up. I finished out the number, and laugh about it now. Not every performance is going be perfect; it is how you handle those imperfect moments that help you grow as an entertainer.

❀Dakota Rain: I was performing at the Rainbow in Lake Wylie, South Carolina, USA, and the CD I had burned was skipping. Thank GOD, I had a backup! Another time, I was doing a duet with my son, Ked BlackRain, and I forgot my words, but he stepped up and saved the day.

❀Ashton The Adorable Lover: My biggest mistake, or fail, was actually during a national pageant. My prop was cheaply made, and it made it standing for the whole pageant, and then stage set up. As soon as the music for my talent came on it completely fell down, and came a part on me. My face cracked and I had a minute of fear, sadness, and more. Then I came back, and gave my all for second part of my talent. Remember, "$*it happens, keep rolling."

✦**Pierce Gabriel**: Two major wardrobe malfunctions. I forget which happened first, but both left me mortified, and reluctant to ever go on stage again. I had not tried on a new pair of pants until I was changing before my next number. They were too tight. I spent so long trying to get them to button and zip that I was not paying attention to how much time passed, and suddenly they were announcing me on stage and the music was starting. I had to go on stage with my pants undone, one shoe untied, and my shirt unbuttoned over the tee shirt I had worn my previous number. The tips I got that night were out of sympathy. The other incident was not as bad as it could have been, but I am still scarred by it. During an all-ages show I had dressed completely open-shirt, and my part of my binding came undone, revealing a little more of my feminine body than I would have liked, even at a 21+ show. My mistake there was insisting on going open-shirt when I was sweating too much for the binding to stay in place. In the two years since, I have never gone fully open-shirt since.

✦**Brandon KC Young-Taylor:** I think the most embarrassing thing to watch is when an entertainer is on stage not getting tipped and the immediately show how discouraged they feel. It is heart breaking to watch but I totally understand how it feels. My personal most embarrassing moment by far did not happen on the stage during my number but afterward. We did a political theme show and I chose to do White America by Eminem. In true Eminem fashion I pushed the boundaries by wearing an American flag on my back. I felt I did the number very tastefully and never allowed the flag to touch the floor, be stepped on, or disrespected, but what I did not know is that the bar owner had served and had flags flown in wars for her. She did not agree with the way I did the number, and I was very embarrassed to have disrespected her. I am so thankful she took a moment to talk to me about it, and I have never made this mistake again. Oh, to be young and dumb!

✦**Ryder Knightly:** Oh my, the perks of live performances, anything can happen! I had a routine where I did 'Great Balls of Fire'. I had my keyboard on stage, but I did not have it fully connected to the stand. In the middle of the song, I am pounding of my keyboard, and it nearly went flying of the stand. I basically almost turned a full length keyboard into a guitar version. I have also fallen, and sent my glasses flying off my face into the crowd. I am blind as a bat.

✦**Kruz Mhee:** My most embarrassing mistake was my cock sliding down the leg of my jeans and poking out by my boot. My second most embarrassing moment was one night when I did not wear my pack and I was in a tuxedo. A fan decided to cup check me and instead of cup checking Kruz, he felt up Paula. To this day I still cannot see him without blushing. The mistakes are what make you a better entertainer. We all have to learn by mistakes, not just from each other. When something goes wrong, believe it or not, more often than not, I point it out. If I show the audience what went wrong then we all laugh about it. Mistakes have not killed my career as a DRAG King.

🍀Silk Steele Prince: The most embarrassing mistake I made on stage is wearing pants that pull up and down instead of pants with snaps for a wardrobe change on stage. My shoes got stuck and someone had to come step on the pants so I could pull my leg out. It looked so amateur and it was embarrassing.

🍀Flex Jonez: When your pants split in half during a dance routine, make sure you have a pair of funny or matching underwear to compliment the number.

🍀SirMandingo Thatis: Getting on stage to perform a song you do not know all the words to. People come to see a show not someone who gets up there and flubs.

🍀Cody Wellch Klondyke: When I was walking up the stairs I tripped in fell. I picked myself up and continued. Then last time I was doing "Locked Out of Heaven" and I dropped to my knees, I could not get back up for a minute.

🍀J Breezy St James: Tripping over your own feet on the catwalk because you were not paying attention.

🍀George De Micheal: Forgetting my words, as I am a live singer, I do not mime. I was told to carry on with the show if anything happened on stage, which I always do.

🍀Colin Grey Smooth: Lost it and said, "fuck" where you could hear it, when I got mad because of a CD screwing up. It was very unprofessional.

🍀Kameo Dupree: My biggest mistake onstage was caused by the biggest prop: myself. It was St Patrick's Day. I consumed too much green beer. I went up the steps, as the music started, all proud in my green outfit that took me three days to make. Suddenly the room took a spin (that is how it felt) and I crashed to the stage. Yes, I was my worst prop that night.

🍀Phantom: When I first started using prosthetics, I was not that knowledgeable on how to keep them on correctly, or how to make them look proper while performing. The first time I used them, my face fell off. My advice to anyone having this issue: use it in your performance and keep going. There is no use in stopping; you get a lot more respect for keeping in character even though everything is falling off.

🍀Stefan LeDude: Once in a rap I wrote and sang, I accidentally sang the wrong verse, so then I just switched and sang the second verse last, though I missed a couple of lines. Also missed cues, wrong steps, nothing too embarrassing really. I would say that the most important thing to remember is, many mistakes are not really noticeable. The audience does not know what is supposed to happen.

🍀Jamel Knight: The most embarrassing mistake I have had is my binding coming loose on stage. I just had to roll with it and figure out a way to make it work. Comedy always helps in a situation like that. At the end of the day, even the most seasoned professionals will occasionally make a mistake. It is not the fact that a mistake was made, but what you do after it is done that matters.

❋**Master Cameron Eric Leon:** I have a number where I throw a bunch of baby powder at my nose. I missed and got it all in my eyes. I could barely see to walk off stage.

❋**Bootzy Edwards Collynz:** Most embarrassing mistake that happened to me on stage? My piece fell out. I did not have my usual piece (with harness) because I forgot it at home. I always try to carry spare parts to shows, but I did not have an extra harness, and there was no way the extra one was just going to "stay" in place without a harness. I ended up taking a regular old bar towel, with some duct tape to fashion a piece I could use. I ended up loop in it through my underwear and duct taping it together, somewhat. Through the course of my second number, with sweat and all, I could feel the tape loosen, and my piece start to move and slowly slide down my right leg. I was wearing jeans for the performance, and decided to dance a little bit less and keep my foot flexed hoping I could make it to the end of the number and regroup (so to speak). I could feel it resting close to my ankle. As I turner to walk back down the aisle and took my first step it flew out from my pants leg. I had no idea where it went. Thank goodness, it had flown under the table of some friends at that show. My friend Jill brings it to me on a shot tray with another bar towel covering it. She comes up and presents to tray to me, whips off the towel and says in a French accent, "I believe this belongs to you. But the color and texture look a bit goofy. You might want to get that checked out before they attach it." First and last time for that.

❋**DeVery Bess:** Biggest mistake? When I was on stage the first time I took the stage for a solo, I did a poi number (swinging balls that glow). It was an improved number and I was performing, dancing like a beast, starting to do poi, when the poi wrapped around itself and hit me in the... sensitive area. So through the pain I kept going cause that what I do, and that what should be done. But if I would have practice more that probably wouldn't have happened.

❋**Welland Dowd:** I was supposed to pull off a burlesque dancer's stockings, but could not get them off! Then I was so flustered I tripped over a monitor on the stage. But people afterwards said they thought it was part of the act, so I guess it was not so bad!

❋**Michael Christian:** Motor City Pride, couple summers ago. It was around 90 degrees and I had four layers of reveals on. I was in my third show of the day and sweating more than I thought. By the time I got to my last reveal, I unbuttoned the shirt and realized I had sweated through even the spray adhesive, and one side of my chest was undone. I put my shirt back on and finishing my number with little movement. Things happen all the time. Just do not panic, laugh it off, and get through it. We are live theater after all. No editing. It all makes for great stories and laughs for years.

🌸**Sam Masterson:** When my DRAG princess and I changed clothes on stage.

🌸**Julius M. SeizeHer:** Forgetting the words. It is a common mistake, and it is always the worst as a performer. It has happened numerous times. I just pretend like it did not happen, and move on.

🌸**Jonah Godfather of DRAG:** It was during a show. I was in the dressing room trying to hurry so I could get out to the audience to watch a queen that I just love. I ran out to the table where my wife was sitting. I was trying to be all cool, and was ready to tip the queen. She made a beeline to me. I thought I was being suave as she leaned in close. Instead of kissing me, she whispered in my ear that my zipper was down. We laughed as she thought that was my way of trying to impress her with my "package."

🌸**Howie Feltersnatch:** The most embarrassing thing that has ever happened to me is falling on stage and actually injuring myself pretty bad. I was performing at Edmonton pride and fell. Once I recovered I got back on the stage, better than ever. I am still dealing with the injury, as now I have to go for surgery on my knee to ensure that I can do the crazy dance moves I want to do.

🌸**Lyle Loves-It:** ALWAYS CHECK YOUR FLY!

🌸**Jack E. Dickinson:** My very first gig, the CD skipped! I turned it into a joke, and pretended I had the hiccups until the DJ, who did not seem to be paying attention cause it went on for almost a minute, finally fixed it. I think acknowledging it and turning it into a joke often works. Unless the number is serious.

🌸**Xavier Bottoms:** While helping a DRAG queen with a performance, I was dancing on top of a piano. One of the other dancers told me to put his shorts down. I did. He had on boy boxers underneath. Then he thought it would be cute to down my shorts. I had nothing under my shorts. After the show, a patron came up to me and said how much he appreciated my "high and tight" style.

🌸**Clark Kunt:** On my one year DRAGiversary, I performed at a Halifax Pride event, the same event where I had gotten my start a year earlier. I actually went straight from a hockey game to the show, so incorporated part of my gear into the number and made it a whole story. Problem was my feet were sweaty so when I took my shoes off and stripped out of my hockey pants, I was trying to be all sexy in my boxers except I slipped and fell on my ass... twice! Sock feet = bad idea.

🌸**Emilio:** Just. Keep. Going.

🌸**Juan Kerr:** I think a lot of people do not even realise if a performer has made a mistake onstage. They do not know the act, unless they have seen you do it before anyway. Plus, a lot of it is how you recover from whatever the mistake is. Do you freeze, forget all the words, or do you laugh it off, make light of it and carry on. If there is a positive or a negative way you can deal with something I had prefer the former. What's the point of the latter?

Trey C. Michaels: The first time I went completely open shirt, my tape popped on my left side and I flashed the crowd. I finished my number holding my boob, and looking like I was having a heart attack, or just really emotional about my song.

Aaron Phoenix: I popped my duct tape at a talent show one night, doing an open shirt number. Miraculously, no one saw anything explicit and only a few people realized that anything had "malfunctioned", but I ended up holding my shirt closed for the rest of the number, terrified that I had just flashed the crowd in a "family-friendly" establishment. I have also slipped on a dance floor where someone had spilled a drink and sprained my ankle right in the middle of a number. I did not do half the dancing I had intended to do, but I let the good leg do as much of the work as possible and made it work through the rest of the song. Also, about 1/3 of the way through a high-energy number, my packer somehow came loose and the next thing I knew, I had a rubber penis creeping down my pants leg. I was extremely lucky, I had on baggy pants so no one noticed it (or noticed when it was gone), and the lighting was dark (small club, no spot light). I had on a long trenchcoat, so at the transition into the next song, I turned my glittery, embellished back to the audience just long enough to reach into my pants and toss my "package" behind the DJ Booth. Someone even took video of the performance, and I can tell when the moment happens, but the "incident" was completely unseen by the audience. I was mortified all night, but it goes to show that if you keep it professional, roll with the punches, do not take yourself TOO seriously, keep your confidence and remember "the show must go on," you can play off a mistake without your audience knowing anything is wrong. My advice, just roll with it, the show must go on. Everyone makes mistakes, it is how you recover from them that shows your professionalism.

Thug Passion: There was one time I backed up into one of the lighting stands that was around the stage and I fell backwards. All I could think of at the time was "tuck and roll". So I did that, and landed on my knees and did some type of dance move to make it look like it was a part of the show. Afterwards, I laughed so hard at myself.

Soco Dupree: One of my worst mistakes was not being taped down correctly. I was in a rush and assumed I had been able to miss a few pieces of tape to reassure I was secure. However, during my first number, my left boob popped and then soon after, my right followed suit. Not a fine moment in performing.

Stefon Royce Iman: Wardrobe malfunction. Always make sure your tape is really completely stuck on. My chest popped out. I did not use spray adhesive; I thought I was secured. Guess again, buddy! I was not. Another embarrassing moment was my strap coming loose. I was dancing and it fell down my leg. Now I do not have that problem; I have special underwear on to secure my dildo.

Jensen C. Dean: I had finished performing. I was taking down a table that was used as a prop while the host was talking and I stepped back on to the trench coat I was wearing and the table and I fell backwards, me right on my butt, the table made a bunch of noise. Everyone saw it and heard it.

E. M. Shaun: Not being taped up all the way. So while performing, my tape came undone. Another time I forced myself into some pants that I had partially sewn together, and right at end of my number I was getting all passionate with my performance, that when I bent down I ripped the seam in the crotch of my pants. I did not realize how bad the tear was, until I walked off stage and I heard all the whistling while my boxer briefs were showing to everyone. I was a little embarrassed, but all in all the show must go on, even if you have a mistake or costume malfunction.

Smitty O'Toole: I have been in different performance art venues for a while now, before I started DRAG, so I know that DRAG is a living art that you prep for, but really create on stage. I have had my binding tape pop with an open shirt, and tripped a couple of times on the stairs of the stage, but I just play them off. If you work through it on-stage and just keep rolling, usually the mistake will be easily forgotten and usually not noticeable. Just remember only you know your performance, the crowd does not know what is on purpose and what is not, so play it off.

Luke Ateraz: I had tear away pants on, and had recently broken my arm and could not get my pants off all the way. Luckily, I had a good friend sitting right in the front row so I walked over and had her take them off me. I did not have enough strength yet in my arm to rip them off myself.

Boi Wonder: My packer falling down my leg for sure.

William Vanity Matrix: Me falling on stage, and another time was me breaking a mirror. Not to mention some of my very poorly executed ideas I have had. One is even caught on video, and it was on a National Stage. Since then I have redeemed myself but people still like to give me hell for it, which keeps me humble.

Devin G. Dame: Any mistake can happen, from a costume mishap to missing your words. The real key is to keep going.

Chapter Thirty-Five
"Many performers ignore the patron tipping them. Other entertainers stop and acknowledge the dollar with intimate gratitude; in the middle, are the rest of the impersonators. Where do place and why?"

❦**Clark Kunt:** I try to acknowledge every tip, unless I am in the middle of a choreographed section of a number. I give a hug or at least sing directly to the tipper while I accept. With the smallest Canadian bill being a $5, your tipper is saying I value your performance more than another drink; that's saying something to me.

❦**Shook ByNature:** I have had entertainers, who personally do not like me, tip me during a number, and I have done the same. It shows a respect for the craft. When my "Lovers", as I call my fans, tip me, I try and make it special to show them I appreciate them coming to every show. I do not ignore those who don't tip. Just because they are not tipping, does not mean they do not like the show. I have seen Kings not get tipped, and ignore the "non-tipping" section, or get ticked and give up halfway through the number. It is not about the money!

❦**Scorpio:** I never ignore anyone. I try my best to make it a special one on one show with those around and close by. The reactions vary, and some tip and some do not. It is not about the money to me. It is about making an impression so they will remember me, and enjoy the show.

❦**Travis Hard:** I always acknowledge with a head nod and or by saying "thank you". I am grateful for every dollar.

❦**Travis Luvermore:** I was taught early on to acknowledge and thank each person tipping, including other performers, with a wink or a nod. I was also taught not to throw the tip on the floor, that it was a sign of disrespect. If I can, I will put in my pocket, or place them on my partner's table. Some places have tip buckets for you to hold your tips in.

❦**Stormm:** I will nod and smile to the person, that is my way of saying thank you. When I perform, it is not about the tips, but when I get them, I am grateful.

❦**Justin Cider:** You have to acknowledge the money. When I am putting together a more choreographed routine, I try to at least have a section for grabbing tips. The people in the audience are why we are here. You never want to leave them high and dry. Any veteran performer will not only tip when they are not on stage, but encourage you to always be grateful for every tip you get.

❦**Coti Blayne**: I say thank you, and give a smile and a nod unless it breaks my character then I will just do a head nod. If it is a good friend or someone I haven't seen in awhile I will totally give huge hugs and say hi for a second before getting back into finishing the song.

✿**Alexander Cameron:** I try my best to acknowledge every patron who tips me. Very often, I will pay them special attention by singing lyrics directly to them or "play" with them in some way. I want everyone who comes to see me perform to understand how much I appreciate their patronage and show my gratitude by including them into my performance.

✿**Shane Rebel Caine:** If someone is tipping, I interact with them personally. I will think them by a smile or a head nod. Tips are what I am working for so I try to earn it the best I can when someone is generous enough to tip. Never ignore your tippers! I dislike tipping entertainers that ignore the tipping crowd, as it is rather rude.

✿**D-Luv Saviyon:** I acknowledge my tips, simply because they do not have to tip. It is an honor, and I appreciate them for it. What I do has never been about making tips, it is something I love to do, so tips are the icing on the cake. I give them each a bit of personal attention, and a kiss (on the hand or cheek, unless it is an unfamiliar place). I also give hugs . Without the crowd and supporters, there is no King or Queen.

✿**Campbell Reid Andrews:** Intimate gratitude is all me. I love to show the tippers a little something extra. If they are giving me their hard-earned money that is the least I can do. It also gives me a chance to interact with the crowd more. Gives me a reason to move about the crowd, you know. They appreciate it, for the tips they are giving.

✿**Adam DoEve:** I do my best to acknowledge everyone, tipper and non-tipper, because they did not have to come to see the show, they could have gone anywhere. I love to try and draw the crowd into my number. I know I should not leave the stage area, but sometimes you just have to.

✿**Chance Wise:** I am always gracious when someone tips me; I give them eye contact and give their hand a light squeeze, or stay with them for a second and sing a certain part of a song to them. If they lean in to kiss my cheek, I reciprocate the gesture. I do try to show them that I appreciate the tippers, and even those who do not tip.

✿**Dakota Rain:** I try to acknowledge all people that tip, and I do my best to tip all performers when I can. I feel it is a matter of respect, whether you like each other or not. As for the fans, I do my best to make sure I hug them or make eye contact with them, to let them know I do care and that it means the world to me.

✿**Ashton The Adorable Lover:** In the middle, more towards the personal side. I do not want to make it about the money, but also not all about me, and my performance. I do acknowledge with a kiss, wink, a thank you, something to each person that comes up and tips me, and those that come and find me after the performance.

❀**Rasta Boi Punany:** I always acknowledge each patron that I see while performing, even if it means missing a move I may have done during a performance. I want them to know I appreciate their acknowledging ME, and I have learned to give an affectionate squeeze as I accept their money.

❀**Freddy Prinze Charming**: I always acknowledge everyone handing me a dollar. I try not to break character, but will give them a head nod, a smile, a squeeze of the hand.

❀**Joshua Micheals:** I always show acknowledgment through a nod, or a squeeze of the hand, but always pay attention to everyone. You never know why they are not tipping, and I perform for the love off the art not the tips. I also NEVER throw my tips on the ground during my number. That is disrespectful. People work too hard for the money they tip you with for you to just throw it away.

❀**Ben Eaten:** I acknowledge every person that tips me. I feel like it is rude to not let them know it is appreciated, and I thank them.

❀**Clint Torres:** I never ignore tipping patrons. I do not altogether stop either. I accept the tip with a tip of my head during the performance (hopefully not missing a beat), and then I will respectfully thank them after the show. I have a good memory for it.

❀**Spacee Kadett:** I think learning how to accept dollars is a major process for anyone. I remember starting out, the panic of seeing that dollar and trying to perform! Or missing untold numbers of dollars because I was so focused on the performance, or the loud side of the stage, or I couldn't see with that blasted spotlight in my eyes!! I WILL NEVER BE ABLE TO DO THIS! Now I am comfortable enough on stage to have fun with dollars. I hug friends and patrons I know, or do an extra quickstep for random people. We dance and sing together. I blow kisses, kiss girls on the hand, bow my head to performers I respect, or verbally thank people and slip back into performance mode (this is great when you're sketchy on words, too. If there is a dollar I know I cannot get to yet, I will visually acknowledge the person with a smile of gratitude before I make my way to their end of the stage. Accepting tips is just as much an art form as impersonation itself. I have found that taking advantage of that moment to make a personal connection is also a great way to ensure future tips and a following beyond that performance.

❀**Adam All:** We do not get tips in the United Kingdom. This kind of sucks. We tend to get heckling and or joining in. The art is in quick-witted responses whilst remaining in character. I try to catch the eye of as many people as I can, draw my audience into my story, give a shout out to someone enjoying the show. Wish we got tips.

❀**Kameo Dupree:** I am the middle. Many times I am so caught up in my element, that I do not see the patron's money. When I do see it, I will give total acknowledgement. After the show is over, I spend time with the patrons prior to going home.

♣Kenneth J. Squires: I always thank the person who is giving a dollar or two. Saying thank you to the person is what is best. You have to look at it as this person is giving up their hard-earned money to tip me.

♣Pierce Gabriel : I try to show the gratitude whenever possible. But, I also always try to bring the audience into my performance whenever possible. I like making people feel special. Shaking their hand, caressing their cheek, a kiss on their knuckle. Sometimes I will even be more flirtatious or sexual about it. It depends on the song.

♣Koomah: It depends on the show and the performance. Many shows I am in that involve group numbers with choreography encourage the audience to wad up bills and throw them onto the stage, while other shows have a tip bucket. If I am doing a solo, I will often take a tip and interact with the fan. If I go out into the audience and do fan service, I will interact will tipping fans longer/more closely. I never wear my glasses onstage so there have been times where I did not see a fan tipping.

♣Vinnie Marconi: I am in the middle, leaning toward intimate. Choreography of a number, and what I have going on as far as back-up dancers, will determine how much time I spend with a tipper. I NEVER toss the tips on the stage! This tells them that their money is inconsequential to me and I do not care. At the very LEAST, I will take their hand and nod in acknowledgement that they are enjoying the performance.

♣Kruz Mhee: You never ignore anyone that paid to get in. I always acknowledge the patron tipping, and the people around them as well. I always try to remember that not everyone has the money to tip but they came up with the money to get in the club, and see me perform. I do not do it for the money, I do it for the fun.

♣Alec Allnight: You have to acknowledge the love! It is hard with choreography, but for the most part, the audience is aware and will wait for the acknowledgement.

♣B J Bottoms: I fall in the middle. I look the person in the eye smile and take their tip. A few seconds of acknowledgement goes a long way to the person.

♣SirMandingo Thatis: I never ignore patrons, tipping or not, they are the reason I still do what I do!

♣Jonah Godfather of DRAG: I give gratitude whether it be saying "thank you," giving a kiss or a hug, or a kiss on the hand. I have a vision problem so I do not always see a tipper and sometimes they think I am ignoring them, which I would never do.

♣Silk Steele Prince: I am in the middle with intimate gratitude. When I am in the middle of choreography, I want to nail it, and I usually acknowledge patrons during chorus parts. Sometimes I feel bad that they are just standing there with their arm extended out, so I will try to ease out of transformation.

❋**Flex Jonez:** In all my performances, I see to it there is a point in my routine that I can check the crowd for the tips. It gives me time to thank them, kiss a few, and hug a few. The audience is the reason the venue is open for me to perform.

❋**Mike Oxready:** If I am in the midst of choreography, I will not receive tips unless the patron put the tip in my costume. Generally, I graciously accept and acknowledge all patrons who are tipping, but I also want to keep the performance going.

❋**Abs Hart:** If someone tips me, I acknowledge it. I am probably more on the intimate side. There are times, when I will focus on the performance and then take time to accept tips. If someone is handing me a tip, they are saying they appreciate what I am doing. I want them to know I appreciate them. After all, I am there for the audience.

❋**Cody Wellch Klondyke:** Some reactions vary, and some tip and some do not. It is not about the money to me. It is about connecting with the crowd and letting them be a part of it all, so they will remember me and enjoy the show.

❋**George De Micheal:** I wish we got tipped! In England, we do not have this system.

❋**DeVery Bess:** People tip? I want in this. Some places in Canada tip, others do not.

❋**Colin Grey:** I take the time to offer a hand squeeze while I am taking the dollar. I bow my head in thanks, sometimes I wink. It just depends on the song and the person tipping, but I always recognize the person handing me money.

❋**Sam Masterson:** I always acknowledge, especially to royals. It is a sign of respect.

❋**B J Armani:** I acknowledge each and every tip. This fan took the time to show you that they enjoy you, the very least you can do is reciprocate!

❋**Jamel Knight:** I am in the middle. I try to acknowledge every tipper but at times give more attention to family, friends, and those fans who show me the most support.

❋**Stefan LeDude:** Tipping is a new thing for me, as people do not do it back in Montreal. I have only had two so far, and one was from someone in the same show. It is very flattering, but also makes me a little shy. I have to get used to it.

❋**Welland Dowd:** People do not seem to tip in Montreal, so I have never had that experience. It would be pretty sweet though!

❋**Michael Christian:** I acknowledge every tip, with a thank you or gesture. I squeeze the hand, or wink, if I am in the middle of lip sync. I hug or mouth thank you at other times. I NEVER throw money on the ground. I believe people worked hard for their money. If they chose to spend it on me, they deserve my gratitude and respect. Ignoring them when they tip or throwing it on the ground, kind of gives the air you are not thankful they are there. Without the audience, we are nothing.

❁**Harry Pi:** Either kiss or hug, depending on the person tipping. I did a split for someone who wanted to see it, with them placing the tip in my pants pocket.

❁**Julius M. SeizeHer:** It is hard to see when I cannot wear my glasses. As a performer, I acknowledge everyone. I am legally blind, so I may not see you.

❁**Howie Feltersnatch:** I only got a tip for go-going, never for a number before. If I were to, I would give them a hug or flirt with them a little.

❁**Emilio:** I always acknowledge a person who tips, make them part of the show. I want to make sure they know I see them, and appreciate them.

❁**Juan Kerr:** We are not tipped in the United Kingdom. If someone did slip me a note, I give their hand a little peck and look them deep in the eye. It would be rude not to.

❁**Trey C. Michaels:** Depending on the number, I will always grab their hand with both of mine, look them in the eye, smile and then nod my head at them. If it is a faster number, I will look them in the eye and flash them a smile.

❁**J Breezy St James:** I acknowledge when they tip me. It is the respectful thing to do.

❁**Bailey Saint James:** I attempt to ignore tips until the last third of my performance. If you take tips too soon, in my most humble opinion, makes you look greedy.

❁**Xavier Bottoms:** I acknowledge everyone, even if you are not waving a dollar to tip me. When being tipped, I keep eye contact with them. If it is a gentleman doing the tipping, I usually kiss them on the kiss or wink. If it is a lady doing the tipping, I will kiss their hand and wink. If it is a little child, I will get down on my knees and give them a hug. Sometimes, I swoop them up and bring them back on stage with me.

❁**Aaron Phoenix:** I always acknowledge someone tipping me, be it with a wink, an air-kiss to the cheek, a kissed hand, a hat tip, a hand squeeze, even just pointed eye contact - something. Without the audience there tipping us and enjoying our shows, we're just playing dress-up, so acknowledge and appreciate them!

❁**Atown:** I try my very best to not miss a tip. Not because of the money, but because the patrons do not have to take their time, and money, to walk to the stage to hand you a tip. Sometimes it is just as nerve wracking for the tipper to get the courage to approach the performer. I do like to thank everyone, or somehow acknowledge that I am appreciative, by smiling, dancing in front of them, singing to them, or somehow get them involved in that split second to make them feel appreciated. It is difficult to grab a tip during choreography, or bad lighting, where you cannot see them.

❀**Thug Passion:** I acknowledge every tip by dancing, singing to them at a specific place in the song, winking, and giving them a hug. I try to say thank you so they know I appreciate them. If I just did not see the person until the song goes off I tell them thank u and let them know I will give a little extra special attention on the next song. It is not about the money for me it is about if the crowd is enjoying the show and trying to make people feel special for the 3 to 5 minutes I am on the stage

❀**Stefon Royce Iman:** I always acknowledge who is tipping me. I never ignore them.

❀**Soco Dupree:** A kiss on the cheek, hand, or whispering "thank you" to them. Remember, we are here for them, not the other way around.

❀**Santana Romero:** I am in the middle. I try to give everyone tipping me a few seconds of attention, since they are giving me their hard-earned money. If I am doing a performance that requires me to move around, personal attention is difficult. I try to make the last number a little slower to give the audience love, a dance or a sexy look in the eyes usually does the trick, so they know I appreciate them. I also never snatch tips, under any means. I had hate to seem rude.

❀**E. M. Shaun:** I always acknowledge a patron whom is tipping. I will dance with them, hug or kiss their hand and I will tell them thank you when I am close to them. It is always fun to add them into the act, and always be appreciative to the tipper because they do not have to tip. I do not expect anything but it is great to see that the fans want to compliment you.

❀**Smitty O'Toole:** It is important to acknowledge patrons when they are tipping you. I also make a point to make myself available after I perform to mingle with the crowd.

❀**Jensen C. Dean:** I make every effort not to ignore anyone. If they give me money they earned, they deserve to be recognized in some way. I try not to break character when accepting tips, i.e. a darker number means no big smile, but I will slip in a wink or a hand squeeze, if I take a tip during a lull in the lyrics, I will say thank you.

❀**William Vanity Matrix:** I try to be as sincere as possible, and at least do some sort of little head bow and make eye contact with my tipper.

❀**Bootzy Edwards Collynz:** I like being tipped, but it is not the end of the world if I am not tipped either. I see tipping as the patron showing appreciation for your art/talent and your performance. They want to get in close to "really" check you out; figure out the illusion because it is so cool (See the "Goods" so to speak). To me, tipping is a high compliment and very flattering. It is a great form of recognition on a good job/performance. To know that people like what you do enough to jump up outta their chair and hand you a dollar is amazing. I think about the shows (as a performer) that I attend. There have been acts on stage that make me want to jump up and give them a dollar. The performance "moves me" and definitely makes me take notice, that is pretty cool recognition. I mingle with/in the crowd for performances. I try to keep/make it fun; but keep it real/honest to the performance. I try to make an effort not to miss/ignore anybody during or after my performance. I try to show my appreciation for their "compliment" every time during a show. Whether that is a slight head nod, quick dance, handshake, peck on the cheek, or a quick hug, I always try to say "thank you." It is very important to keep your words/Lip-synching; you are performing at a show. It is a little hard not to break character with certain patrons, especially friend you have not seen for a long time, fun patrons in the crowd, or the patron/friends who I know can dance a bit. Yeah, they are prop for a little bit, but I think it does add a bit of a personal touch to the song (depending on the song). It also gives the patron a chance to step on stage for some fun too. I see it as a way of bringing that person into our world of performing for one brief moment. I try to give each patron their own "personal show" every show.

✿**Master Cameron Eric Leon:** I think the problem with tipping is that it makes it harder to have a really smooth, well-choreographed performance, which is the end goal of what I do. I am from Canada, where tipping is not usually done, so when it is, normally the patron waits for an appropriate moment, or for me to come down into the audience. Overall, I think I like that it is more rare here because it means I can plan my performances more thoroughly.

✿**Devin G. Dame:** I always acknowledge every tip with eye contact, a head nod, a hug, and/or a squeeze of their hand. They work hard for their money that they are giving me and I am very thankful for that!

Chapter Thirty-Six
"How do you like to be introduced to the stage?"

❀**Shook ByNature:** "Now for your DRAG king enjoyment, all the way from Wilmington, North Carolina, USA, the Port City Loverman, Mr. NC Unlimited FMI 2014 Mr Shook by Mutha Fuckin' Nature!"

❀**D-Luv Saviyon:** "Welcome to the stage, your male illusionist, D-Luv Saviyon."

❀**Travis Luvermore:** No need to list awards unless a reigning king.

❀**Clint Torres:** "And now for the up and coming, very talented, very sexy Clint Torres!" I heard one of the hosts do it one time, and the audience went crazy so that's the way I like it now.

❀**Gus Magendor:** "And now welcome to the stage, the king of kings, the amazingly sexy, Gus Magendor."

❀**Phantom:** "I want you to welcome to the stage giving you some "Face Off" realness, Phantom."

❀**Adam All:** Depends on what set I am performing but generally, "One of the United Kingdom's finest and most long established DRAG Kings, the cheeky dapper chappy with a geek chic streak, he's Adam All."

❀**Spacee Kadett:** Anything with HE. For God's sake, stop saying "SHE is your current-reigning Mr. Such-and-Such!"

❀**AJ Menendez:** Since Master Male Illusionist is more than just a title, it is actually part of my stage name, I get introduced as "AJ Menendez, Master Male Illusionist".

❀**Joshua Micheals:** Nothing frustrates me more than to be called by female pronouns when performing and it happens a lot. The queens that do it do not mean harm they just do not think about it.

❀**Chance Wise:** A huge pet peeve of mine is when someone refuses to use your whole stage name. You can give me almost any decent lead in, just call me Chance Wise.

❀**Justin Cider:** I like it nice and slow. Many people take a minute to even get my name so the slower you say it or my personal favorite is to say "I love being Justin Cider."

❀**Travis Hard:** I like to be announced as Travis Hard, pure and simple! Or my classic, "Trav... is hard for you."

❀**Corey James Caster:** I love being announced as Corey James Caster.

❀**Rychard "Alpha" Le'Sabre:** Every host is different. It is fun to hear what they have to say. I do not mind what they say, so long as they pronounce my name right.

❀**Shane Rebel Caine:** I like it when they announce my name with enthusiasm. It gets me hyped when the DJ has a creative line leading up to my name as long as it is not anything mean. I like it most when they draw out my middle name Rebel as it is my personal family name. I hate when they only call me by my first name, though.

❀**Atown:** "Get ready because Atown is about to put-i t-down on this stage right now!"

❀**Freddy Prinze Charming**: As long as they get my name right, that's really all I care about. If I have a recent title or award, it is professional courtesy if they acknowledge it, but it does not always happen.

❀**Rasta Boi Punany:** "Next to the stage is a DRAG king who has taken Philadelphia, Pennsylvania, USA by storm by winning several titles. He is smooth, sexy, and suave. Please welcome to the stage, the one, the only, Ratsa Boi Punany." I include my titles in my intro of every song (unless it is a pageant). That way I do not get shortened, when they do not give my titles as I ask them to.

❀**Ashton The Adorable Lover:** "He's one sexy and adorable man, one of many talents, your current Mr. Gay Minnesota USA 2014, Ashton The Adorable Lover."

❀**Dakota Rain:** Well something simple, "Are you ready for this next entertainer, he is our own little boi toy and he loves to make you smile, so give it up for the one the only, Dakota Rain."

❀**Adam DoEve:** As long as you get my name right, and you do not say "she" we are good. One time the DJ said "Adam Duvay." I might lay on a bed but come on! Adam DoEve, please.

❀**Stormm:** "Next to the stage, Wausau's favorite king, ready to put a smile on your face, STORMM!"

❀**Vinnie Marconi:** "Our next entertainer is sure to make you smile! Vinnie Marconi." If the audience knows my name, that is all that is needed. If they do not already know it, if I do my job right, they will remember it next time! I have one of our favorite Queens here in Tampa Bay, Daphne Ferraro, who mistakenly called me Vinnie Macaroni at our first benefit, and has introduced me the same way ever since as a running joke and everyone knows it! I get a wink when she says it right for call backs."

❀**Ben Eaten:** Any title I hold or about to give up is what I want them to say. Like, "And now for your entertainment is your current Mid Mo Pride King Mr. Ben Eaten."

❀**Brandon KC Young-Taylor:** "And now welcome to the stage, the handsome, the sexy, Mr. Brandon KC Young!" (I always like when they make me feel good-looking right before I go on stage. It gives me that extra boost of confidence!) Also, do not mind if titles are added in, if I am currently holding one.

❀**Kruz Mhee:** "Ladies and gentlemen, please welcome him to the stage, the one, the only Kruz Mhee!"

❀**Hawk Stuart:** "Welcome to the stage, the one, and the only Mr. Hawk Stuart."

✤**Ryder Knightly:** Anything is fine, except for female pronouns. It is really irritating, but also messes with your mind frame a bit right before going on stage.

✤**Alec Allnight:** Because I know all the local hosts, I prefer they come up with something of their own. When I do my strip number though, I like them to say something like, "And now, giving you a little boi-lesque, Mr. Alec Allnight!"

✤**Silk Steele Prince:** However they would like, as long as they get my name right and say my entire stage name: Prince Steele Silk.

✤**SirMandingo Thatis:** "Next, coming to the stage is one sexual chocolate drop. Check him out, Sir Mandingo Thatis."

✤**Flex Jonez:** "Ladies and gentlemen, we bring to you the god-daddy of kinging, Mister smooth and sauve, Flex Jonez."

✤**Cody Wellch Klondyke**: For a closing, "What would you do for a Klondyke?"

✤**Viciouse Slick:** Just my name, if they want to announce titles or describe my style of DRAG, that is all fine with me.

✤**Kenneth J. Squires:** "Now coming out to the stage, he is an up and coming king, male Illusionist, Kenneth J. Squires."

✤**George De Micheal:** "Ladies and gentlemen, please put your hands together for your next entertainer, Mr. George De Micheal."

✤**DeVery Bess:** I like just being announced with respect. If the MC respects your introduction, then it is all good.

✤**Thug Passion:** I like any positive creative line with enthusiasm, and I also like it when they DRAG out the first part of my name.

✤**Bootzy Edwards Collynz:** I like just a simple respectful introduction. I love positive, creative intros, especially with people who have seen or worked with me. Handsome, sexy, good dancer work too.

✤**Colin Grey:** "Ladies and gentlemen, your man of many talents, Mr. Colin Grey!"

✤**Jack King:** "And now ladies and gentleman, here is a delicious man, I was tempted out there behind the scenes, please welcome our only king, here comes Jack King!"

✤**Kameo Dupree:** "Up next, he is our Mr. Everything, let's hear it for Kameo Dupree." (Yes, this is how numerous local bars introduce me and I like it!)

✤**Xavier Bottoms:** "For your viewing and entertainment pleasure, I will like to introduce Mr. Xavier Bottoms, DMV's (District of Columbia, Maryland and Virginia, USA) one and only cowboy. Enjoy."

✤**Stefan LeDude:** "And now, the always sexy, Stefan LeDude!"... or something, I am not really fussy.

❀**Jamel Knight:** "And now, introducing the always debonair king of R&B, the ladies love him and you will too. Give it up for Jamel Knight."

❀**Howie Feltersnatch:** "Now introducing the king with the dirtiest name in the troupe, Howie Feltersnatch."

❀**Welland Dowd:** "Hello, I am Welland Dowd."

❀**Julius M. SeizeHer:** "And now, coming to the stage, Julius Seizeher!" (I am not fancy. Basic is good.)

❀**Lyle Loves-it:** "Mister Lyle Loves-It, current reigning Mister Borderline USProud M.I. 2014, THE King of Hearts."

❀**Jensen C. Dean:** Jensen Dean, Jensen C. Dean, either is fine. Male pronouns. Please, please, please, do not call me "she".

❀**Jonah Godfather of DRAG:** "And now for your entertainment, here is your show director for the FRatPack, The Godfather of DRAG, Jonah!"

❀**Campbell Reid Andrews:** With an amazingly witty intro. Hopefully they announce that I am a male illusionist, so the crowd knows what they are looking at.

❀**Jack E. Dickinson:** "And here is Jack E. Dickinson, with more absurd gender-fucking shenanigans!"

❀**Clark Kunt:** I love a little banter of some kind, but it can be a fine line. I have been referred to as lady-boy or man with 'real boobs' within introductions, and that does not sit well. As a gender non-conforming person and persona, I love a good "Kunt" joke, but nothing that boarders on transphobic language.

❀**Emilio:** "Emilio, Latin DRAG King come to us all the way from Rosario, Argentina, and has been shaking his Latino hips for audiences since 2008!"

❀**Juan Kerr:** I like being called a family favourite, that's nice. Anything positive. A good compere will be able to think of something cool.

❀**Trey C. Michaels:** I love it when they give me crap. Most recent line before I went on stage was "Folks, this next performer is bisexual... buy him something and he'll be sexual!" It got people to laugh and they paid more attention to my performance.

❀**Bailey Saint James:** "Coming straight out of Milwaukee, he is no sinner, but still is Bailey A. Saint."

❀**Aaron Phoenix:** I always appreciate any reference to my physical attractiveness before going on stage! A queen MC expressing her "confusion" by her attraction to me always tends to get an easy laugh and let the audience know what they're about to see. Otherwise, a quick mention of my current title if it is appropriate, and then my stage name is plenty. I prefer to let the performance do the talking.

❀**Stefon Royce Iman:** "Ladies and gentlemen, please prepare yourself for an experience like no other. Often imitated, but never duplicated, please help me welcome to the stage Mr. Stefon Royce Iman."

❀**E. M. Shaun:** "Ladies and Gentlemen, get ready to experience the amazing and creative stylings of the mix master himself, Mr. E. M. Shaun."

❀**Santana Romero:** "Please welcome next to your stage, he is the spicy Latin dancer with a hip-hop twist, Santana Romero!"

❀**B J Armani:** "The King of Comedy, and the most handsome, butch, man's man there ever was and ever will be, the total stud muffin, B J Armani!"

❀**Smitty O'Toole:** I am usually announced as, "Houston's All-Star DRAG Race winner, Smitty O'Toole." I do not like a biographical introduction.

❀**Luke Ateraz:** Does not matter how I am introduced, just say my name right.

❀**Dixon Heat:** "The king that packs Heat... Dixon Heat!"

❀**William Vanity Matrix:** At my home club I am usually announced as, "And now for your Mister Wreckroom, William Vanity Matrix! (Or Will Matrix)." I am not really picky, just prefer the Matrix is in there because Facebook will not let me change it.

❀**Devin G. Dame:** "National Promoter for Mister USofA MI, Classic, & Diva, owner of Master Male Illusionist, please help me welcome Mister Devin G. Dame."

❀**Dionysus W Khaos:** When you can pronounce my name right, I am ecstatic. I am not too picky when it comes to introductions.

❀**Mike Oxready:** "Mike has strutted his stuff as a Male Illusionist and DRAG King since 2009. He got his start by winning DRAGnomenon as a first time performer, and went on to co-found the now retired DRAG king troupe, New Cocks on the Block. Mike has been hitting the stage solo since, expanding his performance horizons to distant DRAG-lovin' audiences in New York, USA and North Carolina, USA."

Name the performers without checking on DRAG411.com

Place Faces Without Peeking At The Answer Key In Book Two

Chapter Thirty-Seven
"How do you handle a heckler in the crowd, sidetracking your performance?"

❀**D-Luv Saviyon:** Ignore them or thank them for their critique.

❀**Shook ByNature:** I have yet to deal with this. I may get the occasional person saying "I can do that," to which I reply, "Can and do are two different things, so when you do this let me know so I can watch."

❀**Alexander Cameron:** I have never experienced a heckler before. There is almost always a patron who wants to become "part of the show", and draw a lot of attention to themselves. In those cases, I ignore them. I want everyone to has a good time, but there is a show going on so be respectful.

❀**Campbell Reid Andrews:** Never had this kind of disrespect during my number. But if it did, I would turn the negative into a positive and give them the attention they so desperately wanted. Incorporate it into my number somehow. Always in the most professional way.

❀**Travis Luvermore:** Ignore them and focus on the rest of the crowd.

❀**Gus Magendor:** I push myself harder to show I am better than their criticism.

❀**Freddy Prinze Charming**: If it is my show, and the person is distracting and disruptive, I will have them removed. They can ruin the entire evening, not just for the entertainers, but for the other patrons. If it is not my show, I will generally have a word with the bartender and/or show director, for the reasons I mentioned above.

❀**Adam All:** I have some set phrases I can turn to, if I am thrown, but usually confronting them jovially disarms them quickly. Use your words in character to get the audience to laugh at them, they will quickly give up when they realize their opinion is not wanted. I have never had someone really disrupt a show. There is always the 'ignore them' tact, if you think they will be abusive. Just remember 90% of your audience are interested to see you. This one idiot can bugger off.

❀**AJ Menendez:** I smile or laugh and I keep right on going. I never give them the fuel they want to keep going. I look at them like a small child having a tantrum; if you ignore them long enough, they will stop.

❀**Chance Wise:** I mostly just ignore them though.

❀**Hurricane Savage:** I am kind of in my own world when I am on stage, and just work the ones that I know are in to what I am doing.

❀**Marcus Mayhem:** I laugh and just keep going, or play with them a little and go on.

❀**Travis Hard:** I actually was just performing at Pridefest in Milwaukee, and during my performance, while lip-syncing, an audience member asked to perform. This was odd and I shook it off, they proceeded to say they could do better than anyone could on that stage, and watched the show in disgust. All I could do was keep on performing and tell my performers just to give their all. People are going to love you or hate you, but it should never stop you either way!

❀**Rychard "Alpha" Le'Sabre:** Lap dance.

❀**Shane Rebel Caine:** I mess with those people the most. I was told, when I first started, demand attention, and it is the best way is to mess with someone who is giving attitude while you perform!

❀**Dakota Rain:** I mess with them during the show, I will pull them on stage if they will come, I will not force anyone and show them that that can have a good time if they just pay attention.

❀**Ashton The Adorable Lover:** Never had one. I have had girls try to pull me off stage by my tie or something, but most venues have great security if it gets too wild. Otherwise, I act charming and keep on getting it with my performance.

❀**Spacee Kadett:** I was hosting, getting people hyped for a long weekend. A gentleman in the audience started making cutting gestures across his throat: "NOT FUNNY!!" He exclaimed. "YOU'RE NOT FUNNY!" I do not expect everyone to laugh at my crazy ass. Many of my campy numbers win blank stares. There is nothing funny about being hyped for a long weekend. I laughed and said, "Well, someone thinks I'm funny if they gave me this mic!" Then I moved on and hyped the weekend. The gentleman was swiftly removed by management for chronic heckling of the entire cast not just me. Remember that people heckle because they want attention. YOU are the one onstage. Just move on...do not let their idiocy make you react like an idiot too.

❀**Pierce Gabriel:** Generally I will try to embarrass them. Go over and stand behind them, wait until they wonder why everyone is looking over their shoulder and then I wave when they turn around and jump. Or I will pull them into my act, dancing on them, etc. Whatever I feel like, and whatever fits the mood of the song.

❀**Vinnie Marconi:** I do not have to handle them; other audience members usually shut them down! If not, security takes them for a walk. I will do some antics on stage to keep the focus on me and not the ruckus in the bar.

❀**Stormm:** If ignoring them does not work, I mess with them. I do not have an issue.

❀**Kruz Mhee:** If they are with someone, I bring their partner on stage to play with them. Sometimes I just take their drink or make them part of the show.

❀**Atown:** They motivate me.

❀**Silk Steele Prince:** I ignore them and aim higher in my presentation.

❀**SirMandingo Thatis:** I just get them involved in the performance by going over to them and singing or rapping straight to them they always love that, especially when that light hits them in the face.

❀**Flex Jonez:** The audience handles the matter.

❀**Cody Wellch Klondyke:** I guess if I did I would say I would ignore them.

❀**Viciouse Slick:** I would ignore them, or go straight to them. Because sometimes they may start to be quiet when they see you are willing to interact back.

❀**Kenneth J. Squires:** I usually ignore them. If they continue, I go over to them and try to embarrass them. Once they realize they look like a total ass, they quit.

❀**George De Micheal:** I make a joke out of it and they end up the fool.

❀**Chasin Love:** Stay in your zone. I go somewhere else in my head. There is always drama in the DRAG world, but if you can stay focused on yourself, you are a head of the game, no worries.

❀**DeVery Bess:** Punch them in the face! I am just joking. It depends on the situation, but being in a troupe, there is always someone who has my back, and will let the heckler know it is not appropriate. I have had to help a brother out also.

❀**Colin Grey:** Ignore them. My fellow performers will take care of those kinds of issues. One of the perks of performing in a close knit group.

❀**Eddie C. Broadway:** I usually ignore them. Unless it gets out of hand. Then I will embarrass them somehow.

❀**Sam Masterson:** I use it to my advantage, flip it and reverse it.

❀**Jack King:** Ignore them and do your show.

❀**Kameo Dupree:** Honestly, I have not experienced a heckler. I do get the "front row cellphone users." I usually dance around then and make them notice me, then focus my attention on all the other patrons who came to enjoy a spectacular show.

❀**Stefan LeDude:** Never really had a heckler, but I am guessing I would ignore them and stay focused on my performance.

❀**Jamel Knight:** There are two ways you can handle a heckler: either ignore them, or come up with a way to make them a part of your show. If you can find a way to make them a part of the show, and get a few laughs, then go for it. It is important to be able to think on your feet. Sometimes things like that can make for an amazing show.

❀**Welland Dowd:** I have never experienced a heckler!

❀**Michael Christian:** I have never experienced more than a loud person maybe a little too deep in their cups. With that, I just try to play it up with them. They usually just want to feel special and we can all move on with the show.

❀**Julius M. SeizeHer:** I ignore them. Do not give them the satisfaction.

❀**MaXx Decco:** When I am performing, I usually tune everything else out, kind of like tunnel vision, so I do not notice or pay attention to hecklers, if any. Luckily, it hasn't been an issue, but if a patron is a problem there is always security.

❀**Lyle Loves-It:** No hecklers, encountered. If I did, I would try to ignore them.

❀**Jonah Godfather of DRAG:** I have often thought about what I would do if I did. I would probably just focus on the people in the crowd enjoying the show and my performance. I would try my hardest to ignore the heckler.

❀**Jack E. Dickinson:** I would either ignore it or, if I had a witty reply that fit with the act, just go with it. They are the ones that look like a fool.

❀**Xavier Bottoms:** Never had one, but I think if I did, I would hand him my business card and tell him that I think he needs to be educated on the art of DRAG. You may not like me, but eventually I will earn your respect.

❀**Clark Kunt:** I once had a patron interfere with my ability to do a choreographed dance by tipping me then trying to stay on stage and dance (in a ridiculously large Halloween costume). I just shrugged to the audience and played it up as a joke, then made sure to land my choreography the next time the chorus came along. As long as the audience is having fun, I am not too worried what happens on stage.

❀**Emilio:** No hecklers, but security normally handles the drunk ones. I just continue doing what I do onstage.

❀**Juan Kerr:** I do not tend to get hecklers. I just get the people trying to grab my crotch when I am packing, but most of the time I am offering it them to grab anyway.

❀**Howie Feltersnatch:** If ignoring them is not working for me, I will use it to my advantage and go up to them and flirt with them, and just embarrass them. If they come on stage, I will usually act like it was planned, and I will dance with them then kick them off stage.

❀**Brandon KC Young-Taylor:** It all depends on the situation. If the heckler is being friendly then I may include them in the performance. Very rarely have I ever had anyone being a heckler in a rude way. When that has happened, I just move on to the next person tipping.

❀**Trey C. Michaels:** I have had a couple of times when there was a heckler or disturbance in the crowd. I will try to not let it sidetrack from my performance, and usually will give an extra 100% to help the audience focus more on the show then the person causing problems.

❀**Bailey Saint James:** Much like a comedian, I love to play with hecklers.

❀**Aaron Phoenix:** I have not had any hecklers, per se, but there is, of course, the occasional person who's had too much to drink or wants to stumble onto the stage or get too hands-on with me. I just work with it or around it the best I can. If someone comes up on stage, dance or mess with them for a few seconds and then guide them back to their seats. If someone gets too grabby, I can usually give them a cheeky "shame on you" look and dance off in the other direction before it gets out of control. If someone was being downright ugly and rude, I had just look past them and focus on a different area of the crowd.

✤**Stefon Royce Iman:** I never had one, but if I did I would ignore them.

✤**E. M. Shaun:** Never experienced that, but if it did occur, I would ignore it. If it would persist further, then I would get security if necessary or just keep on performing, and either earn their respect later or they do not have to be present when I perform again, if my presence makes them feel some kind of way.

✤**Mike Oxready:** I have never had this issue, but ignoring them as others have said, and then having security remove them if it continues.

✤**B J Armani:** There's always someone that feels the spotlight should be on them. It never fails that alcohol induced excitement can become a potent mix. As a host I have made fun of them back or I have acknowledged that they will be our next DRAG Act. Once a person realizes an entire crowd is looking at them they usually simmer down. I love my hecklers in that usually it is another performer's friend throwing shade and making a jerk of themselves. Let us me know I am doing well!

✤**Smitty O'Toole:** I make them a part of my act. I walk up to them and perform in their face. It diverts the crowd to that person and puts them on the spot and in the light. I have only had to do it once, but it worked like a charm.

✤**LoUis CYfer:** I kill them with kindness.

✤**Jensen C. Dean:** For the most part, I try to ignore them, the reaction is what they want most of the time. If it gets really bad, then try to catch the eye or bar staff or another performer and get a hand from someone not in the middle of a performance.

✤**Luke Ateraz:** People come to see a show. I have had fans take care of the hecklers. They get annoyed with people who are not paying attention to the entertainer on stage. While I am on stage, I just keep doing what I am doing. Do not let one person ruin the fun for the rest of the crowd. That one person will probably get the hint by the end of the night anyways.

✤**Devin G. Dame:** You can either ignore them, or play to them as part of your performance.

✤**Dionysus W Khaos:** I try to ignore them, and not let it mess with the performance.

Chapter Thirty-Eight
"When everything is said and done, and you leave the stage for the very last time in life? What do you hope your fans will say about you?"

❧**Spacee Kadett:** I will never have a retirement show, because I know my sorry ass will keep getting back onstage. With that in mind, "Please welcome back to the stage one last time, that crazy old ball of arthritic fun, Spacee Kadett!"

❧**D-Luv Saviyon:** I contributed to the advancement of Kings and represented them in a positive light.

❧**Kameo Dupree:** It is not really a "saying" but more of a feeling. "I was able to warm a heart, make a bad day better, and lift a spirit through my actions using music."

❧**Adam Allthat:** I am a groundbreaker and father to the scene.

❧**Marty Brown**: That I made them smile and left them wanting more.

❧**Travis Luvermore**: That I touched them with the songs.

❧**AJ Menendez:** I would like to think they would say that I touched them both on and off the stage as well.

❧**Adam DoEve:** I brought some fun, laughter, and maybe a little head scratching to brighten up their life.

❧**Gus Magendor:** I am well remembered and was freaking awesome!

❧**Dixie Shuffle:** That I helped the United Kingdom DRAG King scene out of the lesbian margins and opened up opportunities in mainstream cabaret.

❧**Chance Wise:** That I gave them a good time and I am remembered well.

❧**Coti Blayne:** I hope that when it comes time for me to retire from DRAG that I am missed. That people remember how I made them smile or laugh even if they were having a horrible day, that I made their day better.

❧**Clint Torres:** I was an inspiration to young DRAGs and a supporter of my community.

❧**Justin Cider:** That I was original and that I will be missed. That I always gave it my all and people just enjoyed watching me perform.

❧**Hurricane Savage:** I have not really thought about it. Hope this is something I can do for many years in one form or another.

❧**Stormm**: I hope I will be missed and that I was an inspiration to others. I hope they know I worked hard trying to entertain the crowd.

❧**Marcus Mayhem:** I have stepped away from DRAG and miss it. People say they miss my creativity. I did songs most people do not know.

❧**Travis Hard:** I do not want them to say anything. I want them to remember me.

❧**Emilio:** "Wow! It was always fun to watch Emilio perform!"

❀**Rychard "Alpha" Le'Sabre**: I do not care, as long as I am remembered for my good deeds and the fun I put in people's lives

❀**Shane Rebel Caine**: I hope I will be missed and I will leave a lasting impression not only on stage, but also within the community. I hope I made a difference, a successful entertainer, and helped pave the way for future Kings.

❀**Dakota Rain**: I hope to leave a great impression. I hope they look back to say, "I remember that guy. He was awesome. I loved to see him perform."

❀**Ashton The Adorable Lover**: That I affected them some way, whether they were entertained, swooned, smiled, had similar feelings, stories, or just thought I was a cute and adorable guy that loved what he did!

❀**Rasta Boi Punany**: The DRAG King with long hair doing big stuff every time!

❀**Xander Havoc**: To consider me an inspiration as I do with some of my idols.

❀**Freddy Prinze Charming**: I hope people will remember me as a creative entertainer, a mentor, who gave back to his community, who entertained audiences, and made people feel something; even if it was just a smile.

❀**Ben Eaten**: I hope that I have inspired someone and that I am remembered. Whether I was the first King they saw or they liked my number or a costume.

❀**Kenneth J. Squires**: I can only hope to be remembered for making a difference in the art of DRAG King and M.I. That I grew and got better at what I was doing. Maybe have a chance to help a young person; I would be honored to do that.

❀**Pierce Gabriel**: I want people to say that I reminded them of the passion in life. The importance of emotion, and how beautiful it is to feel.

❀**Koomah**: I empowered, encouraged them, or inspired them in some way.

❀**SirMandingo Thatis**: He is so freaking entertaining and awesome. There will never be another King to grace the stage like him.

❀**Campbell Reid Andrews**: "Out-fucking-standing performance," because I completed the reason I started in the first place. My last show in life will have pyrotechnics, a billion dancers, a light show, and celebrity cameos.

❀**Vinnie Marconi**: "I just love how he stoned that wheelchair!"

❀**Kruz Mhee** Kruz had fun. He made me feel I was part of his time on stage.

❀**Hawk Stuart**: "I love he can still bring down the house and rock the stage."

❀**Chasin Love:** I had fun. I was a good performer and will never forget me.

❀**B J Bottoms**: I hope someone will feel touched by me. That I have made an impression on them because of either a performance or a conversation.

❀**Silk Steele Prince:** They will think of me when they hear my signature songs. That it is always a treat to see me perform and I am the best performer they ever encountered. Most of all I hope they say that I made them happy.

❀**George De Micheal:** I made them proud and they enjoyed watching me entertain.

❀**Colin Grey:** I hope I am missed. I hope they would say I am one of the most talented people they ever had the pleasure of watching perform.

❀**Eddie C. Broadway:** I hope that people will remember my creativity, out of the box ideas, my humility, and integrity.

❀**J Breezy St James:** I put on a damn good show. They enjoyed my time on the stage.

❀**Phantom:** I just hope that my craft and my life's work will keep inspiring people and Kings to push the limits of DRAG.

❀**Sam Masterson:** I also have a signature song and whenever it plays, I hope they always think of me, how I truly entertained and got everyone involved.

❀**Jack King:** That I did a good show and they will have more.

❀**Stefan LeDude:** That I was an awesome performer and HOT.

❀**Clark Kunt:** Simply that they will see me at the next show, because they know I will be there supporting my family.

❀**Jamel Knight:** I hope they say that each time I stepped on stage I entertained them and gave them all that I had. I want to be an entertainer that will be remembered and inspire other entertainers long after I am gone.

❀**Welland Dowd:** I hope people recognize my performance in the context of Montréal's, Quebec, Canada, long history of DRAG to say, "Wow, he was one hot dude!"

❀**Michael Christian:** I feel like I will not purposely retire. If I ever fade away I hope people remember me like Peter Pan. The stage kept my heart young even when I need to use a walker. I hope that I made them smile.

❀**Julius M. SeizeHer:** That I did my job well, and that I will be missed.

❀**Jonah Godfather of DRAG:** I would like to say I am never retiring because I love DRAG and performing. I would like the audience to say I was always entertaining and gave it my all; I was a good and caring person.

❀**Howie Feltersnatch:** Hope DRAG is always in my life. I could not do without it. If for some strange reason it had to come to an end, I hope that people would think I was funny and entertaining and that the stage is not the same without me.

❀**B J Armani:** "Every show was full of talent, love, and laughter. She never stopped thinking about the audience and did as much as she could to help the community."

❧**Lyle Love-It**: "What an ICON, he performed with all his heart and LOVED to entertain. Inspired many and a positive role model in art of Male Illusion."

❧**Jack E. Dickinson:** I hope that people will feel inspired to reach beyond what they thought they were capable of doing, inspired to be themselves, inspired to be creative, and inspired to share their gifts with their communities.

❧**Bootzy Edwards Collynz:** Remember me as a "Southern Gentleman," a lover not a fighter, but will knock you out. I was full of laughter and joy, always dancing, singing and cutting up backstage. I hope I am remembered as a great performer, friend, and supporter of the community. Big hearted and always open to help and get dirty if needed. High-energy performances, great dance, smooth and sexy, a craziness. He keeps it spicy and fun, and has a shyness that makes him so sweet. I just want to be remembered for making people smile dance and sing. Sharing my joy.

❧**Santana Romero**: I have thought about this a lot. I guess I would want people to remember me for my moves on stage. When people talk about me when it is all said and done, it would be nice if they said, "Yeah, I know who he or she is! His or her dancing was amazing!" If I can leave that mark on the ones who have seen me perform, my job is complete. I love making people happy through what I do and it is even better when I inspire them to tap into something they thought they never had.

❧**Juan Kerr**: I was funny, awkward, and sexy all at the same time. I want to confuse people into not knowing what they think or feel about me. That would be good. If they thought I was cute that might be enough.

❧**Brandon KC Young-Taylor:** To be remembered for being a part of a generation of Kings paving the way for Kings to rule as fierce as the Queens!

❧**Trey C. Michaels:** I hope people will see I used the stage to support local causes and fundraisers. I also want people to see I am a genuine person.

❧**Xavier Bottoms:** "It is about time." I hope they say, "Xavier Bottoms, a legend. He poured his heart out on stage for every performance. He never let anyone down, always there to help. The community will miss his charity work. He was a very entertaining gentleman. We are glad he helped the future of DRAG, showing how it is done, and making sure the art of Male Illusion lives on. He will truly be missed."

❧**Aaron Phoenix:** I hope they remember me for positive energy, compassion, a playful smile, and always a fun show.

❧**Thug Passion:** I hope my audience will say I miss seeing you perform on stage, I enjoyed watching you, that I was nice and respectful, that I made a difference in their lives somehow, that I would never be forgotten.

❊**MaXx Decco**: Me retire? I hope one day I will be spotted at a show and someone will say, "There goes MaXx f'ing Decco, the reason why I started doing DRAG." I want to know I inspired and supported people as much as I was inspired and supported.

❊**Soco Dupree**: One word, encore!

❊**Dominic**: I have not performed in a long time but I just wanted people to remember me by my passion and making every song I did MINE. I succeeded because I still have many people that stop me or find me on Facebook asking if I am Dominic from Perfect Gentlemen or Dominic that performed at Sports Page or Chiq Bar. It is nice to know people enjoyed my art and performances.

❊**E. M. Shaun**: I would want people to say that I had respect for the craft and the audience and that I put my heart and soul into my performances. I want people to know I had a message with my craft and that I wanted to bring happiness and entertainment to the community, gay or straight.

❊**Stefon Royce Iman**: I would hope they respect the craft of Male Illusion and remember the shows and great things I have done for the community.

❊**Chasin Love**: That my fans enjoyed my show and that I did not hold back.

❊**Jensen C. Dean**: I hope they will say that they enjoyed the time they had with Jensen, both as a performer and for his contributions to the community.

❊**Cody Wellch Klondyke**: I hope they will say; they hate that I am going, they really enjoyed the show, and they hope that it is just a temporary thing because they love to see me on stage and watch me perform.

❊**Mike Oxready**: I hope that I will have made a difference, and some of my performances made people think and question the social construct of gender.

❊**Smitty O'Toole**: I brought them enjoyment with my performance. I hope that they have respect for me because I do not conform to gain status.

❊**LoUis CYfer**: I will never leave!

❊**Luke Ateraz**: I would hope my audience would say that I was entertaining. That I was passionate about my song choices. That they will miss me.

❊**Devin G. Dame**: I would hope that everyone knew I put my heart and soul on stage.

❊**Napoleon Bonerparte**: I hope they would say I put on a good show and that I moved them in some way. That is my ultimate goal as an entertainer! I also hope they would know that I always tried to return the favor of giving new entertainers an opportunity to perform. Lastly, I hope they would remember that I was one of the ones fighting for the day when DRAG Kings and female performers receive the same respect as anyone else in the show bar world.

Chapter Thirty-Nine
"If you were to sit down with a new performer, one on one, to say an important message about the craft, what would you say?"

❈**Adam All**: Know yourself, know your character, and know the differences and the similarities. Know your message and your product and when you know all this, do not ever let it go. You can adapt, you can evolve, you can revamp and reintroduce, but hold on to the core of why you did it in the first place. Eventually you will not be able to stop. It can bring you joy, pride, anger, humiliation, and endless questions. If you get on that stage and you know yourself, nothing can bring you down. Polish your craft and be true to yourself. You will never be as good as you could be tomorrow until you get to tomorrow so do not be hard on yourself when you are not there yet. Do not think yourself the best when you could still have so far to go. Arrogance will destroy you, avoid it at all costs, and above all try to fucking enjoy it!

❈**Travis Luvermore**: Enjoy what you do, take time to put energy into your craft; you do not have to be rich to dress classy on stage. Check out thrift stores, take time to not only learn your songs, but also on your total look.

❈**AJ Menendez**: Never go out on stage unless your illusion is complete, nor go on stage with your everyday clothes. Maintain a sense of professionalism both on and off the stage. Never let them see you sweat, always know your lyrics as if you wrote the song, and own the stage. Have fun with it!

❈**Chance Wise**: All the above advice, I also add that you should listen to more seasoned performers and use their advice, and to stay humble.

❈**D-Luv Saviyon**: Remain humble. Always stay open to learn and receive criticism. Never get complacent, always try to be better. Learn and do what works for you, then try to perfect it. Be your own King; never try to replicate someone else. Have fun and never feel anyone owes you anything but common decency and respect. If at any point, you no longer get nervous or think you have mastered Male Illusion, get off the stage.

❈**Marty Brown**: When it stops being fun and enjoyable, it is time to quit.

❈**Coti Blayne**: The biggest thing I tell performers is to stay out of the drama. Sure, it might get you very famous very quick, but it will not be in a good way. In the long run it is going to hurt you because no one wants to book or perform with a drama queen. You will lose friends and bookings. Just be nice and friendly and do not get involved if it does not concern you. Please do not air out your dirty laundry on Facebook. Be famous, not infamous.

❋**Clint Torres**: Be yourself, trust in your fellow brothers, be confident, and have fun. Those are the most important things to remember about this craft. Find what you are comfortable doing, what looks and feels good, something that will get the audience involved. Then kill it.

❋**Justin Cider**: Have fun; if you are having fun on stage, the audience will be way more receptive.

❋**Hurricane Savage**: I have a new DRAG son and I tell him all the time to stay out of the drama, stay true to yourself and do not become what others think you should be. Just do you the best you can.

❋**Jonah Godfather of DRAG**: Preparation is key. Try to bring your A game every time you are on stage. There are Kings who are complacent with their DRAG and it shows. The audience comes for show and we as entertainers have a responsibility to them and the venue owner to give a great show every time.

❋**Stormm**: Have fun, know your words, and make sure you hide the girls...

❋**Marcus Mayhem**: Duct tape is your friend and your foe. A paper towel over the nipples keeps you from ripping them off. Duct tape is not like a Band-Aid stuck on with craft glue. Never use your street cloths. Pick music the crowd likes as well as what you like. KNOW YOUR WORDS. Watermelon, bubble gum, or banana will not cut it, we are not Queens. Be better than that. Be on time! It takes time to do your face right. Have fun with your crowd.

❋**MaXx Decco**: Do not enter lightly, performing is a passion! LEARN as much as you can, WORK HARD, IT IS WORTH IT. Let your creativity flow, push boundaries, have fun, and you will SHINE.

❋**Freddy Prinze Charming**: Listen and learn.

❋**Kameo Dupree**: Never think you know it all; there is always room to improve. Things change every day so never get comfortable with the same thing. Perform what you feel and feel what you perform. If you do not believe in what you are doing, how can you expect someone else to?

❋**Adam DoEve**: When it is no longer fun, walk away, never stop learning and just be you.

❋**Dominic Von Strap**: Do not be offended when seasoned Kings offer you feedback. The simple fact that they think you are worth the time to provide those critiques is an honor, not an insult. Take in whatever feedback you can but do not dare try to be someone you are not. There is only one you in this world, do not rob any of us from that presence.

❋**Koomah**: You can always learn from everyone and always be willing to share what you know. Someone will always be better than you are at certain things. Do not take it too seriously. Be open to change. Know your audience. There will always be room for improvement. Anxiety before a performance is good, it is adrenaline, and it means you will bring it onstage. Take a break from any number that feels like you are performing it on autopilot. Have fun.

❀**Trey C. Michaels**: Listen to the seasoned Kings when they give advice. Avoid drama. Nothing kills your love for the art like petty drama.

❀**Travis Hard**: I would tell them to not let their first few years get to their head. Stay humble. Love what you do!

❀**Shane Rebel Caine**: The number one rule is to avoid drama at all costs. Most venues do not want to book someone that is associated with a lot of drama. Also, realize that your first few years will be difficult, especially depending on the town you are in; do not let a lack of tips or bookings discourage you from continuing. Listen to the other Kings when they give you advice. Even some Queens can have helpful advice.

❀**Rychard "Alpha" Le'Sabre**: Never think you are done learning; listen to advice from every corner of DRAG, try to expand and grow with each and every performance. Always know your words.

❀**Dakota Rain**: Do not lose sight of YOU, or your personal life. Avoid drama at all costs, watch and learn things and make sure you are doing this for you, not just because someone wants you to.

❀**Ashton The Adorable Lover**: Know who you are and who your Illusion is. Never go on stage to perform out of Illusion. Be professional, know all your words; connecting with your music helps you connect to the audience. Own the stage, be confident, mistakes happen, so roll with the punches and most importantly have FUN!

❀**Rasta Boi**: Be yourself. People will you respect you more.

❀**Xander Havoc**: I would say that it takes lots of hard work and dedication but nothing feels better than stepping out and leaving your heart on the stage. The impact you have on people's lives makes it all worth it!

❀**Ben Eaten**: Take all the advice you can get. If you get advice that you are not sure about, try it for one number. If it does not work then do not try it again. You do not have to change what you want to do because someone gives you a suggestion. It is YOUR performance and they are only suggestions. Do not just write it off without actually listening. Ask for advice and bounce ideas off performers that are more knowledgeable about the craft.

❀**Spacee Kadett**: The beauty of this art form is that you can take it as casually or seriously. I have known many great entertainers who just do occasional benefit shows and open mic nights; their art is pure fun. I also know many great entertainers who make a living or a good portion of their living as DRAGs. Kings are at the threshold of more opportunities than we ever could have imagined. If that is what you want, go for it. Blow their minds! Blaze a trail. Just know that there is no such thing as overnight success. Crowns are not all-access passes. They are keys that you must use to unlock doors. Nobody in this business is entitled to anything. Be kind. Be resilient. Work hard. Gobble up every opportunity, no matter how big or small, because you never know where it may lead. Remain humble. Learn. Grow. Be mindful of whom you ask for advice and be respectful of who has paved your way, do your research. Most of all do not lose sight of yourself, your character, or where you want to take him. Do not let petty drama kill your art or your spirit. Move on. Light up audiences. Live in that moment. Be different. Go where they told you. Be entertaining. Be you.

❀**Pierce Gabriel**: Never give up. You may have to change how you do things, make sacrifices. Learn new tricks to please a different crowd. Never give up.

❀**Vinnie Marconi**: If you really want to do this, know it is a lot of work. I have a blast getting on that stage and pulling one emotion or another from the audience. You have to decide what persona best fits you and what style you want to bring to the stage. It takes me weeks to put together just one number, from concept to stage. I never have been able to memorize well and it takes me that long to learn lyrics. Then I figure out costuming and if I need back-ups. Then the hard part is learning every nuance in the words and music so you can really pop. The fun is seeing the reaction from the people. What do you want them to think of your number? Did the number fit the venue and the crowd? Always keep in mind where you are performing and the audience you are performing to. Do not do rap in a country bar; do not do old school to a 20's crowd. Neither will "get it." Stay true to you! I have heard, go outside your comfort zone, and I can tell you, there is no fun in that. The stress and worry about doing it "right" makes me have a bad performance. If you are not comfortable doing it, then do not!

❀**Kruz Mhee**: Never walk on stage without makeup or unprepared. Look the part. Know your words. If you are doing this for money, you are doing it for the wrong reasons. Connect with the crowd. Make them part of the show.

❀**Hawk Stuart**: I would help them out the best I can and if I do not know how to do something, I would tell them whom to ask.

❀**B J Bottoms**: Have fun. You have three minutes and some change to perform as this character you created. Make every second count. Treat every song as if it is the last one you will ever do.

❀**SirMandingo Thatis**: Stay true to yourself in your music and clothes styles. Let your personality shine through the performance.

❀**Silk Steele Prince**: For some people the stardom is slow for some it is fast paced. Overall, love what you do and do what you love. Always be open to learn from others and allow others to learn from you. Be creative. Think outside the box. Aim high and give it your all.

❀**Flex Jonez**: Be physically fit, figure out the image of a King you want to bring to the stage, always be professional, and mentally leave everything but yourself and your routine away from the stage. Lastly, be prepared to eat many peanut butter and jelly sandwiches because you will not get rich doing this.

Kenneth J. Squires: Put everything they have into this art. Put in your time, willingness to learn, develop stage presence. Be yourself. Have fun with performing. Stay out of the drama, and stay true to yourself. Then I would thank the person and feel honored that they came to me for advice.

George De Micheal: Focus on your image and stay away from negativity.

Chasin Love: Know your songs. Go into your own zone and have fun.

DeVery Bess: All you need are the 4 C's, Character, costume, choreograph, and charisma. Develop your skills.

Colin Grey: Have fun. Be yourself. Do not let negative people steer you away from what you love doing. Do not wear your street clothes on stage. Always be open to advice and accept criticism with grace.

Eddie C. Broadway: Be open to advice and be willing to learn. Once you have those down, BE YOURSELF. Take care of you and show the world who YOU are. Do not be a replica of someone else before you.

Sam Masterson: Always entertain and look real.

Phantom: Do what makes you happy with your DRAG, ask as many question as you can, you learn something new every time you step on the stage.

Jordan Allen: To be confident is important, but being humble is VITAL.

Joshua K. Mann: The ones that take the risks, do the right thing, and learn this business are the ones people remember.

Jack King: Be yourself and do not give up, do what you heart says.

Jamel Knight: I would say find who you are as an entertainer, figure out what it is you do best and grow from there. Continual growth is the key to maintaining and gaining new fans. Definitely stay confident and understand that not everybody that grins in your face is your friend.

Welland Dowd: I am a big believer that numbers have to have some kind of hook, message, or story. I get bored when Kings just dance around the stage with no message other than, "Look at me I am dancing."

Michael Christian: Humility is key. You will never know it all so don't act like you do. Life is to be lived. Light fires. Knock down doors. Inspire minds. Be inspired. Learn. Never close your mind. Be professional. Even if you are in it to have fun as a hobby the person next to you may be running a full business in this art. Respect that. This is a world of magic and imagination. You have a five minute window to be someone else and to take the minds of an audience anywhere you want. Take their troubles away and make them smile. This is a very rare opportunity to be paid for what is essentially playing dress up with your friends. Live it up. Enjoy your time in Never Land!

❦**Julius M. SeizeHer**: Do not set your sights too high. Be prepared for anything, and have fun!

❦**Campbell Reid Andrews**: You are only as good as your last performance, so make it count. Focus on the passion first and then the money. Remember where you came from and who you are because when you take off the makeup at night you are still a regular person.

❦**Howie Feltersnatch**: I have done this many times. I tell them that their nerves are normal and they never go away. Just get up on stage, flash that smile and have fun. The rest will come to you. Do not be afraid to make mistakes, because that is how you grow as a performer and a person.

❦**B J Armani**: Never forget about the audience! Without the people that come, we are just performers in costumes. Be willing to put in your time and never forget what it is like to be new. Never put anyone else down as a performer, it makes you look catty. Always be willing to push the envelope and as long as you are having fun, the audience will too. Above all, MEMORIZE YOUR WORDS.

❦**Lyle Love-It**: Present yourself with self-respect, give a good impression, and be PROFESSIONAL.

❦**Jack E. Dickinson**: Go with your gut instinct and do acts that YOU enjoy and are passionate about. Your passion will show through!

❦**Clark Kunt**: Find your persona, but do not lose yourself in the character. Keep grounded and always having fun. If performing stops being DRAG and becomes "a DRAG," step away until you find the love for it again.

❦**Bootzy Edwards Collynz**: You MUST love doing it. There is a heart and a passion in performance and that holds true here. The pay is more experience and emotional than with money. Most passion driven professions don't pay unless you hit a certain level in that profession. Your passion (love for it) must be for ALL the good, bad and ugly, because that's what makes it great. Your passion must be resilient, open, humble, reflective, and stubborn at times. Stay true to your craft, but be open to new challenges. It's ok to be nervous about the challenge. Nerves show you care about your craft, and that's always good. Always look for newer, fresher, bigger, better, brighter. There is always something to improve, so work on making your weaknesses your strength. Presence and confidence in your character, always show your pride in what you do and who you are. Lend a helping hand to those who might need it. We all have to start somewhere; and there are those people who help us get here- pay it forward. And above all these, it don't mean nothing if you DON'T KNOW YOUR WORDS. Perform!!!

❦**Emilio**: Be sexy. Have fun. Entertain.

❦**Juan Kerr**: Be yourself. Do not let anyone say that you are doing it wrong. You cannot do yourself wrong. Have fun and work at your routines. Find songs you love and enjoy!

❀**Brandon KC Young-Taylor**: You are about to take the ride of your life. The ride is what you make of it and only you can make it what you want it to be. Enjoy every smile and every frown along the way. Make it beautiful!

❀**J Breezy St James**: Learn from other performers and do not ever think you are the best. Stay humble and enjoy performing.

❀**Bailey Saint James**: Learn from your audience and step out of your comfort zone. The more fun you have, the more fun the audience will have fun.

❀**Xavier Bottoms** I would ask them why they want to perform. Because if you do not have the passion, do not start. DRAG is not about money, but having fun and loving the craft. Choose songs you are comfortable with. Do not try to do too much. Open your mouth when lip-syncing, as you do when singing in the car by yourself, but never let a sound come out of your mouth. This takes a lot of practice. Try to stay away from doing a ballad in the beginning. That is how you lose the audience. Upbeat, sing along songs are great. Keep the audience involved as much as possible. Practice your dance moves, try not to look like a puppet, unless you are portraying one. Try to match your outfit with the song. My two biggest pet peeves: never draw on facial hair and know the words to your song. Lastly, enjoy the ride. You get out what you put into it. I will always be here for you if you need anything.

❀**Aaron Phoenix**: Be confident, but not cocky. Push yourself, but not so much that you resent it. Take it seriously, but have fun.

❀**Thug Passion**: I would say be yourself. Find who you are on that stage. Make sure you give back to the community whether it is benefit shows, taking pictures with fans, or just simply taking five minutes to converse with a fan. Most of all have fun because if you are, so is everyone else. I also would tell them that in the LGBT, Lesbian, Gay, Bi, Transgender, community you become a celebrity when you are an entertainer. You will become someone people look up to; they will want to take pictures with you. There will be fans, and there will be groupies but just remember to stay humble and appreciate your fans. You could always get dressed and ready to do a show but they might not always be there to watch.

❀**Dominic**: Always be yourself. The best thing about performing is, for those few minutes, the stage is yours, and ALL EYES are on you. Savor every moment because this is where your hard work shows. Do NOT get involved with the drama surrounding this art. People can damage your name without a reason so always stay neutral and true to who you are and your beliefs!

❀**E. M. Shaun**: I would say have fun and be yourself. You can always learn from vets so be open to suggestions and criticisms. Do not let anyone change you or the performer you want to be. Be confident and be around supportive people to aid you with your career.

❀**Stefon Royce Iman**: I would say research the craft, be genuine, and be unique. Remember, be yourself always, and have fun.

❀**Santana Romero**: Practice, stay current, avoid drama and know who you are as an entertainer. Never let anyone or anything take away the love of what you do. Appreciate every aspect; learn from the good and bad. Be humble and thankful. Last but not least, NEVER forget where you came from because at any point, you can end up back at square one.

❀**Cody Wellch Klondyke**: Be you and enjoy what you do, take time to put energy into your craft; you do not have to be rich to dress classy on stage. Check out thrift stores, take time to not only learn your songs, also take time on your total look. You are an entertainer so stay creative and just be yourself!

❀**Soco Dupree**: Stay humble!

❀**Smitty O'Toole**: Never lose yourself in the craft. Always remember where you come from, stay humble, and remain open to new ideas.

❀**Jensen C. Dean**: Overall the message to a new entertainer would be to make sure they are having fun and that they are always able to say they are proud of what they bring to the stage.

❀**LoUis CYfer** Do not take no for an answer and do not take part in DRAG drama. Most of all be confident and true to yourself. You are an artist. Enjoy it

❀**Luke Ateraz**: Be yourself. Do not come into this looking for a get rich quick scheme. DRAG is an expensive hobby. Always take advice from those who came before you, never think you know it all. Go to shows and watch other performers. Be respectful of your elders. Do not sit on a cell phone at a show. Learn to do everything on your own, but do not be afraid to ask for help.

❀**William Vanity Matrix**: The higher you get on your high horse, when you start feeling cocky, the harder you will fall. Pick yourself up and be humble from there on out. Take it from someone who made the mistake.

❀**Devin G. Dame**: Be true to yourself, have fun, watch, learn, and never stop growing.

❀**Diseal Tanks Roberts**: Be confident; do not act better than anyone else. Know your music and learn your words!

❀**Chasin Love**: Never stop learning, listening, and most of all, know that you are important, not what anyone else thinks of you.

❀**Napoleon Bonerparte:** Follow your calling, follow your heart. Be adventuresome, be unique. Listen to advice, but always follow your own gut! Make contact with the people who hand you those dollars, look them in the eye. Introduce yourself to the audience before and after the show. Connect with your community! Make new friends. Be grateful for everything.

Chapter Forty

"The Pageantry system has adjusted many times since its inception. Explain your belief of where it is now and what it needs to accomplish in the future."

NOTE: 44% of the respondents commented, they refused to address this comment in fear of retaliation by the systems and their followers.

🎭**D-Luv Saviyon**: King pageants and King competitions have grown by leaps and bounds over the years. Some systems are wide-open, sky is the limit, and they are not looking for a specific type of King. For others, I think they are so stuck with a certain format that they are not open to more varied types of Kings. I wish there was not such a separation of systems where performers are harshly judged or disadvantaged for being a former in another system or because they do not fit their usual format. The familiarity factor, the resistance to accept Kings outside of their comfort zones and the fear of competing in systems that are dominant in one nationality or the other is another problem. We should just have pageants and compete. Some systems are imploding for many of these reasons.

🎭**Spacee Kadett**: The other night, my home venue hosted a television-famous Queen who was inquiring with our house cast about a national pageant she wanted to enter. My advice? "You are already 'SO and SO!' You do not need the title!" To which my cast mates immediately responded, "Yes, but the prize package is $XX,XXX!" I smacked my head and apologized. "Ha ha! I am so sorry, I was not thinking, the King prize package is only one tenth of that." To which one of my cast mates sharply responded, "Well if it is such an issue, then be a Queen!" Thanks, sis. There are a lot of angles we could take with this question. But for the purpose of this King book, I am grateful for the opportunity to express my sheer sadness over the blatant sexism that runs rampant in USA DRAG pageantry. I have watched, with a lump in my throat, as my fellow Queens paraded around expansive, multi-million dollar venues in their walk of formers and final night grandeur, knowing that I will NEVER walk that stage in any capacity. Knowing that NO King pageant takes place at such grand venues, on such optimal nights, with prizes that could well cover the down payment of a HOUSE. We Kings are a newer breed, and we are forging new opportunities. For that, I remain passionate about pushing the boundaries of King contests, and grateful to those who do the same. And so, while I firmly believe that money should be the least of our focus in DRAG, I also strongly believe in fairness. It is not fair that a Queen wins a prize package ten times that of her King. It is not fair that a King represents a system for half the pay of his Queen the entire year, or that Queens are handsomely compensated to appear as formers, while their Kings receive nothing. This is where our pageantry is now, and from where it must rise. I was so naïve when I started DRAG, I did not understand the difference between King, Queen, boy or girl. We were all just doing DRAG. This is where I would like to return. How about a pageant that puts all of us on equal footing? THROW ME IN WITH THE QUEENS! Because at the end of the day, I believe our art should be about entertainment, not about what is between our legs.

✺**Adam All:** in the United Kingdom, there are no pageants for Kings and we do not get tips. In fact, we are often not paid at all. It is ridiculous that one cannot live on the income of a DRAG King regardless of the number of gigs they book. It is mostly down to the lesbian scene not supporting the King network, not having the balls to step up and have a go themselves. The gay scene does not involve women, keeping Male Impersonators at arm's length or for the sake of eye candy only. I push every day for equality, but without a following, it is not going to happen. How many Prides do we have to work the women's stage before people take notice?

✺**Travis Luvermore**: The national systems are definitely growing and expanding, though it seems that most preliminaries are limited to certain areas of the USA. I moved to the northeast, some Kings who would like to compete for these systems do not have the start up money to travel for a preliminary. If it is a national system, preliminaries should be scattered more evenly across the USA so it is easier for up and coming Kings to compete.

✺**Orion Blaze Browne**: I believe a huge problem in the pageantry systems is the unfair packages between Kings, Queens, femmes, and males. We are all entertainers If you can compete at the caliber of a national system and win then you should be rewarded despite what gender you started as before getting into character. There are many systems that performers will claim are "rigged" because they are looking for a certain face to represent them instead of looking for a well-qualified entertainer.

✺**Marcus Mayhem**: The only thing I know for sure is, I do not run, have not run and do not plan on running. This is not to be mean or single anyone out, but it is the ones who are on testosterone or have changed their bodies who are competing. It does not seem fair to say you are impersonating a male when you are changing into a male. Then the fake hair is not fake. The taping down of the chest is not happening, for you no longer have one. It is the same for Queens. If they are transitioning and got a boob job, then they are no longer impersonating the opposite sex. These is where I think there should be a different set of pageantry systems to keep it fair. For myself to compete against a female who is becoming a male is just not fair. The age limit is another thing too. I am 36 and the moment I said, "Hey I would not mind having a bar crown then maybe go for the state one." I learned I am too old. I know this is for the young but I enjoy doing DRAG too.

❋**Kameo Dupree**: Pageants should be about brotherhood, giving back to the community, and meeting new people while displaying yourself to show the world who you are as an entertainer. I know many systems state in their packets that if you win there are so many benefit shows, charitable actions, ect. you must perform. Many do not follow this. My biggest hang up with many of the MI pageants is it is ok for females that are transitioning to compete. I love all my brothers and sisters but on a competition level where is the line drawn? If you live everyday as a male, where is the illusion? This keeps me from competing in several systems because one thing almost all systems judge on is male realness. If someone has taken multiple steps to transform their body, then how is that fair to those who have to still apply facial hair, bond, and pack. Not saying that cannot compete but I think there should be separate systems.

❋**Freddy Prinze Charming**: I have the same issue regarding prize packages for Kings. The focus is always on the Queens. They get bigger and better venues, better prize packages, and higher booking fees. From preliminaries to nationals, the Kings always get the short end of the stick. There were recent preliminaries here for a national system. The Queens received a cash prize, five nights of their hotel covered, a gown, and more. Kings and male entertainers got two nights covered for their hotel, less than half the cash prize, and far less recognition than their Queen counterparts. I would not necessarily say certain systems are rigged, but when winners become predictable, it starts to make one question the system's integrity.

❋**Koomah**: I know several folks who love being involved in pageants and it is awesome that they found a space and a sub community that works for them! I am not competitive and have no desire to do pageants. I have seen pros and cons in the system from a spectator perspective. As someone who makes their living solely as an artist and performer I can not imagine paying to perform in an event with the aspiration that I am chosen as the one who gets paid. The King prize packages have never impressed me much compared to the Queen prize packages either.

❋**Travis Hard**: This subject is very touchy for me. I love that many systems are growing as an actual brotherhood. I was a part of a system that seemed to neglect and look down on transgender participants. With the growing amount of transgender persons, it was only a matter of time that people opened their eyes and got over it. It was disgusting for me to sit and watch how my friends were treated for the simple fact that their facial hair was real. The systems are growing and including everyone now and that makes me happy. My friends can compete without worry!

❋**Chance Wise**: I have always been apprehensive about pageants, I consider doing them, and perhaps at some point I will. My experience with serving on a pride board a few years back was the discussion that Miss and Mister Pageants were less than fun. I was pushing for the Mister to get the same prize package with a crown. There was a well-known Queen on the board who said that Queens should get twice the prize package because, "They have to buy gowns." My reply to that was, "Well, when was the last time you bought a good suit? Tailored of course, with a vest, and a pair of shoes?" I was pretty much ruled out and the Queen got twice the package including a crown, and the King got a sash. It was discouraging to say the least.

🏵**Campbell Reid Andrews**: Here comes the bad guy! Pageantry now, when I came back to the surface of my performance career here in Texas, USA, pageantry was everything. Every year the bio boys and the Queens spend thousands of dollars they do not have or spread IOUs around town to get ready. For their big WIN. However, the King's titles are minimal. Bar titles, or charity titles. No one takes the time or wants to put the money into an M.I. division here. How can you blame them they just want to make money off the pageant, right. "No one will come to that pageant," they say, "Besides there is only one King who would compete anyway." Even with my attempts to convince other Kings to compete they flake, making us look even worse. To know hey I am not getting paid the same as a Queen, I am not getting cash prizes for bar titles, and I have no opportunity to grow in any of the rinky dink titles that are so generously thrown my way. But wait, why would they want to extend any major pageantry here? None of the Kings show their faces outside of their own cities. A pageant promoter wants to know the title will be visible and well taken care of. I do not blame the ones here for not trying because the Kings are not either. As for pageants as a whole, no there is no growth, they all just want your money. I have participated in this industry a lot because I had to get my name out there and titles matter here. To be quite honest it is a waste of money. Some systems say, "Hey it is about the talent," yet every year the national winning King looks the same as the rest and has "ok" talent. But nothing, WOW. I think it is wrong to lead people on with all their hard work and then have other random people from the system judge them and say, "Maybe next year we need to see you are loyal to the system." What the F! Why do I have to come back ten times and support you? Should not my hard work and putting a great package together specifically for your system be enough? I love the systems that are crowing their friends or DRAG family. Why? I am no longer going to funnel my hard-earned money into systems that do not believe in change. Whether a King lives in a different state, does not wear facial hair on a regular basis, or first time competing with your system; these things should not matter. It should be about the talent and their personality. I am not trying to start fires I just want Kings to realize that for systems to change, who have been doing the same things for years, all Kings have to follow through not just ask without action. If you want things to change we will all need to prove we are worth it, not just some of us. On the other hand do what they do here, appoint yourself.

✤**Rasta Boi Punany**: ANY system needs to be fair and not pick their favorite.

✤**Dakota Rain**: I personally do not like to do pageants, but a lot of people do. I do feel they need to be fair and should not be picked if they are a favorite of the bar or judges. This is something people work hard at so they should be rewarded for their effort and given constructive criticism.

✤**Stefon SanDiego**: With this being the year of equality and change within our communities as we know them, I believe pageants find themselves outdated. Pageantry systems sparked a frown in many aspects within our communities. Often I hear my brothers and sisters of the stage exclaim the unfair and unruly decisions as well as requirements. Honestly, I believe pageants need a more firm foundation of their criteria as transgender is becoming more frequently questioned.

✤**Vinnie Marconi**: Pageantry Systems need to grow with the times. There should be more transgender opportunities. Have a Mr. for biological boys, Mister for transgender men and maybe Ms.Ter for women as Kings. The same should apply to Queens. There needs to be more than one title for those six or nine, including alternates, that could be KING of the system. I love my transgender brothers, but there HAS to be some way to cut the animosity between us all. We need MORE definitive descriptions of categories. Styles change and what works for one system does not for another. The hems of pants, sleeve length, and a GOOD FIT need to be better defined so money is not wasted on trying a new system that has different standards or ideas of each category. Pageant Packages are NOT CHEAP and it is a shame to be turned off by a system because: 1) It does not have standardized guidelines for all judges. 2) It is not run professionally and timely. 3) They are not equipped for different possibilities of talents at the chosen venue. 4) REQUIRING contestants to stay at a host hotel when there are more cost effective alternatives for some. What should set apart the different systems would be what is written in the contract for the title winner. The requirements of the title are VERY important when competing! If you do not have a job that allows you to travel and the contract states MUCH traveling is required, then DO NOT compete! Too many systems keep the contract a secret until it is time to sign it, therefore I will not spend the time, energy, or money on that system.

✤**Stormm**: It would be nice if it were in most of the bars.

✤**Kenneth J. Squires**: I have seen many pageants for DRAG Queens, and it does seem like they have it better. I would like to see bigger and better pageants for DRAG Kings and Male Illusionists.

✤**Kruz Mhee**: I have only entered local pageants. I did run my own pageant at a local club for four years. I have yet to find the correct link in getting into the pageant system overall. I would truly love to see the King pageant system become more accessible.

✿**Hawk Stuart:** There should be more for the Kings and transgenders. There are a lot for the Queens but not enough for the rest.

✿**Flex Jonez:** Pageantry for Kings has grown widely over many years. When I began there were no King pageants. We had to enter the Queen pageants with hopes to win. Pageantry is like any other venue. If there is a demand for it, then it will be accessible.

✿**SirMandingo Thatis:** I am happy to see pageants specifically for Kings.

✿**Atown:** There is still a lot of work to do as far as expanding the systems of pageantry and getting the word out about Kings. I am a strong believer of the pageantry system I am currently involved in, and it is only getting bigger.

✿**E. M. Shaun:** Pageant are not cheap and the rules need to be clearly defined in a systems handbook and should be used as their standard by all that are used as judges. People get turned off by pageant bc they feel that they are rigged or that everyone wasn't judged by the same rulings. King pageants have grown over the years but the participation in them has not been very large for the most part. For eh future... There needs to be more promotion and maybe even pageantry school to aid/teach new kings of how to prepare for pageant. It feels really bad to work so hard, use all your time, spend all your money and then get judged so harshly especially if you did know about certain rules or structure.

✿**Cody Wellch Klondyke:** The DRAG King MI system is growing leaps and bounds. I am glad to see that. A few years ago you did not hear of DRAG Kings or Male Impersonators. You hear it more now today then yesterday. My titles are, Mr. Gay North Shore 2013, Slidell, Louisiana, USA. Mister USofA M.I. 2013, second alternate.

✿**George De Micheal:** I would like to see more DRAG Kings in the United Kingdom. DRAG Queens are more prominent. I hope also to inspire many other people to try it and be there for guidance and advice.

✿**Colin Grey:** I would like to see more entry-level pageants for Kings in my area. It seems they have more or less died out and it makes me sad.

✿**Jamel Knight:** I would like to see more pageants in different areas. There are quite a few National pageants but the majority of the contestants are from one of a few select regions. The more pageants and preliminaries there are in different areas the greater the variety of contestants and competition.

✿**Welland Dowd:** In Montréal, Quebec, Canada, we do not do pageants. Kings here are wary of a system based on hierarchy. No one cares if you hold a title; they care what you bring to stage. I find titles a little pretentious, but I also understand it is a big part of the DRAG scenes in other parts of the world.

✿**Jonah Godfather of DRAG:** I have not been involved in many pageants. I have done a few local ones and one national one. But just as a weekly show, Queens get more. I would like the pageantry system to do more to promote equally for Kings and Queens. It is true that Kings have not been as popular in the past but the King scene is growing and the pay should reflect that.

❊**B J Armani**: There are so many pageant systems! Problem is there are systems that are very large but have no M.I. or DRAG King division because they do not believe that Kings bring it as Queens do. It is sad but we just need to keep pushing our craft harder and smarter and NOT take any title that is out there for granted! It is not that hard to have a pageant system come to your area if you have the backing and the drive. Many bars do not even need a rent fee since they are making money on bar sales! Just make sure you are aware of travel costs and expenses: crown, sash, and potential money for nationals that you need to come up with for the winners.

❊**Crash Bandikok**: I have been in a few pageants and I am not sure all of them are one-hundred percent true. I do not perform anymore so I cannot speak for what it is like now, but I know back when I did perform it went off who you knew. I would like to see more King activity for sure

❊**Bootzy Edwards Collynz**: I am not involved with the pageant system. I have a few friends who hold titles and places in and on courts. I am always at the shows to support, but it is not appeal to me in joining right now.

❊**Lyle Love-It**: Find the ones available, give it your A-Game and dress to IMPRESS. Support the Female Illusionists and, for the most part, they will support us. FIGHT LIKE A GIRL. I learned my weak points, how to strengthen them, met NUMEROUS great people. Made many memories and hope to have made POSITIVE memories in others of myself.

❊**Xavier Bottoms**: Most pageantry systems are doing away with the At-Large title. I personally feel that whether you a biological boy, transgender male, male impersonator, large, tall, small, purple or orange, we are all entertainers, one category. As a M.I., it has really stepped up my game competing against biological males.

❊**Clark Kunt**: I love that some pageants here are moving towards accepting all kinds of different performance artists, giving those who do not fit the classic DRAG pigeonholes an opportunity. I am currently the King of Hearts and Mr. Menz. I have only competed in the two pageants; I have found that changing facial hair and hairstyle for each number, costuming and displaying a range of performance styles can separate performers during competition.

❊**Emilio**: Although I have won a pageant, they are not my cup of tea. I do not want to compete with other Kings; I just want to be me. It was great because it got my name out there, but I am not a fan of pageants. No competing for me.

❀**Juan Kerr**: We have a thing called 'DRAG Idol' and another called 'King of the Castle.' Whilst I applaud the people who have the flaps to enter, (why do we have to say balls?) I personally do not like them. I also think they can sometimes just be a popularity contest, who has the most friends there? I do not like competitions though because I am a very bad loser, so I will not do them.

❀**Brandon KC Young-Taylor**: There are several systems run by different people for a reason, we all fit in differently. What is great for one, may not be great for another and that should always be okay! I won the very first pageant I ever competed in. It was an amazing experience and I think that is why I love to compete. The best part is that it was the Brotherhood of Kings in my hometown all competing against each other! Since this time, I have won and lost several pageants. Losing never feels good but it is something I think every person should experience. How else is a national titleholder going to be able to understand what those other Kings are feeling after he is crowned?

❀**Santana Romero**: I believe that most pageant systems are set up for Queens to dominate and the Kings to be thrown a bone every once in a while. Even National titles with King and M.I. categories are still treated as third best in comparison to Queens and male leads. I believe we need more systems that are run by KINGS for KINGS and KINGS only. In order for this to happen, we all must come together and really step up to the plate for ourselves. As shady as Queens can be, they really know how to come together for the betterment of their own community and Kings should really learn to do the same. I believe the only way we can be taken more seriously in EVERY aspect of our craft, is to create our own paths to success and stop relying on people who do not understand what we do to make them for us. That way we can get better prize packages, better treatment and more acknowledgement for what we work so hard for because our fellow brothers understand why we are here.

❀**Smitty O'Toole**: I have not participated in pageants because I have seen rigged pageants and creativity that is out of the box. I am Houston's DRAG Race All-Star winner, Texas, USA. I was the only King among eleven Queens.

❀**Jensen C. Dean**: In the future I hope to see the Kings having as many pageant options as our Queen counterparts have.

❀**Devin G. Dame**: There are still good National Pageant Systems out there for Kings. My suggestion is to research anything and everything about the system before getting into it. Know who is running it and for what reasons. The promoters and titleholders will continue to promote their pageants. Kings need this growth to create good strong avenues to express their want and desire to see who may be the best.

Chapter Forty-One
"Where do you see this craft in ten years? What do impersonators need to do, to enable it to positively move in the right direction?"

❀**D-Luv Saviyon:** My HOPE is that the art of Male Illusion will be equivalent to bookings, prize packages and respect received by our Queen counterparts. I also hope that we get on one united page as Male Illusionists. There is so much separation between us from one area to the next, and from system to system. At the end of the day, we all should have one common goal and that is not just furthering ourselves as entertainers, but to further the art of Male Impersonation as a whole.

❀**Adam All:** I think we need to engage with our audiences more. See what they want and not just put out what we think is working. I think the 'Lesbian' arm of the LGBTQI, Lesbian, Gay, Bi, Transgender, Queer, Intersex, with Steven Fry; family is hopelessly appalling when it comes to supporting the art. Maybe that is just the United Kingdom, but I feel it is going to take some innovation to do what they want and bring them out to the clubs. There is enormous scope for diversity in styles and talent, we could easily have Kings that juggle, do magic, contemporary dance, mini plays, unicycling, and break dancing. I have introduced beat boxing, which has gone down well, ukulele, and guitar playing are well received. We have more room to play with ideas than the Queens because the rules are not yet set in stone.

❀**Travis Luvermore:** I would hope all cities and states embrace the craft; I am in an area where there are no venues that totally embrace the King community. I would love to see the DRAG communities work hand in hand.

❀**Travis Hard:** I hope to see our craft get as big as the Queen's craft or bigger. I hope I can turn on the television one day and watch a show similar to RuPaul's DRAG Race.

❀**Chance Wise:** We need to persevere and continue to grow. Kings will have the same respect as the Queens as long as we do not give up and continue to up the game as many performers have done. Ten years from now, I see the art of Male Illusion celebrated alongside our Queen counterparts.

❀**Shane Rebel Caine:** Kings are respected more and seen as equals to Queens. As impersonators we need to encourage those around us who express interest in it, help our fellow entertainers no matter how young or old they are and no matter what do not put down anyone who wants to try or is just starting to perform.

❀**Dakota Rain:** I think as Kings we need to show respect, honor, and show everyone that, we too can draw a crowd, perform, and have fun doing it. I would like to see the art of DRAG Kings as a better form of entertainment, meaning, we as Kings work hard to do what we do. We want to make people smile and be happy and want them leaving saying, "Now that was a show and I cannot wait to see him again!"

❀Ashton The Adorable Lover: I hope we become equal to our DRAG Queen counterparts, to unite more and come together. We also need to keep doing it, introducing shows to areas that have none and bring up more talent rather through a talent show, work shop and bring them into our family.

❀Freddy Prinze Charming: I would love to see more Kings take pride in the art that is Male Illusion. It is more than just dressing like a dude and strutting about on stage. There is potential in this craft, so much that can be done, but not enough are doing it. I do not want people to have puzzled looks when someone says they are a King or an Illusionist. We should be just as well known as the Queens, but we need to work to get there. I would love to see bar owners and show directors hold Kings to the same esteem they hold the Queens. We need to push those boundaries, push our own limits, and try new things. Make people stand up and take notice.

❀Ben Eaten: My hope is to see the King community soar and grow. I wish that the communities, King and Queen, could work together to grow the entertainment together instead of it being a battle between the two. I have been turned down for shows because, "They do not book Kings." which I do not think is a mindset one should have. I hope that mindset is on its way out.

❀Clint Torres: In ten years I hope male impersonators will be freely excepted on RuPual's DRAG Race or maybe we'll even have our own with Landon Cider and King Phantom. What I hope for is for people to know what a DRAG king is as easily as they know the queens and we'll all be on equal playing fields. I believe that in order to obtain this we kings need to start leaving our mark more on the world. Let them know that we're here and that we're not going anywhere. We work just as hard and just as long as the queens do and we deserve the same type of recognition

❀Rasta Boi Punany: Hopefully, this craft will get stronger and those who are on this journey will continue to do the best that we can to promote and maintain a positive presence in the world of entertainment.

❀Kenneth J. Squires: I would like to see DRAG Kings and Male Illusionists have the same venues as DRAG Queens. To be equals in the world of entertaining. I also hope that DRAG Kings and Male Illusionists are more popular in the years to come.

❀Pierce Gabriel: I can see DRAG becoming a big entertainment field. I think the biggest obstacle is that most people do not know what it is all about. We need to start bringing in more people who have never been to DRAG shows before. Invite your friends, coworkers, and family. Awareness is the key to appreciation.

❋**Vinnie Marconi:** It would be nice when I go to a regular Queen Bar to perform, that they don't have to explain WHAT a King is!!! I would LOVE for newbies to take this art form seriously, as queens do, and not just as a hobby or to impress their friends. A LOT of work goes into perfecting the "look" so people don't believe I'm a woman, and the performance is the icing on the cake. I believe it is important to take on the whole persona when I'm in "Vinnie mode" and that is the characteristics of a man. It's hard for me to appreciate a King who comes off the stage and squeals like a little girl back stage... Have fun, YES, but it IS a job and as a professional, act accordingly.

❋**Kruz Mhee:** Kings will be as respected as Queens. It would be awesome to be addressed accordingly. I think the craft will be huge in comparison to what it is now.

❋**Flex Jonez:** Performers need to be more visible, need a venue for the craft to be seen, and should join forces with each other toward presenting the craft.

❋**Silk Steele Prince:** I see myself teaching newcomers and guiding them in a good direction that suits their style and needs as a great performer. I believe impersonators need to embrace each other in a brotherhood fashion to enable a positive outcome.

❋**SirMandingo Thatis:** I would like to see all my Kings united and helping one another to better the craft and to keeping going in a positive direction.

❋**Stormm:** I hope to be around teaching the young ones that are coming on, uniting the Kings so we can be just as big and respected as the Queens.

❋**Colin Grey:** I hope that it is still alive and well in my area. I hope to see some talented, humble, and dedicated Kings in ten years.

❋**Phantom:** I hope to leave an imprint on the DRAG world. I hope to start a makeup line for Kings. I would love to have a place where I can teach makeup, sewing, and prop making. The dream seems far away but my goal is to put Kings on the map.

❋**B J Armani:** I do not see our craft leaving existence anytime soon. I see TV shows that may be like RuPaul's DRAG Race but geared towards DRAG Kings. I see more and more Kings becoming mainstream and popular. The only way to keep this momentum is to be kind to each other as performers and to continue to push every envelope. NEVER be satisfied and ALWAYS continue to drive yourself and remember THE SHOW IS ABOUT THE AUDIENCE.

❋**Jamel Knight:** In ten years we will have a much bigger presence in the LGBT entertainment world and in mainstream society, in general. If we continue to grow as entertainers and push the envelope as far as performance, costumes, and productions, I can see DRAG Kings being just as visible as DRAG Queens. Respect is earned and not given therefore we have to continue working collectively to perfect this craft and show that we can be just as entertaining as the Queens and should be seen just as much.

❦**Howie Feltersnatch**: In ten years I see myself still performing outrageous numbers, but to bigger crowds. I think that with exposure of Kings on mainstream TV we could have more respect from the other art forms.

❦**Welland Dowd:** I am hoping people will be more aware of DRAG Kings in the future. I always get a "Whaaaaaa?" when I tell people I am a King.

❦**Julius M. SeizeHer:** Kings and Queens will be all over. People will be booking us left and right.

❦**Lyle Love-It:** KEEP SONGS and PRODUCTION respectable!

❦**Jonah Godfather of DRAG:** I hope to see Kings bigger, better, and with the same equality as Queens for bookings and pay. Kings need to learn and improve.

❦**Campbell Reid Andrews:** In ten years I would hope that the King community would really come together. Not just in our own towns or systems but as a nation. I feel that right now we are still somewhat divided, even in some city communities there is division. I also feel if we would find the time to help newcomers in the art, along with friends and family, then we will succeed. There is so much that each of us can learn from one another. If we utilize all of our resources, we will grow this industry and community farther than others would expect. I would hope that in ten years new and seasoned performers realize that how they portray or execute their performances really does reflect on all of us. So take pride in costumes, concepts, makeup, binding, and everything else.

❦**Jack E. Dickinson:** I hope that people will increasingly avoid imposing limits on their performances based on social attitudes toward gender. DRAG performers should not impose gender rules on each other. We can be at the vanguard of gender exploration; show the world what is possible! I would hope that the DRAG community can model anti-oppression in all its forms and become more and more accessible to people from various marginalized communities. Finally, I would hope that the focus moves away from competition and closer to mutual support. We should all work together to help each other realize accomplishments We all have our own gifts to share and to appreciate amongst ourselves and with our audiences.

❦**Clark Kunt:** I truly hope that we will be able to remember the history of DRAG, as a space for marginalized performers to break the mold. I hope that we are able to expand our concept of what it means to be a DRAG performer beyond the King and Queen binary, to open the boxes and our minds to a whole variety of gender performances. DRAG Queers, Gender Fuck DRAG, Gender Benders, DRAGlesque, there are so many ways of performing that are deserving of the spotlight and our attentionWe will have shows that blend multiple styles, and that performers of all types can respect and work with one another to advance the art form. ❦**Emilio**: I think in ten years DRAG Kings will be mainstream. It is not just for the Queens anymore.

❀**Juan Kerr**: In the United Kingdom the scene will be as big as it is in the USA. Kings will stop with the bitchiness and get behind each other, to be mainstream like Queens.

❀**DeVery Bess**: I do not plan on leaving any time soon, but I want it to be common for Kings to get paid to do what they do. I would like to not have to explain my craft, and erase the stigma that, "Kings just wear their day clothes and perform."

❀**Trey C. Michaels**: I hope in ten years that Kings will be seen on the same level as Queens. That what we do is an art and that we put a lot of time into our art.

❀**Bailey Saint James**: Kudos to Landon Cider and his attempt at making RuPaul's DRAG race! This is where our craft is going. One day we will be a DRAG Queen's equal.

❀**Xavier Bottoms**: in ten years, I would hope that my efforts to "pave the way" would go unbroken. Keep the brotherhood going. Books like this one will help. Reach out to each other. Our art of Illusion has to be seen and heard everywhere. I truly see a bright future for these kids. There are some amazing, talent and beautiful people in this craft. There are so many pageantry systems, a great brotherhood. Get involved. Do not be afraid to take the next step.

❀**Aaron Phoenix**: Kings will have stepped up to the level of recognition and respect that Queens have in the LGBT, Lesbian Gay, Bi, Transgender, and Queer community. Kings need to pave the way by keeping up with the Queens in costuming, productions, energy on stage and entertainment value in general.

❀**Thug Passion**: I see the craft for the Kings continuing to grow. There will be more pageants out there for Kings. In order for it to continue, Kings need to keep the brotherhood going. Continue to work together. It is a lot easier to make an impact as a group then it is as an individual.

❀**MaXx Decco**: The DRAG King art and scene is growing. Excited to be part of it. Today's Kings are stepping up to become tomorrow's leaders; teaching newcomers, blurring lines of gender and standing tall next to our beautiful Queen counterparts.

❀**Soco Dupree**: I would love to see us just as mainstream as the Female Illusionists on RuPaul's DRAG Race.

❀**Stefon Royce Iman**: DRAG Kings as the new line of entertainment on TV and movies.

❀**Cody Wellch Klondyke**: I would like to see DRAG Kings and Male Illusionists have the same venues as DRAG Queens. I would like the Kings and Queens to share the stage because we are one big family and for everyone to be treated as equals in the world of entertaining. I also hope that DRAG Kings and M.I.'s are more popular in the years to come since we are growing and moving mountains.

❀**E. M. Shaun**: As Kings, we need to keep the truthfulness of the brotherhood going. I think DRAG Kings will get more respect for their craft and maybe one day there will be a male version of RuPaul's DRAG race.

❀**Smitty O'Toole**: I am not sure where I see the craft in ten years. I hope it has evolved to be a bit more original to each performer's performance. I would hope it continues to become more diverse and open.

❀**LoUis CYfer**: In ten years, I think DRAG will be mainstream all we need to do is keep positive and remember why we do this. For our audience!

❀**Spacee Kadett**: Remember when "Survivor" premiered on CBS? Remember when it was THE "it" reality TV game show...the ONLY one? For our genderbending community, that is RuPaul's DRAG Race. So many projections about RPDR adding a king. Or a king version. Maybe. Possibly. But no. In ten years (which will be 2024, at the time I am writing this), I don't entirely know if RPDR will still be churning out new seasons...I mean, really, does RuPaul herself want to keep doing this that long?? Today, casting directors are already pitching king shows to major networks. Within the next decade, we will see an explosion of gender-bending entertainment on a number of major networks -- yes, bigger than LOGO -- that will showcase queens, kings, males and femmes alike. In ten years, we kings will have nearly matched our queen counterparts with make-up, contouring, high-quality wigs and elaborate costumes as our norm. We will see a much wider spectrum of identities celebrating our art at professional levels: transmen, butches, femmes, bisexual and straight women all bringing incredible illusion and performance to the stage. We will have major casts with equal balances of kings and queens -- not six queens to one king, for example -- and the prestige and compensation in pageantry and performance to match our queen counterparts as well. But we MUST do our part. We MUST hit the stage with the make-up, hair, costuming, and entertainment value of our long-celebrated queen counterparts. It's extra hard for us kings: male illusion does NOT naturally lend itself to the stage. And even with the time and effort, a fully-painted king face, for example, is never appreciated as a queen face. We don't have the luxury of rouge, lashes, lipstick, big wigs, high heels, jewelry, ruffles, curves, lace...but we can overcome that and prove how amazing we are. I truly feel that today, in 2014, society is just at the threshold of recognizing that. We are moving faster than ever, and by 2024, we will be celebrating male illusion as an art form that is as well-refined, commanding, respected and acknowledged as that of the greatest DRAG queens.

❀**Jensen C. Dean**: In ten years, I hope that we have grown to have a presence as large as the Queens. Maybe our own version of DRAG Race. The best thing we can do to help progress things along in a positive way is to make sure that we hold ourselves to high standards, pass those standards to new performers, and help them do the same.

✿Luke Ateraz: Hopefully it will have expanded in recognition. With the younger generation of Kings coming out like, Cody Ateraz, Mr. Jr. Phoenix Gay Pride 2013, age sixteen. The youngest King I know of is Wayne Depain who just turned ten years old. I hope that Kings and M.I's will be more mainstream in the future.

✿William Vanity Matrix: In ten years, I want to see our Kings as commonly well known as DRAG Queens. Maybe have our own DRAG Race, or shows on TV dedicated to our craft. I would like Kings to be as mainstream as our Queen counterparts.

✿Kameo Dupree: Ten years from now, if health allows, I will still be on the stage. I live the life I love and love the life I live!

✿Bootzy Edwards Collynz: Ten years from now, I think I would still like to be performing if the good Lord is willing to keep me going. I see the art of Male Impersonation becoming as big as it is for the Queens. Maybe even our own DRAG Race and other shows that deal with the art. I also see the art forming more categories for recognition, like the Queens' androgynous subsets. I definitely feel that our presence will be a lot stronger and more equally recognized on the same scale as our Queens. I love performing and dancing. As long as I am able to produce good quality work, I will do it.

✿Master Cameron Eric Leon: I want to see it grow as a respectable profession. It is not enough to be equally recognized as DRAG Queens because even they deserve more commendation. I want to see us in the mainstream; I want to see us hired for all kinds of events because we belong there and have the entertainment value, not simply as a novelty or second thought.

✿Devin G. Dame: I hope to see both Queens and Kings truly on the same level. We have come a long way but still have a long way to go. The Kings continue to go above and beyond and we will be on the same page across the country sooner than later.

✿Napoleon Bonerparte: I really hope that before the ten-year mark is reached, that we see equality between all performers along with a sense of pride and solidarity! There is far too much division in our community. I think the only way to enable positive growth in the DRAG and queer entertainer's world, is to reach out to fellow performers, troupes and casts. Communicate, support each other's shows whenever possible, create a community, work together, have a support system. Be kind.

Pass this book on to another male impersonator…
or better yet, go on DRAG411.com
to get them their own book!

The interns of both DRAG Guides. Content: Feddy Prinze Charming, Spacee Kadet, Gail Hoffmeyer, Napoleon Bonerparte, Anna Hairfield, along with Vincent and Lynn Marconi helped format the book set to maximize included content created by the impersonators.

Counterclockwise
Spacee Kadett (Out of face) credit: BravoBravo!
Freddy Prinze Charming Credit: Gabe King Photography
Gail Hoffmeyer photo credit - Kiki Colunga
Napoleon Bonerparte photo credit - self
Karen J. Melchionne, aka Vinnie Marconi photo credit - Alex Melo Photography

Ten Black Books

Book 1 DRAG411's
"DRAG Bully, A Survivor's Guide"

The Largest Bullying Project in LGBT History for Struggling Entertainers. Advice from over a hundred male, female, and androgynous impersonators around the world to help entertainers struggling with their family, peers, relationships, neighbors, regular jobs, venues, and successfully overcoming self-doubt. Best Selling author Todd Kachinski Kottmeier created DRAG411 to document the lives of male, female, and androgynous impersonator years ago. It is now the largest organization for impersonators on earth with over 7,000 entertainers in 32 countries. DRAG411 also operates The International Original, Official DRAG Memorial with almost a thousand names (2018). This is his 25th book, 20th World Record, and 12th book on this subject. Thousands of invitations to contribute were send out. This book contains the best of their responses, in their own words, to you.

Book 2 DRAG411's
"Original DRAG Handbook"

Over 155 female impersonators (and 1 male impersonator) from around the world share over a thousand insightful comments in the first handbook created of this art form.

Commentary shared with Todd Kachinski Kottmeier included the following contributors of The Original, DRAG Handbook to include Ada Buffet, Adora , Adrian Leigh, Afeelya Bunz, Alisa Summers, Alanna Divine, Alexis De La Mer, Alexis Mateo, Alex Serpa, Allure, Amanda Bone, Amanda Love, Amy DeMilo, Anastaia Fallon, Astasnaia Rexia, Angel gLamar, Angela Dodd, Anita Cox, April Fresh, Ashleigh Cooley, Aurora Sexton, Babette Schwartz, Bailey St. James, Barbra Herr, Barbra Seville, Beverly LaSalle, BJ Stephens, Blair Michaels, Brandon M. Caten, Brianna Lee, Brittany Moore, Brookyln Bisette, Bukkake Blaque London St. James, Cartier Paris, Cathy Craig, Champagne T. Bordeaux, Cherry Darling, Christina Paris, CoCo LaBelle, CoCo Montrese, CoCo St. James, Conundrum, Crystal Belle, Daniel Murphy, Danika Fierce, Daphne Ferraro, Dasha Nicole, Dee Gregory, Deva DaVyne, Diamond Dunhill, Diedra Windsor Walker, Dmentia Divinyl/Eva LaDeva, Echo Dazz, Esme Russell, Estelle Rivers, Eunyce Raye, Felica Fox, Felina Cashmere, Geraldine Queen Cabaret, Ginger Minj, Glitz Glam, Gilda Golden, Horchata, Ima Twat, Ineeda Twat, Jade Daniels, Jade Jolie, Jade Shanell, Jade Sotomayo, Jaeda Fuentes, Jami Micheals, Jay Santana, Jeffrey Powell, Jenna Chambers Tisdale, Jessica Jade, Jocelyn Summers, Jodie Holliday, Joey Brooks, Joshua Myers, J.P. Patrick, Juwanna Jackson, Kamden Wells, Katrina Starr, Kenny Braverman, Khrystal Leight, Kier Sarkesian, Kiki LaFlare Santangilo, Kitty D'Meaner, Kori Stevens, Krystal Amore Adonis, Lacey Lynn Taylors, Lady Clover Honey, Lady Sabrina, Lady TaJma Hall, Lakeisha Pryce, LeeAnna Love, Leigh Shannon, Lisa Carr, Lola Honey, Madisyn De La Mer, Makayla Rose Devine, Maxine Padlock (Maxi Pad), Melissa Morgan, Melody

Mayheim, Michael Wilson, Mike Astermon-Glidden, Mis Sadistic, Miss Conception, Miss Gigi, Mr. Kenneth Blake, Misty Eyez, Monique Michaels, Myah Monroe, Mystique Summers, Nairobi V. D'Viante, Naomi D-Lish, Naomi Wynters, Nicole Paige Brooks, Nikki Dynamite, Nova Starr, Ororo, Patrica Grand, Patricia Knight, Patrica Mason, Pandora DeStrange, Penelope Reigns, Polly FunkChanel, Phiore Star Liemont, Purrzsa Kyttyn, Pussy LeHoot, Raquel Payne, Rhyana Vorhman, Rickie Lee, Rusti Fawcett, Scarlett Fever, Selina Kyle, Shae Shae LaReese, Shealita Babay, Shugah Caine, Stephanie Roberts, Stephanie Stuart, Stormy Vain, Summer Breeze, Sybil Storm, Tabatha Lovall, Tatum Michelle, Teri Courtney, Tiffani Middlesexx, Timm McBride, Toni Davyne, TotiYanah Diamond,Trixie LaRue, Trixie Pleasures, Vegas Platinum, Venus D Lite, Vivika D'Angelo, Wendel Duppert and Wendy G. Kennedy.

Book 3: DRAG411's
"Crown Me! Winning Pageants"

Hundreds of invitations sent to the titleholders, pageant promoters, judges, and talent show hosts to share their insight on not only winning pageants and contests but also owning the stage every time they perform. Their topics included auxiliary steps to success needed for song selection, dancing, movement on stage, props, backup dancers, creating your own edge, personal interviews, steps to success for winning the talent category every time you step on stage, on stage questions, eveningwear, and creative costuming. They discussed in their own unedited words, wardrobe changes, makeup, hair, shoes, when is the time to compete, qualities needed for a judge, and the top misconceptions of contestants competing in the pageantry systems.

Commentary shared with Todd Kachinski Kottmeier included the following contributors of Crown Me! to include AJ Menendez, Amy Demilo, Anastacia Dupree, Anson Reign, Bob Taylor, Breonna Tenae, Brittany T Moore, Coco Montrese, Dana Douglas, Darryl Kent, Denise Russell, Dey Jzah Opulent, Freddy Prinze Charming, Gage Gatlyn, Jay Santana , Jayden Knight, Jennifer Foxx, Joey Jay, Kori Stevens, Mis Sadistic, Mykul Jay Valentine, Natasha Richards, Rico Taylor, Sam Hare, Stephanie Stuart, Taina T. Norell, Tiffani Middlesexx, Tori Taylor, Ty Nolan, Vinnie Marconi, and Vivika D'Angelo.

Book 4: DRAG411's
"DRAG King Guide"

Over 155 male impersonators around the world share over a thousand insightful comments in forty-one chapters.

Commentary shared with Todd Kachinski Kottmeier included the following contributors of The Official DRAG King and Male Impersonators Guide to include Aaron Phoenix, Abs Hart, Adam All, Adam DoEve, AJ Menendez, Alec Allnight, Alexander Cameron, Alik Muf, Andrew Citino, Anjie Swidergal, Anson Reign, Ashton The Adorable Lover, Atown, Ayden Layne, B J Armani, B J Bottoms, Bailey Saint James, Ben Doverr, Ben Eaten, Bootzy Edwards Collynz, Brandon KC Young-Taylor, Bruno Diaz, Cage Masters, Campbell Reid Andrews, Chance Wise, Chandler J Hart, Chasin Love, Cherry Tyler Manhattan, Chris Mandingo, Clark Kunt, Clint Torres, Cody Wellch Klondyke, Colin Grey, Corey James Caster, Coti Blayne, Crash Bandikok, Dakota Rain, Dante Diamond, Davion Summers, DeVery Bess, Devin G. Dame, Devon Ayers, Dionysus W Khaos, Diseal Tanks Roberts, D-Luv Saviyon, Dominic Demornay, Dominic Von Strap, D-Rex, Dylan Kane, E. M. Shaun, Eddie C. Broadway, Emilio, Erick LaRue, Flex Jonez, Freddy

Prinze Charming, Gabe King, Gage Gatlyn, George De Micheal, Greyson Bolt, Gunner Gatlyn, Gus Magendor, Hawk Stuart, Harry Pi, Holden Michael, Howie Feltersnatch, Hurricane Savage, J Breezy St James, Jack E. Dickinson, Jack King, Jake Van Camp, Jamel Knight, Jenson C. Dean, Johnnie Blackheart, Jonah Godfather of DRAG, Jordan Allen, Jordan Reighn, Joshua K. Mann, Joshua Micheals, Juan Kerr, Julius M. SeizeHer, Jude Lawless, Justin Cider, Justin Luvan, Justin Sider, K'ne Cole, Kameo Dupree, Kenneth J. Squires, King Dante, King Ramsey, Jack Inman, Kody Sky, Koomah, Kristian Kyler, Kruz Mhee, Linda Hermann-Chasin, Luke Ateraz, Lyle Love-It, Macximus, Marcus Mayhem, Marty Brown, Master Cameron Eric Leon, Max Hardswell, MaXx Decco, Michael Christian, Mike Oxready, Miles Long, Mr-Charlie Smith, Nanette D'angelo Sylvan, Nolan Neptune, Orion Blaze Browne, Owlejandro Monroe, Papa Cherry, Papi Chulo, Papi Chulo Doll, Persian Prince, Phantom, Pierce Gabriel, Rasta Boi Punany, Rico M Taylor, Rock McGroyn, Rocky Valentino, Rogue DRAG King, Romeo Sanchez, Rychard "Alpha" Le'Sabre, Ryder Knightly, Ryder Long, Sam Masterson, Sammy Silver, Santana Romero, Scorpio, Shane Rebel Caine, Shook ByNature, Silk Steele Prince, SirMandingo Thatis, Smitty O'Toole, Soco Dupree, Spacee Kadett, Starr Masters, Stefan LeDude, Stefon Royce Iman, Stefon SanDiego, Stormm, Teddy Michael, Thug Passion, Travis Luvermore, Travis Hard, Trey C. Michaels, Trigger Montgomery, Tyler Manhattan, Viciouse Slick, Vinnie Marconi, Welland Dowd, William Vanity Matrix, Wulf Von Monroe, Xander Havoc, and Xavier Bottoms.

Book 5: DRAG411's
"DRAG Stories"

Funny stories shared with Todd Kachinski Kottmeier including the following contributors of DRAG Stories to include Chance Wise, Anson Reign, Tiffani Middlesexx, Rico Taylor, Todd Kachinski Kottmeier, Bob Taylor, Stefon Royce Iman, Candi Samples, Alexis Mateo, Naomi Wynters, Dmentia Divinyl, Bruce Lacie, Kennedy Wendy, Chastity Rose, Miss GiGi, Angel gLamar, Patricia Grand, Shook ByNature, Lady Guy, Eunyce Raye, Charley Marie Coutora, Jezzie Bell, Lamar Kellam, Jayden St. James, Rachelle Ann Summers, Champagne T Bordeaux, Gilda Golden, Daisha Monet, Vivika D'Angelo, Rachel Boheme, Esme Rodriguez, and MaNu Da Original.

Book 6: DRAG411's
"DRAG Mother, DRAG Father" Honoring Mentors

Performers look to DRAG mothers, DRAG fathers, friends, and fans for insight, compassion, and guidance as mentors. This book honors those special people. Over 140 entertainers contributed wisdom and words for this historical book, making it the largest project of its nature in GLBTQ history and the first published book on male and female mentors.

Commentary shared with Todd Kachinski Kottmeier included the following contributors of DRAG Parents to includee AJ Menendez, Vinnie Marconi, Mis Sadistic, Todd Kachinski Kottmeier, Bob Taylor, Taina Norell, Andrew Stratton, Horchata Horchata, David Warner, Gianna Love, Trinity Taylor, Domunique Jazmin Vizcaya, Brittany Moore, PurrZsa Kyttyn, Jake Lickus, Shelita Taylor, Adriana Manchez, MiMi Welch, China Taylor, Armondis Bone't, Monique Trudeau, Simeon Codfish, Diamond Dupree, Stefon Royce Iman, Jayden Stjames, Demonica da Bomb, Colin Grey, Christopher Todd Guy, Celyndra Lashay Clyne, Candice St. James, Justin Barnes Williams, Ivanna Dooche, London Taylor Douglas, Christina Alexandria Victoria Regina Lowe, Bianca DeMonet, Critiqa Mann, Jazmen Andrews, AJ Allen, TotiYanah Diamond, D' Marco Knight, Chip Matthews, Mirage Montrese, India Starr Simms, Jade S Stratton, Emerald Divine, Elysse Giovanni, Vanity Halston, Kristofer Reynolds, Akasha Uravitch, Adriana Fuentes, Erykah Mirage, Felicity Ferraro, Joey Payge, Rhiannon Todd, Vicious Slick, Amirage Saling, Tori Sass, Chy'enne Valentino, and Robbi Lynn.

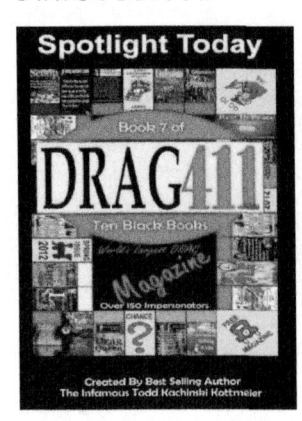

Book 7:   DRAG411's
"Spotlight Today"

It was the World's Largest Paperback Magazine for Impersonators and Fans when it premiered with over 175 pages. DRAG411 no longer prints Spotlight Today Magazine, but here is the re-release of the groundbreaking first edition. Complete articles by Vinnie Marconi, Denise Russell, Tiffani T. Middlesexx, Kristofer Reynolds, Magenta Alexandria Dupree, Butch Daddy, Vivikah Kayson-Raye, Makanoe, Amanda Lay, Thomas DeVoyd, Kevin B. Reed, Glenn Storm, and over 150 impersonators from around the world.

Book 8:   DRAG411's
"DRAG Queen Guide"

Almost two hundred female impersonators around the world share over a thousand insightful comments in forty-one chapters.
Commentary shared with Todd Kachinski Kottmeier included the following contributors of Official DRAG Queen and Female Impersonator Handbook to include Alana Summers, Alexis Marie Von Furstenburg, Alize', Aloe Vera, Alysin Wonderland, Amanda Bone DeMornay, Amanda Lay, Amanda Roberts, Amy DeMilo, Anastasia Fallon, Angie Ovahness, Anita Mandinite, Appolonia Cruz, Ashlyn Tyler, Aurora Tr'Nele Michelle, Azia Sparks, Barbie Dayne, Barbra Herr, Beverly LaSalle, Bianca DeMonet, Bianca Lynn Breeze, Blair Michaels, Boxxa Vine, Brittany T Moore, Britney Towers, Brandi Amara Skyy, Brooke Lynn Bradshaw, Candi Samples, Candi Stratton, Candy Sugar, Cathy Craig, Catia Lee Love, CeCe Georgia, Cee-Cee LaRouge-Avalon, Celeste Starr, Chad Michaels, Chevon Davis, Cheyenne Desoto Mykels, Chi Chi Lalique, Christina Collins, Chrystal Conners, Claudia B Eautiful, Coca Mesa, Coco St James, Damiana LaRoux, Dana Scrumptious, Danyel Vasquez, Dee Gregory, Delores T. Van-Cartier, Demonica DaBaum, Denise Russell, Diamond Dunhill, Diva Lilo, Diva Savage, Dove, EdriAna Treviño, Elle Emenopé, Elysse Giovanni, Erica James, Esmé Rodríguez, Estella Sweet, Eunyce Raye, Eva Nichole Distruction, Faleasha Savage, Felicia Minor, Felicity Frockaccino, Gigi Masters, Ginger Alley, Ginger Gigi Diamond, Ginger Kaye Belmont, Glitz Glam, Grecia Montes D' Occa, Heather Daniels, Hennessy Heart, Hershae Chocolatae, Holy McGrail, Hope B Childs, Horchata, India Brooks, India Ferrah, Ivy Profen, Izzy Adahl, Jaclyn St James, Jade Iroq, Jade Sotomayor, Jade Taylor Stratton, Jamie-Ree Swan, Jennifer Warner, Jessica Brooks, Jexa Ren'ae Van de Kamp, Joey Brooks, Jonny Pride, Kamelle Toe, Karma Jayde Addams, Kelly Turner, Mama Savannah Georgia, Mr. Kenneth Blake, Kamden T. Rage, Kira Stone-St James, Kirby Kolby, Kita Rose, Krysta Radiance, Lacie Bruce, Lady Jasmine Michaels, Lady Pearl, Lady Sabrina, Latrice Royale, LaTonga Manchez, Leona Barr, Lexi Alexander, Lilo Monroe, Lindsay Carlton, Lucinda Holliday, Lunara Sky, Lupita Chiquita Michaels Alexander, Madam Diva Divine, Mahog Anny, Makayla Michelle Davis Diamond, Mariah Cherry, Maxine Padlock, Melody Mayheim, Menaje E'toi, Mercede Andrews, Mi$hal, Mia Fierce, Michelle Leigh Sterling, Miss Diva Savage, Miss GiGi, Misty Eyez, Mitze Peterbilt, Monica Mystique, Montrese Lamar Hollar, Morgana DeRaven, Muffy Vanbeaverhousen, Natasha Richards, Nathan Loveland, Nicole Paige Brooks, Nikki Garcia, Nostalgia Todd Ronin, Olivia St James, Paige Sinclair, Pandora DeCeption, Pheobe James,

Reia'Cheille Lucious, Robyn Demornay, Robyn Graves, Rhonda Sheer, Rose Murphy, Ruby Diamond NY, Ruby Holiday, Ryan Royale, Rychard "Alpha" Le'Sabre, Rye Seronie, Sable Monay, Sabrina Kayson-Raye, Samantha St Clair, Sanaa Raelynn, Sapphire T. Mylan, Sasha Phillips, Savannah Rivers, Savannah Stevens, Selina Kyle, Sha'day Halston-St James, ShaeShae LaReese, Shamya Banx, Shana Nicole, Shaunna Rai, Sierra Foxx White, Sierra Santana, Sonja Jae Savage, Stella D'oro, Strawberry Whip, Sugarpill, Tasha Carter, Tanna Blake, Taquella Roze, Tawdri Hipburn, Taylor Rockland, Tempest DuJour, Tiffani T. Middlesexx, Traci Russell, Trudy Tyler, Vanessa del Rey, Velveeta WhoreMel, Vera Delmar, Vicky Summers, Vita DeVine, Vivian Sorensin, Vivian Von Brokenhymen, Vivika D'Angelo-Steele, Wendy G. Kennedy, Willmuh Dickfit, Wynter Storm, Yasmine Alexander and ZuZu Bella.

Book 9: DRAG411's (Two Comedy Scripts) **"Best Said Dead"** and **"Following Wynter"**

Best Said Dead examines in funny conversations those brief minutes after a person dies. Many religions and beliefs define different paths for each of us. Rarely do we discuss those precious moments between death and the final destination. This comedy opens the possibilities that for a moment, a person vanishes into the memories in their mind. Any part can be male, female, or ambiguous.

Following Wynter is a hilarious comedy play. Ethan discovers his newlywed husband is the flamboyant DRAG queen Wynter Storm in this whimsical farce with an important message of believing in yourself and your friends. . . even if your friend is Serena Silver. Any part can be male, female, or ambiguous.

Book 10:   DRAG411's
"DRAG World"
The contributing writers of DRAG411's "Spotlight Magazine," the World's Largest Paperback Magazine for Impersonators and Fans when it premiered in 2012 with over 175 pages, created this companion book. DRAG411 no longer prints Spotlight Today Magazine, but above you will find Book 7 is the re-release of the groundbreaking first edition. Complete chapters on DRAG Marketing by DRAG411.
Complimentary articles on Confidence, Duct Tape, Music Selection, Living Divinely, authentic stage presence, Pageants, having fun performing, jewelry, legislative information from the United States and around the world, the Old School performers, Virgin stage performers, and payday from contributing writers including Denise Russell, Jay Santana, Chance Wise, Vivikah Kayson-Raye, AJ Menedez, Glenn Storm, Freddy Prinze Charming, Gage Gatlyn, Kevin B. Reed, and over 100 impersonators from around the world!

Other books from the Best Selling author
The Infamous **Todd Kachinski Kottmeier**

"Turn Around Bright Eyes, The DRAG Queen Killer"

Few crimes in gay history rocked a nation as great as The DRAG Queen Killer. The country seemed paralyzed from the first ring of the chain tapping on the concrete, as they pulled Cassandra to her death, until the very last brutal killing. The murderous rampage seemed buried amongst the media suffering from a barrage of tales from the 9-11 terrorist attacks.

"CommUnity of Transition"

We sent over a thousand invitations to the transgender community around the world asking them to share wisdom, advice, and compassion for those questioning or struggling. No restraints, using topics they created, as they guided the conversation over forty chapters and fifty topics. By the close, these remarkable people had created the largest compilation book in transgender history. They opened their heart with these words.

NOTE: *This book is "lightly edited" to reflect the intent and form of over one hundred transgender contributors. Unedited photographs "before and after" come from actual contributing transgender writers.*

"Joey Brooks, The Show Must Go On"
By Joey Brooks and Todd Kachinski Kottmeier

Joey Brooks, The Show Must Go On is the story of The First Lady of Ybor from the days of El Goya to present day. Female Impersonator, Show director, hostess, author...
"Old school, new school, no school... who gives a shit? I'm too old to go to school. I barely remember last week. When I get too old to remember what the fuck I did when I was young ...ger, I'll just open one of these books and laugh my ass off. I wonder how many other queens had this much fun becoming one of the icons of their community. Too funny. I just called myself an icon. Hell, I must be a queen. Only a female impersonator could call themselves a diva, a queen, a star without people giggling behind her back. Giggling is good. A twenty-dollar bill is better."

"Two Days Past Dead"

The Author's First Published Book

It is hard to be the good guy when you succeed so well being bad. This is the Auggie Summer's dilemma his entire life. The story, based loosely on the tales of The Infamous Todd, follows the precocious child. His story begins with selling candy in 9th grade where he catches not only the attention of the press but also amusement of the drug cartel early in its' own infancy. Auggie Summers finds himself in the forefront of one of the most dangerous organizations on Earth.

"Waiting On God"
The Author's Humorist Novel

Learn to live after the doctors tell you "that are dying." A humorist essay on embracing funny moments and to create an environment around you that makes people not only laugh, but also be inspired by your strength.

Printed in Great Britain
by Amazon